MW00586773

POCKET SIZE

LAW DICTIONARY

**Contains Over 4,000
Legal Terms & Phrases**

THIRD EDITION

Mat #41549726

© 1984 by Harcourt Brace Legal and Professional Publications, Inc.
© 1997 by Harcourt Brace Legal and Professional Publications, Inc.
© 2014 LEG, Inc. d/b/a West Academic

      444 Cedar Street, Suite 700
      St. Paul, MN 55101
      1-877-888-1330

West, West Academic Publishing, and West Academic are trademarks of West Publishing Corporation, used under license.

Printed in the United States of America

ISBN: 978-0-314-29069-4

Summary of Contents

Preface

To someone first encountering the terminology of American law and the legal profession, "legalese" may seem somewhat like a foreign language. Indeed, the Latin phrases, complicated definitions of unfamiliar terms, and the specialized meanings of common words do give the legal field a language all its own. The purpose of the Gilbert Law Dictionary is to provide the beginning law student (or any person encountering legal jargon) with a convenient, easy-to-understand reference guide.

The Dictionary defines over 4,300 words and phrases in straightforward, layperson's language, without sacrificing the substantial legal meanings and applications. But defining these terms is only part of learning a new vocabulary. To aid the law student in the considerable task of learning to *use* the legal vocabulary, the Dictionary includes the following features:

1) Examples to clarify and apply the defining terms;

2) Clear distinctions between shades of meanings;

3) Cross-referencing between related entries; and

4) Notations as to specific areas of law to which the terms apply.

Also included as reference materials are a color map of the United States Courts of Appeals Circuit, the Constitution of the United States of America, and a Table of Federal Governmental Agencies and Departments.

Commonly used pronunciations have been given for non-English words and phrases. The words have been divided into syllables, with the accented syllables in capital letters. Pronunciation symbols have not been used; instead syllables should be pronounced as if they were the English words that they resemble. Thus a syllable written as "eye" is pronounced as a long letter "i." And, the final syllable of "de-LIK-tie" should be pronounced like the neckwear. Note that few, if any, of the pronunciations conform to the conventions of classical or ecclesiastical Latin, or standard French.

The entries in the Gilbert Law Dictionary encompass the most common words and definitions in the legal vocabulary. The Dictionary is designed as a portable reference guide, abridged for convenience and facility. With this book in hand, you should soon come to understand the language of the law.

A.B.A.
See American Bar Association.

abandoned and malignant heart
A state of mind indicating the malice aforethought necessary for murder; reckless indifference to an unjustifiably high risk to human life.

abandonment
1. Knowing relinquishment of one's right or claim to property without passing rights to another and with no intention to reclaim possession. 2. Desertion of one's spouse or child.

ab ante
(ab AN-tee) Lat. Before; in advance.

abatement
A decrease or termination of something (*e.g.,* abatement of taxes: a rebate of taxes previously paid or a decrease in an assessed valuation; abatement of action: ending or dismissal of lawsuit; abatement of legacy: reduction or extinction of a bequest due to insufficient funds or payment of debt).

abdicate
To give up completely; to renounce.

abduction
1. The criminal taking of a person by fraud, persuasion, or violence. 2. Common law: taking of females for purpose of marriage, cohabitation, or prostitution. 3. Civil law: taking of another's wife.

abet
To encourage, incite, instigate, or assist another in the commission of a crime with knowledge of its wrongfulness.

abettor
Person who incites, encourages, or commands another to commit a crime. An abettor must share criminal intent.

abeyance

State of being in waiting, expectation, or suspension; an undetermined or unsettled state of affairs. Property held "in abeyance" means there is a lapse in succession of ownership, and title is held in expectation of rightful owner.

abide

1. To comply with a decision; to accept the consequences of. 2. To await a result.

ab initio

(ab in-ISH-ee-o) Lat. From the beginning (*e.g.,* a contract, deed, or marriage is said to be either lawful or void ab initio).

abjuration

The act of taking an oath to renounce or abandon an allegiance or right (*e.g.,* a citizen of a foreign country abjures allegiance to that country upon becoming a citizen of the United States).

abnormally dangerous activity

An activity that always carries with it a serious risk of harm, even if the actor uses reasonable care. A person who engages in an abnormally dangerous activity may be held strictly liable for the harm caused by it.

abode

A person's home, place of dwelling, or residence.

abortion

The premature termination of a pregnancy. It may be spontaneous (*i.e.,* taking place unexpectedly) or induced (*i.e.,* intentionally removing a fetus from the womb, thereby terminating its life).

abrogation

The annulment or cancellation of a law by legislative act, constitutional authority, or usage.

abscond

To hide or secretly travel out of a court's jurisdiction in order to avoid the legal process.

absolute

Final, complete, unconditional (*e.g.,* an absolute bond is perfect in itself and has no restrictions upon it).

absque hoc

(ab-skwee hock) Lat. Without this. Words of denial used to

introduce the negative part of a plea.

abstention

Doctrine whereby a federal court relinquishes its jurisdiction to a state court. It is often used to avoid conflict between federal and state affairs.

abstract of title

A condensed history of the title to a piece of land listing all conveyances, liens, and liabilities on it.

abuse

Misuse; to mistreat physically or mentally.

abuse of discretion

Failure to exercise sound legal discretion. The term is used as a rationale by an appellate court when it is of the opinion that a lower court made an error of law by ruling contrary to evidence, logic, or reason.

abuse of process

The improper use of the legal process, after it has been issued, for a reason other than that intended by-law (*e.g.,* prosecuting a person in order to intimidate him).

abut

To touch; to border on, as where one lot touches another.

abuttals

1. The boundaries to a piece of property. 2. The end (as distinguished from side) boundary lines of a property.

Accelerated Cost Recovery System (A.C.R.S.)

A depreciation method of accounting, wherein the cost of an asset is written off over a set period of time.

acceleration

A shortening of the time required before an event will take place, such as the enjoyment of property rights.

acceleration clause

A provision in a credit agreement that allows a lender of money to call a debt due for failure of borrower to meet some obligation, such as to pay taxes or a special assessment on mortgaged property.

acceptance

1. Consenting to specific terms of an offer, thereby forming a

binding contract. 2. Act of receiving goods with the intention of keeping them. Act by which a buyer takes title to property. 3. Act of a bank promising to pay person named on a negotiable instrument.

access

The means or right to approach, as in the unobstructed ability to get to and from one's property. The ability to get from a street to a place of business.

accession

1. Acquiring a right to the thing that becomes part of something else already owned (*e.g.*, the vegetation that grows on one's property). 2. Under the Uniform Commercial Code, goods that are installed in or affirmed to other goods. *See* U.C.C. § 9–314(1).

accessory

One who in a secondary role, knowingly aids or contributes to the commission of a crime. An "accessory before the fact" counsels, encourages, or commands another to commit a crime, but is not present during its actual commission. An "accessory after the fact" knows of the crime yet still aids the criminal afterwards, such as by comforting or hiding the criminal.

accident

An unexpected, unforeseen event happening by chance. The term does not eliminate consideration of negligence on the part of the person who caused the accident.

accommodation paper (note)

A bill or note signed, without consideration, by one person to help another get a loan. The person who signed the note freely lends her credit to the accommodated party, and is called the "accommodation maker."

accomplice

1. One who knowingly, voluntarily, and with common criminal intent aids another in the commission or attempted commission of a crime. 2. One who is guilty of complicity in a crime.

accord

Agreement to settle differences; agreement that a debt obligation be settled for less than the person owed. It constitutes a contract and, after performance, bars further action.

accord and satisfaction
Payment of a disputed debt, often for less than the amount to which the creditor is entitled, which satisfactorily settles the obligation for all concerned.

account
1. A written record of money received or paid. 2. An unsettled claim between a debtor and creditor. 3. Money deposited in a bank, such as a savings or checking account. 4. A detailed statement recording the debits and credits between parties.

accountant
Person skilled in keeping financial records. A Certified Public Accountant (C.P.A.) is one who has met specific requirements and is licensed.

accounting, action for
Action to obtain a statement of account, to clarify the rights of parties in a shared asset.

accounting method
The method by which income and expenses are tracked, for tax or other purposes.

accounts receivable
1. List of money owed to a person or entity. 2. A debt.

accredit
To give official recognition or approval, especially to approve of a school for having met academic standards, or to recognize an envoy to a foreign country.

accredited investor
One who qualifies to buy securities in dealings which are exempt from registration under the Securities Act of 1933.

accretion
1. The act of adding to something, especially small bits of land added by action of water. 2. The right of an heir to add to his estate the inheritance of a coheir who is unable or refuses to take his inheritance.

accrual basis
Method of accounting which shows expenses incurred and income earned during a tax year; expenses need not have been paid to be deductible nor income received to be taxed.

accrue

To increase; to grow (*e.g.*, accrued interest is added to principal; accrued profits on an investment are those due and payable).

accumulative sentence (judgment)

An additional sentence imposed on a person already convicted of and sentenced for another offense. The second sentence begins when previous one expires.

accusation

A formal charge, made in court, that an individual or corporation is guilty of a punishable offense.

accused

Person charged with the commission of a crime; the defendant. He is not called "the accused" until after an indictment or information is returned against him, or until he is restrained after an arrest.

acknowledgment

An admission or declaration that a thing is genuine (*e.g.*, "acknowledgment of paternity": an individual admits his parental relationship; "acknowledgment of debt": debtor admits his obligation to creditor; "acknowledgment instrument": a formal document attested to before a proper public officer).

a coelo usque ad centrum

(a COY-lo uskwee ad SEN-trum) Lat. From the sky all the way to the center of the earth. An early principle of property law, by which owners marked boundaries of their property.

acquiescence

Quiet approval or compliance; lack of disapproval. When questioned about a crime, for example, a person's acquiescence may imply guilt or consent.

acquit

To set free or discharge from accusation or obligation; to declare an accused innocent.

act

1. A law passed by a legislative body. 2. A deed performed voluntarily.

action

1. A judicial proceeding in which a person demands the protection of his or her rights, or in which he or she prosecutes another for a

wrong done. The term covers all the formal court proceedings, including the decision and the enforcement of penalties. "Action" is used with various words to designate a particular area of lawsuit (*e.g.,* class action, civil action, criminal action). 2. Conduct; behavior.

actionable
An act or occurrence that provides grounds for a lawsuit.

act of God
An event caused solely by the forces of nature (*e.g.,* an earthquake).

act of state doctrine
In international law ,the principle that one nation may not judge the acts of another nation done within its own territory.

actual cash value
The fair and reasonable price for which an item or piece of property would sell on the open market. Also "fair market price."

actual damages
See damages.

actual notice
Express information of facts or circumstances from which it can be reasonably inferred that a party was notified of those facts and circumstances; the notice actually given to convey such information.

actuary
Statistician who calculates insurance and pension rates and premiums, and the value of annuities based on known risk and probability factors.

actus reus
(actus RAY-us) Lat. At common law, the requisite criminal act accompanying the mens rea resulting in criminal culpability.

ad damnum
(ad DAM-num) Lat. To the damages. The clause in a complaint that states the amount of damages or money loss being claimed.

addict
A person who habitually uses narcotics, alcohol, tobacco, or other substances, or who engages habitually in certain conduct, such as gambling.

additur

(ADD-it-tur) Lat. It is increased. The power of the court to increase the amount of damages awarded to a plaintiff by a jury as a condition for denying a new trial to a plaintiff if the defendant agrees to pay the plaintiff extra money. *Compare* remittitur.

adduce

To present, introduce, or state; used especially with reference to proof or evidence.

ademption

Revocation or taking away of a legacy by an act of the testator. It occurs when a testator, while living, gives the bequest to the legatee or substitutes another bequest for that mentioned in the will. It also can occur when the testator does something to make it impossible for his or her will to be carried out (*e.g.,* if testator disposed of property before he or she died).

adequate

Sufficient; suitable; enough. "Adequate consideration" is a fair and reasonable consideration (or a thing of value) under the circumstances. "Adequate com-

pensation" is the fair market value of property.

adhesion contract

A one-sided contract, unilaterally written by a party who offers it to another on a "take it or leave it" basis. The accepting party has virtually no choice or bargaining power in reference to the contract's terms.

ad hoc

Lat. For this, for a particular purpose (*e.g.,* ad hoc committees are set up to handle special problems).

ad hominem

Lat. To the person. Most often used with argument. Ad hominem arguments are personal attacks directed not at an opponent's position, but at his person.

ad idem

(ad EE-dem) Lat. To the same thing, result, or idea (*e.g.,* when two pieces of evidence prove the same thing).

ad infinitum

(ad in-fin-EYE-tum) Lat. Infinitely, without end.

adjective law

The body of law that governs the procedure of the courts as opposed to the law that the courts administer (substantive law). It prescribes the method by which the courts operate.

adjourn

To postpone, put off, or suspend business until a later time.

adjudicate

To act as a judge; to settle.

adjudication

The formal rendering of a final judgment in court.

adjudicative facts

In an administrative proceeding, factual matters concerning the parties (*e.g.,* intent). Contrast with legislative facts, which concern more general facts (*e.g.,* public policy).

adjuration

An oath.

adjuster

Person who settles or adjusts a matter, as an insurance adjuster settles a claim against the insurance company by an insured person.

adjustment

The process of settling a claim; the actual settlement. An insurance adjustment ascertains the value of a property loss and the liability of the parties involved.

ad litem

(ad LIE-tum) Lat. For the suit. A guardian ad litem, for example, may be appointed by the court to handle a suit of an infant.

administration

1. The management of the estate of a deceased person. 2. The management of a business or country. 3. The body of people who work in the executive branch of government.

administrative law

1. Body of law that governs the running of administrative agencies. 2. The rules and regulations created by administrative agencies (*e.g.,* the income tax regulations).

administrative law judge

An official who presides over hearings conducted by an administrative agency. Administrative law judges engage in many of the same functions as other judges, including administering oaths, ruling on questions of evidence and procedure, and making findings of fact. Also called a hearing officer.

Administrative Procedure Act
Federal or state provisions governing practice and procedures before administrative agencies.

administrator/administratrix (female)
A person appointed by the court to manage an estate, as compared to an "executor," who is named by a person in his or her will. *See* personal representative.

admiralty law
Maritime law; body of law relating to activities at sea such as commerce, navigation, contracts, or torts.

admissible evidence
Evidence that may be introduced in court and considered by a jury; evidence that the court is bound to allow to be introduced. Note, though, that evidence that is otherwise admissible may be withheld from consideration if a judge determines its probative value is outweighed by other factors, such as if it misleads or prejudices the jury.

admission
A voluntary acknowledgment of the existence of facts that are usually favorable to an adversary. An admission is not limited to statements, but may be inferred from a person's conduct. An admission is not the same as a confession and does not imply guilt.

admonition
A judge's or tribunal's statement of advice, warning, or reprimand given to a jury, counsel, or an accused person.

adoption
1. The act of accepting a child born to another person as one's own with all the rights and responsibilities of parenthood.
2. Passage of a bill into law.
3. The acceptance or appropriation of a thing, such as property, as one's own.

adulteration
The act of mixing an inferior substance into a superior or pure product. It occurs with reference to drugs, cosmetics, foods, and

drinks, and produces an inferior or even harmful product.

adultery
Voluntary sexual intercourse between a married person and someone not his or her spouse.

ad valorem
(ad va-LORE-em) Lat. According to value. An ad valorem tax varies according to the value of the thing taxed (*e.g.*, property tax or sales tax).

advancement
Money or property a parent gives her child (or prospective heir) in anticipation of inheritance from parent's estate; sum is later deducted from child's (heir's) share of estate.

adversary
An opponent in a lawsuit.

adversary proceeding
Legal proceeding involving opposing parties.

adverse interest
Interest opposed to one's own interest. Having an adverse interest sometimes disqualifies a person from being a witness.

adverse party
The party whose interests are opposed to another party in a lawsuit.

adverse possession
Method of acquiring title to real property by openly occupying land for a continuous period of time set by statute. Occupancy must be hostile, that is, occupying party does not recognize title of actual holder, and he uses property without permission of the title holder. Occupant should visibly display his intent to claim and hold property.

advice
Opinion given by counsel to a client.

advisement
Consideration; deliberation. A case "under advisement" means the judge postpones a decision until after a period of consideration of evidence and arguments.

advisory opinion
Formal opinion given by a judge about a matter of law which has no binding effect. It is often given in response to questions of law asked by a legislative body

or government official. Federal courts cannot issue advisory opinions.

advocate
1. (n.) One who speaks in favor of a cause or another person. A lawyer. 2. (v.) To speak in favor of; to support.

affiance
To promise to marry.

affiant
Person who makes and swears to the truth of a written statement or affidavit.

affidavit
A written statement sworn to or affirmed before a person with authority to witness the oath.

affiliate
1. (n.) Something allied, connected, or closely associated with a larger group. 2. (v.) To join or closely associate with.

affiliation
A close association; used legally to mean the act of determining the parentage of a child.

affinity
Close attraction or relationship between persons, especially the relationship a person has to his or her spouse's blood relatives.

affirm
1. To confirm, reassert, or agree with, especially when a higher court supports a lower court's decision. 2. To make a formal declaration about the truth of something in place of an oath.

affirmative action
Action taken to remedy a situation, especially discriminatory practices against minorities, the handicapped, or women. Action may involve hiring, promotion, or testing practices, and can be court-ordered, voluntary, or result from the organization's status as a federal contractor.

affirmative defense
A defendant's answer to a complaint that does not deny the facts of the charge or the plaintiff's complaint, but which presents evidence or arguments in favor of the defendant that mitigate or excuse the defendant's actions (*e.g.,* insanity, self-defense, and duress are pleas used in criminal

cases which are affirmative defenses).

affirmative relief

Relief which may be sought by defendant, independent of the success, failure, or abandonment of plaintiff's claim.

affix

1. To attach, fasten to, or add on, as when a building is affixed to property. 2. To inscribe or impress upon, as when a seal is affixed to a document.

Affordable Care Act

See Patient Protection and Affordable Care Act.

affray

A fight in a public place that disturbs others.

affreightment

Contract made with a shipowner in which owner agrees to carry goods.

aforesaid

Already mentioned.

aforethought

Planned; premeditated; thought of beforehand.

a fortiori

(ah for-tee-OR-ee) Lat. With greater reason. Term is used in logic to mean if one thing is true, then a thing that it encompasses or is less than it, is also true (*e.g.,* if a person is dead, then a fortiori, he is not breathing).

after-acquired

Acquired after a particular date or occurrence (*e.g.,* after-acquired property is property debtor acquires after security transaction is perfected and that is covered by security agreement).

against the weight of the evidence

Contrary to the evidence presented. A trial judge may set aside a verdict and order a new trial if she feels the verdict is clearly contrary to the evidence of the case. It is not proper for a judge to do this unless it can be clearly seen that the jury made a mistake or acted under a bias or with an improper motive, any of which would result in a miscarriage of justice.

age discrimination

The unequal treatment of persons, based on their age. This practice was barred in employment situations by the Age Discrimination in Employment Act of 1967.

agency

1. A fiduciary relationship in which one party represents another by the latter's authority. The relationship can be between an agent and a principal, in which case the agent acts for the principal by, for example, handling his finances; between a master and a servant, that is, between an employer and an employee; or between an employer and an independent contractor. 2. The place where an agent operates. 3. A branch of government (*e.g.*, a police department).

agent

A person who is authorized to act on behalf of another.

age of consent

1. Age at which persons may marry without parental consent. 2. Age at which a person may consent to sexual intercourse without subjecting his or her partner to prosecution for statutory rape.

aggravated assault

Purposely causing or attempting to cause serious bodily injury to another. Definition varies according to statute, sometimes referring to an assault with intent to commit murder, rape, or robbery, and other times to the degree of fear inflicted by an assault. *See* assault.

aggravation

Circumstances tending to increase the seriousness or add to the injury of a crime, but that are not part of the actual crime itself (*e.g.*, malicious threats to inflict bodily harm on a kidnap victim).

aggrieved party

1. One whose personal or property rights have been violated or threatened. 2. One who suffered a loss, which may have resulted from a judgment or decree operated against him.

agreement

A meeting of minds; a consensus between two or more parties that affects their legal rights and duties. Term is broader than "contract," as it may lack some requirement of a contract.

aid and abet

To knowingly, purposefully, and actively help in the commission of a crime. It can be by words, acts, or presence so long as person assisted in the perpetration of a crime. One who aids and abets is liable as a principal.

air rights

Right to use the air space above a piece of real estate (*e.g.*, the right to build a bridge over a road).

a.j.

Abbreviation for associate justice or associate judge.

alderman

Person elected to a city council; councilman.

aleatory

(AY-lee-a-tory) Dependent on risky or uncertain outcome.

aleatory contract

A contract in which performance by one party depends on the occurrence of an uncertain or contingent event (*e.g.*, life insurance is aleatory).

Alford plea

A guilty plea in which a defendant does not admit her guilt, but agrees that the evidence against her is such that she probably would be convicted.

alia enormia

(a-lee-a e-NOR-mee-a) Lat. Other wrongs. Term used to claim additional injuries for a plaintiff.

alias

Otherwise called, or another name by which a person is known. Abbreviation is a.k.a. for "also known as."

alibi

Account of a person's activities and whereabouts at the time a crime was committed that is used as a defense to show it was impossible for him to commit the crime.

alien

A foreigner; a person who is not a citizen of the country in which she is living. An alien does have the right to protection of life, liberty, and property afforded under the Due Process Clause of the Constitution. A "resident alien" has permanent resident status but is not a citizen.

alienate

To transfer or convey title to property.

alienation

The voluntary and complete transfer of title and possession of real property. "Alienation clause" is a provision in an insurance policy that voids the policy when a transfer of ownership occurs.

alienation of affection

A malicious and willful interference with a marital relationship by a third party. It deprives a person of the affection of his or her spouse, and can result from embarrassing, disgracing, humiliating, or inflicting mental anguish on one of the spouses. *Note:* Almost every state has abolished this as a cause of action.

alimony

Payments made by a divorced or separated husband to his ex-wife (or vice versa) for her support. The amount is court-ordered. Alimony is based on the common law duty a husband has for the support of his wife. In many states, it is called "spousal maintenance" or "spousal support."

aliquot

(AL-ee-kwot) Lat. Literally means contained an exact number of times in something *else.* As applied to trusts it means a fractional interest.

aliunde

(al-ee-YUN-dee) Lat. From another source. Term is used with "evidence," meaning evidence is from another source. An ambiguous will, for example, is clarified by evidence aliunde (*i.e.,* a source other than the will).

allegation

An assertion of fact, made in a pleading, stating what a person intends to prove.

allege

To charge; assert; to make an allegation. "Alleged" means only charged or asserted and not proven.

allegiance

Loyalty and obedience to a country and its government in return for the protection it affords. Allegiance can be natural: that owed to one's native country; acquired: that which applies to a naturalized citizen; or local and actual: that obedience owed to a foreign government in whose territory one is temporarily present.

all fours

Two cases alike in all legally relevant respects are said to be on "all fours."

allocation

Placement or assignment of something in or to a particular place, such as the allocation of cash dividends to income or principal.

allocution

A court formality of the sentencing procedure in which a trial judge asks the defendant if he has any legal reason why judgment should not be passed against him and a sentence imposed.

allodial

Owned without obligation to another with superior rights; owned freely.

allograph

A signature made for another person.

allonge

(a-LONZH) A separate piece of paper attached to a negotiable instrument to provide extra space for endorsements. *See* U.C.C. § 3-204(a).

allotment

A portion or share of something, usually property (*e.g.*, an allotment of land, or an allotment of shares in a company).

alternate dispute resolution

Methods for settling or resolving disputes without litigation. *See* arbitration, mediation.

alternative pleading

A form of pleading in which a person presents two or more separate, and possibly inconsistent, sets of facts that may form the basis for a claim or defense.

alternative writ

A court order commanding a person to do something or show reason why he should not.

amalgamation

A union of two or more different entities, usually corporations, to form a single concern. Term is also used when referring to the consolidation of unions, associations, organizations, and stock.

ambiguity

An uncertainty, doubtfulness, something that lacks specific meaning. Term is used in referring to an uncertainty in written documents, such as wills or contracts. There are two kinds of ambiguity: latent and patent. Latent ambiguity exists when the document itself is clear but some extrinsic factor makes the document's execution unclear. Patent ambiguity exists when the language of the document itself is obscure.

ambit

A boundary line marking the limit of something, such as the bounds of a district, jurisdiction, or sphere of influence.

ambulance chaser

A person who pursues accidents for the purpose of representing the injured party in the ensuing litigation or for the purpose of soliciting such a case for a lawyer; generally, an unethical lawyer.

ambulatory

Movable, changeable, revocable. An ambulatory will is one that can be changed or revoked. An ambulatory disposition is a changeable judgment or sentence. Ambulatory jurisdiction is not limited to one location.

amend

To correct or change.

amendment

A change or modification. An amendment of a pleading is any change (such as a correction of an error) in a pleading already made. An amendment of a bill is a change in the bill, and can be made while the bill is being debated in the legislative body or by the governor or president before signing it. An amendment to the Constitution is one of the changes made in or added to the original document.

amenity

In easement law, a restraint on the property owner keeping her from doing something on the property that she could do but for the grant or covenant (*e.g.*, a negative easement).

American Bar Association (A.B.A.)

Voluntary organization of attorneys, the primary function of which is the improvement of the legal profession.

American Civil Liberties Union (A.C.L.U.)

Association dedicated to the protection of civil liberties guaranteed by the federal and state constitutions.

American Constitution Society

A group comprised of lawyers and law students that promotes civil liberties and law reform.

American Depository Receipt (A.D.R.)

A receipt denoting indirect ownership of stock in foreign companies, issued by U.S. banks to U.S. investors.

American rule

The rule that states that all parties to a lawsuit must bear their own costs of litigation. Exceptions to the rule are found in fee-shifting statutes, court rules, or contract clauses that provide for shifting the expenses of litigation.

Americans with Disabilities Act

A federal law that prohibits discrimination against persons with disabilities, or perceived disabilities, in employment, public accommodations, or public services.

American Stock Exchange

Formerly, the second largest stock exchange in the U.S.; since 2008, a part of the New York Stock Exchange.

amicus curiae

(a-MEE-kus KYUR-ee-eye or A-mi-kus KYUR-ee-eye) Lat. Friend of the court. A person who is not party to the law suit but who is permitted, upon petition, to submit information or arguments for the court's consideration.

amnesty

An act by a sovereign power by which a general pardon is granted to a class of persons who have been guilty of some offense, usually political in nature. Amnesty differs from a pardon in that a pardon excuses an individual for an offense against the peace of the nation.

amortization

The payment of a debt by equal, periodic payments over a course of time (*e.g.*, a mortgage on a house is amortized by making monthly payments on the loan for the number of years the mortgage runs).

analogy

A comparison of similarities in unlike things (*e.g.*, comparison drawn between two different kinds of cases, each of which *is* governed by same general principle).

ancestor

1. A person from whom another is descended (*e.g.*, a parent or grandparent). 2. A former possessor.

ancillary

Something that acts to assist or is subordinate to something else. Ancillary jurisdiction is the power of a court to rule on a matter not normally within its primary jurisdiction, such as the power of a federal district court to handle actions from a circuit court. An ancillary proceeding is one that grows out of, aids, or is subordinate to another action.

animus

Lat. Will, intention, being of the mind. Term is used in conjunction with other terms (*e.g.*, animus cancellandi (an-i-mus cancel-LAN-dee): with the intention of destroying or cancelling; animus furandi (an-i-mus fur-RAN-dee): with intent to steal; animus testandi (an-i-mus tes-STAN-dee): with intent to make a will).

annex

To attach to, to bind, to add to or join, as a piece of personal property is annexed to real property and so becomes a fixture (*see* fixture) or as a piece of land is annexed to a city.

annotation

1. Note on a passage in a book intended to explain the meaning of the passage. A legal annotation is an explanation that follows the text or the decision on a case. 2. History of cases construing a statute.

annuity

A fixed periodic payment for life or a specified number of years usually from an insurance company. The payments are a partial return of a capital investment (insurance policy) plus interest. The person receiving the payments (annuitant) does not have an interest in the principal from which this money arises, but only in the periodic payments themselves.

annul

To cancel, void, to do away with, as a marriage or judicial proceeding can be annulled.

annulment

Act of making something void. A marriage annulment differs from a divorce in that a divorce ends a marriage in existence; an annulment voids the marriage from the beginning, as if it never existed.

answer

1. A reply, response. 2. The first response or pleading made by a defendant to the charges leveled against him in a lawsuit. It must contain a denial of the allegations, and may also contain affirmative defenses, and any permissive or compulsory counterclaims.

antenuptial agreement

A contract made before marriage by the future spouses, usually to settle questions of support and distribution of wealth should one spouse die or should the planned marriage end in separation or divorce. Also called a "prenuptial agreement."

anticipation

1. Doing or taking something before its proper time, such as paying off a mortgage before it comes due. 2. Expectation; knowledge of the probability that something will occur; principal by which negligence is determined if a prudent person could have reasonably expected a thing to happen.

anticipatory breach
The breaking of a contract after it has been entered into but before the actual time of performance arrives. In some jurisdictions, the aggrieved party has a right to sue for breach once the repudiating party states his intention not to perform.

antitrust acts
Federal and state statutes enacted to protect trade and commerce from unlawful restraint and monopolies. *See* Sherman Antitrust Act of 1890 and Clayton Act of 1914.

a posteriori
(a pos-teer-ee-OR-ee) Lat. From effect to cause. In logic, term means that first one observes effects, then ascertains their causes.

apparent authority
In law of agency, authority a principal permits an agent to have, or holds agent out as having (*e.g.*, an employer permits an employee to have a certain amount of authority in the performance of his job). It includes authority a prudent person would reasonably assume the agent to have.

appeal
To ask a superior court (*i.e.*, an appellate court) to review a decision of a lower court. The process is called "an appeal."

appearance
A coming before the court either as a plaintiff or defendant and thereby submitting oneself to the court's jurisdiction. It can be in person or through an attorney, the latter being the case in most civil suits.

appellant
The party who appeals a decision of one court to a higher court.

appellate court
A court with jurisdiction to review cases from a lower court. The U.S. Supreme Court is the highest appellate court in the country. *See* appeal.

appellee
The party against whom an appeal is made, usually the winner of a case in a lower court.

appoint

In testamentary or probate law, disposing of property pursuant to a power of appointment. To give "power of appointment" in a will or deed is the authority to determine who gets one's property and how it is to be used.

appointment of receiver

The process by which a party obtains receivership of a provable property interest.

apportionment

1. A fair and proportionate division and distribution of something, such as property, corporate shares, or estate taxes. 2. Process of determining the number of representatives to a legislative body an area is entitled to (*i.e.*, their proportionate distribution throughout the state based on population).

appraisal

An estimation of the value of a property by a qualified, disinterested person.

appreciation

The increase in the value of property for reasons other than improvements (*e.g.*, due to infla-

tion or greater demand for property).

appreciation test

A criminal defendant will be found not guilty by reason of insanity if she shows by clear and convincing evidence that, at the time of the crime, she suffered from a severe mental disease or defect that prevented her from appreciating the wrongfulness of her conduct.

apprehend

1. To seize, capture, take hold of bodily. 2. To grasp in the mind, as in to understand, conceive or fear.

appropriate

1. To set something apart for a particular use, such as land for a public park or funds for highway repair. Appropriation is the governmental act of taking private property and setting it aside for public use. (*See* eminent domain.) 2. To take something as one's own. 3. To set apart money or goods for a particular purpose.

appropriation of likeness

Taking or using the name or identity of another person without permission, and using it for one's own financial or other gain.

appurtenance
(a-PURR-ten-ants) Something that is attached or belongs to something else of greater value, such as a barn or a fence to the land it is on. In property law, term refers to a burden attached to land that restricts the use or enhances the enjoyment of the land (*e.g.*, easement, covenant, or servitude). *See* easement, covenant, and servitude.

a priori
(a pree-OR-ree) Lat. From what goes before; from the cause to the effect.

arbiter
Person chosen to decide a controversy according to the rules of equity and law; a referee; arbitrator.

arbitrage
The purchase of stock or other security in one market and its sale in another market for the profit made in the exchange.

arbitrary
1. By mere opinion; by will alone; not according to reasoned judgment, rules, or determining principles; non-rational. 2. Legally, without substantial legal cause. 3. In trademark law, an arbitrary mark is made up of common words that do not describe or relate to the product represented by the trademark, or to any qualities of the product.

arbitration
The submission of a dispute between two parties to a third, impartial party (arbitrator) with the agreement that the decision of the arbitrator will be binding and final. It is a quasi-judicial procedure that avoids the formality, delay, and expense of a normal trial. *See* mediation.

arguendo
(ar-gyoo-EN-do) Lat. In the course of an argument. A hypothetical statement made and assumed to be true for the sake of argument. A judge may make a statement arguendo to illustrate a point.

argument
1. An attempt to persuade through a course of reasoning that sets forth facts and laws. 2. Legally, statements made by counsel to a judge or jury in an attempt to further her cause.

arm's length
Relationship that exists between parties who are unrelated, and have no duty or obligation to each other. An arm's length transaction is one in which parties act entirely for their own interest. Term is often used in transactions that determine the fair market value of property.

arraignment
The initial step of a criminal proceeding in which an accused person is brought before a judge to be informed of the charges against him, and during which time defendant enters a plea.

array
1. (n.) The body of persons summoned from which a jury is selected. 2. The list of persons impaneled on a jury. 3. (v.) To select jurors.

arrears, arrearages
Debts unpaid and overdue.

arrest
The taking of a person into custody for the purpose of bringing her before a court. The arresting person must have legal authority, must adequately communicate his intent to arrest, and must actually restrain the arrested person for the act to be called an arrest. He must have probable cause to seize and detain (*i.e.,* suspicion is not enough).

arrest of judgment
Act of withholding judgment on legal action because of some error on the face of the record that, if ruled on, may result in a reversal of the verdict on appeal.

arson
The malicious, willful, and unlawful burning of a building or other property. Several states divide arson into first degree, second degree, and third degree depending on the time of the burning and the nature and occupancy of the structure. At common law, structure had to be the dwelling place of another.

article
A separate and distinct part of a document, such as a distinct paragraph in a constitution or statute.

articles of incorporation
The document filed with the state upon the formation of a corporation. It lists, among other things, the purpose of the corporation, its place of business, and the names of its directors. Also called "certificate of incorporation."

articles of organization
The document used to form or organize a limited liability company (LLC). The document is filed with the state in which the LLC is organized.

artifice
1. A trick; a contrivance. 2. A fraudulent device used to accomplish some evil.

artificial person
An entity created by law that has some of the rights and duties of a natural person (*e.g.,* a corporation).

as is
A phrase denoting a thing is being sold just as the buyer sees it, with no promise from the seller that it is in perfect condition. The buyer takes all risk as to the quality of the item.

asportation
(as-por-TAY-shun) The unlawful carrying away of something. It is an essential element to constitute a crime of larceny.

assault
1. The attempt or threat, accompanied by the apparent present ability, to inflict bodily harm on another. 2. The display of force as to cause fear of bodily harm. *Cf.* battery. In many states, the crime of assault may include common law battery as well as assault.

assay
The testing of ores and metals, especially gold and silver; examination to determine characteristics of weight, measure, or quality.

assessment
1. The process of determining the value of property for taxation

(*e.g.*, a property tax assessment). A special assessment is a burden put upon a piece of land with reference to the benefit the property owner gains (*e.g.*, a special assessment for street repairs). 2. The determination of the amount a person will pay into a common fund (*e.g.*, an assessment of condominium owners for the construction of a swimming pool for the building). 3. In relation to corporations, a call made to stockholders to pay the amount of money mentioned in their subscriptions.

assessment of deficiency
The amount of tax due to the Internal Revenue Service by a taxpayer, after I.R.S. review.

assets
Property of any kind that can be used for the payment of debts. Assets include money, land, personal property, and intangibles such as patents and copyrights.

assign
1. To appoint to or designate for a particular purpose or duty. 2. To formally transfer one's legal rights or interest in property

or a contract, as when a deed is assigned to another. 3. To point out or specify, as in to assign mistakes in an assignment of error (*see* assignment of error).

assignment
The transferring to another of one's rights or property interest.

assignment for benefit of creditors
A debtor's transfer of a substantial portion of property to another person in trust for payment of debtor's debts, with the return of any surplus to the debtor.

assignment of error
The complaint made by an appellant in which he specifies the alleged errors made by a lower court and on which he relies for reversal of the decision.

assignment of income
The transfer of income earned by one taxpayer to another person, so that the transferred income is taxed to the assignee.

assize
(as-SIZE) The writ of an ancient court of assize, determining ownership of title and/or directing the recovery of property.

association

A body of persons united for a common purpose. Term sometimes refers to an organization that acts and is treated as a corporation for federal tax purposes although legally it is not one; an unincorporated society. Professionals and nonprofit organizations, for instance, form associations; also certain business trusts are called associations.

assumpsit

(as-SUMP-sit) Lat. He promised. In contracts, it is a promise, either oral or written but not under seal, by which a person agreed to do or pay for something. The term is used in connection with the recovery of damages for breach of contract.

assumption

Act of taking over; assuming responsibility (*e.g.*, the assumption of a mortgage on a house to make oneself personally liable for the mortgage debt).

assumption of risk

An affirmative defense used by a defendant in a negligence suit in which he asserts plaintiff knew of a danger and voluntarily exposed himself to it. Assumption of risk by plaintiff would relieve defendant of legal responsibility for any resulting injury.

assurance

1. The act of assuring; a declaration which inspires confidence. 2. A pledge, guaranty, or surety. 3. Insurance. 4. A document showing title to real property; a deed. 5. The act of conveying or transferring title.

assured

The person covered by an insurance policy; the insured.

asylum

1. A sanctuary; a place of safety and shelter from arrest or prosecution. Certain states and countries are places of asylum. Term denotes both the place and the protection it affords. 2. Neutral waters where ships take refuge during warfare. 3. Archaic: An institution for the protective housing of the insane, blind, lame, or destitute.

at bar

Before the court. A "case at bar" refers to the specific case presently before the court.

at large

1. Free, not restrained or controlled (*e.g.*, an escaped prisoner is said to be at large until apprehended). 2. Unlimited; open to debate. 3. At large elections are those in which all voters cast ballots for a candidate (*e.g.*, U.S. Presidential or Senatorial elections are at large as opposed to state legislative elections which are limited to in-district voters).

atrocious

Extremely evil, cruel and vile.

attachment

1. The remedy which involves the taking of property to be held as security by the court for the purpose of satisfying an anticipated judgment. 2. A writ issued by the court to the sheriff ordering her to bring before the court a person guilty of contempt. 3. A document affixed to another.

attainder

A form of punishment involving the elimination of the civil rights of a person guilty of a crime punishable by death. The doctrine of attainder was once used as a punishment for treason, but is no longer constitutional.

attempt

Effort to commit a crime where effort goes far enough toward the actual start of the crime yet falls short of its accomplishment; contemplation and preparation are not enough. Thus, the elements of criminal attempt are intent, an overt act coupled with the real possibility to commit a crime, and the failure to accomplish it.

attendant circumstances

Facts surrounding an event; often required to satisfy elements of criminal law (*e.g.*, the defendant's state of mind during an alleged homicide).

attestation

Act of witnessing the signing of a document, such as a will, and then signing name as such a witness.

attesting witness

The person who witnesses the signing of a document. *See* attestation.

attorney

1. A lawyer; an officer of the court who has a duty toward a client and the court for the ad-

ministration of law. 2. An agent; a person appointed to act formally for another.

attorney-client privilege

A client's privilege to refuse to disclose and to prevent others from disclosing anything said in confidence to his attorney.

attorney general

The chief nonjudicial legal officer in the country or a state who advises the chief executive and other heads of the executive department on legal matters. On the federal level, she is a Cabinet member appointed by the President and confirmed by the Senate, and is the head of the Department of Justice. On the state level, she is sometimes appointed by the Governor, but more often is elected at large.

attorney in fact

An agent with authority to do some particular act, not of legal character, for another. The agent is granted such authority by a written document called "power of attorney."

attorney's fees

The charge for services rendered by an attorney. Determination of fee may vary, depending on whether the attorney's contract stipulates a contingency fee, hourly fee, or retainer, or whether the fee is subject to other regulations (*e.g.*, the American rule or the common fund doctrine).

attornment

The recognition of third party as an acceptable successor to a contract, especially the agreement in which a tenant agrees to pay rent to a new owner of property.

attractive nuisance

Dangerous piece of property that may be attractive to children; the doctrine which states that a person who has such a possibly dangerous property or condition on his premises has the duty to take reasonable precautions to guard against injury to children attracted to it. The fact that a child is a trespasser does not relieve owner of responsibility for injuries (*e.g.*, a swimming pool is an attractive yet potentially dangerous condition, and its owner has a responsibility to put a fence around it).

auction

The public sale of personal or real property to the highest bidder. The person who conducts an auction is a licensed individual called an auctioneer, and she operates on behalf of the seller.

audit

1. (n.) An examination of something, especially financial records, accounts, or tax returns, to determine their truth and correctness. 2. (v.) To conduct an audit; to examine; to adjust; to ascertain; to verify.

auditor

Person qualified to conduct an examination of financial records; may be a public official or private accountant working for a business. In court, an auditor, also known as a master, examines an account in controversy and reports to the court, which then uses the report's information in rendering its judgment.

authentication

To officially recognize a thing as genuine; in evidence, the act of legally recognizing a document, such as a will, a deed, or a law, to be what it is claimed to be.

author

The creator of a work protected by copyright.

authority

1. The right, permission, or power to act, as in the permission a principal gives to his agent to act in his behalf, or the power a police officer has in the lawful exercise of his duties. Authority can be "express" (*i.e.*, that which is explicitly given as in a document of Power of Attorney); it can be "implied," as in that which can be inferred from a person's conduct or from circumstances; and it can be "apparent," as when a principal permits an agent to act. 2. Judicial precedent (*i.e.*, higher court decisions have authority over those of lower courts). 3. A body with power to act.

authorize

To give the right to act; to empower with authority. Sometimes term connotes "permitted" or "directed" to act.

automatic stay

In bankruptcy law, an order barring actions to collect a debt from a debtor, that is deemed entered when the bankruptcy petition is filed.

automatism

Act performed in a state of mental unconsciousness; conduct occurring without will or intent. Used as affirmative criminal defense to negate mental intent based on voluntary acts.

autopsy

An examination of a corpse usually to determine the cause of death; a post mortem examination.

avails

Profits or proceeds, such as the avails from the sale of land.

aver

1. (v.) To state clearly; allege; assert. (*See* averment.) 2. Old Eng. (n.) Property; especially livestock.

averment

In pleading, a positive statement alleging facts; an allegation.

avoid

To annul; make void; cancel; eliminate the efficacy of something.

avoidance

1. In pleading, the statement in which a person admits facts in an allegation against him, yet also shows why those facts should not have their normal legal effect (*i.e.*, to avoid them). (*See* affirmative defense.) 2. An annulling or voiding of something. 3. Evasion.

avoidance of tax

The means by which one legally minimizes his tax liability (*e.g.*, taking valid deductions to reduce taxable income). In contrast, "tax evasion" is the fraudulent reduction of tax liability.

avowal

A declaration or offer of proof made outside of the jury's hearing, by a witness not permitted to testify before the jury, in order to have the statement recorded should the case be appealed.

avulsion

The removal of soil by the action of water, and its placement on the land of another. It differs from accretion (*see* accretion) in that avulsion is a sudden, perceptible change, and in that the ownership of the land does not change. Avulsion also denotes the sudden change in the course of a river or stream; this does not change the boundary line marked by the previous course of the water.

award

1. (v.) To give or grant, as when a jury awards damages, or when a contract is awarded to a firm.
2. To adjudge, as when a court rules on a matter in controversy.
3. (n.) The decision rendered by a tribunal.

B

bad debt

An uncollectible debt, worthless to the creditor (*e.g.*, a loan made with the intention it would be repaid but which appears unlikely to ever be repaid). A bad debt is deductible for tax purposes.

bad faith

Dishonesty in dealing with another person. Term implies a willfulness on the part of one person to trick or mislead another, and is not the same as negligence or mistake. It may or may not constitute fraud.

badges of fraud

A general term used to indicate suspicious circumstances surrounding a transaction, especially suspicion of defraud of creditors. A particular "badge" does not prove fraud but only implies it (*e.g.*, if a transaction takes place to avoid a creditor and in antici-

pation of a suit, the conveyance is called a badge of fraud).

bad title

A defective title, insufficient to legally convey property, not marketable.

bail

1. (v.) To give a security (often money) to procure the release of a person being held for an offense, and to insure that person's future appearance in court. 2. (n.) The person in the position of a surety (*see* surety) who gives such a security.

bail bond

A written instrument of debt made by a person in custody and by others for him (*see* surety) which procures his release. Surety promises to pay amount mentioned on bail bond should defendant fail to appear in court at a designated time.

bailee

1. Person to whom property of a bailment (*see* bailment) is delivered. 2. Person who temporarily possesses personal property in trust for another.

bailiff

1. A sheriff's deputy or court officer who keeps order in a courtroom. 2. Person given authority for the care of another; a guardian. 3. A keeper of the property of another who is responsible to manage it for the best benefit of the owner.

bailment

1. The delivery of personal property to another under express or implied contract, for some specified purpose, to be returned or accounted for after purpose is fulfilled. "Bailment for hire" is the relationship created upon delivery of goods to someone (bailee) for some purpose in exchange for compensation (*e.g.*, when a broken television set is delivered to a TV repair shop). 2. The lawful possession of property belonging to another, with the duty to account for it (*e.g.*, a finder of a mislaid camera).

bailor

Person who gives personal property to another to be held in bailment. *See* bailment.

bait and switch

A deceptive advertising practice in which a retailer entices customers into the store with attractive advertising, and then fails to stock sufficient quantities of the advertised product or disparages the product. Both tactics are done with the intention of selling a higher priced product.

balance sheet

A summary of financial data showing assets, liabilities, and owner equity of all the accounts of a company at a certain time.

balancing test

A constitutional test wherein the court weighs the right of individuals to certain constitutionally guaranteed rights with a state's right to protect its citizens from invasion of their rights. Used in cases involving equal protection and freedom of speech.

bank

1. A commercial institution that receives deposits of money, cashes checks, makes loans, and handles other money-related matters. Banks are chartered under federal and/or state laws, and are usually incorporated.

2. The raised ground at the edge of a watercourse.

bankrupt

1. The state of being unable to pay one's debts when due and payment is demanded. 2. A person, partnership, or corporation so unable to pay its creditors. *See* bankruptcy, insolvency.

bankruptcy

A legal procedure, by which a debtor is relieved of his debts. Under the Federal Bankruptcy Act, a debtor's assets may be liquidated to pay his creditors, or, under a provision of the Act, debtor's assets are not liquidated, and debtor is allowed to reorganize, continue business, and pay creditor from future earnings.

bar

1. A prohibition or barrier to the relitigation of a case which has already been adjudicated (*i.e.*, a court decision sometimes "bars" further action on the same case). 2. A position in a courtroom; a defendant "at bar" stands before the judge. 3. "The bar" is the entire body of lawyers. 4. A case "at bar" is the particular case before the court.

bar association

An organization of lawyers whose primary purpose is the betterment of the legal profession. Bar associations are formed on national, state, county, and municipal levels.

bargain

1. (n.) A mutual agreement between parties; a contract. 2. (v.) To negotiate the terms of an agreement.

barratry, barretry

1. Offense of provoking or exciting quarrels and suits, sometimes done by lawyers for the profit that can be gained from an ensuing lawsuit. 2. In maritime law, act by a master or mariner of a ship, done for a fraudulent or unlawful purpose which results in injury to the ship's owner.

barrister

In England, a legal counselor; a person who argues a case at bar; similar to a trial lawyer in America, except a barrister does not prepare a case from the beginning but gets the case material from another type of legal professional—a solicitor.

barter

The exchange of one good or service for another that does not involve money.

basis

1. The foundation of something. 2. The value of a property on a certain date. The basis of a property is used as a baseline in determining appreciation (gain) or depreciation (loss) of value over time, and is used for taxing purposes.

bastard

An illegitimate child; a child not born during a lawful marriage. The term "child out of wedlock" is more commonly used now.

bastardy proceedings (action)

Legal action in which the father of an illegitimate child is determined and support obligations are enforced. Now, more commonly referred to as a "parentage action" or "paternity suit."

battered woman syndrome

A psychological or medical condition of a person who has suffered abuse from a spouse or partner; sometimes advanced as a defense to a prosecution for

assaulting or killing the abusive spouse or partner.

battery

The unlawful, undesired, and unprovoked use of force on another person with the intention to harm or create fear of harm in that person; harmful touching. In tort law, all parts of a person's body and anything closely attached to it (such as clothes or a car being driven) are protected. Assault is the threat to use force; its actual use in an offensive way, even though slight, is battery.

bawd

An operator of a house of prostitution; a madam.

bearer

Person who possesses a negotiable instrument, title, or security marked "payable to bearer," "cash," or is indorsed in blank (*i.e.*, the payee is unnamed). The instrument itself is called a bearer bond or bearer paper and is payable upon presentment.

bench

1. A court while sitting in its official capacity. 2. All judges

together. 3. The place in a court-room where the judge sits.

bench trial

Trial held before a judge, without a jury, during which the judge acts as the factfinder.

bench warrant

A judge's written order to authorities to arrest a person, often issued to bring a person before the court to answer a contempt charge or to appear as a witness.

beneficial interest

1. An interest, or right to profits, in a property. 2. That interest in property which one holds entirely for her own benefit. 3. The remainder of an estate after obligations have been met.

beneficiary

1. Person or organization entitled to benefits in a will, insurance policy, or trust. 2. One who benefits from acts of other persons.

benefit of clergy

1. In Old England, the exemption the clergy possessed from the jurisdiction of the secular courts. It then came to mean the exemption of any church officers from capital punishment, though it did not apply to certain crimes such as high treason. Abuse led to its abolition in 1827. 2. "Without benefit of clergy" means cohabitation without being married.

bequeath

To give a gift of personal property in a will, distinguished from "devise," which is to give a gift of real property, although terms are often used synonymously.

bequest

A gift of personal property given in a will; a legacy; distinguished from a "devise," which is a gift of real property.

Berne Convention

International agreement first proposed in 1886 on the protection of copyrighted material that sets out the minimum standards for national copyright laws. The United States became a member of the Convention in 1989.

best evidence

The best proof or evidence available under the circumstances; primary evidence; the original (*e.g.*, the actual written document, not a copy).

bestiality

Sexual intercourse between a human and an animal; constitutes a crime against nature.

best interests of the child

Principle that courts determine questions relating to a child's custody or other living arrangements according to what will provide the greatest benefit to the child.

beyond a reasonable doubt

Phrase used to refer to the level of certainty required in the mind of an honest, conscientious juror before convicting a person of a crime; it is not absolute certainty, containing not the least bit of doubt (for this is impossible), but that degree of certainty a moral person seeking the truth is required to have. It is the highest degree of proof required in a trial.

bias

1. Preconceived opinion; a leaning toward one party or side of an issue; a predisposition. 2. A judge's state of mind toward a litigant that tends to sway her judgment and which may be cause for disqualification.

bicameral system

A legislature divided into two houses, as is the Senate and House of Representatives.

bid

An offer to buy or sell a product or service at a stated price (*e.g.*, building contractors submit bids for work on construction projects, and public agencies accept bids before awarding contracts).

bid shopping

A practice whereby general contractors use low sub-bids from other subcontractors to compel potential subcontractors to submit even lower bids.

bifurcated trial

Separate trial of separate issues (*e.g.*, criminal trials involving guilt and punishment; civil trials involving liability and damages).

bigamy

Criminal offense committed by marrying a person when one knows his previous marriage is still in existence.

bilateral contract

An exchange of mutual promises in which each party is both a promisor and promisee; each is bound to perform some duty for the other (*e.g.*, a contract for the sale of a car is bilateral because one party promises to pay for the car while the other promises to give it). Differs from a unilateral contract in which there is a promise on one side only, usually a promise to pay for a service rendered.

bill

1. In legislation, a draft of a proposed law that is introduced to the legislature for enactment. 2. A written account of indebtedness stating items sold, services rendered, or work performed. 3. The first pleading by a plaintiff in equity action; a complaint.

bill of attainder

Any form of legislative action that singles out an individual or group of persons for punishment without trial. Such an act is unconstitutional.

bill of exceptions

A formal written statement of the objections a party has with the rulings, decisions, or instructions given by a trial judge that is submitted for the information of an appellate court. A bill of exceptions is no longer necessary to preserve an objection in federal courts or in most state courts.

bill of exchange

A written order made on a second party to pay a third party a certain sum of money; a check, a draft.

bill of indictment

The document containing the accusation(s) against a person before it is given to a grand jury. *See* indictment.

bill of lading

A receipt for the goods issued by a person contracted to transport and deliver them to a specified person or place. It names the person from whom goods are received, states the place of delivery, describes the goods, and states the terms of the contract to transport them.

bill of particulars

An amplification of a pleading or a more detailed statement of the offense charged against a defendant to inform him of the specific nature and extent of a plaintiff's claim. It allows defendant to properly prepare his defense, but does not mention the specific evidence plaintiff will use against him.

bill of review

Proceeding in equity that seeks the reversal or revision of a decree already rendered. It is usually applicable only to correct errors of law on the face of the record, when new evidence is discovered, when new matter arises, or where there is evidence of fraud impeaching the original transaction.

Bill of Rights

The first ten amendments to the U.S. Constitution that guarantee fundamental rights and liberties of the individual, many of which limit the power of legislature.

bill of sale

A written agreement that transfers title of personal property to another; not the same as a receipt for payment.

bind

To legally obligate, especially by a contract, bond, or decree; to hold responsible for duties or obligations.

binder

1. A temporary insurance policy issued before determination of risk and the issuing of a final policy. 2. A receipt for a deposit on the purchase of a home that binds buyer and seller to agreed-upon terms.

binding

Legally obligatory; compulsory adherence to a contract, bond, decree, or duty.

bindover

1. The act by which a court requires a person to post bond and appear in court, or enter into a recognizance. 2. To transfer a case to a higher court or grand jury after finding probable cause of guilt.

***Bivens* action**

An action brought against a federal agent or official for violations of the plaintiff's constitutional rights. *See Bivens v. Six Unknown Named Agents*, 403 U.S. 388 (1971).

blacklist

1. (n.) A list of persons to be avoided (*e.g.*, employees who have been fired for unacceptable

41

performance or behavior, or troublesome union members). 2. (v.) To put someone on such a list.

blackmail

Extortion of money by threat to do bodily harm, expose a wrongdoing, or disgrace the character of another.

Blaine Amendment

A provision in a state constitution that provides for a higher level of separation of religion and the state than is provided by the First Amendment.

blank indorsement

The signing of a promissory note or bill of exchange without naming person to whom payment is to be made. It is payable to the person who possesses it (*see* bearer) and is negotiable upon delivery.

blasphemy

1. Act of maliciously reviling or reproaching God or religion; speaking of God so as to harm or destroy reverence toward Him. 2. At common law, a misdemeanor that is seldom enforced.

blue chip stock

Highest quality stock, issued by companies with enduring financial success, and promise of further success.

blue sky laws

State laws that regulate sale of stock and other securities to protect investors from fraudulent offerings.

board

1. An organized body of persons that acts in the interest of others by performing managerial, representative, and administrative duties for a corporation or government (*e.g.*, board of directors, board of health, board of aldermen). 2. Regular meals, though term sometimes includes lodgings.

Board for International Broadcasting

Created in 1973, and disbanded in 1994, this agency was responsible for overseeing broadcasting by stations serving Eastern Europe.

bona fide

(bon-na FAYD) Lat. In good faith; honest; without deceit. A

bona fide possessor is one who holds property with the honest belief that he is the proper proprietor.

bona fide occupational qualification (B.F.O.Q.)

A provision that allows employers to discriminate against potential employees on the basis of sex, religion, or national origin, provided employers can show that those qualifications relate to an essential duty of the job and are reasonably necessary for normal operation of the employer. Such a qualification is, thus, a B.F.O.Q.

bona fide purchaser (BFP)

In a purchase transaction, one who pays valuable consideration, has no notice of outstanding rights of others, and acts in good faith.

bond

1. An instrument of indebtedness issued by companies and government bodies that pays holder an interest for a specified amount of time. Some bonds have detachable coupons redeemable by the bearer for the interest payments. 2. A contract between a surety and the government that states surety will have defendant appear in court at a specified time, or forfeit bond money; bail bond. 3. A binding agreement, backed by securities, to do or not do something (*e.g.*, a "performance bond" guards against loss due to failure on a construction project). 4. A deed that obligates a person or his heirs to pay a sum of money by a specified date.

bonded warehouse

A government-designated building where goods are kept. Owner or lessee of building posts bond to protect government from loss connected with stored goods.

bondsman

A surety. One who posts bond for the release of a person in custody is called a bail bondsman.

bonus

Extra pay given gratuitously to an employee often in appreciation or as an incentive; any extra payment above regular remuneration. Bonuses are given, for instance, for extraordinary performance on a job, for prepayment of mortgage debt, and to professional athletes.

bookmaking

The taking and recording of wagers, most often on sporting events such as horse races, boxing matches, and football games. It is a form of gambling and is usually illegal except where permitted by law for specified events.

book value

The net worth of something, such as a company, as recorded in its account books; value of something after deducting liabilities from assets.

bootlegging

The illegal possession, use, transportation, or sale of intoxicating liquor, often done to avoid taxes.

booty

Personal property taken by a land army.

borrowing statutes

Laws of one state used by another state in deciding conflict of laws questions (*e.g.*, statute of limitations of state where claim accrued as opposed to limitations statute of forum state).

bottomry

A contract in which a shipowner borrows money to repair or equip his vessel, while offering the ship and its cargo as security for the loan. Usually made by the master of the ship while in a foreign port in times of emergency.

brownfield

Real property that is vacant but that is difficult to develop due to environmental contamination.

bureaucracy

1. An organization with a hierarchy of authority, specialized functions, and fixed positions, rules and procedures. 2. A governmental body of non-elected officials that makes and/or administers policy.

burglary

Entering a building or room with intent to commit a felony, usually theft. Common law required a burglary to be a breaking and entering a house at night, but modern statutes have broadened the definition.

business cycle
The sequential growth and shrinkage of economic activity.

business judgment rule
States that business managers are immune from liability when making careful, honest decisions under corporate authority.

business method patent
A patent that protects the invention of a process or series of steps that makes up a unique method of doing business.

business record exemption
Exemption to the hearsay exclusion rule that permits routine records, such as police reports, to be admitted in court as evidence.

business trust
An unincorporated form of business organization in which property is conveyed to a trustee (*e.g.*, a bank), according to specified terms, to be held and managed for the benefit of a beneficiary.

buyer
A purchaser, especially of movable property (chattels).

buy-sell agreement
1. An agreement between co-owners of a business to purchase the interest of a co-owner who withdraws from the business. 2. A restriction on the transfer of shares of a corporation that requires a shareholder to sell, or offer to sell, her stock to the corporation or to other shareholders when a stated event happens

bylaws
Rules and regulations of corporations, associations, and other organizations. Sometimes term is used synonymously with "ordinance" to mean the laws or statutes of a locality.

C.A.B.
See Civil Aeronautics Board.

cabinet
Body of officials that advises chief executives (*e.g.*, the heads of the major executive departments of the U.S. government, such as the Secretary of State and the Secretary of Defense).

cadaver
A dead human body; a corpse.

c.a.f.
Cost and freight. In sales contracts, the price includes the cost of goods and freight charges.

calendar
A list of cases to be tried; a docket.

call
1. Corporate law: A demand made on subscribers for payment of an unpaid portion of shares. 2. Securities: Option to buy an amount of shares of stock at or within a specified time and for a specified price. 3. Conveyance: An object or landmark that serves as a boundary marker.

callable bonds
Instruments of indebtedness redeemable before maturity (*i.e.*, the issuer has the option to pay off debt early); redeemable bonds.

calumny
(cal-OOM-nee) False accusation of a crime; defamation; libel; slander.

camera
Lat. A judge's chambers. A case heard "in camera" is heard in private, with no spectators.

cancel
To make void; to invalidate; to revoke. An instrument is cancelled by destroying it or writing on it so as to show it has been terminated. Regarding wills, the maker's intent to revoke is a necessary ingredient for its termination.

canon

Law or rule, especially of church discipline and doctrine, but also used with reference to inheritance, ethics, and taxation rules and those that guide the construction of written documents.

canon of ethics

Standard of conduct expected of lawyers that includes both a minimum level of conduct lawyers must maintain and ideal principles to which they should aspire. *See* Model Rules of Professional Responsibility.

capacity

The mental ability to comprehend the nature and effect of one's acts, especially in the making of a will or contract or in the commission of a crime. Regarding wills, capacity includes one's ability to understand the nature and extent of one's property and the claims made upon it. Regarding contracts, capacity requires one to be of legal age, of sound mind and sobriety to make a contract. Regarding criminal acts, capacity means one is able to understand the criminality of an act and be able to conform to the law.

capias

(CAP-ee-as" or "CAPE-ee-as) Lat. That you take. General term for various writs issued by a judge to the police to take someone into custody, (*e.g.*, a "capias pro fine" is a writ authorizing the taking into custody and detention of someone until a fine is paid).

capital

1. (n.) All property or monies of a business (*see* assets) such as the machinery a company owns to make its product, or the money stockholders have invested in the business. 2. (adj.) Major; chief; principal.

capital assets

Income tax law: All property owned by a taxpayer except for certain business property such as inventory or real estate.

capital crime

Crime that may be punished by death.

capital expenditure

Money spent to improve a property (*e.g.*, the construction of a building on a company's proper-

47

ty). The expenditure adds to the value of the property, but it is not deductible as an ordinary business expense.

capital gain

Profit made when a capital asset, such as a house or stock, is sold. Capital gains are classified as long term (property held more than 12 months) and short term (property held less than 12 months).

capital investment

1. Money spent to increase the value of an asset. 2. Money spent to purchase new equipment for a business.

capitalization

1. All the liabilities of a business such as the stocks, bonds, and debentures it has issued; the total value of those liabilities. The structure of a company in reference to the stocks and bonds issued by it. 2. To record an expenditure as a future asset rather than a present expense. 3. A computational method of giving value to a property according to the income it produces.

capitalized value

The present value of an expected future payment. The present value of that payment is determined by discounting the amount, taking into consideration the time value of money.

capital punishment

Punishment by death.

capital stock

1. All the shares of stock a company has issued or may issue. 2. The amount of money or property investors have contributed to a company. Capital stock represents a company's liability to its investors.

capitulation

1. Act of surrendering under certain terms. 2. Certain immunities from the law granted to aliens living in a foreign country.

caption

1. The introduction to a pleading that includes the names of the parties in the case, the title of the court it is held in, the presiding judge, the docket number, and other facts. Sometimes term refers to just the heading on the legal paper (*e.g.*, *Smith v. Jones*,

34 Cal. App. 3d 234 (1974)).
2. The seizing part of common law larceny, the other part being the carrying away.

captive audience doctrine
A principle that allows government restriction of speech that is so intrusive that a listener cannot, as a practical matter, escape it.

captive insurance
Insurance provided by a subsidiary to its parent company, especially when the subsidiary was established solely for the purpose of providing insurance only to the parent company.

cargo
The freight carried on a ship, train, airplane, or truck, as distinct from the transport vehicle itself.

carnal knowledge
Sexual intercourse; any penetration, however, slight, of the female sex organ by the male.

carrier
Someone who transports persons or goods for hire. A "common carrier" is one whose regular business is to transport the general public; one who transports

all persons or goods indifferently (*e.g.*, a railroad or bus company). A "private carrier" transports persons or goods in specific instances under contract.

cartel
1. A grouping of individual companies that conduct similar business in order to gain advantage from their union, such as for the fixing of prices or the creation of a monopoly. Cartels are restricted in the United States under antitrust laws. 2. An agreement between hostile nations made during wartime, especially for a prisoner exchange.

carve out
The practice of setting aside the income stream of a piece of property, for tax purposes.

case
1. A lawsuit; an action; a cause in controversy before the court. 2. The evidence and arguments used to support one side of a lawsuit. 3. In general, the word means a situation, an event, or a happening, as in "in this case."

case law

Law based on judicial precedent rather than legislative enactment (*i.e.*, the body of law founded in adjudicated cases as distinguished from statutes); common law.

case system

The method of studying law by the examination and discussion of past cases.

cash surrender value

The cash amount a life insurance policy is worth when terminated.

cash value

1. The price a property would bring if sold in an unrestrained, open market by an uncompelled seller to an uncompelled buyer. 2. Market value; fair market value; actual cash value.

castle doctrine

A man's home is his castle. At common law, a person is justified in using deadly force to protect his home and its inhabitants. Statutes have modified the rule to permit reasonable use of deadly force without first attempting to retreat in order to protect the home's inhabitants

(*e.g.*, against violent entry, threat of imminent harm, commission of a felony).

causa

(KAOW-sa) Lat. Cause, motive; lawsuit, case.

causa mortis

(KAOW-sa MOR-tis) Lat. In anticipation of death, such as a gift causa mortis.

causa proxima

(KAOW-sa PROX-i-ma) Lat. Proximate cause. The immediate or most closely related cause for a happening. The real cause of an accident (*see* proximate cause). It carries the liability.

causa sine qua non

(KAOW-sa SEE-nay kwa non) Lat. Cause without which a thing would not have occurred, used especially in relation to the cause of an injury in a negligence case.

causation

A necessary link between a wrongful act and resulting damage which grounds liability. In tort law, an act must be the "proximate cause" and the "cause in fact" of the plaintiff's injury.

cause

1. That which produces a result; the reason for something. 2. A legal action, suit, or case.

cause of action

Facts which give a plaintiff the right to bring a legal action against another. *See* claim.

caveat

(KAV-ay-yat *or* KAV-ee-yat) Lat. Let him beware. 1. A warning or caution, especially given to a judge or ministerial officer to prevent him from performing certain acts. 2. Statement which opposes the probate of a will. 3. Notice formerly filed with the U.S. Patent Office by an inventor to prevent a patent from being issued to another.

caveat emptor

(KAV-ay-yat *or* KAV-ee-yat EMP-tor) Lat. Let the buyer beware. A maxim which means the buyer purchases something at his own risk and should examine the item before taking possession of it. It applies to purchases where item is not under warranty. This maxim has been weakened by recent laws.

cease and desist order

An order from an administrative agency or court demanding that certain activities be stopped (*e.g.,* an order from the National Labor Relations Board to an employer to stop an illegal labor practice).

cede

To give up; to assign; to transfer. Usually used to mean the transfer of territory from one country to another.

censorship

Restriction of the public dissemination of printed material, movies, plays, or spoken words. Such restriction is sometimes done on the grounds of morality or in order to keep peace and order. Censorship has been challenged as a denial of First Amendment rights of freedom of speech and of the press.

census

A counting of people who live in a city, state, county, or nation, usually for the information of a government. A census also compiles social and economic information on those counted.

Central Intelligence Agency (C.I.A.)
Established by National Security Act of 1947. Agency makes recommendations to the National Security Council and gathers foreign intelligence and counter-intelligence information.

CERCLA
(SERR-kla) *See* Comprehensive Environmental Response, Compensation, and Liability Act.

certainty
Without doubt; clearly known; definiteness.

certificate
A written statement by someone with official status assuring that something has or has not been done, that certain facts are true, or that a legal requirement has been met.

certificate of deposit
A document issued by a bank acknowledging a deposit of money to be paid back with interest.

certificate of stock
A document issued by a corporation acknowledging the interest the stockholder has in the corporation.

certification
Procedure used by a court to suspend proceedings until another, usually higher, court rules on a specific question of law (*e.g.*, U.S. court of appeals may certify a case to U.S. Supreme Court or to state supreme court).

certification proceeding
An action by the National Labor Relations Board to determine whether a company's employees want to be represented by a particular union.

certified check
A check drawn on deposits in a bank where the bank guarantees or "certifies" there is enough money on deposit to cover the check. The bank becomes liable for payment of the amount of the check.

certiorari
(serr-shor-RAR-ree) Lat. To make sure. A writ issued by a superior court to an inferior court ordering the inferior court to produce records so that they may be examined for any irregulari-

ties, jurisdictional problems, or errors apparent on the face of the record. Most commonly used to refer to U.S. Supreme Court. The writ acts as a discretionary device for the Court to choose the cases it wishes to hear.

cession

Act of giving something up, especially property or rights. *See* cede.

cestui que

(sess-twee kuh) French, meaning "the one who." For instance, the term "cestui que use" refers to the person whose usage rights in a property are held by another.

C.F.T.C

See Commodity Futures Trading Commission.

chain of custody

Description of the physical location of evidence, and the names of the persons who had possession of it, from the time the evidence was obtained to the time it is offered at trial.

chain of title

The history of a title to a piece of property that traces the successive conveyances starting with the earliest known owner and ending with the present owner.

challenge

To object, to call into question, or to take exception to something, especially a person serving as a juror, but also to the personal qualifications of a judge to hear a case. There are two types of challenges to a juror: peremptory and for cause. Peremptory challenges do not need to state causes for the objections, whereas a challenge for cause does require causes to be stated.

chambers

1. A judge's private office. 2. Rooms in a courthouse where court officers can conduct business that need not be done in court.

champerty

A bargain made with a party to a lawsuit in which a third person, called a champertor, offers to pay for the litigation in return for part of any award given. It is a form of maintenance and is illegal.

chancellor

1. In some states, a judge in the court of chancery. 2. The highest

executive officer of a university.
3. An ecclesiastical officer who assists a bishop in matters of church law.

chancery
Equity, jurisprudence exercised in a court of equity (*i.e.*, matters decided according to reason, good conscience, and fairness as distinct from strictly according to law).

change of venue
The removal of a suit begun in one location to another location, often because of prejudice in one venue that may hinder a fair trial. May also occur in civil cases for the parties' convenience or in the interests of justice.

Chapter Eleven
Chapter of the Bankruptcy Code that allows a corporation or other organization to reorganize and restructure, while continuing to operate under Bankruptcy Court protection.

Chapter Seven
Chapter of the Bankruptcy Code that requires the liquidation of a debtor's assets, and payment of the proceeds to his creditors.

Most of a debtor's debts will be discharged.

Chapter Thirteen
Chapter of the Bankruptcy Code that allows an individual to repay her debts through the Bankruptcy Court.

character evidence
Evidence of a person's moral attributes which may be shown by reputation testimony, consisting of opinion or specific acts. Such evidence is generally inadmissible in civil cases, unless character is directly in issue. In criminal cases, a defendant may introduce evidence of her good character to which the prosecutor can then respond.

charge
1. An accusation. 2. A lien, claim, or encumbrance on land that gives the chargee a right to payment of debts owed him. 3. The liability on an estate imposed in a will for the payment of testator's debts on legacies. 4. A judge's summation of a case and instructions to a jury on matters of law, given before the verdict is rendered.

chargé d'affaires
(shar-ZHAY da-FAIRZ) Fr. 1. A diplomatic representative to a foreign government. 2. A substitute for an ambassador, usually appointed on an interim or temporary basis.

charge-off
An accounting term for the elimination of an item from assets, such as an uncollectible debt; a write-off.

charitable
For the public good, for the promotion of the general welfare, not for private profit. For something to be called "charitable," such as a trust or a bequest, it must be for the benefit of general public, not for a specified person or persons. Charities are for the benefit of the poor, the advancement of education, for the advancement of religion, and other causes beneficial to society.

charitable contribution
A contribution to a charitable organization or tax exempt group (*e.g.*, a charitable, educational, literary, public safety, religious, or scientific institution). Such contributions are often used to reduce a person's tax liability.

charitable remainder
A future interest in property given to a charity after an intervening estate.

charter
1. A document that establishes a corporation setting forth the laws that will govern it; the corporation's constitution; also an act by a legislature that creates a corporation. 2. A document issued by a sovereign power that grants a group of people certain rights, liberties, and powers such as the "Magna Charta." 3. The organic law of a city or town. 4. To hire a vehicle, airplane, or ship for transportation purposes.

charter-party
A written contract between a merchant and a shipowner for the transportation of goods.

chattel
An item of personal property as opposed to real property. If the item is moveable and is not attached to or has no connection with land, it is called a personal chattel (*e.g.*, car, stereo (*see*

personalty)). An interest concerning property is called a real chattel (*e.g.*, leasehold estate).

chattel mortgage

1. A mortgage on personal property rather than on real property (*i.e.*, the putting up of personal property as security for payment of money or performance of some other act). 2. A bill of sale with a defeasance clause (*i.e.*, a clause that cancels the lien on the property when all payments have been made). Used before existence of U.C.C.

chattel paper

An instrument representing both a debt and a security interest in specific goods.

check

A written order made on a bank for payment of money from funds the writer of the check has in his account with the bank to be paid on demand to the party named on the check. The check must be signed by the maker of the demand, and contain an unconditional promise to pay a certain sum in money to the order of the payee. A check is evidence of the drawer's promise to pay, and if it is a bad check (*i.e.*, there are insufficient funds on deposit to cover the amount drawn) the holder may sue for the amount owed him. *See* certified check, draft, promissory note.

Chief Justice

The senior or principal judge of a court that has three or more judges sitting together (*e.g.*, there is a Chief Justice of the Supreme Court as well as of the court of appeals).

child and dependent care credit

A tax credit allowed for a full-time worker who maintains a household for a dependent child or a spouse (or dependent) with mental or physical disabilities.

chose

(shows or chose) A personal chattel; personal property. *See* chattel, chose in action, chose in possession.

chose in action

A claim or right to possess something not presently in one's possession, such as money owed one in a debt. It includes the right to recover the item by lawsuit. Also, the thing itself that is recoverable by suit.

chose in possession
Personal property in one's possession including the right to possess and enjoy it.

churning
Excessive trading by a stockbroker solely to generate commissions.

C.I.A.
See Central Intelligence Agency.

c.i.f.
In commercial law, term signifying the cost of goods, insurance, and freight are included in the sales price.

circuit court
A court with jurisdiction in several districts or counties; some are immediate appellate courts and some are trial courts. *Compare* district court.

circumstantial evidence
1. Secondary facts from which a primary fact may logically be inferred. 2. Evidence gained not from direct observation of facts or personal knowledge, but from deductions made from related facts and circumstances; indirect evidence. Such evidence is capable of supporting a decision in a case if it consistently and reasonably points to one conclusion.

citation
1. A writ issued from a court of jurisdiction compelling a person to appear in court at a specified time; a summons. 2. An order from a police officer for a person to appear in court (*e.g.*, traffic citation). 3. The reference to the legal authority for a point of law that includes the case name, the volume of the report or reporter, the page number on which it appears, and court—if more than one is in reporter (*e.g.*, *Skalnik v. Town of Sperry*, 527 P.2d 860 (Okla. 1974)).

cite
1. To summon a person to appear in court. 2. To refer to a passage in a book, especially to the legal authority that supports one's argument. 3. To quote.

citizen
1. Person who is a member of a political community, who enjoys its rights and privileges, and who

owes allegiance to its government. 2. United States citizens are persons born in the United States or its territories, persons born to U.S. citizens while they are abroad, persons naturalized according to law. The term also includes municipalities, local governments, and national banks.

Citizenship and Immigration Services

Division of the Department of Homeland Security responsible for processing immigration and naturalization applications, and for establishing policies regarding immigration services.

civil

Branch of law pertaining to rights and remedies (*e.g.,* torts, contracts, real property) as opposed to criminal law.

civil action

A suit brought to protect a private right or to redress a wrong, as distinguished from a criminal proceeding; equitable action; legal action.

Civil Aeronautics Board (C.A.B.)

Created in 1938 to regulate airlines and interstate air commerce, including rates and fares. Abolished as of January 1985.

civilian

1. A private citizen. 2. A person not in the armed services. 3. A person well versed in the civil law.

civil law

1. Body of law that nation or state has established for itself as distinguished from natural law (*see* natural law) and international law; municipal law. 2. Law determining private rights and liabilities as distinguished from criminal law. 3. Roman law as set forth in the Justinian Code and distinguished from England's common law and the Church's canon law.

civil penalties

Punishment for certain activities, usually in the form of fines or money damages, and typically stipulated by a statute or regulatory scheme.

civil rights

Rights granted by positive law (*i.e.,* law established by legislative enactment or tacit acquiescence), as distinguished from civil liberties that grant rights by negative law (*i.e.,* law that restricts governmental power); specifically, rights guaranteed by the Constitution or by statutes such as those against discrimination on the grounds of race, religion, or national origin.

civil service

Governmental employment, excluding service in the armed forces.

civil union

A legal status recognized by some states that grants couples some of the benefits of marriage. Same-sex couples are eligible to enter into civil unions, even if the state would not allow them to marry. Also called a domestic partnership.

civitas

(SIV-i-tas) Lat. A group of people who live under the same laws, or in the same political community.

claim

1. The assertion of a right to property, money, or remedy (term is used as noun and verb). 2. The facts giving rise to the assertion. 3. Cause of action. 4. In patent law, a statement that describes an invention.

claimant

Person who makes a claim or asserts a right. *See* claim.

claim for refund

The means by which a taxpayer obtains a refund of taxes paid to the government. Such a claim is submitted to the government in writing.

clandestine

Secret, hidden, usually for an illegal purpose (*e.g.,* a clandestine mortgage is a second mortgage given on a property while concealing the first; clandestine introduction is the secret introduction of an item into a country in order to avoid customs).

class action

A lawsuit brought on behalf of a plaintiff and an ascertainable group of persons the plaintiff represents. For a class action to exist, the group of persons must: share a common interest with the plaintiff, be too large to feasibly be joined as parties, and benefit in some way from a successful outcome of the plaintiff's suit.

classified information
Information designated by its source (usually the government) to be for limited distribution.

classified stock
Common stock which has been divided into two or more classes; typically for the purpose of rewarding one class of stockholders with privileges not accorded to the other class(es).

clause
A single part of a legal document be it a paragraph, subdivision, sentence, or part of a sentence.

Clayton Act
An amendment to the Sherman Antitrust Act, enacted in 1914, which extended the prohibition against monopolies, price discrimination, certain mergers, and exclusive dealing contracts between companies.

clean hands
A maxim in equity law that holds that a person seeking equitable relief must not have acted unfairly in relation to the transaction at issue. If the action appears to arise out of an illegal or immoral matter, the person bringing it is said to have "unclean hands," and the court will not grant relief to such a person.

clearance
1. In maritime law, the right of a ship to leave port. 2. In contracts involving the showing of motion pictures, the amount of time between the close of the showing of a film in one theater and its start in another. 3. An amount of space needed around a moving vehicle, such as a train or bus.

clear and convincing proof
The degree of proof required to produce a firm belief concerning the truth of facts in the mind of the person(s) trying matters in issue; the degree of proof is greater than the "preponderance" (*see* preponderance) required in most civil cases, and less than "beyond a reasonable doubt" (*see*

beyond a reasonable doubt) required in criminal cases.

clear and present danger
Constitutional doctrine concerning speech which is not protected by the First Amendment guarantee of freedom of speech. Restrictions may be imposed if the speech provokes an illegal action or presents a danger to society (*e.g.*, yelling fire in a crowded theater and using "fighting words" are not protected).

clearinghouse
1. An association through which banks exchange checks and make adjustments on accounts. 2. An association within a stock or commodity exchange which handles daily records of the transactions between its members.

clear title
1. Title free from any obstruction, encumbrance, burden, or limitation. 2. Good title. 3. Marketable title.

clemency
1. The reduction of the punishment given a criminal by an executive commuting the sentence or by pardon. 2. Mercy; leniency.

clerical error
A "mechanical" error, or error of technique, as opposed to a judicial error (*e.g.*, a typing or copying mistake, a failure to properly record elements of a case, or an inadvertent omission of a clause from a document).

client
One who retains a lawyer for legal advice, representation in court, or for other legal matters.

close
1. (n.) A piece of land enclosed by a boundary, whether clearly visible such as a fence, or invisible and found only in the title. 2. (v.) To end a case.

close corporation
Corporation owned and run entirely by one person or by a small group of persons. In many states, such a corporation need not meet some of the usual requirements of a corporation such as annual meetings and election of officers.

closed-end management company

A management investment company for which a fixed number of shares are issued.

closed season

A time of year during which the hunting or fishing of a particular type of animal is prohibited.

closed shop

A company which requires its employees to be members of a particular union. Closed shops were declared illegal by the Taft-Hartley Act.

closing

The conclusion to a sale of real estate, whereby payment is made, mortgage is secured, and deed is transferred.

closing agreement

A written agreement between the Internal Revenue Service and the taxpayer for determining tax liability.

cloud on title

An outstanding claim or encumbrance on the title to a property which casts doubt on the validity

of that title. Such a claim itself may be valid or invalid.

co

1. Prefix meaning with, jointly, together, or in conjunction with.
2. An abbreviation for company or county.

code

A systematic collection of laws, statutes, or rules that have been enacted by the legislature (*e.g.*, commercial code, penal code, motor vehicle code).

Code of Professional Responsibility

Rules of conduct for the legal profession published by the American Bar Association in 1969 and adopted by most states. The Code has been superseded by the Model Rules of Professional Conduct. *See* canon of ethics.

code pleading

The system of pleading which conforms to state codes of civil procedure. These rules have descended from the New York Code of 1848, which was enacted to simplify pleading procedures.

codicil

A supplement to a will which adds to, subtracts from, restricts, qualifies, or modifies the will. A codicil must be written in clear, distinct language and executed according to testamentary rules.

codification

The process of systematically collecting and arranging by subject the laws of a particular locality.

coercion

1. Threat, intimidation, or force used to pressure a person to act against her will (*e.g.*, coercing another to commit a criminal act by threatening her with bodily harm or death). 2. Testamentary law: Coercion is pressure which causes testator to act against her free will (*e.g.*, pressuring her to include an undesired beneficiary).

cogent

Appealing to the intellect or reason; convincing.

cognizance

1. The exercise of jurisdiction (*e.g.*, the power to try and rule on a matter). 2. Judicial notice or knowledge (*i.e.*, the recognition of the truth of facts without evidence, such as a law of nature, which is recognized to be true without having to prove it).

cognovit note

(kog-NO-vit) Lat. A promissory note signed by a debtor that gives an attorney the right to enter a judgment against him should he fail to pay his creditor on time.

cohabitation

1. To live together as husband and wife, with or without sexual relations. 2. To illegally have sexual intercourse.

co-heir

One who inherits property jointly with another; one of several persons to whom an inheritance descends; joint tenants; tenants in common.

coinsurance

A clause in an insurance policy which makes the insured person responsible for a percentage of the property not specifically covered in the policy. This scheme divides the risk between the insurer and the insured (thus the term coinsurance), and it encourages the policyholder to carry greater coverage.

collateral
1. Secondary; auxiliary. 2. Parallel; on the side. 3. Property offered as security for the performance of an obligation, such as a bank account offered to back a loan.

collateral attack
A challenge to the integrity of a judgment, decree, or order brought in an action separate from the one which rendered the original judgment, decree, or order. It is not an appeal or review, and although it seeks to avoid or defeat the judgment, it must have a stated purpose other than that of impeaching the judgment (*e.g.*, a challenge to proper jurisdiction often constitutes the basis for a collateral attack).

collateral estoppel
Doctrine stating that issues litigated and determined in a proceeding are binding for the parties involved should those issues arise in any subsequent proceeding. A defendant may plead collateral estoppel to an issue to prevent double jeopardy. *See* double jeopardy, res judicata.

collateral heir
A person related to but not directly descended from a decedent (*e.g.*, brother, aunt).

collateral security
Additional security attached to an obligation to insure its performance (*e.g.*, valuable jewelry offered in addition to a bank account as collateral for a loan). It is subsidiary to the principal obligation and runs parallel to it (*i.e.*, if it is sold, its proceeds go to pay off the original debt).

collateral source rule
A payment to an injured person from a source other than the tortfeasor (*e.g.*, liability insurance is generally not deducted from damages received from the tortfeasor). The existence of the collateral source is usually inadmissible evidence.

collation
1. The comparison of a copy to the original; also the report by the person who made the comparison. 2. "Collation of advancements" is the grouping of

the assets of an intestate to determine the value of what he has already given to some heirs during his lifetime (advancements) so that the estate may be fairly distributed among all the heirs.

collective bargaining
A procedure by which employers and representatives of their employees negotiate a bargain regarding conditions of their employment such as wages, working hours, benefits and working conditions. The procedure is used to settle labor disputes, and must be conducted in "good faith" (*i.e.*, with an open and honest desire to solve the differences between them).

collision
The striking together of two objects

colloquium
(ko-LO-kwee-um) That part of a libel or slander complaint which connects the offensive words of the defendant to the plaintiff.

collusion
A secret agreement between two or more persons to commit a fraudulent act; term especially applies to manufacturing evidence to obtain a divorce.

color
1. Appearance or semblance, something that seems true, but is not actually so. 2. A prima facie right. 3. In pleading, the hiding of facts behind insufficient legal theory (*i.e.*, grounds that are apparently valid but are actually insufficient).

colorable
That which appears to be true or real but is not actually so; counterfeit; feigned.

color of office
Appearance of having official authority to act while not actually possessing it; an act so performed.

color of title
1. Mere appearance or semblance of good title; any fact or instrument which gives the appearance of passing good title but which, due to some defect, actually does not pass good title (*e.g.*, a counterfeit deed has only color of title). 2. Apparent title.

combination

1. The union of two or more persons for a common purpose.
2. A union of persons to achieve an unlawful end; conspiracy.
3. Patent law: An invention produced by uniting other inventions, some or all of which may have already been patented. The combination may be patented if it produces a new and useful result, and not a mere aggregate of the results of its parts.

comity

A doctrine of courtesy by which courts recognize the laws and judicial decisions of other sovereignties.

comment

A statement of opinion by a judge or counsel based on alleged facts. If a judge comments on the credibility of a witness or weight of the evidence, he must make it known it is his opinion. Contrary to federal courts, most states prohibit a judge from commenting on evidence or credibility.

Commerce Clause

Article I, section 8, clause 3, of the U.S. Constitution, which states, "Congress shall have the power to regulate commerce with foreign nations, and among the several states and with the Indian tribes."

commercial code

A compilation of laws dealing with most aspects of commercial transactions such as sales, bank deposits and collections, letters of credit, and investment securities. The Uniform Commercial Code (U.C.C.) was originally published in 1954 by the National Conference of Commissioners on Uniform State Laws and the American Law Institute and has been adopted in its entirety by all states except Louisiana.

commercial law

Law relating to the rights of those engaged in commerce and trade.

commercial paper

Negotiable instruments; written documents that serve as money; bills of exchange (*e.g.*, checks, bearer bonds, certificates of deposit, and promissory notes).

commercial speech

Speech that advertises a product or service for business purposes. It is now afforded some First Amendment freedom of speech protections although false advertising is not protected.

commingling

To mix together. Often used regarding the combining of goods belonging to several persons (*e.g.*, grains). It is considered a breach of fiduciary duty when funds are mingled by a fiduciary (*e.g.*, lawyer-client; trustee-beneficiary).

commission

1. Authority from the government empowering someone to perform certain acts, such as the authority an officer in the navy or a police officer has to perform his duties. 2. The authority to take a deposition. 3. A public board or administrative body. 4. An amount of money paid to an agent for his services, such as that paid to a stockbroker. 5. The performance of a criminal act.

commitment

1. The order or process by which a person is sent to jail or to a mental institution. 2. A promise to do something.

committee

1. A body of persons entrusted with authority to consider, determine, or manage some matter or to perform a duty. 2. The guardian of an insane person.

commodity

1. A thing produced, bought, or sold; an article of commerce; movable item; personal property. 2. Farm or mining products, such as wheat or iron ore, that are traded on a commodity exchange.

Commodity Futures Trading Commission (C.F.T.C)

Created in 1974; regulates trading on the 11 U.S. futures exchanges and actions of commodity exchange members.

common area

In landlord-tenant law, the portion of premises used in common by all tenants (*e.g.*, stairways, hallways, and entrance areas), which the landlord controls and for which the landlord is liable.

common fund doctrine
Principal that states that a litigant may recover the expenses of litigation from a fund that was recovered by the litigant, and that benefits persons other than the litigant or her attorney.

common knowledge rule
Exception to the usual requirement that a medical malpractice claim be supported by expert evidence. The exception applies when the act of malpractice or negligence is of a kind that a layperson would understand that it was negligent (*e.g.*, leaving a sponge inside a patient's body after an operation).

common law
Law based on judicial principles found in court decisions rather than law based on legislative enactment. It originates and derives its authority from usage and custom rather than statute. In England, that law distinguished from Roman Law, Civil Law, and Ecclesiastical Law. In the U.S., common law is that background law of England and the American colonies before the American Revolution. Generally, common law is the system of legal concepts upon which laws are based. It is adaptable by judges to the changing needs of society.

common-law marriage
One created without ceremony by mutual agreement to form a marriage relationship, cohabitation as husband and wife, and an assumption of marital obligations. Such a marriage is invalid in many states.

commonwealth
1. U.S. territory that is not a state, but that is self-governing under a constitution of its adoption and whose right of self-government will not be unilaterally withdrawn by Congress. 2. Official designation of the state in Kentucky, Massachusetts, Pennsylvania, and Virginia.

community property
Property owned jointly by a husband and wife, each having an individual one-half interest; it includes property acquired by either spouse during the marriage (except by gift, devise, legacy, or descent). In states with community property systems, income

earned by either spouse is owned jointly and equally by each. In common law systems, income is owned by the person who earns it.

commutation

1. Act of changing, altering, or substituting one thing for another. In criminal law, it is the act of lessening the punishment given to a convicted criminal. In commercial and civil law, it is the act of substituting one form of payment for another such as accepting an amount of money for performance of a job.

compact

An agreement or contract, especially of a serious nature. Compacts are made between nations to settle disputes, as well as between persons to create enforceable rights and obligations.

company

An association of persons united to perform a business or commercial activity and made a legal entity by a charter or incorporating document. It may divide its interest into transferable shares sold to the public in order to raise capital. Some companies are incorporated for religious or charitable purposes and do *not* sell shares. *See* corporation, partnership, firm.

comparative negligence

A doctrine that compares the relative degree of fault attributed to a defendant and a plaintiff in a negligence suit; it states that a plaintiff may recover damages from a defendant in a negligence suit even though the plaintiff may be guilty of some negligence himself, provided that the negligence of the defendant was greater. In states with pure comparative negligence, a plaintiff may recover even if his negligence is greater than that of the defendant. The damages awarded the plaintiff will be diminished in proportion to the degree of negligence attributed to him.

comparative rectitude

A principle applied in divorce cases that compares the relative degree of responsibility attributed to each spouse for the marriage termination. Relief is awarded to the person least at fault.

compensation
1. Payment for injury or loss sustained. 2. Giving something of equal value for something lost. 3. Making of amends; recompense. 4. Payment for work performed.

compensatory damages
Those recoverable for the precise injury sustained; damages that make an injured party whole as opposed to punitive, nominal, or exemplary damages. Compensatory damages include medical expenses, pain, mental suffering, and injury to one's reputation.

competent
1. Having the proper legal qualifications, ability, or authority. 2. Having the capacity to understand and act reasonably.

competent evidence
Evidence which is legally admissible; it is relevant and is of the proper form required to assist a jury in determining a point in question.

complainant
1. Person who makes a complaint. 2. One who initiates a lawsuit; plaintiff; petitioner.

complaint
1. Criminal law: A formal charge made under oath before a magistrate stating that a person has committed a crime or offense. (*See* affidavit.) 2. Civil law: A statement of the plaintiff's claim for relief and the grounds on which it is based; the original pleading in a civil action.

compliance
Act of complying, obeying, or submitting to someone or something, as in "compliance with the law."

composition
An agreement between a debtor and his creditors whereby the creditors accept a lesser amount than is owed them in exchange for some consideration, such as immediate payment. There are two types of composition agreements: a "composition with creditors" in which creditors voluntarily release the debtor from some part of his obligation, and a "composition in bankruptcy" in which creditors must, by law, release the debtor. *See* accord.

Comprehensive Environmental Response, Compensation, and Liability Act
Federal statute that fixes liability for the costs of cleaning up hazardous waste sites.

compos mentis
(com-POES MEN-tis) Lat. Of sound mind; sane.

compounding a felony
Refusal by a party injured in a felony to prosecute or inform against the offender in exchange for some considerations, such as a cash bribe.

compound interest
Interest on interest (*i.e.*, interest added to principal creates an aggregate sum upon which interest begins to accrue).

compromise
An agreement to settle differences by making mutual concessions; it can be made in or out of court.

compromise verdict
An improper verdict resulting from a juror relinquishing her sincere opinion or conclusions regarding an issue in return for other jurors doing the same regarding other issues solely in order to reach an agreed verdict.

comptroller
An official who examines and audits accounts, keeps records, supervises the collection of money, and reports on the financial status of a public body or private company.

compulsion
The exertion of physical or mental force to compel a person to act against his will. *See* coercion, duress.

compulsory counterclaim
A counterclaim that must be asserted, or it is waived.

compulsory process
1. Process which compels a person to appear in court. 2. The constitutional right a defendant has to call a witness into court. Subpoenas, summons, and warrants of arrest are writs utilized in this process.

compurgator
In old Anglo-Saxon law, one of several neighbors of an accused person who swore he believed in the defendant's innocence. A

compurgator is the forerunner of a juror in English law.

concealment

The withholding of information which one in honesty and good faith is bound to reveal (*e.g.*, the concealment of a hidden medical problem from an insurer).

concerted action

1. Action involving joint plans, arrangements, and agreements between persons pursuing some goal. 2. Conspiracy. 3. In labor relations law, it is a joint action by employees to further a common goal, such as a work stoppage to present a wage grievance; concerted activity.

concession theory

In corporations law, a theory which views a corporation as "indivisible, immortal, and [which] rests only in intendment and consideration of the law." *Case of Sutton's Hospital,* 10 Coke 1, 23 (1613).

conclusion of law

1. Conclusion reached by a judge after applying the law to the facts in a case, as distinguished from conclusion of fact, which is a conclusion drawn by a jury from evidentiary facts; final judgment or decree. 2. A judge's statement as to what law applies to the facts found in a case. 3. In pleading, it is a statement which does not plead the facts (*e.g.*, a defendant's reaction to the facts).

concubine

Archaic term for woman who lives with a man as his wife but who is not married to him.

concur

1. To agree with (*e.g.*, a concurring opinion of an appellate judge is one that agrees with the majority opinion though it may be for different reasons). 2. To happen simultaneously, as in "the two events concurred." 3. To act jointly with other claimants in making demands against an insolvent debtor.

concurrent

1. Running together, as concurrent prison sentences are served at the same time, which differs from consecutive sentences which are served one after the other. 2. Agreeing with, as a concurrent opinion by a judge who agrees with the result of a

majority opinion, but uses different reasons to reach that result. 3. Acting in conjunction, as in, concurrent causes act together at the same time to produce a result. 4. Having the same authority. *See* concurrent jurisdiction.

concurrent jurisdiction
Authority possessed by two or more different courts to hear and decide on the same matter within the same territory. The choice of which court will be used is left up to the plaintiff.

condemn
1. To sentence a person to death upon conviction of a capital crime. 2. To declare unfit for use. 3. To take private property for public use. *See* condemnation.

condemnation
The process of taking private property for public use under the power of eminent domain. The owner's consent is not necessary, but just compensation must be paid. *See* expropriation; *contrast with* confiscate.

condition
1. A possible future event, the occurrence of which creates a

right or attaches a liability. 2. Contract law: A provision in a contract that limits or modifies the duties under the contract. 3. A clause in a will which suspends, revokes, or modifies the bequest. 4. Real estate law: A qualification, restriction, or limitation annexed to a conveyance of land which states that the estate will commence, be enlarged, or be defeated upon the occurrence or nonoccurrence of an event, or the performance or nonperformance of an act. A condition can be express (*i.e.*, made known by clear, direct words); or implied (*i.e.*, known indirectly or inferred from surrounding circumstances); or constructive (*i.e.*, judicially imposed). *See* condition precedent, condition subsequent.

conditional
Depending on the occurrence or nonoccurrence of a possible future event; contingent.

conditional bequest
(legacy) A gift of personal property by will that either takes effect or is defeated depending on the occurrence or nonoccur-

rence of an uncertain future event.

conditional fee

An estate in land conditioned to terminate on the occurrence of some particular event which may or may not occur; also known as "fee conditional," "fee simple conditional," and "base fee."

conditional sale

A sale of goods whereby the buyer takes possession of the goods but does not have ownership until they are paid for in full.

condition precedent

A condition that must exist before a right or obligation is created. The term is used in real estate law to refer to a condition that must exist before an estate can take effect. It is used in contract law to refer to an event that must occur or an act that must be done before a contract becomes effective. In insurance law, the term refers to a condition that must exist before a policy is effective. *See* condition.

condition subsequent

A condition which, after occurring, cancels a right or obligation. In estate law, a condition subsequent is one attached to an estate already vested, and which will make the estate conveyed liable for defeat if a breach of the condition occurs. In contract law, it will void a contract if the specified event or action occurs. In a lease, a condition subsequent will give a landlord the right to revoke the lease. *See* condition.

condominium

1. A jointly owned, multiple-unit building whose residents have exclusive ownership of a single unit (apartment) and ownership as a tenant in common of all the common areas, facilities, and grounds. 2. A system of owning a building.

condonation

Voluntary forgiveness of a spouse's actions that may constitute grounds for divorce, with the implied condition of future good behavior. It is a valid defense in a divorce action.

confederacy

1. An association of nations united for their mutual benefit; confederation. 2. An association of persons united for an illegal purpose; conspiracy.

confession

An admission of guilt. A confession is admissible as evidence against a defendant only if it is given voluntarily. A confession may be indirect or implied (*i.e.*, inferred from the defendant's conduct or pleading).

confession and avoidance

Pleading in which a person confesses (admits) the truth of an allegation against him but seeks to avoid the effect of the admission by presenting new matter; affirmative defense.

confession of judgment

Entry of a judgment against a debtor who has agreed such a judgment will be entered should he fail to pay his debt on time. The procedure saves the time and expense of a normal legal proceeding, but has been prohibited in many states due to abuse and due process considerations. *See* cognovit note.

confidence game

A swindle whereby the swindler falsely represents himself or some fact, gains the victim's confidence, and abuses that confidence, usually to enrich himself.

confidential communication (information)

Privileged communication intended only for the knowledge of a particular person (*e.g.*, communication between client and attorney or between husband and wife).

confidential relation

Relationship in which one person puts trust and confidence in another to act in good faith for his best interest. It arises where one person has an influential or superior position over another because of the confidence placed in him by the person in a dependent position. Confidential relations exist between client and attorney, employee and employer, principal and surety, child and parent, and in many other relationships. *See* fiduciary.

confirmation

1. (n.) An affirmation; a contract or document affirming something. 2. To give approval; to make firm or binding. A confirmation of estate is a conveyance of an estate or right in land in which a voidable estate is made unavoidable or made larger. A confirmation of sale is the probate court's approval of an executor's sale of estate property.

confiscate

To take private property for public use without compensation. *Contrast* expropriation.

conflict of interest

A term describing a situation in which a public official's private interests clash with his duty to serve the public interest. A conflict of interest may disqualify the official from acting on a particular matter, such as a judge from hearing a case in which he has a monetary interest.

conflict of laws

1. Differences and inconsistencies in the laws of different localities. 2. The system of jurisprudence which determines which law applies or reconciles inconsistencies of conflicting laws when the jurisdiction of different states or countries is involved. Such matters are often decided by determining which jurisdiction had the most significant interest in the matter in controversy.

Confrontation Clause

The clause in the Sixth Amendment which prescribes the right of an accused criminal "to be confronted with the witnesses against him."

confusion of goods

A mixing of the personal property of different persons so as to make the individual property of each indistinguishable. The mixing may be accidental, but if it is willful and tortious, the person who did the mixing suffers the loss of his property.

conglomerate

A corporation that controls a number of companies not in competition with one another.

conjecture

Judgment or inference that is based on weak or tenuous evidence.

conjugal rights

Marital rights which include the right to companionship, love, sex, and joint property.

Connivance

1. Secret consent to the commission of an illegal act. 2. In divorce actions, it is plaintiffs corrupt consent to offense charged against defendant.

consanguinity

Blood relationship; kinship; having common ancestors. Consanguinity is either lineal (*i.e.*, being directly descended from another), such as a son is from his father; or collateral (*i.e.,* being related but not directly descended from the other), such as cousins are related.

conscience of the court

In a court of equity, the power of the court to base decisions upon commonly held principles of fairness and expediency.

conscious parallelism

Following a competitor's course of action independently, without colluding or conspiring with the competitor.

consecutive sentence

See accumulative sentence.

consent

1. Free, voluntary agreement by one who has proper physical and mental capacity; it is an act of reason and deliberation; acquiescence. 2. A unity of opinion.

consent decree

1. A decree in equity court sanctioning an agreement between parties; an agreed judgment. 2. An agreement by a defendant to stop certain activities.

consent judgment

A judgment sanctioning an agreement between parties, which is immune to collateral attack as a judgment rendered.

consequential damages

1. Indirect damages or losses not flowing immediately from an act, but rather from the consequences of the act (*e.g.*, loss of business as a result of a fire). 2. Damages resulting from special conditions which are not ordinarily predictable. Some contracts have provisions against consequential damages which limit liability for injuries caused by unusual, un-

predictable circumstances. Same as special damages.

conservator

A guardian appointed by the court to take charge of the property or manage the affairs of an incompetent person.

consideration

The thing of value each party to a contract agrees to give in exchange for what he receives; the reason a contract is made. Consideration is necessary to make a contract binding. The term includes both the benefit gained by one party and the corresponding responsibility undertaken by the other (*e.g.*, if a builder makes a contract with a homeowner to build an addition to the homeowner's house, he undertakes the responsibility to do the job in exchange for the promise he will be paid an agreed-to amount; the homeowner's promise to pay for the addition is consideration for the builder's promise to do the work, and vice versa).

consignment

1. The handing over of goods by their owner (consignor) to a carrier for delivery to a third party (consignee). 2. Bailment for hire; also, the goods so sent. 3. Commercial law: Sending goods to an agent to sell without transferring title to the goods to the agent.

consolidation

A joining together of separate parts into one, such as a consolidation of companies to form a new corporation (also called a merger), or the joining of suits to be tried as one.

consortium

1. Marital rights, the company, companionship, affection, and aid one spouse gives to another. "Loss of consortium" may be grounds for a lawsuit, for example, by the spouse of a person negligently injured in an accident, or if disaffection occurs as a result of an intentional interference with a marriage. 2. Civil law: The joining of several persons as parties to one action.

conspiracy

An agreement of two or more persons made for the purpose of committing an illegal act, or for the purpose of doing a lawful act by unlawful means. Each person must know the purpose of the conspiracy and agree to join in the plans to further that purpose. Many jurisdictions require that some overt act accompany the planning for conspiracy to exist.

conspirator
One of the persons involved in a conspiracy. A conspirator may simply agree with another person's criminal aims, or he may actually aid in the planning, commission, or attempted commission of a crime.

constable
A municipal or county officer who keeps the peace, serves writs, and executes court process (*see* process). Constables have been replaced by sheriffs.

constitution
A system of basic laws and principles by which a nation, state, corporation, or other organization is governed. It may be unwritten, but the term generally refers to a written document containing those laws and principles.

constitutional law
The branch of law that involves the interpretation and application of the fundamental laws and principles stated in the U.S. Constitution. Those laws and principles apply to the organization, function, and power of the government, and to the rights of the governed.

constitutional right
Right guaranteed by the U.S. Constitution or by a state constitution which is not to be violated by any legislative, judicial, or executive acts.

construction
Act of determining the meaning of something that is unclear, such as a statute, law, or written document. There is strict (or literal) construction which determines exact, technical meaning, and liberal (or equitable) construction which expands on and interprets the meaning of a statute or law.

constructive
That which is not so in its essential nature, but which is regarded as such in the mind of the law; not actual, but legal. Constructive is used as an adjective with

79

many terms to mean that which, through inference, presumption, or interpretation, the law holds as existing. "Constructive eviction" is a situation where a landlord causes a tenant to leave his premises without actually asking him to do so (*e.g.,* by turning off the heat in winter). "Constructive fraud" lacks the element of intentional dishonesty of purpose actual fraud requires, but the law regards it as fraud because its consequences in equity are similar to fraud. A "constructive trust" is one raised by a court of equity against a person who obtains or holds legal title to property through fraud, abuse of confidence, or some other unconscionable conduct, that is, title which in good conscience he should not hold.

consul

An officer assigned to a foreign country to promote and protect a government's economic interests and the interests of its citizens in that country.

consumer

One who purchases, rents, or uses a product or service primarily for personal rather than business purposes.

consumer credit

Credit offered to individuals for personal, family, or household purposes as opposed to business purposes.

Consumer Credit Protection Act

Truth-in-Lending Act; federal law that protects consumers by requiring, among other things, full disclosure of terms and conditions regarding credit transactions.

Consumer Product Safety Commission (C.P.S.C.)

Created in 1972, federal agency responsible for reducing unreasonable risks of injury associated with consumer products.

consummation

1. The completion of something, such as an agreement by the mutual signing of a contract. 2. The act of making a marriage "complete" by having sexual intercourse.

contemplation

Expectation; anticipation; consideration of an action with the thought that it will occur. "Contemplation of bankruptcy" refers to the expectation a business will fail. A transfer or assignment of an asset made in contemplation of bankruptcy is made with the intention of protecting the asset from the distribution that results from the bankruptcy proceedings. Acts done in "contemplation of death" are those done in anticipation of death, such as the transfer of property to avoid inheritance taxes. In such transfers of property, death need not be imminent, but thoughts of death must be the primary motive for the transfer for it to be said that it was made in "contemplation of death."

contempt

Intentional disobedience of or disdain for a known order from a court or legislative body.

contempt of court

Conduct which tends to interrupt the dignity and order of a court or the administration of justice; intentional disobedience of a court order. Direct contempt openly disregards the authority of the court in its presence (criminal contempt), and indirect (or constructive) contempt disrupts the administration of justice outside the courtroom (civil contempt).

contentious

That which involves an argument, contest, or dispute between adversaries. A trial is a contentious proceeding. "Contentious jurisdiction" is jurisdiction concerned with hearing and ruling on disputed matters.

contest

1. To challenge, to dispute, to call into question, such as to contest a will. 2. To oppose, to defend, to resist, such as to contest a lawsuit in court.

contingent

Liable or possible, though not certain, to occur due to dependence on some possible future event; provisional. With a "contingent claim," liability does not exist until the occurrence happens. A "contingent estate" is a right to property that vests only after the occurrence of a specified event. A "contingent fee" is one paid to a lawyer depending on the amount awarded in a civil suit, which may be nothing if the suit is lost. *See* conditional.

continuance

The adjournment or postponement of a court action to a future time or date. A continuance may be granted at the request of one or both of the parties to the action, or it may be ordered by the court for its own reasons.

contra

(KON-tra) Lat. Against; in opposition to; contrary to; disagreeing with.

contraband

1. Goods that are illegal to produce, possess, export, or import. 2. Goods which a neutral country is not permitted to carry into a country at war.

contra bonos mores

(KON-tra BOE-noes MORE-ays) Lat. Against good morals.

contract

An agreement between two or more parties which creates legally binding obligations. A valid contract must involve competent parties, proper subject matter, consideration (*see* consideration), and mutuality of agreement and of obligation. The Uniform Commercial Code defines contract as "the total legal obligation which results from the parties' agreement." Contracts are classified in many ways, some of which follow:

Bilateral or *unilateral*. A bilateral contract is one involving mutual promises between parties. A unilateral contract is a one-sided promise where one party undertakes an obligation without a reciprocal promise or obligation being made or undertaken.

Executed or *executory*. An executed contract is one which has been carried out (*i.e.*, where both parties have met their obligations). An executory contract is one where an obligation is to be carried out in the future.

Express or *implied*. An express contract is openly expressed in writing or orally. An implied contract is one inferred by law to exist because the parties' conduct or surrounding circumstances indicate a contractual relationship exists.

Contract Clause

Constitutional provision (Art. 1, § 10) that prohibits states from enacting any law that retroactively impairs existing contract rights.

contra pacem

(KON-tra PAY-sem) Lat. Against the peace.

contravention

Act of going against or breaking a law or agreement.

contribution

1. That which one person does or gives to meet his share of a jointly held responsibility. 2. The right to demand a person bear his portion of a shared burden, such as a jointly held debt or a concurrently caused injury. (*Contrast* indemnity.) 3. Civil law: A proportional division of the proceeds of the property of an insolvent debtor among his creditors.

contributory

1. (adj.) Additional; supplementary; auxiliary. 2. (n.) A person who is a member of a joint stock company and who is liable to contribute to the assets of the company when it is being wound up.

contributory infringement

Supplying the means for another to infringe on the copyright of a work, with the intent that the means be used for infringement.

contributory negligence

Lack of ordinary care for one's safety on the part of an injured plaintiff that, when added to the negligence of another, contributes to the cause of an injury. It is an affirmative defense to a negligence charge, but it has often been replaced by the doctrine of comparative negligence. *See* comparative negligence.

controlled substance

A chemical whose possession, sale, and use is regulated by state or federal law.

controversy

1. A definite, concrete issue concerning legal relations among parties whose interests conflict. The term is used in Article III of the U.S. Constitution to limit the exercise of judicial power to concrete cases involving the legal rights of adversary parties,

that are based on alleged facts, and that would result in a decision granting specific relief. 2. A civil proceeding as distinguished from a criminal proceeding (called a case).

contumacy

Intentional disobedience or defiance of a judicial order, whether in or out of court (*e.g.*, refusal to appear in court when summoned to do so).

convention

1. Treaty. 2. A formal statement of principles by a group of nations.

conventional

That made by agreement between parties rather than by law (*e.g.*, a conventional lien or a conventional estate).

conversion

1. Tortious act of depriving an owner of his property without his permission and without just cause. An illegal taking, detention, use, assumption of ownership, or destruction of the property of another all constitute conversion. 2. A change of real property into personal property,

or vice versa is equitable conversion. 3. Act of exchanging one type of security for another.

conveyance

1. A transfer of title to real property (verb is convey). 2. The deed or written instrument that transfers title to real property; deed of conveyance.

convict

1. (v.) To adjudge a person guilty of a crime. 2. (n.) Person in prison after being found guilty of a crime by a court.

conviction

A final judgment of guilt reached after a criminal trial that is based on a guilty verdict, a guilty plea, or a plea of "nolo contendere." Term often includes the subsequent act of imposing punishment on the guilty person.

cooling time

1. Criminal law: That time between provocation and reaction that allows a person to become calm and composed, and thus become able to comprehend the results of his actions. 2. Labor relations: Time provided for settling disputes between labor

and management. 3. Divorce law: An automatic period between the initiation of a divorce action and the divorce hearing. 4. Consumer law: A time during which a buyer may cancel a purchase. Also called a "cooling off period."

cooperative association
A group enterprise jointly owned or run by those who use its activities or services.

coparceners
(ko-PAR-senn-ers) Persons who jointly acquire an estate by descent. They are co-heirs who jointly and severally hold an interest in an entire estate. "Coparcenary" is an estate so jointly inherited and held. Coparcenary differs from joint tenancy in that it can only come about by descent, whereas joint tenancy can be created by a written instrument.

copyright
Statutory protection of work such as a literary work, musical composition, or film or other audiovisual creation giving the creator (or the holder of the copyright) the right to regulate the publica-

tion, reproduction, distribution, performance, or use of the copyrighted material for a certain period of time. It is an incorporeal right (*i.e.*, a right to something intangible as opposed to tangible, such as a right to land).

coram nobis
(kor-ram NO-biss) Lat. In our presence; before us. A writ of appeal that brings before the court then hearing a case errors of fact, and seeks relief from the consequences of those errors. It differs from a writ of "coram vobis" (before you) in that the latter is directed by a court of review to the trial court. These writs have been abolished by *Federal Rule of Civil Procedure 60(b)*.

co-respondent
1. A codefendant in an equity suit. 2. Person charged in a divorce action with having committed adultery with the plaintiff's spouse.

corner
Controlling a large quantity of a commodity for the purpose of manipulating its price. This is done by buying, for future deliv-

ery, a greater quantity of the commodity than is at the time available in the market. The buyers withhold the commodity from sale until increased demand for it artificially pushes its price up.

coroner

A public official who conducts inquiries into violent deaths or deaths that occur under suspicious circumstances. A "coroner's inquest" is the name of the investigation conducted by such an official.

corporal punishment

Physical punishment; punishment inflicted on the body, such as beating or slapping. The term may also include imprisonment.

corporate bond

An instrument representing a corporation's promise to pay a fixed sum with interest at some future time and given in exchange for money or something of value.

corporate opportunity

The advantage of one who is close to a corporate entity to benefit from knowledge gained

from that relationship. A corporate director who takes unfair advantage of such knowledge for personal gain breaches his fiduciary obligations.

corporation

An artificial person (*see* artificial person) created by and operating under law, thus possessing only the properties its charter gives it; a legal entity having an existence and personality distinct from that of the individual members that form it, but having the capacity of acting as a single person in matters related to its purpose. "Public corporations" are created by the state for political purposes (*e.g.*, a town government or a school district). The term also refers to corporations that sell shares to the general public (these are more accurately described as "publicly traded corporations"). "Private corporations" are created by private persons for nongovernmental purposes. *See* close corporation.

corpus delicti

(KORE-pus de-LIK-tee) Lat. Body of the crime. The substantial fact a crime has been committed; the thing upon which a crime has been committed coupled with proof a crime has indeed been committed (*e.g.*, in a murder case, the body of the victim and proof that the victim died by a criminal agency).

corpus juris
(KORE-pus JUR-ris) Lat. Body of law. The substance of the law. A book or books containing a compilation of the law. "Corpus Juris Secundum" is an encyclopedic work on American law.

corroborate
To strengthen, confirm, or support (*e.g.*, corroborating evidence supports evidence already presented).

corruption of blood
A doctrine of feudal English origin that prevented a person from inheriting or passing property to his heirs because of attainder (*see* attainder). It has been abolished.

co-sign
A joint signature of a document, often indicating the signers' common obligations under that document.

cost of completion
A measure of damages for breach of contract, representing the total amount the injured party would have to receive in order to place him in the same position he would have been in had the contract not been breached, by having another person complete the task that was not performed as promised.

costs
1. Money paid by the loser to the winner of a court action to cover the expenses incurred by the litigation. Generally, costs do not include attorney's fees. 2. Charges and fees that statutes require be paid for the services of court officers, witnesses, jurors, and others.

costs to abide the event
A court order requiring the losing party to pay legal expenses of the prevailing party, sometimes including the costs of all appeals.

co-tenancy
Ownership of property by two or more persons who have unity of possession (*i.e.*, a right to possess the entire property). Term includes joint tenancy, tenancy in

common, and tenancy by the entirety (*see* joint tenancy, tenancy in common, and tenancy by the entirety).

counsel

1. An attorney; counselor.
2. Advice given regarding legal matters.

count

1. In indictments, an allegation of a distinct offense; a charge.
2. In civil procedure, the statement of a specific cause of the action.

counterclaim

A counter demand made by a defendant against a plaintiff (*i.e.*, between opposing parties in the original action) in a civil suit. It is not a defense, answer or denial, but an independent cause of action made to diminish or defeat the plaintiff's claim. A counterclaim may be compulsory, arising out of the subject matter of the claim against the defendant, or permissive, not arising out of that subject matter. *See* set-off; *compare* cross-claim.

counterfeit

To forge, fabricate, or unlawfully copy something with the intention of deceiving another by passing the copy as the original. Used also as a noun and an adjective in reference to the thing so fabricated.

countermand

To revoke or cancel an order previously given. An order that is inconsistent with a previous order countermands the first order by implication. Used also as a noun.

counteroffer

An offer made in response to an offer that changes the terms of the original offer (*e.g.*, by making acceptance dependent on the performance of a condition).

countersign

To sign a document in addition to a principal signature so as to attest to the document's validity. The signature itself is called a countersignature.

county

A geographical subdivision of a state made for political, judicial, or administrative purposes. In some jurisdictions, counties have incorporated in order to facilitate the administration of local government.

course of dealing
The history of business conduct between parties that establishes a basis of understanding their behavior.

court
1. A governmental institution charged with the administration of justice according to laws or principles of equity. 2. The place justice is administered. 3. A Judge or all Judges.

Courts are classified as "superior" and "inferior." Superior courts have general original jurisdiction in the first instance (*i.e.*, unlimited jurisdiction in their jurisdictional area) and have a degree of control over lower courts. Inferior courts have limited jurisdiction (can only hear certain types of cases) and are subject to review by higher courts. Courts are also classified as civil and criminal. Civil courts adjudicate controversies between individuals involving private rights. Criminal courts adjudicate cases involving criminal laws. A court of equity administers justice according to principles of equity.

court-martial
1. A military court established to adjudicate cases of members of the armed forces. 2. (v.) To prosecute before such a court.

court of appeals
A court that hears cases on appeal from the lower courts. *See* appellate court.

court of assize and nisi prius
(as-SIZE and NYE-see PREE-us or PRY-us) Early English trial courts commissioned by the king, that traveled throughout the kingdom to hold jury trials.

Court of Claims
Since 1982, Court of Federal Claims. A federal trial court that hears and determines claims against the United States Government. These claims may be founded upon acts of Congress, regulations of executive departments, contracts with the government, and upon matters founded upon the Constitution. Many states also have courts of claim for claims against the state.

court of exchequer

An early English court with jurisdiction over matters of government law and revenue.

covenant

A written agreement; a promise or obligation contained in an instrument under seal, such as a deed. The term is often used in relation to land, such as a "covenant for quiet enjoyment," which is a promise by the conveyor of land that he will protect the buyer against lawful claims made on the land. A "covenant of seisin" is a promise made by a grantor of property that he lawfully possesses the property and has the right to convey it. Covenants are classified in many ways. "Covenants in gross" are those that do not run with the land (*i.e.*, they do not pass to succeeding owners). "Covenants running with the land" do pass to succeeding owners. "Covenants against encumbrances" are promises made by the grantor stating that an estate has no burdens on it, such as claims or liens. Covenants are usually express, but may be implied from the agreement.

covenant marriage

A form of marriage recognized in some states in which the spouses agree in advance that they may not obtain a divorce unless they meet stricter requirements than normally required for a divorce in that state.

covenant not to compete

A contractual agreement in which the parties consent not to compete against each other; generally invoked in the sale of a business or as a part of an employment contract.

coverture

At common law, the status of a married woman that combines her civil existence with her husband's. Coverture gives the husband equal control over his wife's property (as is the case in community property jurisdictions). Modern statutes have changed this and have given the woman complete control over her own property in many jurisdictions.

C.P.S.C.

See Consumer Product Safety Commission.

crashworthiness doctrine
Principle in products liability law that holds a manufacturer strictly liable for injuries from an accident that were due to a cause other than the defective product, but that were made worse or aggravated by a defect in the product.

Creative Commons
A type of license to use copyrighted work that does not require the user to receive prior permission, or to pay a fee. Creative Commons licenses often require that the person who makes use of the work attribute the work to the original author.

credit
1. (n.) The trust or confidence a buyer gains from a seller based on the buyer's ability and reputation for payment. It allows a person to pay for a purchase over time or to borrow money. 2. The time allowed a buyer to pay for a purchase. 3. The amount of money at one's disposal (*e.g.*, in a bank account or other security). 4. In accounting, money one is owed; opposite of debit. 5. (v.)

To acknowledge payment of a debt.

credit bureau
A firm that collects information on the character, reputation, and credit rating of persons or corporations for distribution to subscribers, such as banks; commercial agency; credit agency; mercantile agency.

creditor
Person to whom a debt is owed; one who extends credit to another; anyone to whom an obligation is owed; opposite of debtor.

creditor's bill (or suit)
An equity proceeding whereby a party who has been found by the court to be owed a debt (judgment creditor) seeks to collect on that debt from the assets of the debtor (judgment debtor) that cannot be reached by execution (*i.e.*, the seizure and sale of the assets). *See* execution.

credit score
A statistical analysis of a person's creditworthiness, expressed as a number. The formulae or logarithms used to generate a

credit score are usually proprietary secrets.

crime

A violation of penal law. Crimes are classified in many ways, most generally as misdemeanors and felonies. They are also classified as "mala in se" (immoral or wrong in themselves) and "mala prohibita" (prohibited by law but not necessarily immoral). Crimes are also petty and major, infamous and not infamous, and there are those that involve moral turpitude and those that do not.

crime of passion

A crime committed in the heat of passion (*e.g.*, a husband attacks his wife's rapist upon discovering the crime). This may be used as a defense to charges of a premeditated crime.

crimen falsi

(krim-men FALL-see) Lat. A crime involving some element of deceit, fraud, or untruthfulness (*e.g.*, embezzlement, perjury, forgery). At common law, such a crime disqualified its perpetrator from appearing as a witness.

crimes against nature

Deviant sexual acts considered to be crimes (e.g., bestiality).

criminal

1. (n.) One who has been found guilty of committing a crime.
2. (adj.) Pertaining to or having the character of a crime, as opposed to civil, which pertains to private rights and remedies; criminal generally pertains to law that protects society at large from harm.

criminal coercion

Unlawful compulsion or restraint. A person commits criminal coercion when, in attempting to restrict another's freedom, he threatens to: commit any criminal offense, accuse anyone of a criminal offense, expose any secret tending to subject any person to hatred, contempt or ridicule, impair his credit or business repute, or take or withhold action as an official, or cause an official to take or withhold action. *Model Penal Code § 212.5.*

criminal conversation

Adultery; sexual intercourse with a person not one's spouse. A cause of action in tort formerly was recognized for criminal conversation, but most states have abolished the action. *See* alienation of affection.

criminal law
The branch of law that defines what public wrongs are considered crimes and assigns punishment for those wrongs.

criminal maintenance
Unlawful meddling in a lawsuit by a non-party, in which a person helps one party to prosecute or defend the litigation, and thereby sustain an unnecessary litigation, obstruct justice, or promote community unrest.

criminal negligence
Omission or commission of an act that a reasonable, prudent person would do or not do under similar circumstances. Such negligence endangers another's life or safety and is punishable as a crime (*e.g.*, reckless driving with complete disregard for the safety of others is criminal negligence that may be punishable as manslaughter if the death of another occurs).

cross-action
An independent action by a defendant against a plaintiff or codefendant that grows out of the subject matter of the plaintiff's suit. Same as "cross-complaint." Term is often used interchangeably with cross-claim, but accurately, a cross-claim is between parties on the same side of the action.

cross-claim
A claim made by a person against a party on the same side of an action. Cross-claims arise out of transactions or occurrences that are the subject of the original suit, a counterclaim to the original suit, or the property involved in the original suit. *Compare* counterclaim, cross-action.

cross-examination
The questioning of the opposition's witness in order to test the truth and accuracy of that witness's testimony given on direct examination.

cruel and unusual punishment
Excessive punishment that inflicts unnecessary pain, such as beating, torture, or starvation;

punishment not in proportion to the crime. The term also applies to inhumane or substandard conditions in prisons. The death penalty is not cruel and unusual punishment per se, although some states have held it to be so. The Eighth Amendment prohibits cruel and unusual punishment.

cruelty

Willful and malicious infliction of physical or mental pain. Term is used in divorce actions to mean that conduct that inflicts physical suffering, mental distress, or fear of bodily harm on one's spouse so as to seriously harm the marital relationship. Cruelty to animals inflicts unnecessary suffering on animals and is usually a misdemeanor.

cuckold

1. (n.) A man married to an unfaithful wife. 2. (v.) To seduce a man's wife.

culpable

Worthy of blame; morally at fault. "Culpable negligence" is sometimes defined as more than ordinary negligence in that it is a conscious and wanton disregard of one's legal duty or of the rights and safety of others.

culpable mental state

The state of mind necessary to commit a crime (*e.g.*, the recklessness, malice or negligence with which a person commits an unlawful act). The mental state of the accused is widely used to qualify the severity of the crime. *See* mens rea.

cumulative

Additional; added together; consecutive. "Cumulative sentences" are served one after the other, as distinguished from "concurrent sentences" that are served at the same time. "Cumulative evidence" is additional evidence that serves to prove a fact already proven by other evidence; corroborating evidence. A "cumulative remedy" is a remedy (*see* remedy) added to one already in force.

curative instruction

A judge's instruction to a jury that corrects a previous erroneous instruction.

cure

1. To remedy defects or errors. 2. Under the U.C.C., a seller's right to correct a delivery of goods that does not conform to the terms of the sales contract.

curia

(KYUR-ee-a) Lat. A court or judicial tribunal.

curia regis

(KYUR-ee-a REE-jiss) Lat. The king's court.

curtesy

(KURT-see) At common law, a husband's right to his deceased wife's estate, dependent upon the birth of a child capable of inheriting the estate. A "curtesy initiate" exists when such a capable child is born, but before the wife dies. After her death, the right is called a "curtesy consummate." *Compare* dower.

curtilage

(KURT-ill-adj) Space around a house often, though not necessarily, enclosed by a fence or shrubbery; also "curtillium."

custodial interrogation

Questioning initiated by law enforcement officers that triggers a person's right to be advised of certain constitutional rights (*"Miranda rights"*) if she is in custody. Custody can occur any place where the person's freedom to leave has been curtailed, or when a reasonable person would believe that she was under arrest.

custody

Care or control of a person or piece of property (*e.g.*, the custody a guardian has over the child under his or her care or the custody a person has of a car loaned to him). Custody is not possession (which entails the exercise of dominion and control) but is a mere keeping and caring. Also, a person whose liberty is restricted, in prison or out, is said to be "in custody."

custom

A practice that, through long, repetitious use and common acceptance, has gained the status of unwritten law in a particular area. "General custom" prevails throughout the country and is called common law. "Particular custom" or local custom applies to a smaller locality, such as a town.

customs

1. Duties on imported or exported goods. 2. Governmental agency that oversees the importation of goods into a country.

Customs and Border Protection

Division of the Department of Homeland Security responsible for preventing people from entering the U.S. illegally, or from bringing anything harmful or illegal into the United States.

cybersquatting

Registering an internet domain name without a good faith intent to use the domain. Cybersquatting often involves registering a domain name that is the same or very similar to a company's name or trademark, with the intent of selling the name to the company.

cyberstalking

Using the internet to threatening or harass another person, especially by sending him multiple e-mail or text messages.

cy pres

(sigh PRAY *or* sigh PRESS) Fr. As near as possible. A doctrine that allows the court to carry out a will or trust that, for some reason, is impossible to carry out as directed. In such a case, the court will follow the general intention of the testator as nearly as possible. This doctrine is commonly applied in regard to gifts to charity.

D.A.
See district attorney.

damage
The loss or harm caused by the negligence, design, or accident of one person to another person or his property. Damage is distinguished from injury in that injury is the wrong committed whereas damage is the harm suffered. *See* injury, damages.

damage feasant
(damage FEE-zant or FEE-zunt) Doing damage. The term originally meant the harm caused by trespassing animals.

damages
The monetary compensation awarded to one who suffers a loss or detriment which is the fault of another. Damages are classified in several ways.

Actual damages are awarded for the real loss suffered; synonymous with *compensatory damages* and *general damages*.

Exemplary or *punitive damages* are awarded in excess of actual damages to punish the defendant.

Hedonic damages are awarded to compensate for a loss of enjoyment of life.

Incidental or *consequential damages* are awarded to compensate for costs incurred by a buyer which are incident to a breach of contract by a seller, or vice versa. *See* liquidated damages.

Nominal damages are awarded as a token for an infringement of a right; a small amount awarded where no substantial loss has been suffered or where the plaintiff cannot show the amount of his injury, but where the law recognizes that some slight injury has occurred.

damnum
Lat. Damage.

damnum absque injuria
(DAM-num AB-skwee in-JUR-ee-a) Lat. Damages without

injury. A loss suffered where there is no cause for legal action.

day in court
1. The right to appear in court to answer a complaint or to defend a right; due process. 2. The opportunity to appear in court to present claims or defend rights. 3. The day one is to appear in court.

deadlocked jury
A jury that is unable to agree on a verdict in a criminal case. Also called a hung jury.

deadly weapon
Any instrument which can cause death or serious bodily harm whether it is designed to do so (*e.g.*, gun, knife) or merely capable of doing so (*e.g.*, hammer, ax).

dead man's statute
A law that prohibits the introduction of a statement by a deceased person into evidence.

dead peasant insurance
Colloquial term for life insurance taken out on lower-level employees. The employer is the beneficiary of the policy.

death
The ending of life; the cessation of all vital life signs such as brain function, movement, respiration, heartbeat, reflexes, and responsiveness to external stimuli. The precise definition of death varies, yet most states' definitions involve the cessation of brain function.

"Civil death" means a person loses all civil rights, such as when he is sentenced to life imprisonment. "Natural death" is that which results from natural causes as distinguished from violent death. "Presumptive death" is presumed death due to long, unexplained absence.

death penalty
The supreme penalty imposed for murder and other capital crimes. The Supreme Court has held that the death penalty does not, under all circumstances, constitute cruel and unusual punishment, which is barred by the Eighth and Fourteenth Amendments.

debauchery
A broad term for excessive indulgence in sensual pleasures, such as unlawful sexual behavior

or habitual drunkenness; sexual immorality.

de bene esse

(day BEN-nee ESS-ee) Lat. Conditionally; provisionally; for the present. Phrase applies to a thing done in the present in anticipation of future use (*e.g.*, de bene esse evidence is taken out of court and before a trial to prevent it from being lost, due to the death of a witness, for instance).

debenture

A certificate, promissory note, or bond acknowledging or creating a corporate obligation, usually unsecured. A "mortgage debenture" is one where specific property or funds are used as security.

debit

1. Bookkeeping term for sum charged as due or owing. 2. As a verb, to enter an amount on the left-hand side of a ledger as being owed the account.

de bonis non administratis

(day BONE-iss non ad-min-i-STRAT-is) Lat. Of the goods not administered. When an executor dies without completely adminis-

tering an estate, the administrator appointed to succeed him is granted administration de bonis non.

de bonis propriis

(day BONE-iss PROP-ree-is) Lat. Of his own goods. Term used for a judgment against an executor or administrator which is settled out of that person's property and not out of the estate of the deceased. It is rendered, for instance, when the executor or administrator has wasted the deceased person's property.

debt

That which is owed to another, whether money, services, or goods; an obligation one person owes to another.

debtor

1. One who owes a debt; one who is under obligation to pay money to another. 2. In bankruptcy law, the debtor is the party who initiated the proceedings, or against whom the proceedings were initiated.

debtor in possession

The debtor in a Chapter 11 bankruptcy proceeding.

decedent

A deceased person, especially one who has recently died.

deceit

A fraudulent representation whereby one person, while having knowledge of the falsity of a material fact, intends to deceive another, thereby causing the latter to suffer damage due to her acting on the misrepresentation.

deceptive act

An action that is likely to deceive a consumer acting reasonably under the circumstances.

declaration

1. Act of declaring, asserting, or formally stating. *See* declaration of intent. 2. An unsworn statement made out of court, such as a "dying declaration" when the victim of a homicide speaks about the circumstances surrounding his fatal injury. 3. The formal complaint by a plaintiff where the cause of action is stated.

declaration against interest

A statement that is so vastly contrary to the speaker's pecuniary or proprietary interests that it is assumed that a reasonable man in his position would not have made the statement unless he believed it to be true. Such a statement is an exception to the rule against hearsay.

declaration of intent (or intention)

A formal statement made before a court by an alien intending to become a U.S. citizen. 8 U.S.C. § 731.

declaratory judgment

A statement of the court declaring the rights and duties of the parties in a case or stating an opinion on a question of law without awarding relief. This judgment is binding whereas an advisory opinion is not.

declaratory statutes

Statutes which merely declare the existing law, for the purpose of resolving doubts or conflicting legal decisions.

decree

A decision in a court of equity, admiralty, or probate which includes the remedy ordered to correct the injustice. A distinction once was made between decrees and judgments, the former referring to decisions in a court of equity and the latter to decisions in a court of law, but today judgment commonly applies to both.

decree nisi

(decree NYE-sigh or NEE-see) A provisional decree that takes absolute effect unless a reason can be shown why it should not.

de die in diem

(day dee in DEE-em) Lat. From day to day.

deduction

An amount subtracted from a taxpayer's calculation of her gross taxable income.

deed

A written instrument which transfers real property or the right to real property. A "bargain and sale deed" is a conveyance with a consideration regarding its use attached. A "quitclaim deed" releases and conveys only the interest the grantor has in the property involved. A "warranty deed" insures the validity of the title. The covenants of title are warranty of seisin, quiet enjoy-

ment, and right to convey, freedom from encumbrances, and defense of title as to all claims.

deed of trust

A conveyance of title by written instrument creating a trust in real property which is used as security for performance of an obligation, such as payment of a debt on land. It is similar to a mortgage, though it differs in form. The deed of trust is executed in favor of a disinterested, third-party trustee, whereas a mortgage is executed to the creditor directly. *See* mortgage,

deed poll

A deed made by and obligating only one party as opposed to an indenture which obligates two or more persons.

deem

To hold; construe; adjudge; treat as if (*e.g.,* a fact deemed to be true is treated as if true).

de facto

(dee FAK-to) Lat. In fact; in actuality (*e.g.,* a de facto corporation exists in actuality though it may not meet all the legal requirements of a corporation). De facto is used in contrast with de jure, which means lawful.

defalcation

1. Failure to account for or pay money entrusted to one when due. Term is broader than misappropriation and embezzlement in that it does not necessarily imply criminal fraud. 2. The making of a claim against a claim. *See* recoupment, counterclaim.

defamation

The publication of material injurious to a person's good name and reputation. Includes both libel and slander.

default

Failure to perform a legal duty; neglect; omission (*e.g.*, a default on a mortgage is the failure to pay on the loan when due, and a default in legal proceedings is the failure to perform a procedural step, such as to appear or plead in an action when required to do so).

default judgment

A judgment entered against a defendant who fails to appear in court or to enter a plea when required to do so.

defeasance

1. An instrument attached to some other deed or estate which cancels or defeats the latter. 2. A collateral deed containing conditions which, when met, cancel the original deed. A "defeasance clause" is a clause in a mortgage which states that the mortgage is ended when all payments on it have been made.

defeasible

Subject to being canceled, annulled, revoked, or avoided upon the occurrence or nonoccurrence of a future event or action (*e.g.*, a mortgage is a defeasible instrument because it is subject to cancellation upon payment in full).

defect

A deficiency; a lack of completeness or perfection; the absence of a requirement needed to make something legally sufficient. A defect can be in a product, in performance, or in a title.

defendant

The person accused in a criminal case or sued in a civil action.

defendant in error

The party who, after prevailing in a lower court, becomes a defendant in an appellate court due to alleged errors of law in the lower court. *See* appellee.

defense

1. All the evidence and argument offered on behalf of a defendant to refute a plaintiff's charges or to diminish or defeat his recovery. 2. Evidence offered by a defendant in a criminal action to refute charges against him.

Defense of Marriage Act

Federal law stating that the states are not required to recognize same-sex marriages entered into in other states, and defining marriage for purposes of federal laws as solely between one man and one woman. The federal definition of marriage was ruled unconstitutional in *United States v. Windsor,* 133 S. Ct. 2675 (2013).

deferment

Postponing or extending to a later time.

deficiency

An insufficiency, a lack of something. The difference between the amount a taxpayer shows he owes on a tax return and the amount the taxing body says is owed.

deficiency judgment

A judgment in favor of a creditor which imposes personal liability on a mortgagor for the amount of debt remaining after the sale of his property to satisfy the debt. 2. The debt remaining after sale of repossessed personal property.

definitive

Final; conclusive; that which ends something, such as a lawsuit.

deforcement

The holding of land which rightfully belongs to another. Term includes abatement, discontinuance, disseisin, and intrusion, but is broader, and it especially applies to cases where the rightful owner has never had possession.

defraud

To cheat; to trick; to misrepresent material facts with the intent

103

to deprive another of property, right, or interest. *See* fraud, deceit. Omissions or concealments which breach a duty, trust, or confidence, and which injure or take advantage of another.

degree

A level, step, or grade, such as in first and second degree murder or first and second degree relatives.

degree of proof

The measure of evidence required to prove a case. This measure varies, depending on whether the matter is civil or criminal in nature. Whereas civil matters require a prevailing party to prove a preponderance of evidence, in criminal matters the proof must be beyond a reasonable doubt. Also called "quantum of proof."

de homine replegiando

(day HOM-in-nee re-PLEJ-ee-an-do) Lat. For replevying a man. A writ to release a person from prison or from the custody of a private person where that person (*see* surety) becomes responsible for the released person's appearance in court.

Analogous to writ of habeas corpus.

de jure

(dee JUR-ree *or* JUR-ray) Lat. Lawful; by right; legitimate (*e.g.*, de jure segregation is that intended by law). De jure is used in contrast to de facto, which means in fact.

del credere

(del KRED-eray) Italian. Of belief or trust. An agent who sells goods for another on credit and guarantees that the purchaser will pay for the goods.

delegable duty

A duty that may be performed by another (*e.g.*, duties, under a contract, that are transferred to another party who is obligated to perform).

delegate

1. (n.) A representative; an agent; a person authorized to act for another, such as a delegate at a political convention. 2. (v.) To authorize; to relegate, as in "to delegate power."

delegation

1. A body of representatives or delegates. 2. The act of authoriz-

ing a person to act for others. 3. Civil law: A species of novation whereby another person takes on the obligation of the original debtor. The consent of the three parties to the substitution is required in a delegation, whereas in other species of novation, consent is required of only the two parties to the new arrangement. *See* novation.

delegatus non potest delegare

(del-ay-GAT-tuss non POE-test del-lay-GAR-ray) Lat. A delegate cannot himself delegate (*i.e.*, an agent or representative cannot delegate authority granted to him without the express consent of the person whom he represents).

deliberate

1. (v.) To plan, consider, or think over beforehand. 2. (adj.) Carefully considered; well thought out; planned, as opposed to spontaneous. A crime is deliberate when its perpetrator carefully considers the motives, nature, and consequences of the crime before deciding to commit it.

deliberation

The act of deliberating; weighing and examining the reasons for and against a verdict.

delict

In civil law: A tort or wrongful act.

delictum

Lat. 1. A tort or wrongful act. 2. An injury.

delinquency, delinquent

The condition of failing or omitting to perform a legal duty, such as to pay a debt. "Delinquent" as a noun is the person who so fails; as an adjective, it refers to the object of the delinquency, *e.g.,* a delinquent tax. A "delinquent child" is an underage person who commits a crime.

delisting

Suspending or revoking the privileges of a security for authorized trading on an exchange, usually for failure to meet the exchange's minimum listing requirements.

delivery

The act of transferring possession of goods or title to property. Delivery of goods may be actual or constructive (*i.e.*, implied by law, such as where goods are stored in a warehouse and access to the warehouse is given to the purchaser of the goods). In a transfer of title, delivery takes place when the grantor intends to convey title and puts the deed into the control of the grantee. *Compare* conveyance.

delusion

An unfounded, irrational, or absurd belief held against evidence of its falsity. An "insane delusion" is the product of a diseased or deranged mind.

demand

1. (n.) An assertion of a legal right; a claim; a forceful request to perform an obligation owed to one, such as to pay money. 2. (v.) To assert a legal right; to claim as being owed to one; to seek relief.

demand note

A promissory note which does not state a specific time for payment but rather is payable on demand (*i.e.*, when it is presented).

demesne

(day-MAIN) His own. Domain; held in one's own right, and not of a superior. Term comes from the the land the lord of a manor kept for his own use. It is used today in the phrase "seised in his demesne as of fee" meaning a person has a corporeal inheritance (having physical substance). This is distinguished from an incorporeal hereditament (having no physical substance) which is said to be "seised as of fee."

de minimus

(day MIN-i-mus) Lat. Of small, unimportant matters.

de minimus non curat lex

(day MIN-i-mus non cur-rat lax) Lat. The law is not concerned with trivial matters.

demise

1. (n.) A conveyance or transfer of an estate in fee for life, or at will. Synonymous with lease or let. 2. Death. 3. (v.) To transfer an estate by inheritance or succession.

demonstrative bequest

A testamentary gift that must be paid from a specific fund.

demonstrative evidence

1. Evidence that is shown directly to the court or jury with no intervening testimony. 2. Real, tangible evidence that appeals to the senses (*e.g.*, a gun).

demur

To object in a pleading to the sufficiency at law of the opposing party's pleading. *See* demurrer.

demurrage

A payment due the owner of a ship when it is delayed in port beyond the time allowed in the contract for its hire. Term also applies to railroad cars, and exists to expedite the loading and unloading of freight.

demurrer

A defendant's allegation in a pleading that the legal consequences of the opposition's plea are insufficient to compel him to answer, even though the defendant admits the matters of fact alleged against him are true. A "special demurrer" specifies the defects in *form* of the plaintiff's pleading. A "general demurrer" does not specify defects but rather is worded in general terms, and is an objection to the *substance* of the pleading. In modern procedure, the demurrer has been abolished and replaced by a motion to dismiss for failure to state a claim. Federal Rule of Civil Procedure 7(c).

denial

In pleading, a refuting of the charges made against one; a contradiction; a traverse. Denials can be general and refute all allegations made in a complaint, or specific and address a particular allegation.

denizen

A person whose status is between that of a natural born citizen and an alien. He lives in a foreign country and has many but not all of the rights of a citizen.

de novo

(dee *or* day NO-vo) Lat. Anew; afresh; a second time (*e.g.*, a trial de novo is a new trial which tries a matter as though it had not been heard before).

Department of Veterans' Affairs

Federal government cabinet department created in 1989 that administers the system of benefits for veterans of the armed services and their dependents. Benefits include: medical care, monetary benefits for illness, injury, or death related to military service; benefits to widows and minors of deceased veterans; education and rehabilitation; home loan guaranty; and burial. Formerly known as the Veterans' Administration, or V.A.

departure

1. A deviation from a previous pleading, whether in the substance of the pleading, its legal basis, or by way of a reply, rejoinder, or subsequent pleading. 2. A disagreement between a pleading and the evidence offered to support it. *See* variance. 3. In criminal law, a court's sentence that differs from the sentence that normally would be imposed against a defendant.

dependent relative revocation

Doctrine permitting probate of destroyed will when testator destroyed it because she mistakenly believed that a second will had been validly executed.

deponent

Person who gives a deposition; one who gives a sworn testimony; a witness; an affiant.

deportation

The expulsion of an alien from one country usually to the country from which he came; banishment; exile. Also referred to as "removal."

depose

1. To make a deposition; to give sworn testimony. 2. To forcibly remove from office, particularly a sovereign.

deposit

1. An amount of money given as security for the performance of an obligation, often the purchase of something. A deposit is given as an indication of the buyer's earnest intention to purchase the property, and may be applied to the purchase price and is forfeited if the depositor withdraws from the obligation. 2. A bailment of goods kept by a bailee and returned at the bailor's re-

quest. 3. The placing of money in a bank; the money so deposited.

depositary

The institution or person receiving a deposit.

deposition

The pretrial, sworn testimony of a witness taken out of court in response to oral examination or written interrogatories and recorded in writing for use in court. The adversary is given an opportunity to cross-examine the deponent during the questioning. Federal Rules of Civil Procedure 26 *et seq.;* Federal Rule of Criminal Procedure 15. *See* interrogatories; *compare* affidavit.

depository

The place where a deposit is placed and held.

depreciation

1. Reduction in the value of a property due to deterioration caused by use, weather, or the passage of time. 2. An amount taken as a deduction on tax returns for reduction in the value of property.

deputy

A person authorized to act in place of another; a delegate; an agent; a substitute for a public officer who may perform all the duties of that person.

derelict

1. Abandoned, deserted. 2. Intentionally abandoned personal property. 3. A person without substance or apparent purpose in life; a bum; a vagrant. 4. Land left permanently uncovered by receding waters. *See* dereliction. 5. Maritime law: A vessel abandoned without hope or intention of recovery.

dereliction

1. The process by which land is gained when waters that covered it recede. 2. The land so uncovered. 3. Voluntary abandonment of property. 4. Neglect of duty.

derivative action

A suit by a stockholder on behalf of a corporation to enforce a corporate right or remedy a wrong. The corporation is a necessary party to the action and recovery is made to the corporation.

derivative tort
Tort liability imposed on a principal for a wrong committed by his agent.

derivative work
In copyright law, a work based on or created from another work (*e.g.*, a sequel, a user's guide, or a translation).

derogate
To lessen or detract from so as to impair.

derogation
A partial repeal or abolition of a law by the passage of a subsequent law.

descendant
1. A person who proceeds directly from the body of another (*i.e.*, one's child, grandchild, great-grandchild, etc.). 2. A person to whom an estate descends.

descent
The transfer of real estate by inheritance and the operation of law, not by will.

descent and distribution
Transfer of real or personal property of one who dies intestate. State laws governing such transfers are often referred to as "statutes of descent and distribution." Distribution refers to the process by the court of dividing an estate after the estate has paid its debts. Descent refers to the transfer of property to the estate's lawful heirs, in the proper order of hereditary succession.

desertion
Abandonment of one's duty, such as that which one owes to one's spouse or child, or to one's military post, with no intention of returning.

design patent
A patent granted for the ornamentation attached to a functional item.

de son tort
Lat. By his own wrong (*e.g.*, an executor de son tort is a person who, without authority, acts as an executor of an estate).

destination contract
Sales contract under which the risk of loss passes from seller to buyer when seller tenders goods at their destination.

desuetude

Disuse; referring to an obsolete law that has gone unused for a protracted length of time. When a law is subject to a lengthy desuetude, it is considered repealed.

detainer

1. Lawful detention of a prisoner to insure the prisoner's availability for turning him over to other authorities at the end of his term. 2. Act of keeping property from a person who is legally entitled to it. An "unlawful detainer" is the illegal keeping of goods or real property which may have been originally acquired lawfully, such as when a tenant refuses to leave an apartment after his lease has expired and he has been asked to leave.

detention

Act of holding a person or thing, such as a suspected criminal or a stolen automobile.

determinable

Liable to be determined, settled, or ended after an amount of time or when a certain contingency occurs.

determinable fee

A property interest which may last forever or until an event stated in the grant or devise which creates it occurs (*e.g.,* an estate granted to a widow until she remarries). Also known as a defeasible fee.

determination

1. A final decision, as in the court's determination of a lawsuit. 2. Contract law: The extinguishment or ending of an agreement by judicial order after a contract has been affirmed. 3. An ending in general. 4. An estimate. 5. Tax law: An allowance or disallowance in correcting an error in taxation.

detinue

(DET-tin-oo) At common law, an action to recover specific personal property unlawfully held by another, plus damages caused by its detention.

detriment

In general, term means loss or harm; in contracts it is that which a person gives up in exchange for a promise by the other party. *See* consideration.

devastavit

(de-vess-TA-vit) Lat. He has wasted. Mismanagement of a decedent's estate by its executor or administrator which results in a loss to the estate. Such a violation of duty makes the person personally liable for the loss.

devest

To deprive. *See* divest.

deviation, deviant

A departure from the normal course of travel, operation, or procedure. In employment, it is an employee's departure from his normal duties or scope of employment. In insurance, it is a departure from the risks a policy covers without just cause. The adjective is "deviant."

devise

1. A gift by will; specifically a gift of real property although term sometimes is used to refer to personal property. 2. (v.) To dispose of real property by will *Compare* bequest, bequeath.

A devise may be *contingent* (does not vest until a future event occurs) or *vested* at the death of the testator.

Devises are classified as *specific* (mentions a particular piece of land), *general* (does not mention a specific piece of land but refers to land without additional words attached to qualify it, *e.g.,* "all my lands"), and *residuary* (all the land left after the other devises and debts on the estate have been settled). *See* residue.

devisee

Person to whom real property is given by will.

devolution

1. Transfer of property from one person to another by operation of law. 2. The transfer of a right, liability, title, estate, or office.

devolve

To pass or be transferred from one person to another (*e.g.,* the transfer of an estate from a decedent).

dictum

Abbreviation for "obiter dictum," "a remark by the way." An opinion, observation, or remark by a judge which is not necessary for the decision of the case. Plural is "dicta."

digest

A collection or compilation of books, articles and cases arranged for reference purposes. The American Digest System is the master index system used in the U.S. for reported case law, and is arranged by subject.

Digital Millennium Copyright Act

A 1998 law relating to certain internet-related copyright issues. Key provisions of the Act limit the liability of internet service providers for copyright infringement, and forbid devices that circumvent anti-copying measures.

dilatory

Tending or intended to cause delay

dilatory pleas

At common law, a class of defenses based on a matter not connected with the merits of the case but which serve to delay action on it while not impeaching the right of action itself. Pleas challenging jurisdiction, and those regarding matters of procedure or the capacity of the defendant or plaintiff, are dilatory

as long as they do not defeat the plaintiff's cause of action or result in any relief against the plaintiff. Dilatory pleas have practically disappeared in modern practice. *See* demurrer.

diligence, diligent

Attentiveness; care; prudence. The law distinguishes three degrees of diligence to describe the degree of care various persons exercise in their own affairs: ordinary (prudent person), slight (less than prudent), and extraordinary (exceptionally prudent person). The adjective is "diligent."

dilution

In trademark law, using a nationally well-known trademark in a way that blurs the distinctiveness of the mark, or that tarnishes the reputation of the famous mark. An example would be using the name of a camera manufacturer as a brand name for bicycles.

diminished capacity

A criminal law defense, in which the accused lacks the mental state or intent essential to commit the crime for which he is accused. Such a defense often results in conviction on a lesser offense, rather than exoneration.

diminution

A reduction; an act of taking away or making less. Term is used in phrases such as "diminution of salary" and "diminution in value."

direct

1. (adj.) Immediate; proximate; without any intervention or influence (*e.g.*, the direct cause of an accident is the primary reason the accident occurred). 2. In the usual course or order; opposite of cross, collateral, or remote. 3. (v.) To command, order, instruct, or advise.

direct action

1. An insured's suit directly against her insurer, or a plaintiff's suit against a tortfeasor's insurer. 2. Action by shareholder against the corporation to enforce a right personal to him, as opposed to a derivative suit to enforce a right belonging to the corporation.

direct attack

A challenge to have a judgment reversed, corrected, vacated, annulled, voided, or enjoined, made in a proceeding for that express purpose (*e.g.*, an appeal). It differs from a collateral attack which challenges a judgment in a proceeding instituted for another purpose.

direct contempt

Acts done or words spoken in the presence of the court which tend to interrupt the administration of justice or embarrass the court. *See* contempt.

directed verdict

A jury verdict ordered by the court. In civil cases, a party may receive a directed verdict if the opposite side does not present a prima facie case or a necessary defense. Federal Rule of Civil Procedure 50(a). In criminal cases, a directed verdict may only be for acquittal. Federal Rule of Criminal Procedure 29.

direct evidence

Evidence from a person who actually witnessed the matter in question with his own senses. It is distinguished from indirect or circumstantial evidence.

direct examination

The examination in chief of a witness by the party who called him to the stand.

director

Person elected or appointed to manage the affairs of a corporation. Directors act as a unit called the board of directors.

directory

Instructive; directive; that which is for advisory purposes alone, and carries no obligatory force. A directory provision in a statute should be complied with as nearly as possible, though in fact it is optional. A mandatory provision must be complied with and it carries consequences for failure to do so.

disability

1. Lack of legal capacity to perform an act, such as a minor's incapacity to sue, an insane person's inability to make a contract, or a married person's incapacity to remarry without first dissolving the previous marriage. 2. A physical or mental incapacity to perform one's work; loss of earning power due to such an incapacity. 3. Under Social Security Act: Inability to perform substantial gainful activity due to mental or physical impairment. 4. Under the Americans with Disabilities Act: A physical or mental impairment that limits one or more major life activities, a record of such an impairment, or being perceived as having such an impairment.

disabling restraints

Restrictions on the alienability of real property which are generally void as against public policy.

disaffirm, disaffirmance

To repudiate; to refuse to accept; to revoke a consent previously given, as in to revoke avoidable contract. Noun is "disaffirmance."

disbar, disbarment

To deprive an attorney of the right to practice law by suspending his license. Disbarment is an act of the court taken because of illegal or unethical conduct by an attorney.

discharge

1. (v.) To release, dismiss, free, or relieve (*e.g.*, to discharge a bankrupt is to release him from

liability on his debts; to discharge a worker is to dismiss him from employment; to discharge a person held on accusation of a crime is to set him free; to discharge a jury is to relieve it from further consideration of a case). 2. To perform a duty. 3. (n.) A document by which a contract, such as a mortgage, is ended. 4. A proceeding which releases a bankrupt from his debts.

disclaimer

A renunciation or rejection of a claim, right, or office (*e.g.*, a refusal to accept a right or an interest in an estate offered to one, or a defendant's renunciation of any claim to the thing demanded by the plaintiff).

disclosure

1. A revelation; an act of making known. 2. A thing revealed. 3. As used in the Truth in Lending Act, term refers to the manner in which certain necessary information is to be conveyed to a person seeking credit. *See* discovery.

discontinuance

1. A voluntary termination of a suit by written notice from the plaintiff or by a court order by a judge; a voluntary dismissal; a nonsuit. 2. The abandonment of work on a project. 3. A "discontinuance of an estate" is a termination or suspension of an estate tail due to a grant by a tenant in tail which was larger than such tenant was entitled to convey. *See* tail.

discretion

Use of one's own judgment in making a responsible decision. Judicial discretion is the making of a determination by reference to legal principles and facts of the case or in the interests of justice; decisions must not be arbitrary or capricious. Official discretion is the power of a public official to use her own judgment in determining the action necessary under the circumstances.

discrimination

The unequal treatment of persons where no reasonable distinction exists among them. Federal statutes prohibit discrimination in employment based on sex, race, age, religion, national origin, and disability.

discounted cash flow

A measure of the present value of a future income stream begun by a monetary investment.

disenfranchise

To deprive a free citizen of a right or privilege, especially the right to vote. *See* franchise.

dishonor

To refuse to accept or pay a check or other negotiable instrument (*e.g.*, a bank may dishonor a check if there is not enough money in the drawer's account to cover it).

disinherit, disinheritance

To deprive an heir of his inheritance. This can be done by writing a clause to that effect in one's will. Noun is "disinheritance."

disinterested witness

An impartial, unbiased witness; one who has no interest in the outcome of the case.

disjunctive allegations

Statements in a pleading which charge something in alternative form, with the conjunction "or;" charges which state that the defendant committed one act or another act. When such an allegation obscures that which is specifically being averred, it is inadmissible.

dismiss, dismissal

To discharge or discontinue a suit or action. A "dismissal" is the order or judgment which discharges or disposes of a suit, action, or motion, and may be with prejudice (*i.e.*, based on the merits of the case and barring further action on same), or it may be without prejudice (*i.e.*, not based on the merits and not barring subsequent action). Dismissals may be voluntary (by plaintiff's motion) or involuntary (on motion of court or defendant).

disorderly conduct

A general term for behavior that tends to disturb the peace or shock public sense of morality.

disorderly house

A term of broad definition meaning a place where illegal or publicly offensive practices are frequently carried out (*e.g.*, a house of prostitution or a gambling house).

disparate impact

The effect of an employment practice that is non-discriminatory on its face, but that has the effect of discriminating based on age, race, sex, national origin, or disability.

disparagement

1. A discrediting, belittling, or degrading of someone or something. Disparagement may be of goods for sale or of title, which casts aspersions on a title to property. 2. In old English law, term meant the discredit one sustained by marrying someone below one's rank or character.

dispensation

1. Permission to do something usually forbidden; exemption from a law. 2. An allowance to omit something commanded.

disposition

1. The giving up of something; a relinquishment; a disposal, settlement, or final determination of some matter, such as the disposition of an estate, a debt, or a case. 2. The sentencing phase of a criminal proceeding. 3. Frame of mind; temperament.

dispute

1. A controversy; a demand made or right asserted which is refuted by another party. 2. The subject of a controversy.

disqualify

To render unfit or ineligible, as in to disqualify a juror due to his prejudices.

disseisin

(dis-SAY-sin or dis-SEE-sin) The wrongful dispossession or taking and putting out of an owner from his real property which he presently possesses and enjoys. A disseisin may be a deprivation of the owner of the rents and profits of his property. *See* seisin.

dissent, dissenting opinion

1. To disagree. 2. A judge's disagreement with the majority opinion rendered.

dissipate

1. To use up, destroy, or waste (*e.g.,* to spend funds or dispose of assets foolishly). 2. To disperse a crowd).

dissolution

Act or process of ending, dissolving, or breaking up, as in the

118

dissolution of a contract when the contracting parties themselves cancel it, the dissolution of a corporation when the corporate entity is dissolved, or the dissolution of a marriage by divorce.

distinguish

To call attention to differences; to illustrate why cited case in legal argument is applicable or inapplicable.

distrain

1. To take and keep the personal property of another to be returned upon the performance of an obligation (*e.g.*, a landlord's taking of a tenant's personal property for nonpayment of rent). 2. Any detention of personal property. *See* distress.

distress

1. The act of taking personal property without legal process from a wrongdoer by the party injured, done to secure performance of an obligation the wrongdoer has undertaken. The act is regulated by statute regarding a landlord's taking of a tenant's property. 2. The taking of

personal property to enforce tax payment. 3. Property distrained.

distribution

1. The giving out of something in portions, such as the remainder of an estate, after taxes and payment of debts, to the heirs of a person who dies leaving no will. 2. The division and giving out of the capital assets of a corporation to stockholders.

district

A subdivision of a geographical area for administrative, judicial, political, or electoral purposes (*e.g.*, a congressional district).

district attorney

The prosecuting attorney who represents the United States government in a federal judicial district (U.S. District Attorney) or some state in a state judicial district (State's Attorney).

district court

1. A federal trial court of record having general jurisdiction over a particular geographical area; U.S. District Court. 2. An inferior state court having general jurisdiction, although in some states jurisdiction is limited.

disturbance (disturbing the peace)

1. General term for any act which annoys or agitates another person or interrupts the quiet and orderliness of a neighborhood or a gathering. 2. At common law, a wrong done to an incorporeal hereditament by obstructing the owner from enjoying it (*e.g.*, to put a fence across a piece of land a person has the right to use).

divers

Various; several; sundry.

diversity of citizenship

A ground used to invoke the jurisdiction of the federal courts when parties on different sides of a controversy involving more than $75,000 live in different states, or when one party is an alien. *See* the judicial powers granted the United States under Article III, section 2 of the U.S. Constitution.

divest

1. To take away, deprive, or get rid of something, as in to divest one's property by selling it. 2. To cause a loss of a right or interest in an estate which has already vested in a person.

dividend

1. A sum from the surplus earnings of a corporation, as determined by the board of directors, divided and paid periodically to stockholders. Dividends are sometimes paid in stock rather than cash. 2. A payment to creditors in a bankruptcy proceeding.

divisible contract

A contract susceptible to division into two or more independent parts; severable contract. The separate parts may be considered as independent agreements contained in one instrument, the breach of one not affecting the whole contract.

divorce

A legal separation of husband and wife. A divorce may be absolute (a complete termination of the marriage allowing each person to remarry; known as "dissolution of marriage" in many states), or limited (separation of spouses not allowing either to remarry). A limited divorce is also called a legal separation. *See* annulment.

dock

1. (n.) The place in some courtrooms where a prisoner stays during trial. 2. (v.) To diminish; to deduct from, especially wages due to an employee (*e.g.*, for tardiness).

docket

1. A brief record of the proceedings of a case. 2. A book containing brief entries of court proceedings. 2. A list of cases for trial or appeal. 3. (v.) To enter court activity in a docket

doctrine

A rule or principle of law developed through court decisions.

document

1. Anything with a message on it that can be read (*e.g.*, a deed, contract, receipt, map). 2. (v.) To support with documentary evidence.

document of title

A paper recognized by businesses as granting its holder the right to receive, hold, or dispose of goods mentioned on the document (*e.g.*, a bill of lading, a warehouse receipt, a dock warrant).

Dodd-Frank Wall Street Reform and Consumer Protection Act

Federal law reforming federal regulation of the financial industry, enacted in 2010.

doing business

The carrying on of business for which a corporation was organized. To determine whether a foreign corporation is doing business within a state, it must be determined that the corporation has certain minimum contacts with the state that make it amenable to the courts and/or susceptible to the taxes of that state.

doli capax

(DOE-lee CAP-ax) Lat. Capable of distinguishing between right and wrong. This capacity makes one amenable to the criminal laws.

doli incapax

(DOE-lee IN-cap-ax) Lat. Incapable of distinguishing between right and wrong. Common law recognizes persons under age seven as doli incapax, and thus they cannot be convicted of a crime.

D.O.M.A.
See Defense of Marriage Act.

domain

Absolute ownership and control of land; the land so owned. The state's power to control private land for public use is called the "right of eminent domain." Work that is not protected by copyright is said to be in the "public domain."

Domesday Book

(DOOMS-day or DOMES-day book) An ancient record (1081–1086) published in the time of William the Conqueror, consisting of surveys of the lands in England.

domestic

1. (adj.) Pertaining to home, whether one's house, home state, or country. A domestic corporation is one domiciled in its state of incorporation. 2. (n.) A household servant.

domicile

One's permanent home; legal residence. A person has only one domicile though he may have several temporary residences. For a place to be called one's domicile, one must have an intention of making it one's permanent home. The determination of one's domicile is important because it determines one's voting district and the taxing body under which one falls. *See* residence.

dominant tenement (estate)

A tenement or estate whose owner benefits from an easement on another estate (servient estate). For example, *A,* the owner of a piece of land, sells half of it to *B,* his neighbor, yet retains the right to build a driveway across the land to get to the street. *A* holds the dominant estate, *B* the servient estate.

dominion

1. Ownership and control of something, which includes the right to claim it and the power to dispose of it. 2. Sovereignty. 3. Civil law: Dominion may be "proximate," meaning the owner has possession of the property, or "remote," meaning a person owns something but is not yet in possession of it.

domus sua cuique est tutissimum refugium
(DOE-mus soo-a KWEE-kweh est TOO-tis-sim-um re-FYOO-gee-um) Lat. A man's house is his safest refuge. Old Roman maxim underlying modern principle—a man's home is his castle.

donatio
(doe-NAH-tee-o) Lat. A gift, donation. A voluntary transfer of title and possession of property without consideration.

donee
One to whom a donation or gift is given; a grantee.

donee beneficiary
In a third-party contract, the person who receives a right or benefit of a contract between other parties. A donee beneficiary can sue the promisor for breach.

donee of power
The person to whom a power of appointment is given. *See* power of appointment.

donor
One who makes a donation or gift.

dormant
Inactive, silent, in abeyance, such as a "dormant claim" where title vests in no one, or a "dormant judgment" which remains unexecuted for such a long time that it must be revived before it can be executed.

double damages
Twice the damages normally awarded for certain kinds of injuries. Such damages are awarded according to statute and often for punitive reasons.

double entry
A bookkeeping method which shows every transaction both as a credit and a debit.

double hearsay
Hearsay upon hearsay. An out-of-court statement that incorporates other hearsay. Each separate statement must fall within an exception in order for the complete statement to be admitted into evidence. *See* hearsay.

double jeopardy

Prosecution of a person a second time for the same offense, prohibited by the Fifth Amendment of the U.S. Constitution.

doubtful title

Title whose validity is in doubt; title which exposes its holder to litigation.

dower

A widow's portion or interest in her husband's real estate; a woman's right to one-third of her deceased husband's lands or tenements of which he was seised in fee simple or fee tail at any time during their marriage. Abolished in a majority of states. *See* curtesy.

draft

A negotiable instrument which instructs a second party (drawee) to pay a third party (payee) a sum of money (*e.g.*, a check or bill of exchange).

drawee

The party on whom a draft is drawn (*e.g.*, a bank).

drawer

The party who draws a draft (*i.e.*, one who makes a bill of exchange or signs a check).

droit

(drwah or droyt) Fr. Law, right, justice.

droit moral

(drwah mor-RAHL) Fr. Moral right. The right of artists or authors to preserve the integrity and prevent the alteration of their works. The doctrine is recognized mostly in civil law systems.

drug abuse

State of chronic or repeated use of controlled substances such as narcotics.

drug addiction

Condition of habitual, uncontrolled use of narcotics.

dual purpose doctrine

In tort law, an employee is acting within the scope of her employment if the work necessitates a trip during which she also performs a personal task, thus serving both a business and personal purpose. If the personal errand creates a major deviation from the business purpose, it does not fall within the scope of employment.

duces tecum

(DOO-kess TAY-kum) Lat. Bring with you. A "subpoena duces tecum" is a writ requiring a witness to bring to court any documents, records, or other evidence relevant to a controversy.

due

1. Owing; payable, as when a debt is due it is time for it to be paid. 2. Just; proper; lawful; sufficient; as in "due care" or "due process of law."

due care

The standard of care one legally owes to another under a certain set of circumstances; that degree of care a reasonable and prudent person would exercise under the circumstances. Failure to exercise due care is negligence.

due date

The day on which an obligation must be met, such as the payment of a tax or debt.

due diligence

In corporate and securities law, a potential buyer's pre-purchase investigation of property or securities.

due process of law

A flexible term for the fair and orderly administration of justice in the courts. Essential to the concept is the right a person has to be notified of legal proceedings against him, the opportunity to be heard and to defend himself in an orderly proceeding, and the right to have counsel represent him. Basically, due process is the fundamental fairness principle at the core of the Anglo-American system of jurisprudence. Due process also refers to the actual legal proceedings which serve to protect and enforce individual rights and liberties.

The phrase is expressed in the Fifth Amendment to the U.S. Constitution: ". . . nor [shall any person] be deprived of life, liberty, or property, without due process of law," and also in the Fourteenth Amendment which applied the principle to the states.

Driving Under the Influence (D.U.I.)

Operating a motor vehicle while under the influence of alcohol or drugs.

duplicity

1. The technical fault of combining multiple causes of action or defenses in one plea, multiple offenses in one count of an indictment, or multiple incongruous subjects in one legislative act. 2. Deception, double-dealing.

duress

1. Unlawful threats of harm or other pressure used to force someone to act against his will. An act performed under duress sometimes relieves a person from the legal effect his actions would normally have (*e.g.*, a contract signed under duress is not binding). *See* coercion. 2. Illegal imprisonment or legal imprisonment for illegal purposes.

duty

1. Obligation, as in the duty one has to perform under a contract; obligatory conduct, as in the duty of care one owes to others to avoid negligent injury to them. 2. A tax on imports and exports.

dwelling

The house or building in which a person or persons live (*e.g.*, apartment building, trailer house). Buildings attached to a house are also part of the dwelling.

dwelling house

A person's house or abode; one's residence.

Dyer Act

National Motor Vehicle Theft Act. The act makes it a crime to knowingly transport, receive, conceal, barter, or sell a stolen motor vehicle in interstate or foreign commerce.

dying declaration

Statements concerning the cause and circumstances of a homicide made by the victim who was aware his death was imminent. These statements, introduced into evidence by a witness who heard them, are a common exception to the hearsay rule, and are admissible on the grounds of trustworthiness and necessity. The witness's credibility, though, is

subject to demeanor examination
and cross-examination.

e

Prefix denoting "electronic," as in "e-commerce." Used to refer to internet-based or –related activities.

earned income

Money gained from work as opposed to that gained from invested capital, such as stock dividends.

earnest money

That which is given to secure a contract. "Earnest money" is a sum a buyer pays to a seller to demonstrate buyer's intention and ability to fulfill a purchase contract (*e.g.*, a small downpayment on a house). This money is often forfeited if buyer defaults.

earnings

Income; money earned from work performed or services rendered, without the aid of capital. The term, though, has come to include profits gained from the employment of capital in a corporation.

easement

The right to use, or limit the use of, part of the land owned by another for a special purpose. Its use must be consistent with the general use of the property by the owner. The tenement with this right is called the "dominant tenement" and the one which bears the burden is the "servient tenement."

eavesdropping

Secretly listening to another's conversations without consent, whether by electronic devices or by standing outside someone's window and listening under the "eaves."

ecclesiastical courts

Religious courts established in England which mainly deal with spiritual matters of the established church.

e converso

(ee con-VAIR-so) Lat. Conversely; on the other hand. Equivalent to "e contra."

ecumenical

Universal, worldwide, especially applied to the entire Christian church.

edict

A command or proclamation by a sovereign that carries the effect of law.

E.E.O.C.

See Equal Employment Opportunity Commission.

effect

1. (n.) A result; consequence; the product of a cause. 2. (v.) To accomplish; to execute; to make, as in "to effect a sale."

effects

Personal property; any chattel or movable personal properly, although term may also include real property.

e.g.

Lat. Exempli gratia. For the sake of an example.

egress

A means of getting out; an exit.

Eighth Amendment

Amendment to U.S. Constitution prohibiting excessive bail, excessive fines, and cruel and unusual punishment.

ejectment

An action to recover possession of land claimed by another. To recover, plaintiff must show defendant is in wrongful possession of the property and that plaintiff has a present legal right to possession of same. Also called an "action to recover possession of land," "summary process," "eviction," and "forcible entry and detainer."

ejusdem generis

(ay-YOOS-dem JENN-air-is) Lat. Of the same kind or class. The "ejusdem generis rule" of construction states that when general words follow an enumeration of specific persons or things, the general words are to be interpreted as being in the same category as those specifically enumerated.

election

The act of choosing, as in the election of a candidate to office, a widow's election of whether she will accept what her husband left her in his will or what is provided by statute, or the election of one of several remedies at law.

election of remedies
The choice of one of several remedies afforded by law to redress an injury suffered. Once a party has chosen between two or more possible remedies, he is bound by that choice.

election under a will
A legatee's choice to adopt and conform to the terms of a will. One who is given a benefit under a will must sometimes choose between accepting that benefit or pursuing an estate or interest in the testator's property which he may have a legal claim to. When the party makes that choice, he has chosen to take under or against the will.

elector
1. A qualified voter. 2. A member of the electoral college.

electrocution
Execution by passing an intense electric current through a convict. Verb is "electrocute."

eleemosynary corporation
Charitable; given as alms. An "eleemosynary corporation" is a private corporation created for religious or charitable purposes.

element
1. A basic or essential part, as "breaking and entry" are elements in the crime of burglary. Each element of a crime must be proved beyond a reasonable doubt for a conviction. 2. (Plural) The forces of nature, especially those in violent weather.

eligible
Legally qualified to be selected, as in to be eligible to be elected to public office, or to be eligible to become a citizen.

elisor
Person appointed to perform the duties of a sheriff or coroner when that officer is unable or disqualified to act. An elisor is used especially in the execution of writs of venire which summon a jury.

emancipation
Generally, the act of setting free. Specifically, that time when a parent relinquishes control over a minor thus ending the legal duty to support him and granting him full right to his earnings. This

usually occurs at the age of majority. Emancipation may be express or implied by conduct.

embargo

1. A government's order prohibiting the passage of ships or certain goods into and out of its ports, sometimes issued for purposes of war, and sometimes for the control of commerce. 2. A common carrier's refusal to carry certain kinds of freight, or to carry freight between two points.

embassy

A diplomatic mission in the capital of a foreign nation. An embassy is intended for dealings between the governments of two nations.

embezzlement

The fraudulent taking for one's own use the money or property of another by a person who originally acquired it lawfully. For a crime to constitute embezzlement, a fiduciary relationship must exist between the wrongdoer and the victim, the wrongdoer must have come to possess the money or property through that relationship, and he must have acted with fraudulent intent.

emblements

Crops grown annually by labor of a tenant (*e.g.*, corn, wheat, garden vegetables) and not those that grow spontaneously. The doctrine of emblements states that a tenant has the right to take any crops he has been growing, even after his tenancy has ended.

embracery

The offense of attempting to corruptly influence a jury. Person guilty of this crime is an "embraceor."

eminent domain

A government's power to take, or authorize others to take, private property for a public purpose provided that just compensation is paid for it. In theory, the sovereign has superior dominion over all land, and its "owner" holds it mediately or immediately and must surrender it when the sovereign reasserts its dominion over it. The process of so taking land is called "expropriation" or "condemnation."

emolument

The profit, gain, or advantage arising from office or employ-

131

ment. It includes salary, fees, and benefits.

empirical

That which is based on observation, experiment, or experience.

employee

A person who works for another for salary or wages, and whose work is under the employer's control and direction. The specific definition varies according to statute. Synonymous with "servant."

Employee Stock Ownership Plan (E.S.O.P.)

A qualified profit-sharing plan in which the employee earns stock in the ownership of the company. Such plans are often put in place as retirement benefits for employees.

employer

One who hires another person to work for him, and who is in the position to control and direct that work. Formerly called "master."

employer's liability acts

Statutes which define an employer's liability for injuries suffered by employees while on the job. Many of these statutes state that an employer is still liable even though the worker's negligence may have contributed to the injury (*e.g.*, Federal Employers' Liability Act and workers' compensation acts).

emptor

Lat. A buyer. Used in phrase "caveat emptor" meaning "let the buyer beware."

enabling clause

That clause in a statute or constitution that states by what power it is enacted and enforced (*e.g.*, "Congress shall have the power to enact and enforce this article by appropriate legislation." U.S. Constitution, Fifteenth Amendment).

enabling statutes

1. Any statute which grants new power to do something. 2. An old English statute that gave certain persons the power to make leases for life or for 21 years.

enact

1. To establish by decree or law. 2. To put into effect.

enacting clause

Preliminary clause in a legislative act which states the authority by which it is made. State constitutions and legislative rules often require that a bill have an enacting clause before it may be passed.

en banc, in banc

(en bank) Fr. In full bench. Term refers to situation where all qualified judges of a court take part in a case. This is usually done for important cases in the federal appellate courts.

enclosure

1. Land enclosed by some visible obstruction such as a fence or hedge. *Compare* close. 2. An obstruction that surrounds land. 3. In old English law, the act of freeing land from rights of common and vesting it in one absolute owner. Also "inclosure."

encroach

To intrude unlawfully upon the land, property, or authority of another, usually in a gradual, secretive manner (*e.g.*, to fence in part of another's land is to encroach upon it).

encroachment

1. Act of unlawfully extending one's property boundaries onto the property of another. 2. A fixture that illegally intrudes upon a street or highway. 3. Act by the owner of an easement which alters a dominant tenement so as to create an additional burden upon a servient tenement.

encumbrance

A claim or interest in land held by a person other than its owner (*e.g.*, a mortgage, lien, easement). It does not prohibit passing title, but it does lower the land's value. An encumbrance may also be on personal property (*e.g.*, a chattel mortgage). Also "incumbrance."

endorsement

Act of signing the back of a negotiable instrument to transfer it entirely to another person. An "accommodation endorsement" is one where the endorser extends credit to the holder of the instrument without consideration. A "blank endorsement" is one which does not specify to whom the instrument is payable, and thus is negotiable by the bearer. A "restrictive endorsement" is conditional; restrictions are placed on it as to how it can be transferred. Also "indorsement."

endowment

1. Money or property given to a person or institution the income from which is to be used for a specific purpose; the act of setting up such a fund. 2. The assignment of dower.

enfeoffment

(en-FEEF-ment) Old English term for transferring full ownership in land by a ceremony called "livery of seisin." Today, term means act of investing a person with a fee (estate in real property); the deed by which a person is so vested with possession. Also "feoffment."

enforce

1. To put into effect; to carry out; to cause the performance of; to execute, such as to enforce a contract. 2. To compel obedience.

enfranchise

1. To make free. 2. To give the right to vote.

en gros

In gross; by wholesale; total.

engrossing

1. The making of a clear, legible copy of a document. 2. The cornering of the market on a commodity and gaining of a monopoly.

engrossed bill

A bill in the final form as passed by one house of the legislature.

enjoin

1. To command with authority; to order that something be done or not be done; to require. 2. To issue a writ of injunction. *See* injunction.

enjoy

To have and use with satisfaction; to have the economic benefit of. "Enjoyment" is the exercise of a right, such as the right to peacefully occupy one's property.

enlarge

1. To increase, expand, make larger. 2. To free someone from custody or prison. "Enlargement" or "enlarger testate" is a type of release which enlarges an estate and conveys the interest of a remainderman to a tenant.

enroll

1. To record; to register. 2. To enter into the records of a court or legislature.

enrolled bill

A bill put in its final form as passed by both houses of the legislature for transmittal to the executive.

enrolled bill rule

Rule that states that a duly passed and signed bill shall not be questioned as to its enactment.

entail

1. (v.) To limit the succession to real property to the issue, or certain classes of issue, of an heir; to create an estate tail. 2. (n.) A fee limited to the issue of an heir's body; a fee tail. *See* fee tail.

enter

1. Real property: To go onto land to take possession of it. 2. To become part of something, as in to enter a conspiracy. 3. To formally put into the records, as in to enter a transaction into a ledger, or to enter an appearance in court.

entering judgment

The formal entry of a court's decision into the court records by the court clerk. This record serves as incontestable evidence of the court's judgment.

enticement

Act of wrongfully persuading or inducing person to do something (*e.g.*, to persuade a child to enter a car for unlawful purposes).

entirety

Whole; not divided (*e.g.*, property "seised of the entirety" by a husband and wife is held wholly by both, and neither can convey it without the consent of the other). "Entirety of contract" means the contract is not divisible or severable.

entitle

1. To give right or title to. 2. To qualify for. "Entitlement" is the right to claim something, such as social security benefits.

entity

An existence, a being, be it actual or artificial (*e.g.*, a person, corporation, or trust).

entrapment

Act by police or other government officer of inducing a person to commit a crime he had not contemplated nor would have committed if not for the inducement. It is done to obtain evidence needed to initiate prosecution against the person, and constitutes an affirmative defense if proven by the defendant.

entrusting

The act of transferring personal property to a merchant who deals in goods of that type.

entry

1. Act of writing down an item in a record book, such as a court record or business ledger; the item so entered. 2. The act of going into another's house to commit a crime. The slightest entry by a person, or an instrument used by him for criminal purposes, is sufficient to constitute the "entry" requirement for burglary.

enumerate

To count; to list. "Enumerated" means mentioned specifically or designated.

enumerator

Person who takes a census.

enure

To take effect; to serve to the benefit of a person, as in, "The benefits of the insurance policy enured to *A*." Also "inure."

environmental impact statement

Report that an agency must produce setting out the environmental effects of a proposed law, regulation, or project.

Environmental Protection Agency (E.P.A.)

Federal agency created in 1970 to monitor environmental quality and enforce pollution control laws.

eo instanti

(AY-oe in-STAN-tee) Lat. Immediately; at that moment; instantly.

E.P.A.

See Environmental Protection Agency.

Equal Employment Opportunity Commission (E.E.O.C.)

Created by Civil Rights Act of 1964 to eliminate employment discrimination.

equal opportunity

Employment practices which do not discriminate on the basis of gender, race, religion, national origin., or disability

equal protection of the laws

Constitutional guarantee (Fourteenth Amendment), applicable only to the states, that law shall equally protect all persons under the same circumstances. This does not imply that the law cannot classify persons for specific reasons (*e.g.*, taxation), but only that the classification cannot be arbitrary. Principles of equal protection are enforced against the federal government by application of the Fifth Amendment Due Process Clause (*e.g.*, racial discrimination violates due process).

equitable

Fair, just, based on principles of equity.

equitable estate

A right or interest in an estate the title to which is held by another. The distinction between an equitable estate and a legal estate is that the holder of an equitable estate has the right to the beneficial use and enjoyment of it, whereas the holder of a legal estate possesses title but not necessarily the right to use and enjoyment (*e.g.*, the beneficiary of a trust has an equitable estate).

equitable estoppel

Doctrine which prevents a person from asserting a right he otherwise would have had because of the effect his conduct would have on another. That is, if *A* relies on *B*'s acts and conduct and would be injured if *B* repudiates his acts and conduct, fairness (and the law) holds that *B* should be prevented from so repudiating. Same as "estoppel in pais."

equitable lien

A right to have specific property used, partially or entirely, to pay a certain debt or class of debts. It arises either from a contract or is imposed, as a matter of equity, by a court.

equity

1. Fairness; justice according to principles of fairness and not strictly according to formulated law. 2. "Courts of Equity" are those which administer justice in equity. They originated in England to handle cases where courts of law were inadequate. Today, law and equity have combined, and courts of equity have generally been abolished. 3. The value of property minus all encumbrances on it.

equity of redemption

Right a mortgagor has to redeem an estate after forfeiture. The mortgagor must pay the mortgage debt, costs, and interest.

erasure

Rubbing out or obliteration of words from a written instrument. Also the space where the written words were removed from the document.

ergo

Lat. Therefore, consequently, because.

E.R.I.S.A.

Employee Retirement Income Security Act; federal legislation that regulates the funding, vesting, and administration of pension plans and employee benefit plans.

erroneous

Involving error; deviating from the law. "Erroneous judgment" means a court had the power to act but exercised that power wrongly.

error

1. A mistake in application of law or in matters of fact. 2. Short for "writ of error" which is a writ that authorizes a higher court to review the decision of a lower court for errors that appear on the face of the record.

escalator clause

Clause in certain contracts that provides for an increase in the contract price for specified reasons (*e.g.*, a clause in a labor contract which ties wages to the cost of living; a clause in a construction contract that ties the cost of a building to the price of wood, cement, or labor; a clause in a lease executed subject to price control regulations).

escape

Act of voluntarily and unlawfully fleeing from custody.

escheat

1. The transfer of property to the state because its owner died leaving no one legally entitled to claim it. 2. The property so transferred.

escrow

A document, stock, money or other property given to a third person (escrow agent) to be held by him until the occurrence of an event or performance of a condition, at which time the agent delivers it to the grantee or obligee (*e.g.*, a deed to land held until its purchaser pays for it in full).

E-Sign Act

Abbreviation for the Electronic Signatures in Global and National Commerce Act, a federal statute that provides that digital or electronic signatures have the same legal effect as signatures on paper.

esquire, esq.

A title given to members of the bar and to others.

essence

That which is necessary or essential; the vital element of something, such as a contract, Where "time is of the essence" in a contract, one party must perform on the contract by a certain date or within a period of time for him to be able to require performance by the other party.

Establishment Clause

The provision in the First Amendment of the U.S. Constitution which prohibits the state from enacting laws that establish religion. The provision prevents the state from favoring one religion over another, from forcing a person to believe or disbelieve any religion, from spending public funds for religious schools, and from allowing prayers to be said aloud in public schools, among other things.

estate

1. The interest a person has in real property. This interest varies from absolute ownership to naked possession (actual posses-

sion without color of tide). 2. All the property, whether real or personal, in which one has an interest (*e.g.*, a decedent's estate).

estate at will

A leased estate held at the will of the lessor for an indefinite period of time (*i.e.*, either party is able to end the lease at any time he wishes). An estate at will may be by express contract or by implication of law. Also "tenancy at will."

estate by entirety

Estate held jointly by a husband and wife by virtue of the unity in marriage, and which goes to the surviving spouse upon the death of the other.

The difference between an estate by entirety and a joint tenancy is that the latter may be vested in a number of persons, each of whom have a partial interest in the property, where the former is vested in only two who are regarded as one by law, and each of whom have a right to the entire estate. Also "tenancy by the entirety."

estate for years

An estate in land that will end after a fixed period of time, whether weeks, months, or years (*e.g.*, a leasehold estate). Also "tenancy for years" and "tenancy for a term."

estate tax

A tax on the right to transfer a deceased person's property. It is based on the value of the entire estate. An "inheritance tax" is the opposite; it is a tax on the right to receive property and is based on the value of the property each heir receives.

estoppel

A bar which prevents a person from denying or asserting anything that contradicts what he has, in contemplation of law, established to be true. The elements of estoppel are: reliance on the acts or representations of another, a deception of that person, and a change of position to the detriment of the person who so relied on the acts or representations.

The three categories of estoppel are: *Estoppel by record*, which precludes the denial of truth established in a judicial or legislative record. *Estoppel by deed*, which prevents a party to a deed from denying its existence or the truth of any facts in it. *Estoppel in pais*, or *equitable estoppel*, which prevents a person from denying something his conduct led another to believe.

et al.
Lat. Abbreviation for "et alii," meaning "and others."

ethics
Body of principles of good conduct, especially pertaining to a group or people or a profession.

et seq.
Lat. Abbreviation for et sequentia, "and the following;" also et sqq. for multiple following pages/matters.

et ux.
Lat. Abbreviation of "et uxor," meaning "and wife."

euro
The official common currency of the European Union.

Eurodollar
A U.S. dollar on deposit with a bank in Europe.

euthanasia
See mercy killing.

eviction
Dispossession; act of making a tenant surrender possession of property. Eviction may be by an assertion of paramount title, by disturbing tenant's enjoyment of property thus causing him to leave, by reentry (for breach of a covenant in the lease), or by legal proceedings by the landlord.

evidence
All the means legally presented at trial to persuade the court or jury as to the truth of a matter in question. Evidence includes testimony by witnesses, records, photographs, and exhibits. Although "evidence" and "proof" are used interchangeably, there is a distinction between the terms: "Evidence" is the *means* by which the truth or falsity of a matter is established, and "proof" is the *result* of evidence, although not all evidence establishes proof.

ex
Lat. Preposition meaning from, out of, by, on, on account of, or

according to. Also a prefix meaning "former" and "without."

ex aequo et bono
(ex EE-kwo et boe-no) Lat. From equity and good conscience; in justice and fairness.

examination
1. The questioning of a person under oath, whether by written or oral interrogation. 2. An investigation or search. Examinations are made of witnesses at trial, of persons charged with crimes, of persons filing for bankruptcy, of inventions submitted for patents, and of abstracts of title.

examiner
Person authorized to conduct an examination.

ex cathedra
(ex ka-THEE-dra) Lat. From the chair; with authority.

exception
1. Act of excluding someone or something that would otherwise be included. 2. The thing so excluded. 3. Formal objection to a trial court's ruling made to enter the disagreement into the record, and subsequently to be used in appealing the case. Under the rules of procedure in federal courts and most state courts, exceptions have been replaced by objections. *See* Federal Rule of Civil Procedure 46.

excessive
That which is greater than what is usual and proper (*e.g.*, excessive bail, excessive force).

excessive bail
A bail amount which exceeds the figure reasonably sufficient to prevent the accused from evading the law. Excessive bail is barred by the Eighth Amendment and by some state constitutions.

exchange
1. A barter; a trade; a transfer of property for property, not for money, although some money may be paid in addition to the property exchanged. 2. An organization or association that provides a place where securities are bought and sold (*e.g.*, New York Stock Exchange). 3. A transfer of funds between persons distant from one another at a price agreed upon or at a price fixed by commercial usage.

excise tax

A tax on the manufacture, sale, or use of commodities, or on licenses to pursue certain occupations or on corporate privileges. Also known as "license tax" and "privilege tax."

excited utterance

An evidentiary statement concerning a startling event or condition made by the declarant while under the stress or excitement caused by the event or condition; an exception to the hearsay rule.

exclusionary rule

Rule that prohibits illegally obtained evidence from being admitted at trial (*e.g.*, evidence obtained in an illegal search).

exclusive

Pertaining to one subject only; not shared. A court with "exclusive jurisdiction" has power in certain areas or over certain persons to the exclusion of all other courts. Same as absolute jurisdiction. "Exclusive agency" is the right an agent has to do business in an area to the exclusion of all others. "Exclusive license" is the exclusive right to produce and sell a patented product.

ex contractu

(ex kon-TRAK-too) Lat. Arising out of a contract. An action ex contractu arises from a breach of promise in a contract. It is one of the two divisions of obligations and causes of action. *See* ex delicto.

exculpate

1. To clear or tend to clear of alleged guilt. 2. To provide a justification or excuse. The adjective is "exculpatory."

exculpatory clause

A clause in a trust instrument that relieves a trustee from liability when he has acted in good faith.

excuse

1. (n.) A reason for doing or not doing something; a reason for being exempt from a duty or obligation. 2. (v.) To exempt someone from a duty.

ex delicto

(ex de-LIK-toe) Lat. From a tort or wrongful act. An action ex delicto arises out of fault or malfeasance. Commonly called "ex maleficio." It is one of the two divisions of obligations and causes of action. *See* ex contractu.

ex dolo malo non oritur actio
(ex DOE-low MALL-o non OH-ri-toor AK-tee-o) Lat. From fraud no action arises. A court will not hear an action based on an illegal or immoral act.

execute
To perform; to carry out; to complete; to make, as in to execute a contract or an obligation.

executed
Fully accomplished; carried into full effect; completed.

execution
1. The carrying out of something, such as a court order; the putting of something, such as a contract, into effect. 2. The act by which the state puts a person to death.

executive agreement
An international agreement that usually involves military matters, or matters left to presidential discretion. Executive agreements are not subject to ratification by the Senate.

executive order
A presidential order directing the actions of executive branch agencies.

executor
Person appointed by a testator to carry out the directives of his will. This may be done expressly or by implication. A woman so appointed is an executrix. When a person is appointed by the court to administer a decedent's estate, he/she is called an administrator/administratrix. *See* personal representative.

executory
Something not yet executed or performed; that which requires some performance or occurrence for its completion. An "executory devise" is a gift by will that does not take effect until a future contingency takes place. An "executory interest" vests only after the happening of a specified condition.

executrix
Female executor.

exemplar
Nontestimonial identification evidence such as a blood sample,

fingerprint or handwriting sample taken from a defendant.

exemplary damages

Damages awarded in excess of actual damages (*i.e.*, more than is required to compensate plaintiff for injuries sustained). Such damages are awarded to punish defendant, to discourage him and others from committing acts similar to the one for which he is being punished, and to provide some solace to plaintiff for mental anguish and shame. Same as "punitive damages" and "vindictive damages."

exempt employee

An employee whose job duties place him in a category of employees who are not covered by wage and hour laws, especially the laws relating to overtime pay.

exemption

1. Freedom from a responsibility or duty that one would ordinarily have (*e.g.*, jury duty or military service). 2. A privilege granted by the state to a debtor exempting some of his property of liability to his creditors. 3. A deduction allowed from gross income on income tax returns

(*e.g.*, for self, dependents, or blindness).

ex gratia

(ex GRA-tee-a or ex GRA-shee-a) Lat. Out of grace; as a favor.

exhaustion of remedies

The doctrine requiring a party to exhaust all possible administrative or non-federal remedies before bringing the matter before a federal or state court.

exhibit

1. (n.) An object displayed in court as evidence, such as a document, photograph, or gun. 2. A paper attached to a document. 3. (v.) To display or show.

exigency

An urgent situation requiring immediate action or effort. Such a situation can be used as a justification for not complying with the law or ignoring another's rights or interests (*e.g.*, speeding on the way to a hospital in a life-threatening emergency).

exigible

Capable of being required or demanded.

145

ex mero motu
(ex MARE-o MO-too) Lat. Of his own mere motion; of his own accord; voluntarily without request.

ex officio
Lat. From his office; solely by virtue of office. Powers ex officio are powers necessarily implied by one's office,

exonerate
1. To free from alleged guilt. 2. To find no fault.

exoneration
1. Act of clearing someone of alleged guilt. 2. A removal of a burden; a release from liability, such as an exoneration of part of an estate where liability for payment of debts is removed from one part of the estate (*e.g.*, real property) and placed on another (*e.g.*, personalty). 3. The right to be reimbursed for debts one pays for another. It is similar to "indemnity" though indemnity is usually based on a contract.

ex parte
(ex PAR-tay) Lat. For, by, or in behalf of only one party (*e.g.*, an ex parte injunction may be grant-ed in an urgent situation to one party without notifying the party to be bound by the injunction).

expatriation
Living in a country other than one's native country, especially permanently or for an extended period of time.

expectancy
Something which one expects or hopes for but which one has no present right to possess (*e.g.*, an heir has an expectancy interest in the property he hopes to inherit, yet no interest vests in him until its owner so states it and dies). "Expectancies" are estates in anticipation, and they are of two sorts with regard to the time of their possession and enjoyment: A "remainder" is an expectancy interest created by the act of the parties to the estate, and a "reversion" is an expectancy interest created by an act of law.

expectant heir
Person who hopes and expects to inherit property, or person who actually has a vested or contingent remainder in property.

expenses
1. Costs of objects or services.
2. Expenditures in money or other resources, for the purpose of gaining something else.

expert witness
One whose special knowledge of a subject enables him to express opinions and draw conclusions in his testimony at trial. Persons without such knowledge are not allowed to do so, and are restricted to testifying only to the facts.

ex post facto
(ex post FAK-to) Lat. After the fact. Opposite of "ab initio."

express
Clear, definite, or actual; conveyed in explicit terms (*e.g.*, an express contract, an express warranty). Contrasted with "implied."

expressio unius est exclusio alterius
(ex-PRES-see-o OO-ne-us est ex-KLOO-see-o al-TAIR-ee-us) Lat. The expression of one thing is the exclusion of another. This maxim is used in interpreting documents and laws, and means that when certain persons or things are specifically mentioned, it can be inferred that those not specified are excluded.

expropriation
The compulsory purchase of property by the state under its power of eminent domain. Same as "condemnation." Act of surrendering or renouncing a claim to property.

ex rel.
Lat. Abbreviation for "ex relatione," meaning "upon relation"; on the information of. Suits instituted by the state on its behalf, but at the instigation and on the information provided by an individual who has a private interest in the suit are said to be instituted ex relatione. Captioned: "State of Illinois ex rel. Smith v. Jones."

extend
1. To enlarge; to broaden; to expand; to carry out past a previous limit. 2. To extend credit means to allow a person to defer full payment on a purchase.

extension

A lengthening of time allowed to meet an obligation or of time for which a contract is valid (*e.g.*, an extension given to a debtor allows additional time for payment of debts). The extension of a contract makes an existing contract operative for a greater length of time, and is distinguished from a renewal which requires a new contract be made.

extenuating circumstances

Facts tending to contribute to an illegal act, but which reduce the damages or penalty against the wrongdoer because he had little or no control over those facts.

extinguishment

The ending or cancellation of something, such as a contract, debt, or interest in property.

extortion

1. Offense committed by someone who employs threats to unlawfully obtain money or other property from another. 2. At common law, extortion applies to public officials who use the color of their office to corruptly take money or property. Extortion differs from robbery in that the threat to the personal safety of the victim is less direct in extortion than in robbery. Synonymous with "blackmail."

extradition

The surrender by one country or state to another of a person accused or convicted of a crime in that other country or state.

extrajudicial

1. That which is outside of a regular court proceeding (*e.g.*, extrajudicial oath, extrajudicial confession). 2. That which is outside a court's jurisdiction.

extraordinary remedies

Writs issued to redress or prevent a wrong where ordinary actions in law or equity are insufficient. A writ of habeas corpus might be issued for a child being kept by someone who does not have custody, or a writ of mandamus will order a public official to do something. A writ quo warranto will inquire into the right of a public official to act. These remedies have generally been abolished and replaced by regular court action.

extraterritoriality

A quality some laws have which make them operative outside the state or country which enacted them. Extraterritoriality gives a country jurisdiction over its citizens in a foreign country.

extremis

(ex-TREE-miss) Short for Latin "in extremis," in extremity. Term is used to indicate a situation of extreme circumstances, especially that of imminent death.

extrinsic evidence

Facts outside the body of a document, such as oral statements. Extrinsic evidence is normally inadmissible for the purpose of defining the boundaries of an instrument. *See* parol evidence rule. Such evidence is always admissible for purposes of interpreting an agreement.

extrinsic fraud

Fraud which is additional or supplementary to the issues tried in a case where judgment is rendered. Such deceit may have prevented one party from presenting his case in court, and would provide grounds for equi-table relief against the judgment rendered. Also "collateral fraud."

ex turpi causa non oritur actio

(ex TURR-pee KAOW-sa non or-REE-toor AK-tee-o) Lat. No cause of action can arise out of an immoral (*i.e.*, disgraceful, obscene) matter.

eyewitness

One who testifies as to what she has seen.

eyre

(air) In old England, a court of judges who traveled throughout the kingdom.

F

face

1. Material that appears on a document or statute without any explanation, modification, or addition. 2. Front of check or money order where payor writes the particulars of the instrument. 3. The surface of anything.

face value

1. The value stated on the face of a security or insurance policy (*e.g.*, the value at maturity or death). 2. The value upon which interest is computed. 3. The value that can be ascertained from a document without aid from extrinsic facts or evidence. 4. Par value.

facias

(FAH-she-as or FAY-she-as) Lat. That you do; what you have caused.

facinus quos inquinat aequat

(FAH-shee-nus kwos in-KWEE-nat EE-kwee-tat) Lat. Ail who are contaminated with an evil deed or a crime are equal.

facio ut des

(FAH-shee-o oot days) Lat. I do that you may give; a type of contract in which one agrees to do something for wages or an agreed sum of money.

facio ut facias

(FAH-shee-o oot FAH-shee-as) Lat. I do so that you may do; a type of contract in which one party agrees to do or refrain from doing something in return for the other party's promise to do or refrain from doing something.

facsimile

An exact copy.

fact

1. Something that took place; an act; something actual and real; an incident that occurred; an event. 2. A thing done. 3. Something that exists and is real as opposed to opinion or supposition. 4. Events which are proven in the evidence heard by a court and upon which the law operates.

facta sunt potentiora verbis
(FAK-ta soont po-ten-she-OR-a VER-bis) Lat. Deeds, facts, or accomplishments are more powerful than words.

fact-finder
The person or group responsible for determining the facts in a judicial or administrative proceeding.

factor
An agent who possesses and seeks to sell goods belonging to a client or principal in exchange for a commission. The commission is called a factorage.

Factor's Acts
An English statute and its counterpart in many U.S. states, the purpose of which is to make a factor's possession or property or documents evidence of ownership sufficient to allow him to conduct all acts that the owner might, thus making the owner responsible for the factor's acts and protecting bona fide purchasers in any transaction fairly effected with the apparent owner. 22 Am.Jur. 2d *Factors* § 53.

factum
Lat. Deed or act; fact; central fact or act upon which a question turns; statement of facts.

factum a judice quod ad ejus officium non spectat non ratum est
(FAK-tum a joo-DISH-ee kwod ad AY-yus o-FISH-ee-um non SPEK-tat non RAH-tum est) Lat. An action of a judge which is unrelated to his office derives no force from his being a judge.

factum probandum
(FAK-tum pro-BAHN-dum) Lat. A fact to be proved.

failure of consideration
The neglect, refusal, or inability of a contracting party to perform or furnish the agreed upon consideration after making and entering into a contract (*e.g.*, the thing of value contemplated as consideration becomes worthless or is destroyed).

failure of issue
Dying without children.

failure to state a cause of action
Plaintiff's failure to allege in a complaint facts sufficient, if

proved, to establish a cause of action.

fair comment

A defense to an action for libel based on the common law right to comment, within limits, upon the conduct of public officials without being liable for defamation. Plea states that even if the statements made were untrue they were not intended to create ill will or be malicious, but rather were intended to state the facts as the writer honestly believed them to be.

fair hearing

Flexible term used to describe trial-like decisionmaking process of administrative agencies which contemplates the taking of testimony, with the right of cross-examination assured to the parties, and the rendering of findings of fact supported by evidence. The hearing does not have to use full trial rules or procedures, but it must be conducted in a manner consistent with due process.

fair market value

1. The amount a willing buyer would pay and a willing seller would accept, neither being under a compulsion to buy or sell and both having reasonable knowledge of the relevant facts. 2. The price goods would bring in the ordinary course of trade.

fair trade acts

Laws permitting manufacturers to establish minimum resale prices for name brand goods sold by a retail storekeeper.

fair use doctrine

Principle which allows a person other than the owner of a copyright to use the copyrighted material in a reasonable manner and for certain purposes without the consent of the copyright owner.

false

1. Not true. 2. Intentionally untrue. 3. Wrongful, unjust.

false arrest

1. Tort consisting of unlawful restraint or deprivation of a person's liberty. 2. Arrest without proper legal authority; illegal arrest. False arrest may also be a criminal offense.

false imprisonment

Intentional tort involving the unlawful restraint of the physical liberty of another. If the restraint is imposed by the use of purported legal authority and results in an arrest, then there is a false arrest as well as false imprisonment.

false light

A tort action in which the plaintiff alleges that the defendant has placed facts before the public that depict the plaintiff in a false light, and in an offensive manner.

false pretenses

Untrue statements or misrepresentations knowingly made in order to obtain title to property by defrauding the owner.

false return

1. A report made by a sheriff or other court officer in which false statements are made. 2. Income tax return which has false information on it.

falsify

1. To prove to be false or incorrect; to disprove. 2. To counterfeit or forge. 3. To alter fraudulently.

falsus in uno, falsus in omnibus

(FAL-suss in oono, FAL-suss in OM-nee-bus) Lat. False in one thing, false in everything. Maxim that if a jury believes that a witness has testified falsely in one matter, it may disregard his entire testimony as being false.

Family and Medical Leave Act

Federal law requiring some employers to provide employees with unpaid time off in order to tend to medical or other needs of themselves or of family members. Some states have similar laws.

family purpose rule, family car doctrine

Principle of tort law in some states which holds that the owner of a "family car" is liable for injury caused by its negligent use by members of the family.

famosus libellus

(fah-MO-suss LIE-bel-luss) Lat. A libelous writing.

Farm Credit Administration
Established by Farm Credit Act of 1971 to provide adequate and dependable credit to farmers.

f.a.s.
See free alongside ship.

fault
1. Negligence. 2. An error or defect of judgment or conduct. 3. Any deviation from prudence or duty. 4. Any shortcoming or neglect of care or performance resulting from incapacity or perversity. 5. A wrongful act. 6. Neglect of obligation or duty; mismanagement, bad faith. 7. The responsibility for a misdeed or for negligence. 8. Defect or imperfection. 9. Wrongful act, omission, or breach. *See* U.C.C. § 1–201(16).

favored beneficiary
The party who is favored over others who have equal claim to a testator's estate or interests.

F.C.C.
See Federal Communications Commission.

F.D.I.C.
See Federal Deposit Insurance Corporation.

fealty
Obligation of fidelity which feudal tenant owed to his lord.

feasance
Doing an act, performing a duty.

F.E.C.
See Federal Election Commission.

federal
Joined in a union having a central and predominate authority. In the United States, the national government as opposed to state government.

federal common law
Laws established by the federal courts, uninfluenced by laws and legal decisions made by state courts. The use of federal common law was restricted by *Erie Railroad v. Tompkins,* 304 U.S. 64 (1938).

Federal Communications Commission (F.C.C.)
Created by the Federal Communications Act of 1934. Regulates radio and television broadcasting within the U.S.

Federal Deposit Insurance Corporation (F.D.I.C)
Established in 1933 to insure deposits in Federal Reserve System member banks.

Federal Election Commission (F.E.C.)
Established by the Federal Election Campaign Act of 1971 to monitor campaign practices in federal elections.

Federal Emergency Management Agency (F.E.M.A.)
Established in 1978 to make flood insurance and reinsurance available nationwide.

Federal Employer's Liability Act (F.E.L.A.)
A form of workers' compensation plan for railroad employees.

Federal Home Loan Bank Board (F.H.L.B.B.)
Established in 1932 to provide a flexible credit reserve for member savings institutions engaged in home mortgage lending. Superseded by the Federal Housing Finance Board and the Office of Thrift Supervision.

Federalist Society
An association of lawyers and law students that promotes conservative and libertarian positions on legal and political issues.

Federal Labor Relations Authority (F.L.R.A.)
Created in 1978 to provide leadership in establishing policies and guidance relating to federal labor management relations.

federal offenses
Violations of federal statutes. Congress defines the offenses and prescribes the punishment (*e.g.*, treason, income tax evasion, smuggling, and kidnapping across state lines).

federal question
Issues of law which involve the construction of the United States Constitution, federal laws, or treaties. The federal courts have original jurisdiction over such matters.

Federal Register
A daily publication containing documents issued by the Executive Branch.

Federal Reserve System

Created by the Federal Reserve Act of 1913 to establish a general monetary policy and banking system for the United States.

Federal Tort Claims Act

See Tort Claims Act.

Federal Trade Commission (F.T.C.)

Established by the Federal Trade Commission Act of 1914 to regulate business practices and enforce provisions of the various antitrust laws.

fee

1. A charge for services performed by government employees or by professionals for services performed or to be performed. 2. An estate in property generally denoting complete ownership which entitles the owner to sell the property or to devise it to his heirs.

fee simple

An estate in land without any limitations on it which gives the owner the absolute power of disposition. Today there is a presumption that an estate is given in fee simple unless there is a clear intention to give a more limited estate. Also called "fee" or "fee simple absolute."

fee tail

An estate conveyed by deed or will to an heir and a fixed line of future heirs by the owner of the estate; an estate of inheritance which passes only by lineal descent. Generally indicated by the words "to *A* and the heirs of his body." Almost universally abolished by statute in modern times.

fellow servant rule

Common law rule that an employer is not liable for injuries caused to one employee by the negligence of another employee. Fellow servants were said to assume the risk of each other's negligence. Employer's liability acts and worker's compensation laws have repealed the fellow servant rule in most jurisdictions.

felo de se

(FEL-lo day say) Lat. A felon with respect to himself. A suicide victim; a suicide victim in a jurisdiction where killing oneself is a felony.

felon
One who has been convicted of a felony and has not yet finished serving time for it.

felonious homicide
The killing of a human being without justification or excuse. The term includes suicide.

felony
1. A major or high crime, as distinguished from a misdemeanor. Crimes are declared to be felonies by statute or by common law. 2. As defined by statute, a crime punishable by imprisonment for one year or more or by death. 3. Formerly, every offense at common law which caused a forfeiture of land or goods.

felony murder
The unlawful killing of another during the commission or attempted commission of a felony; first degree murder. In some jurisdictions, only those homicides which occur during the commission of particular, specified felonies are deemed felony murders.

F.E.M.A.
See Federal Emergency Management Agency.

feme (femme) covert
(femm koe-VAIR) Fr. A married woman.

feme (femme) sole
Fr. An unmarried woman.

fence
1. Person who buys stolen property to resell at a profit. 2. A hedge, ditch, wall, or other structure intended to enclose a piece of land, divide a piece of land into distinct portions, or separate two contiguous estates.

feoffment
(FEE-off-ment) Common law method of conveying the title to real estate which includes livery of seisin.

fertile octogenarian
In property and probate law, the legal fiction that assumes that every living woman may conceive and give birth to children as long as she lives.

feud
1. A grant of land made by a superior to a tenant in return for

services in exchange for the superior protecting the tenant. 2. An inherited right to occupy and use the land of a feudal estate. 3. Long continued hostility between two families or two branches of the same family.

feudal system

System of property law from the Middle Ages in England and Europe by which a superior or lord granted the use of land to a tenant in exchange for his services. In return the lord was bound to protect the tenant.

F.H.L.B.B.

See Federal Home Loan Bank Board.

fiat

(FEE-att) Lat. Let it be done. A decree; an order by a judge or other competent legal source.

fiat justitia

(FEE-att jus-TI-shee-a) Lat. Let justice be done.

fiction

An assumption of law that something that is or may be false or nonexistent is true or real. Legal fictions are assumed or invented

for the purpose of accomplishing justice (*e.g.*, constructive trust).

fictitious name

1. An alias. 2. A name taken which is different than a person's real name for the purpose of deceiving someone.

fidelity bond

1. Bond which guarantees payment of a loss if a bonded employee embezzles or absconds with money or valuables in his care. 2. Insurance on a person against that person's dishonesty.

fiduciary

Person entrusted with the duty to act for the benefit of someone else (*e.g.*, trustee, director of a corporation, executor). A fiduciary must exercise a high degree of care and must subordinate her own personal interests in the event that there is a conflict.

fieri facias

(FEER-ee FAH-she-as) Lat. That you cause to be made. Writ of execution commanding a sheriff to seize goods to pay off a debt. Also referred to as "fi fa."

field warehousing

An arrangement by which a wholesaler, manufacturer, or merchant finances his business by pledging goods on his premises; a security device in inventory financing.

Fifteenth Amendment

Constitutional amendment guaranteeing all citizens the right to vote, regardless of race, color, or previous condition of servitude. One of the "Civil War" amendments to the U.S. Constitution.

Fifth Amendment

Amendment to the United States Constitution contained in the Bill of Rights. The Fifth Amendment provides the privilege against self-incrimination, the right to due process, the right to just compensation for the taking of property by government, and further bars subjection to double jeopardy.

FIFO

(FIE-foe) Abbreviation for "first in, first out," an accounting method used in valuing inventories. This method assumes that the first goods bought are the first ones sold.

file

1. The court record of a case. 2. To present a legal document to a public official, usually a court clerk, for the purpose of having it placed on permanent record and preserved.

filiation proceeding

Judicial proceeding to establish the paternity of a child born out of wedlock and to compel the father to contribute to the child's support. Also called "affiliation proceeding," "bastardy proceeding," "parentage action," or "paternity suit."

final

1. Conclusive. 2. End, ultimate, last. 3. Completed. 4. Terminating all controversy, doubt, or dispute.

final decision

Judgment of a court which terminates the litigation in the court that renders it. A final decision settles the dispute between parties unless or until it is set aside or reversed by a higher court. Also called "final judgment" or "final decree."

final judgment

A trial court judgment that leaves nothing open to further dispute and thus terminates the cause of action. Only upon final judgment may a matter be taken up by an appellate court.

Financial Institutions Reform, Recovery, and Enforcement Act

Federal law that revamped regulation of the banking industry.

financial intermediary

An individual or financial organization such as a bank that acts as intermediary between lenders (for banks, its depositors) and borrowers.

financial statement

Report summarizing a company's or a person's financial condition, including assets and liabilities.

financing statement

Under U.C.C. Article 9, a financing statement is filed to provide a public record of security interests in goods.

finding

Decision of a court or jury on issues of fact, which discloses the grounds upon which a judgment rests.

finding of fact

Determination of an issue by the court or jury based on evidence submitted by opposing parties in a lawsuit.

fine

Pecuniary penalty imposed as a punishment for the commission of an offense. In a criminal case, a fine may be imposed instead of or in addition to imprisonment.

firm

1. A partnership or company; an unincorporated business; a business entity, concern, or enterprise. 2. The name or title under which a partnership transacts business.

firm offer

Written offer which will be held open by a merchant for a certain length of time to buy or sell goods. A firm offer requires no consideration in order to be valid and if no length of time is stated then the offer is irrevocable for a reasonable time, not to exceed three months. U.C.C. § 2–205.

F.I.R.R.E.A.

See Financial Institutions Reform, Recovery, and Enforcement Act.

First Amendment

Amendment to U.S. Constitution contained in the Bill of Rights guaranteeing the freedoms of religion, speech, press, and assembly and the right to petition the government for redress of grievances.

first degree murder

Under modern statutes that divide murder into degrees, deliberate and premeditated killings and murders committed during the commission of specific felonies are first degree. Some jurisdictions consider certain additional killings in this category (*e.g.*, by torture, poison, lying in wait).

first devisee

The first person to receive an estate devised by will.

first impression

First discussion, consideration, or examination; new. A case or question is of "first impression" if it presents a new problem to the court and, therefore, cannot be decided by existing precedent.

first instance, court of

Trial court where a lawsuit is first heard as opposed to a court of appeal.

first refusal

Contractual agreement that an owner of property who receives an offer to purchase the property must first offer the property for sale to certain other designated persons at the same price and under the same conditions. If the designated person agrees to purchase the property first, the owner agrees to sell it to her, rather than the other offeror.

first sale defense

In copyright law, the rule that states that a person does not infringe on the copyright of a work if she sells a lawfully acquired physical copy of the work.

fiscal

Broad term referring to financial matters in general (*e.g.*, fiscal report); belonging to the public treasury. A fiscal year is a period of 12 consecutive months used by a business or state as an accounting period for annual reports.

fiscal policy

1. Strategy devised by a government body to achieve economic aims. The setting of tax rates, lending rates and public spending levels are the major means by which fiscal policies are devised.

fixed assets

Property which is essential to operating a business and which will not be consumed or converted into cash during the current accounting period (*e.g.*, land, machinery, and buildings).

fixed charges

Expenses which must be paid whether or not a business is operating, such as rent, taxes, insurance premiums, and depreciation.

fixed income

Income which does not change over time (*e.g.,* income from an annuity or bond interest payments that remains at specified, fixed rates).

fixtures

Items which were once personal property, but which have become so annexed to or physically attached to realty that they are considered to be part of the real property.

flagrante delicto

(fla-GRAN-tay de-LIK-to) Lat. In the very act of committing the crime.

flight

The act of fleeing or hiding when accused of a crime.

flipping

Purchasing real estate in order to resell it quickly at a profit.

float

Funds represented by an unpaid or uncollected check or note.

floating capital

Funds used to meet current expenses.

floating lien

Security interest in current inventory, or accounts as well as after-acquired inventory or future accounts.

flotsam

Goods cast overboard in order to save a ship, goods lost from a vessel, or the debris of a shipwreck found floating at sea.

F.L.R.A.

See Federal Labor Relations Authority.

f.o.b.

Abbreviation for "free on board." Indicates that the selling price of goods includes transportation costs. Title to goods usually passes from seller to buyer at f.o.b. location. *See* U.C.C § 2–319(1).

f.n.u. l.n.u.

Abbreviation for "first name unknown; last name unknown." Placeholder name, used in criminal cases to identify unknown suspects.

F.O.I.A.

See Freedom of Information Act.

forbearance

1. Refraining from action when entitled to act. 2. Act of creditor of holding off demanding payment on a debt that is due.

force majeure, force majesture

(force ma-ZHUR, force ma-jes-TUR) Fr. A higher force; superior, unyielding force; irresistible, natural, or unavoidable force (*e.g.*, floods, earthquakes, lightning, storms, governmental intervention resulting from necessities of war). Also called "vis major."

forced sale

Sale of property by compulsion. Forced sale is usually ordered by a judge to pay off the court's judgment and is done according to statute and rules set by the court.

forcible detainer

The forcible detention of land or buildings by one who is not the owner and is not entitled to possession.

forcible entry

Entering land or buildings with force, threats, or actual violence for the purpose of illegally taking possession thereof.

forcible entry and detainer

Means of eviction by summary proceeding to restore possession of property to person wrongfully deprived of possession.

foreclosure
Cutting off or termination of a right to property. "Foreclosure" describes both the process and the result and is usually done by the person who holds the mortgage. In addition to taking the property away from the mortgagor and ending his rights in it, the property is usually sold publicly to the highest bidder to pay off the mortgage debt.

foreign
Belonging to another nation, country, jurisdiction or subject matter.

Foreign Intelligence Surveillance Court
A federal court that hears requests for warrants that authorize surveillance of foreign intelligence activities in the United States.

foreman
1. Spokesperson selected by a jury from among its members; foreperson. 2. Person in charge of other employees.

forensic
Belonging to, pertaining to, or used in courts of justice.

forensic medicine
Medical knowledge or medical practice involved with court testimony or legal matters. Medical jurisprudence.

foreseeable
Capable of being known in advance (*e.g.*, a reasonable anticipation that injury might result from certain acts or failure to perform certain acts). *See Palsgraf v. Long Island Railroad,* 248 N.Y. 339 (1928).

forfeit
To lose the right to some benefit, privilege or property because of a neglect of duty, an offense, or a breach of contract.

forge
To create a false instrument by making it in imitation of another one with intent to defraud and deceive; to counterfeit a document or signature; to counterfeit or falsify by imitation.

forgery
Criminal offense of making a false document or altering a real

one with intent to commit fraud (*e.g.*, false signature, alteration of the amount of a check, misuse of a document).

form

1. The manner or order of a pleading or legal document as opposed to the essential material of the action or content. Opposite of substance. 2. Model used by attorneys for drafting an instrument, pleading, order, judgment, or other legal document.

forms of action

Procedural devices required for technical categories of personal actions at common law (*e.g.*, trespass, trover, replevin, assumpsit). "Civil action" is the only type of action now for civil suits in most jurisdictions.

fornication

Unlawful sexual intercourse between two unmarried people. Term is often defined by state statute and the offense is usually a misdemeanor.

forswear

To swear to that which the swearer knows is untrue.

forthwith

Immediately; as soon as the nature of the case will permit; as soon as possible; without delay.

fortuitous

1. Unforeseen; happening by chance or accident. 2. Unexpected. 3. Unavoidable; inevitable.

forum

Lat. Court of justice; place where legal remedy can be sought.

forum non conveniens

(FOE-rum non kon-VEEN-ee-ens) Lat. Inconvenient forum. Doctrine which allows a court which has jurisdiction over a case to decline to hear the case out of fairness to the parties if there is another court available which would be more convenient.

forum selection clause

A provision in a contract that establishes the place where disputes arising from the agreement will be heard.

foundation

1. The preliminary evidence required for the admission of other evidence. 2 An attorney's

preliminary questions to a witness, in an effort to establish the admissibility of further evidence.

founder

The person who gives the first funds to a charitable institution; one whose efforts spawn a charitable organization.

four corners

The face of a written instrument. Under the "four corners rule" the intention of the parties is to be gathered from the document as a whole rather than from isolated parts of it and without aid from extrinsic testimony.

Fourteenth Amendment

Ratified in 1868, this amendment guarantees that all persons born in any state are citizens of that state and of the United States, and are thus guaranteed due process, equal protection of the laws, and all of the privileges and immunities due to U.S. citizens. One of the so-called Civil War Amendments, the Fourteenth Amendment was originally intended to guarantee the rights of newly freed slaves. *See* due process of law, equal protection of the laws. The amendment has also been construed to relate to the apportionment of Congressional representatives.

Fourth Amendment

This amendment guarantees the right of people to be secure in their homes and property from unreasonable searches and seizures. It also bars the issuing of warrants without probable cause.

franchise

1. Special privilege conferred on an individual or a corporation by a government. 2. The privileged use of a trade name and the right to market another's product or services. The privilege is usually granted by the owner of the trade name in exchange for consideration (*e.g.*, brand-name gas stations and fast food restaurants). 3. The right to vote. Also called "elective franchise."

franchise tax

A tax on a corporation for the right and privilege of carrying on its business within the sovereign's jurisdiction.

frank

1. To send material through the mail without paying postage; the

166

mark or signature used to indicate that a letter or package goes through the mail free of charge. 2. Free.

fratricide
The killing of one's brother or sister.

fraud
Deception, deceit; trickery. An act using deceit such as intentional distortion of the truth or misrepresentation or concealment of a material fact to gain an unfair advantage over another in order to secure something of value or deprive another of a right. Fraud is grounds for setting aside a transaction at the option of the party prejudiced by it or for recovery of damages. "Actual fraud" involves a deliberate misrepresentation or concealment. A court may infer "constructive" or "legal fraud" either from the nature of a contract or from the relationship of the parties.

fraud in the inducement
A misrepresentation of fact that leads a person to enter into a transaction with a false understanding of the risk, obligations,

benefits, or duties that will later be involved.

fraudulent
1. That which is done with intent to defraud. 2. Something which results in or from a fraud.

fraudulent conveyance
Conveyance or transfer of property to another with intent to deceive creditors by defeating their claims by putting the debtor's property out of their reach.

free
1. Unrestricted. 2. Not subject to legal constraint of another; at liberty to act as one pleases. 3. Without restraint or coercion.

free alongside ship (F.A.S.)
A commercial pricing term indicating that the seller will assume the expense and risk of transporting the goods to the buyer at the buyer's transportation medium.

free and clear
1. Unencumbered. 2. Title to property that is free of liens or other possible hindrances; a good or marketable title.

freedom

The condition of being free of restrictions; without restraints; liberty.

freedom of contract

The right to enter into a contract with another, subject only to civil liability for breach.

Freedom of Information Act (F.O.I.A.)

Federal law which, with specific exceptions, guarantees public access to federal government documents and materials. 5 U.S.C. § 552. Many states also have similar legislation regarding documents of state and local governments.

freedom of speech

First Amendment right to say what one wants without government regulation or restriction. This right is not absolute, but is limited to prevent abuse (*e.g.*, laws against defamation or obscenity, or incitement to violate criminal law).

Free Exercise Clause

First Amendment provision which states that "Congress shall make no law . . . prohibiting the free exercise" of religion. The Supreme Court has held that this principle also applies to state laws.

freehold

1. An estate "in fee" or an estate "for life." 2. An estate of land without a fixed period of duration. An "estate in fee" is owned by the holder and his heirs forever; a "life estate" is owned by the holder for his life or for the life of another. A "determinable freehold" is owned in fee until the occurrence of some condition (which may not occur).

free on board (F.O.B.)

A commercial pricing term indicating that the seller will assume the risk and cost of delivering the goods to an agreed destination.

freeze-out

Action taken by majority shareholders in a corporation to eliminate minority shareholders or to reduce or divest them of their voting power and rights to claim share of corporate assets.

freight forwarder

One who consolidates small shipments into a single lot and

ensures its safe arrival at the destination point.

fresh pursuit

1. An officer's pursuit of the accused, shortly after the commission of the crime. Under common law, this condition is grounds for the officer to cross jurisdictional lines when in pursuit of a felon. This also refers to the Fourth Amendment doctrine allowing an officer to conduct a search and/or arrest without a warrant, when the officer is in immediate pursuit of a fleeing suspect. 2. In defense of property, person may use reasonable force to retake her property if such force is used immediately after taking. 3. Hot pursuit.

friendly suit

An action which both parties agree to take to court in order to obtain a desired judgment about a doubtful question of law, or to confirm the parties' agreement (*e.g.*, a creditor's suit against the executor of an estate to obtain equal distribution to all the other creditors, a suit by an infant to affirm a settlement since the infant is not competent to agree to a settlement).

friend of the court

A person who is not a party to the lawsuit but gives the court, on the behalf of the public interest, information or arguments to aid the court in its decision. Also known as an "amicus curiae."

frisk

A quick patting down of a person in order to detect concealed weapons or contraband.

frivolous

Lacking a valid legal right or disputed fact situation relevant to the pending issue; insufficient for the court to rule upon. A pleading or claim is frivolous if it presents no issue or injury, is meant solely to delay the action or embarrass the other party.

frolic

When an agent or employee performs acts outside the scope of his employment, he is "on a frolic of his own" (*e.g.*, a truck driver who drives off the delivery route for personal activities is on a frolic). *See* dual purpose doctrine.

frontage

The length of property along the street or sidewalk. Thus, "frontage assessments" for paving, sidewalks, curbs, and sewers are made in proportion to each owner's share of frontage.

front-end load plan

An agreement wherein the buyer of a mutual fund purchases shares of the fund incrementally, while the seller withholds sales commission charges from the initial payments.

fructus industriales

(FRUK-tus in-dus-tree-AL-ees) Lat. The fruits of industry. The crops grown through human agriculture, as opposed to those grown in nature.

fructus naturales

(FRUK-tus na-tur-AL-ees) Lat. Natural fruits. Goods produced in the course of nature (*e.g.*, metals, wool, pearls, milk, etc.).

fruit of the poisonous tree doctrine

Criminal law doctrine under which evidence legally obtained may be inadmissible because of the taint of an illegal search by police leading to the evidence. *See also* exclusionary rule.

fruits of crime

Anything acquired in the act of committing a crime.

frustra probatur quod probatum non relevat

(FRUSS-tra PRO-ba-tur kwod pro-BAT-um non REL-e-vat) Lat. That which is proved in vain, because when proved it does not help.

frustration of purpose

In contract law, doctrine that contractual duties are discharged if the purpose of the contract, known to the parties at the time of contracting, has been completely or almost completely destroyed by a supervening act or event not foreseen or caused by the parties.

F.T.C.

See Federal Trade Commission.

fugitive

In criminal law, one who escapes after arrest, prosecution, or imprisonment. A "fugitive from justice" is one who, after committing a crime, flees the state or conceals himself from criminal justice officials within the state.

full faith and credit
Requirement in the United States Constitution, Article IV, section 1, that each state must recognize the legislative acts, records, and judicial proceedings of the other states, giving them "full faith and credit." One state's final judgment in a case is thus conclusive in every other state if it is conclusive in that state.

fund
1. Generally, some collection of money, bonds, notes, securities, or other assets, set aside for a particular purpose (*e.g.*, to pay debts, to purchase particular goods and services, to earn interest). 2. To establish such a fund. 3. To capitalize in order to earn interest.

fundamental error
See plain error rule.

fundamental rights
Those rights expressly granted by the U.S. Constitution, (*e.g.*, right to vote), or those which are necessarily implied from those provisions (*e.g.*, right of privacy).

fungible goods
Goods which are alike in every particle (*e.g.*, oil, milk, flour, grain). *See* U.C.C. § 1–201(17).

furiosi nulla voluntas est
(fyoo-ree-O-see NUL-la vol-LUN-tas-est) Lat. A madman has no will.

future advances
Money loaned after a security interest has attached, and secured by the original security agreement which may or may not include an after-acquired property clause.

future estate
An estate in land without present possession of the land, with the possibility of future possession (*e.g.*, a remainder or a reversion).

future interest
An interest in land or money which will begin in use or possession sometime in the future (*e.g.*, a trust which holds money for the beneficiary until he attains the age of 21).

futures contract

A contract to sell goods or commodities at a future time at a specific price. The buyer agrees to pay that fixed price and the seller agrees to deliver the goods although the parties do not actually contemplate delivery, but rather that the contract calls for a settlement between the parties according to market prices. If the value of the commodity has risen, the seller pays the buyer the amount of the increase; if the value of the commodity fell, the buyer pays the seller the decrease.

gag order
Court order barring attorneys, parties, or witnesses from discussing a case with reporters. Such an order is issued in the interest of controlling publicity and ensuring a defendant's fair trial.

gainful employment
1. Work for which one is remunerated. 2. For purposes of disability insurance, the term refers to an employment situation which could be fairly expected for the employee, given his physical and mental potentialities.

gallows
A raised platform from which convicted criminals guilty of serious crimes are hanged. The superstructure consists of two raised supports with a beam laid horizontally across the supports.

gambling
Playing a game of chance in the hope of winning money or property; making a bet. Gambling is regulated by federal and state laws.

gaming
Gambling.

game laws
Laws enacted to conserve the numbers of wild birds and animals, by regulating the taking of such animals. Such regulations can include the establishment of hunting periods, the restriction of weaponry used, or the prohibition of hunting.

G.A.O.
See General Accounting Office.

gaol
Early English spelling of "jail," now obsolete.

garageman's lien
A lien to secure payment for repairs to an automobile.

garnish
1. To acquire a portion of a person's wages or assets in accordance with a garnishment action. 2. To warn or summon.

garnishee

1. A person against whom a garnishment action is successfully brought. 2. A debtor whose wages or assets are attached to pay off an obligation.

garnishment

The legal process by which a person's wages or assets, under the control of another person or a corporation, are used to pay an obligation owed to a third party. The rights and procedures in a garnishment proceeding are fixed by statute.

gavelkind

A now-obsolete form of common law land ownership originated in England, requiring a father to grant his land rights to each of his sons equally upon his death.

General Accounting Office (G.A.O.)

Federal agency which reports to Congress and whose primary duties are to audit and oversee government programs and to review and investigate their operation.

General Agreement on Tariffs and Trade (G.A.T.T.)

An international, multi-lateral pact requiring nations to give foreign goods no less favorable treatment under law than their domestically produced goods.

general appearance

See appearance.

general assignment

Transfer of all of a debtor's assets to a trustee who has authority to liquidate the debtor's assets and distribute the proceeds to creditors.

General Counsel's Memorandum

A written opinion or position on a legal issue issued by the General Counsel of the Internal Revenue Service.

general creditor

A lender whose loan is secured only by a general promise to repay the debt.

general demurrer

1. Answer of a defendant to an action filed by a plaintiff in a civil proceeding that denies the substance of the plaintiff's suit

but does not state any specific objection. 2. Response by a defendant to a civil action that alleges that plaintiff's pleadings are insufficient at law to support the cause of action pleaded.

generally accepted accounting principles
The rules and procedures that define the approved practices for accounting.

General Services Administration (G.S.A.)
Created by the Federal Property and Administration Services Act of 1949 to coordinate the acquisition and disposition of all government property.

general verdict
1. Decision by a jury that finds in favor of the plaintiff or defendant in a suit but that does not address the specific fact issues in dispute. 2. The ordinary form of a verdict; to be distinguished from a special verdict, where the jury decides facts only.

generation skipping transfer
A transfer in which the transferee is more than one generation removed from the transferor

(*e.g.,* a transfer from a grandmother to her grandchild).

generic
1. Relating to or characteristic of an entire group or class of related things; general. 2. In trademark law, a common or descriptive name for a product.

genericide
Loss or cancellation of a trademark when the mark no longer distinguishes a product as coming from a particular source.

genetic marker test
Analyzing the DNA of tissue samples to determine the parentage or paternity of a child.

Geneva Convention
The Geneva Convention of 1949. A set of international treaties that deal with the law of warfare; specifically, the protection of wounded combatants, the treatment of prisoners of war, and the protection of civilians during conflicts.

gerrymander
1. To arrange or draw the boundaries of a political district with the intent to achieve an unlawful purpose (*e.g.,* to draw the bound-

aries of a legislative district with the purpose of precluding members of a racial group from exercising their constitutional rights to vote and run for office). 2. To manipulate; to rig.

gestation
The period in which a female bears a fetus from time of conception to time of birth. At common law, 280 days.

gift
Present; gratuity; donation of real or personal property by one party to another.

gift causa mortis
Lat. Gift made by a person in contemplation of her impending death.

gift inter vivos
Gifts between living persons, perfected and completed during lifetimes of donor and donee.

gift over
A transfer which takes effect following the termination of a prior estate (*e.g.*, to A for life and then to B).

gift tax
A tax imposed on a living person who transfers property by gift.

gist
1. The principal basis in law for a cause of action without which the suit could not be brought. 2. The basis of an argument, its substance.

going concern value
The aggregate value of an active business, as opposed to simply the book value of its physical assets. Such a measure reflects the value of an enterprise whose role in the marketplace is already established (its good will).

golden parachute
A provision in an executive compensation agreement giving an upper-level management employee enhanced severance benefits if the control of the employer changes.

good behavior
1. Proper conduct; lawful conduct. 2. As used in criminal sentencing the term refers to the procedure whereby a criminal's proper conduct while in prison

will be credited against the time remaining in his sentence.

good cause
1. Legally adequate reason; lawful basis for an action. 2. A satisfactory excuse.

good faith
1. A desire to act in a conscientious and equitable manner with regard to the rights of others. 2. The lack of a desire to take unfair advantage of another. 3. An honest intention to act fairly.

good faith exception
An exception to the exclusionary rule that allows the admission of evidence seized pursuant to a warrant later determined to be invalid if the officers who seized the evidence acted on a good faith belief that the warrant was valid.

good faith purchaser
1. A buyer without notice of circumstances that would cause a person of ordinary prudence to inquire further as to the seller's title. 2. A bona fide purchaser.

goods
1. Merchandise; commercial wares. 2. Personal property. 3. All things moveable at the time of identification to the contract, excluding money and securities. *See* U.C.C. § 2–105(1).

good Samaritan doctrine
Statutory exemption from liability for ordinary negligence for certain rescuers, usually medical personnel, who render voluntary and gratuitous emergency treatment. Gross negligence is not exempted.

good tenantable repair
The obligation of the tenant to maintain the leased property's condition.

good title
A valid and marketable title, free from litigation, palpable defects, and grave doubts.

good will
1. An intangible asset which represents the favorable attitude of clients or customers of a business toward the operation of the business. 2. The value of a business enterprise, above and beyond the value of the business'

tangible assets, which represents the enterprise's reputation with the public and its managerial ability.

government
The control and administration of public policy in a political society by a system of rules.

governmental functions
The functions of a municipality which are conducted in pursuit of the public good.

governmental immunity
Federal, state, and local governments are immune to suits against them unless they have consented to such suits. *See* Federal Tort Claims Act.

grace period
Contract law: The period stated in an agreement, or set by statute, in which performance on the agreement is permitted beyond the date of obligation of performance as stated in the agreement (*e.g.*, in insurance contracts, the period in which insurance coverage continues in force even though the most recent premium has not been paid).

graded offense
An offense for which the offender is subject to a more severe penalty for more serious degrees of the offense (*e.g.*, first degree manslaughter, as opposed to second degree manslaughter).

graft
Corruption involving public officials; any attempt by a public servant to use his public office for his personal pecuniary gain.

grandfather clause
A provision in a statute or an agreement that permits those engaged in certain activities before the adoption of the statute or agreement to carry on with those activities even though the conduct is now prohibited by the statute or the agreement.

grand jury
A group of citizens empanelled by the state or federal government to investigate and hear the government's evidence in criminal cases to determine whether probable cause exists to believe a crime has been committed by a person who should stand trial. If so, an indictment (true bill) issues; if no probable cause is

found, a "no bill" is returned. Grand juries may include up to 23 jurors and thus are larger than trial (petit) juries.

grand larceny
The crime of stealing or converting another's personal property with the intent to permanently dispossess that person of the property. To be considered a crime of this nature the value of the property taken must exceed a minimum value set by statute.

grandparent visitation
In some states, the right of a grandparent to seek a court order granting her an enforceable right to visit her grandchildren, usually after the death of one of the child's parents or the divorce of the parents.

grant
1. To give; to transfer. 2. To permit; to give one's consent to an arrangement (*e.g.*, to transfer real estate by a written contract). 3. A transfer of real property; a conveyance of real property (*e.g.*, a written contract that transfers title to real property).

grantee
A person who receives a grant of real property.

grantor
A person who makes a grant of real property.

gratis
Lat. Free; without reward (*e.g.*, an action performed freely or without compensation).

gratuitous
Dispensed or transferred without compensation or financial remuneration being given.

gratuity
A gift; a donation; a good or service freely given or given without financial remuneration.

gratuitous promise
Promise made without consideration in return. Such a promise is not enforceable as a contractual agreement.

gravamen
The essential part or quintessence of a legal argument, grievance, charge, or cause of action.

gray market

Purchasing goods at a lower price by avoiding a manufacturer's normal supply chain, as by buying foreign-manufactured goods direct from the manufacturer, instead of through authorized dealers or importers.

green card

Colloquial term for an official U.S. government document issued to aliens, which shows that they are as permanent U.S. residents with employment rights.

Green Guides

Publications issued by the Federal Trade Commission to provide guidance on acceptable practices for advertisers who make environmental claims about products or services.

greenmail

Purchasing enough shares in a corporation to effect a takeover, with the intent that the corporation repurchase those shares at a higher price.

grievance

1. One's protest or complaint that an action has imposed upon him an illegal, inequitable, or unjust circumstance. 2. In labor law, a grievance is a complaint filed by the aggrieved party, regarding his employment conditions.

gross

1. Whole; aggregate; overall total exclusive of any deductions. 2. Great; extreme; excessive; extensive.

gross income

1. Total revenue. 2. The aggregate of earnings exclusive of any deductions.

gross national product

The total market value of all goods and services produced by a nation during a period of time (usually 12 months).

gross negligence

The purposeful failure to discharge a duty of care owed in reckless disregard of the consequences as they may affect another's life or property.

ground rent

1. The payment made to a person for use of his real property (*e.g.*, long-time lease for land upon which lessee constructs a building); the lessor still owns the

"ground." 2. The payment made by a lessee to a lessor under the terms of a lease. 3. Under the terms of a sale or transfer of title to real property, a perpetual payment paid to the grantor of the property and his heirs.

growth stock

Type of stock characterized by above-average return on shareholder's equity and potential for future profitability.

G.S.A.

See General Services Administration.

guarantee

1. A person who receives a guaranty. 2. The written instrument or contract of guaranty. 3. As a verb, the act of assuming a guarantor's duties.

Guarantee Clause

Provision in the U.S. Constitution in which the federal government guarantees to the states a republican form of government and federal protection in the event of invasion or domestic violence. Article IV, section 4.

guaranteed security

A type of preferred stock or bond on which principal or interest is guaranteed by another company.

guarantor

1. A person who gives a guaranty. 2. A person who is secondarily liable for another's obligation or debt as established by contract.

guaranty

1. A promise or pledge to fulfill another's obligation in case of that person's default upon that obligation. 2. An agreement to be secondarily liable for the debt(s) of another upon that person's default on that debt.

guardian

1. A person legally responsible for managing the affairs of a person legally incompetent to administer his property or properly assert his rights, such as, a person who handles the affairs of a senile individual. 2. One who is legally responsible for the care of a child or the management of her property, or both.

guest

1. A paying visitor or patron at a motel, hotel, or restaurant. 2. One who is not a member of an organization or association and attends its functions. 3. A person who rides as a passenger in another person's car merely for his own pleasure or business and without compensating the owner or driver.

guest statute

A state law which provides that a gratuitous passenger in an automobile involved in an accident may recover for his injuries against the driver of the automobile only upon a showing of gross negligence or other conduct that exceeds ordinary negligence (*e.g.*, willful and wanton conduct).

guilty

1. Culpable. 2. Responsible for perpetuating a crime; at fault for engaging in a crime or some other type of misconduct.

gun control law

A law restricting or regulating the sale and use of guns and firearms, or a law which establishes a system of registering guns and firearms and/or their owners or users.

H

habeas corpus
(HAY-bee-as KOR-pus) Lat. You have the body. Legal proceeding whereby a writ is brought in order to determine whether a person in the custody of legal authorities is being lawfully detained.

habendum clause
The clause in a deed or a written instrument that transfers title in property and which names the parties to the transaction and defines the nature and quality of ownership in the property that the grantee receives. The clause usually begins with the words, "To have and to hold."

habitability
Status of a dwelling which signifies that it is capable of being safely lived in; the situation where a residence is livable.

habitation
1. The act of living or residing at a certain location. 2. A residence; a dwelling; place of abode.

half brother, half sister
Persons who share only one common parent (*e.g.*, persons who have the same father but different mothers).

halfway house
Residential facility established for persons who have left prisons, medical facilities, or other structured facilities, to help them reenter society.

hallucination
A delusion; an apparently real but actually false sensory perception not caused by any external stimulus but rather by some internal influence.

hamlet
A burg; a small village or town.

hanged, drawn and quartered
An early English punishment wherein the accused was disemboweled while alive, and then beheaded and quartered. This punishment was usually levied for convictions of high treason or other high crimes.

harassment

1. Litigation brought without a reasonable expectation of obtaining a valid result. 2. Words, gestures, or actions of one person which irritate, torment, or impede another.

hard cases

Legal proceedings which because of their facts or the equities present are difficult to apply well-accepted rules of law to, and as a result, a court will deviate from those well-accepted precepts to render its decision. The term is the basis for the adage "hard cases make bad law."

harmless error

1. An error which occurs during a trial, and is small or minor enough to warrant no reversal of judgment by an appellate court. 2. An error that does not prejudice a party's substantial rights or affect the outcome of the case.

Hatch Act

Federal law which prohibits government employees from engaging in specified political activities.

hate crime

A crime motivated by the victim's race, religion, gender, national origin, or sexual orientation. Proof that an offense was a hate crime will often lead to an enhanced penalty for the defendant.

hazing

Physical or emotional abuse used to initiate a new member into a group. Hazing has been made unlawful in many jurisdictions.

headnote

Descriptive summary of a legal argument or principle present in a case that precedes the court's printed opinion.

head of the family (head of the household)

Person who exercises control over members of a family unit, supervises their conduct and affairs, and provides for their general support.

hearing

Session or proceeding conducted under fixed rules where evidence is taken on a given subject and whose purpose is to arrive at some conclusion on the basis of the evidence heard, but it is not a trial that affixes guilt or liability (*e.g.*, a legislative proceeding to determine what changes should be made in defense policy).

hearsay

An oral or written assertion, or conduct which carries with it an assertion, made or carried out by someone other than a witness testifying at a legal proceeding, and which is offered as evidence in court to establish the truth of the matter asserted.

heartbalm statute

A statute that abolishes the common law right of action for alienation of affections, criminal conversation, seduction, or breach of promise to marry.

heat of passion

In criminal law, a sudden and intense passion in the mind of an ordinary person, caused by provocation by another person, causing loss of self-control with a lack of time for the passion to cool. Acts to reduce serious crime to one less severe. *See* provocation.

hedge fund

A type of mutual fund that uses any of several hedging techniques to minimize an investor's risk of loss.

hedging

1. The process of mitigating risk. 2. The means by which a manufacturer, commodities owner, or investor protects against losses due to market fluctuation (*e.g.*, one who has contracted to buy a commodity may hedge by negotiating a counter-contract to sell the same amount of that commodity at a certain price).

heir, heiress

1. A person who will receive the estate and property of another upon that person's death; a person entitled to receive an inheritance at a future date. 2. At common law, the person legally entitled to intestate estate of relative. 3. Legal heir.

heir apparent

A person who has the right of inheritance to an estate or position so long as he outlives his ancestor or the current holder of the position.

heirs of the body
1. A person's issue or offspring.
2. For purposes of property law, heirs of the body are those who are lineal descendants of the decedent, and as such, exclude adopted children, spouses or the decedent's brothers or sisters.

hereditament
Something capable of being inherited or transferred by legal succession.

hereditary succession
The passing of title under the laws of descent; inheritance by law.

heretofore
Prior to this moment; before this time; previous to this instance.

hermaphrodite
A person having both male and female reproductive organs.

hidden asset
An asset carried on a company's books at a value that is less than its market value.

hidden defect
An imperfection which cannot be discovered by simple inspection, and for which a seller or lessor is liable, should the defect cause harm to a user. A buyer may legally revoke a prior acceptance of property upon discovering a hidden defect. *See* latent defect.

hidden inflation
A price increase in which the seller maintains a product's price, while diminishing its quality or reducing its quantity. That product will ultimately cost the buyer more money, thus inflating the per-unit cost to the consumer.

hidden tax
An indirect tax built into the selling price, incurred at some point in the production or distribution of the goods prior to their retail sale. The consumer often unknowingly pays such a tax at the time of purchase.

hierarchy
A group of persons in an organization classified according to their rank, position or level of authority, such as the classification of the officials of a religious sect.

high seas
The open waters of the oceans and seas beyond the territorial control of any country.

hijacking
1. Robbery of goods while in transit; may involve robbery of goods and/or vehicle. 2. To take control of an airplane in flight by force and threats.

H.I.P.A.A.
Health Insurance Portability and Accountability Act. Federal law that protects the health care insurance of employees who lose their jobs or who change jobs, and also authorizes the setting of federal standards for some healthcare related transactions, including privacy standards.

hit-and-run statutes
Statutes requiring a motorist who is involved in an accident to stop at the scene and give certain information about himself to the police and other motorists involved.

H.L.A. test
Human Leukocyte Antigen test, a test to determine the parentage of a child by examining the genetic indicators in his blood.

hoarding
The act of accumulating and holding goods which are in short supply, in anticipation of a future shortage of these items and/or a possible resale at higher prices. *See* profiteering.

hobby losses
For tax purposes, a loss incurred by an individual in an activity which is not intended for profit. Such losses are generally not deductible.

hold
1. To have dominion and control over property by legal title or possession. 2. To determine or resolve a legal question; to sustain an assertion or position. 3. To obligate a person; to render a judgment which affects the legal rights of a person. 4. To conduct; to administer (*e.g.*, to hold municipal traffic court, to hold an election).

holder
Person who is in legal possession of an investment security or some other financial instrument

which is payable to him or the bearer of the instrument. U.C.C. § 1–201(20).

holder in due course

A person who takes an instrument for value, in good faith, and without any notice that it is overdue or has been dishonored or of any defense against it or claim to it on the part of any person. U.C.C. § 3–302.

holding

1. An ownership interest in an asset or a business enterprise. 2. Decision by a court. 3. The rule of law relied on by a court in making its decision in a case.

holding company

Corporation formed to hold equity interests in other corporations and that controls the management of those corporations through the exercise of its equity interests in the corporations.

holding period

The time span in which a capital asset must be held before it can be disposed of, for purposes of determining whether the gain is long term or short term.

holdup suit

An action that lacks a legal basis and whose only purpose is to preclude another event from occurring. Such suits are prohibited by statute.

hold-over tenancy

Possession of real property that exists where a lessee remains in possession of property that he has leased after the term of the lease has expired.

holograph

A handwritten legal document, most often a will or deed, affecting the estate of a person, written entirely by that person and not witnessed by other persons.

homage

In feudal law, a formal acknowledgment or profession of loyalty by a vassal to his lord, upon the lord's granting of land to the vassal.

homeowner's insurance

Liability insurance for the purchasers of residential real estate, providing coverage for non-motor vehicle related negligence on or off the property.

home port doctrine

Principle which states that vessels engaged in foreign commerce are subject to property tax only at their home port; thus prohibiting property taxation in the ports they visit.

home rule

Power granted to local and municipal authorities by state governments to manage their own affairs as established by legislative act or constitutional provision.

homestead

The domicile of a family and the surrounding property (*e.g.*, a farmhouse and the adjoining land and buildings).

home-style exception

A provision of copyright law that allows owners of public gathering places (*e.g.*, bars or restaurants) to play recorded music or air radio or television broadcasts without liability for infringement.

homicide

The taking of another person's life; the killing of a person. The purposeful or intentional taking of another's life is criminal homicide (*e.g.*, murder, manslaughter, etc.).

honor

1. To accept a financial instrument or security as payment for an obligation owed. 2. To make payment with a financial instrument or security on an obligation owed.

honorable

Title of respect given to judges or elected or appointed public officials.

honorable discharge

A formal and final judgment passed by the government upon a soldier's entire military record, and an authoritative declaration that the soldier has left the service in a status of honor. Only those soldiers who are honorably discharged may take advantage of full military retirement or veteran's benefits.

honorarium

1. Fee or recompense given to a person for services performed but for which no fee is legally or traditionally required; such as, a fee given to a person who speaks

at the commencement exercises of a university. 2. A gratuitous payment; a voluntary reward.

honorary
A position that is held without reward, fee or profit, and in consideration of the honor conferred by holding a position of responsibility and trust.

hornbook
Text which summarizes the fundamental precepts of law and cases in a particular legal area.

hornbook law
Those legal principles that are widely known as the basic and generally accepted tenets of law. The term refers to a popular series of legal textbooks which set forth basic principles in a given sphere of law.

hors
(orz or horz) Fr. Outside of; out; without.

hostile environment
In employment discrimination law, a type of harassment in which an employee is subject to severe and pervasive verbal or physical behavior based on his membership in a protected class.

hostile possession
In property law, the occupation or possession of real estate without the permission of the owner.

hostile witness
Witness who is adverse or antagonistic to the interests of the party that called him to testify.

hotchpot
The combining of assets and property of different parties in order to partition and split it equally between the parties (*e.g.*, combining advancement to child with other properties of decedent so as to distribute equal amount to each child of decedent).

hot pursuit
See fresh pursuit.

house
1. Dwelling; residence; abode; home. 2. Term that describes a legislative assembly; name given one of the two elected bodies of a legislature.

housebreaking
The unlawful entry into another's residence; burglary.

household

A family unit that resides together. That which belongs to a family or a residence, such as the home's furnishings and effects.

hue and cry

The loud uproar and clamor that authorities and others made as they pursued criminals under the old English common law and which put all on notice that heard the clamor that they must join in the pursuit of the criminals.

hung jury

A jury whose members are so divided and split in their beliefs that they cannot reach a decision.

hypnosis

The sleeplike state in which the subject of the hypnosis may experience heightened concentration, extreme responsiveness to suggestion, or an increased ability to remember forgotten experiences. Hypnotically induced testimony is admissible in a majority of jurisdictions, often with the requirement that the hypnosis satisfies the standards for the admissibility of scientific evidence.

hypothecate

1. To mortgage resources as collateral for an obligation or debt owed. 2. To pledge assets as security for an indebtedness.

hypothesis

1. A premise or theory advanced by a party at a trial. 2. A theory, assumption, or supposition.

hypothetical question

A query asked in regard to a specific event or situation that is based on a combination of conjecture, assumed circumstances, and proven facts.

I

ibid.
Lat. The same; in the same place (book, page, case). Short for "ibidem." The term indicates that a phrase or word can be found in a book already quoted or in a case already cited.

I.C.C.
See Interstate Commerce Commission.

id.
Lat. The same; the same thing. Abbreviation of idem. This term is used in a citation to avoid repetition of an author's name and title or full case citation in a second successive reference to that item.

I.D.E.A.
Individuals with Disabilities Education Act; a federal law that guarantees to all children the right to a free, appropriate public education regardless of disability.

idem est non esse, et non apparere
(EE-dem est non ess-ee, et non app-a-raree) Lat. Not to appear is the same as not to exist.

identical
The same exactly.

identification
1. Establishment of identity.
2. The proving that a person or an item before the court is the same as it is charged or alleged to be.

idiot
One who is mentally deficient from birth and whom the law therefore considers to be hopelessly incapacitated mentally. The term has largely fallen into disuse.

i.e.
Lat. That is; that is to say; abbreviation for id est.

ignoramus
Lat. We are ignorant. We ignore it. 1. (n.) An ignorant person. 2. (v.) To ignore; not to know. The grand jury would write this

word on the back of an indictment when they considered the accusation against a prisoner to be groundless or unconvincing.

ignorance

The condition of being uninformed, uneducated, or unknowing. Ignorance of the law is not an excuse for unlawful activity. *See* ignorantia legis neminem excusat.

ignorantia legis neminem excusat

(ig-no-RAN-tee-a lejis NEM-i-nem ex-KYOO-sat *or* ex-KOO-sat) Lat. Ignorance of the law excuses no one. A defendant may be punished for a prohibited act even if he did not know that the act was illegal.

illegal

1. Forbidden by law. 2. Contrary to the law.

illegally obtained evidence

Evidence obtained in violation of a defendant's rights, specifically, the right to be immune from unreasonable search and seizure (U.S. Constitution, Fourth Amendment). Evidence obtained in this manner is inadmissible in a criminal case in which the victim of the illegal search is the defendant.

illegitimate

1. Contrary to law; illegal. 2. Improper.

illegitimate child(ren)

Child(ren) born to unmarried parents. Child(ren) born to a married woman in a situation where the presumption of legitimacy has been rebutted. Now often referred to as "children out of wedlock."

illicit

Illegal; unlawful.

illusion

Distorted or misinterpreted perception of an actual object or situation. Differs from hallucination in that illusion is based on actual external stimuli.

illusory

Falsely appearing to conform to a legal act (*i.e.*, an "illusory promise" resembles a legally binding promise but upon examination is illusory because it does not bind the promisor).

immaterial

Not pertinent to the matter in dispute. Evidence is immaterial if it does not bear on an issue on trial.

immediate cause

The most recent in a series of causes that directly produces the result (it may differ from proximate cause), such as a drunken man drowns after falling into water. His intoxication may be the proximate cause of his death if he would not have fallen into the water while sober, but the immediate cause of his death is suffocation by drowning. *See* proximate cause.

immigration

Act of moving into one country from another for the purpose of permanently settling in the second country.

Immigration and Customs Enforcement

Division of the Department of Homeland Security responsible for enforcing federal laws governing border control, customs, trade, and immigration.

Immigration and Naturalization Service

Former division of the U.S. Department of Justice responsible for enforcing immigration laws. The duties of the I.N.S. have been transferred to the Department of Homeland Security.

immoral conduct

Indecent behavior; behavior that is inconsistent with accepted moral standards. This behavior can be grounds for suspending or revoking the license to practice certain professions such as law and teaching.

immunity

1. A privilege granting exemption from a legal duty such as the immunity of charitable organizations from paying taxes. 2. Freedom from prosecution granted to a witness who agrees to testify in a criminal proceeding.

impact rule

Rule which states that when one seeks damages for emotional distress, the distress must have resulted from a situation where there was physical contact with another person or object. This rule is now followed by a minority of jurisdictions.

impair
1. To make worse. 2. To weaken or to affect injuriously.

impanel
1. To list the names of persons subject to jury duty. 2. To list the names of jurors for a particular case. 3. To assemble and select a jury for a particular trial.

impanelling
1. The procedure for selecting and swearing in jurors. 2. The listing of persons chosen to serve on a particular jury.

imparlance
1. Discussion between the parties to a suit in order to settle the controversy amicably. 2. Time granted to the defendant to plead.

impartial
Favoring neither of the parties; equitable. The Bill of Rights requires that the accused be tried by an impartial jury.

impartiality
Lack of bias or prejudice.

impeach
1. To accuse (*e.g.*, to charge a public official with wrongdoing while in office). 2. To discredit a person or a thing (*e.g.*, to call into question the testimony of a witness or the truthfulness of a document).

impeachment
The prosecution of a public official by Congress with the House of Representatives making the accusation and the Senate acting as the trier of fact. Impeachment lies for "treason, bribery, or other high crimes and misdemeanors" and can result in the removal of an official from office.

impediment
1. An obstruction. 2. Contract law: The legal inability to contract for a reason such as insanity. 3. Ecclesiastical law: A situation which affects the validity of the marriage of persons already married or about to be married.

imperative
Mandatory; imposing an obligation.

imperitia culpae adnumeratur
(im-pair-ISH-ee-a kool-PAY ad-NOO-mer-ay-tur) Lat. Lack of skill is considered to be negligence.

impertinence
1. Irrelevance. 2. A statement in the pleading which is immaterial or scandalous.

impertinent matter
1. Information that is irrelevant to the controversy at hand. 2. When pleading, any information which is not relevant to the controversy, or any facts which cannot be supported by evidence, may be struck down as impertinent.

implead
1. To bring into the lawsuit as a party someone other than the original plaintiff and defendant. *See Federal Rule of Civil Procedure 14.* 2. To sue.

impleader
The procedure for joining a person as a party to an action. Under *Federal Rule of Civil Procedure 14,* a mechanism for the defendant to include a third party which may be liable to him for part or all of the defendant's liability toward the plaintiff and thereby determine all liabilities in a single action.

implication
1. Something implied as opposed to something expressly communicated in words. 2. In wills: A "necessary implication" is sufficient to convey an estate. Here, the implication is so strongly probable that any alternative intention of the testator is dismissed. 3. Involvement, as in a crime.

implied
Understood through circumstances or conduct though not communicated in words. *Contrast* "express."

implied authority
The actual authority of an agent implied from circumstances though not expressly granted by the principal.

implied consent
Consent which is manifested by signs, actions, or facts, or by inaction or silence, which raises a presumption that consent has been given; consent that arises

from a course of conduct or relationship between the parties in which there is mutual acquiescence or a lack of objection under circumstances signifying assent. In a rape prosecution, the defendant may claim that his accuser impliedly consented to his actions.

implied consent law

A statute that provides that a person who operates a motor vehicle on the public highways has given her implied consent to an intoxication or sobriety test when such a test is requested by a law enforcement officer.

implied contract

A nonverbal contract implied by the behavior of the parties. "Implied-in-fact" denotes a contract formed by relying on the conduct of the parties rather than on their words (*e.g.*, an implied in-fact contract to pay for services exists when one goes to a doctor for treatment even though neither party discusses compensation for the treatment). "Implied-in-law" denotes a contract imposed by law, regardless of the intention of the parties, in order to prevent unjust enrichment (*e.g.,* an im-

plied-in-law contract for payment exists when a doctor gives emergency treatment to an unconscious accident victim although the injured party did nothing to solicit the doctor's help).

implied intent

Intent inferred from conduct or from language of instrument. In criminal law, general, not specific, intent can be inferred merely from the doing of the act.

implied malice

1. Malice which the law infers from the conduct of a party. The implication from a deliberate act done for a wrongful purpose. 2. In homicide: Where a killing is committed without any factor such as justification or provocation to excuse the murder or to reduce it to manslaughter.

implied warranty

Under the U.C.C., a guarantee implied from the circumstances of a sale of goods that applies unless disclaimed. Implied warranty of merchantability: Goods sold by a merchant must, among other things, be fit for ordinary purposes. *U.C.C. § 2–314.* Implied warranty of fitness for a particular purpose: Where the seller knows of a particular purpose for which goods are to be used and the buyer relies on the seller's skill or judgment to furnish suitable goods, the goods must be fit for such purposes. *U.C.C. § 2–315.*

import
1. (v.) To transport an object into one country from another. 2. (n.) An object which has been transported into one country from another.

impossibility
1. Something that cannot be done. 2. In contracts: Impossibility of performance due, for example, to the destruction of the subject matter of the contract or to the death of one of the parties; may be a defense to nonperformance. 3. In criminal law: Legal impossibility is a defense to criminal charges when the actions of the accused would not constitute a crime even if fully carried out according to her wishes.

impost
A tax; levy; duty.

impotence
1. The physical inability to engage in sexual intercourse. The inability to consummate a marriage is a ground for annulment if the suing party was unaware of the spouse's impotence. 2. In medical jurisprudence: The inability of either party to copulate. 3. Helplessness.

impound
1. To lockup stray animals in a pound. 2. To place documents or goods in the custody of the court pending a determination of their ownership or authenticity.

impracticability
1. In commercial law, contractual performance is discharged where the duty has unforeseeably become extremely and unreasonably difficult to perform (*e.g.,* unexpected war cutting off product supply). 2. In class actions, the difficulty or inconvenience of joining all potential claimants in a single action.

imprimatur
Lat. Let it be printed. 1. Authority or approval. 2. A government license or allowance to print or publish a book. In England, the

government formerly required its imprimatur before allowing a book to be published.

imprisonment
1. The confinement of an individual in a place of detention, usually in a jail or a prison. 2. Any physical restraint or threat of force encumbering the free movement of an individual.

improvement
Any increase in the value of property through the use of labor or the expenditure of money which adds to the property's value by doing more than repairing or restoring the property to its original condition.

impunity
Protection or exemption from penalty or punishment.

impute
To attribute vicariously to a person the charges for another's wrong doing because his relationship with the perpetrator is such that he is responsible for the perpetrator's act or omission.

imputed knowledge
Knowledge that the law attributes to an individual because the circumstances made the facts easily available and the person charged had a duty to know of them.

imputed negligence
The negligence of one person is assigned to a second party because the second party is somehow responsible for the actions of the first (*e.g.*, negligence of an employee may be imputed to the employer if the former is acting within the scope of employment). *See* respondeat superior; vicarious liability.

in absentia
Lat. In absence.

inadequate remedy at law
A situation in which a legal remedy, such as the award of damages, will not make a claimant whole (*e.g.*, refusal of a seller to convey a certain parcel of real estate as promised). Equity will hear a claim if there is no sufficient legal remedy available.

inadmissible
Not acceptable as proof under the law of evidence.

inalienable

Not capable of being transferred or taken away. The Declaration of Independence describes the rights to life, liberty and the pursuit of happiness as inalienable. The U.S. Constitution protects certain fundamental rights such as freedom of religion and freedom of speech.

inarbitrable

A type of dispute not subject to arbitration, generally because it is outside the scope of the arbitration agreement.

in articulo mortis

(in ar-TIK-oo-lo MOR-tis) Lat. In the moment of death.

in bank, in banc

Fr. On the bench. All the judges of the court hearing a case together as a full court. In appellate cases, a litigant can request or the court can move for a consideration of the case by all the judges of a court rather than by a fraction of them. In bank decisions are usually noted at the beginning of the opinion and are often regarded as more influential than decisions rendered by a smaller number of judges. Same as "en banc."

in camera

(in KAM-er-ra) 1. Lat. In chambers; in private. A matter is heard "in camera" in a judge's private chambers or in a courtroom from which all spectators have been excluded. 2. An in-chambers inspection of documents by judge.

incapacity, incapacitated

1. The inability to enter into a legally binding transaction; incompetency. An infant has no capacity to enter into a contract. 2. In Workers' Compensation: Inability to work due either to physical inability to perform or inability to find employment.

in capite

(in KAP-it-ee) Lat. In chief. In early English property law, this term referred to an estate in land held directly by the king.

incarceration

Confinement in a prison or a jail.

incendiary

1. (n.) An arsonist; one who willfully sets another's property on fire. 2. An object capable of

starting a fire (*e.g.,* gasoline). 3. (adj.) Of a fire set by an arsonist.

incest

Sexual intercourse between persons too closely related by blood to be married. Incest is a criminal offense in most jurisdictions, although the degree of prohibited family relationship varies.

in chief

1. Principal; primary. 2. The initial questioning of a witness by the party who called him to testify is an examination in chief.

inchoate

Latent; begun but not completed. In crime: A criminal act that was stopped short of completion. The accused may not be prosecuted for the intended crime, but may be charged with the inchoate offense (*e.g.,* attempt, solicitation, conspiracy). Note that conspiracy defendants can be prosecuted both for conspiracy and the principal crime.

inchoate right of dower

The right, or expectation of a future right, of a wife in her living husband's real estate. Her right does not vest until her husband's death.

incident

A happening or thing of import due to its connection with a main or more important happening or thing.

incident of ownership

An element of ownership in a life insurance policy. If the deceased retained any incident of ownership in a life insurance policy at the time of death, the policy's value is included in his gross estate.

incite

1. To instigate; to arouse to action. 2. To induce others to commit a crime.

inclosure

An area of land surrounded by a tangible boundary such as a fence, wall, or ditch. Also "enclosure."

income

Money received as profits from business, as salary for employment, or as return on investments.

income averaging
A method of calculating an individual's taxable income by averaging her annual income for a number of years.

income statement
A financial statement of operating results for a specific period, usually at quarterly or annual increments. The statement includes revenues, expenses, gains, and losses. Also known as an operating statement, earnings report, and profit-and-loss statement.

income tax
A tax based on the net or gross incomes of persons or corporations. The Sixteenth Amendment allows Congress to institute a tax on incomes.

incompatible, incompatibility
Inability to exist together. In many states, incompatibility between husband and wife is grounds for divorce.

incompetency
1. The state of being unqualified; lacking sufficient ability, knowledge, or physical or psychological capacity. 2. A lack of legal qualifications to discharge the required duty. *See* incompetent.

incompetency proceeding
A hearing to determine the competency of an individual and whether the state should take charge of him and/or his affairs. If the court deems the individual incompetent, it will appoint a guardian to manage his interests until the incompetent satisfies the court of his competency.

incompetent
A person lacking the legal qualifications to manage his own affairs. Usually an incompetent is of full age and is mentally incapable by reason of insanity or chronic illness.

incompetent evidence
Evidence which is inadmissible for some legal reason. A general objection to the admissibility of evidence.

inconclusive
Possible of being disproved or rebutted by additional evidence.

inconsistent
Contradictory; incompatible; mutually exclusive.

incorporate

1. To combine to form one unit.
2. To create a corporation, a legal entity recognized by law as an "artificial person."

incorporation by reference

1. Method of making one document a part of another document by referring to the first in the second, and stating that it should be considered as part of the latter just as if it were actually written out in the first document. 2. The doctrine that a will may incorporate into itself another document which is in existence at the time the will is executed and is sufficiently identified in the will.

incorporeal

Intangible; lacking physical substance or material form. One may have an incorporeal right to intellectual property, for example.

incorporeal hereditament

An intangible right which may be inherited that is derived from or involves the ownership of property (*e.g.*, an easement allowing access to another's property or royalties from minerals discovered on one's property).

incorrigible

Incapable of correction or reform. Usually used in reference to a juvenile whose parents cannot manage his behavior or whose conduct cannot be made to conform to the law.

increment

1. An increase or gain in number or value. 2. That which is gained or added.

in criminalibus probationes debent esse luce clariores

(in krim-in-AL-i-bus pro-bash-ee-O-nees deb-ent ess-ee LOO-see kla-ree-o-rees) Lat. In criminal cases, the proofs ought to be clearer than light.

incrimination, incriminate

Providing evidence that would implicate someone in the commission of a crime. The Fifth Amendment protects persons from self-incrimination while testifying.

incroach

Encroach; to unlawfully intrude upon another's right or possession.

inculpatory
1. Probative of guilt. 2. Evidence which tends to establish guilt.

incumbent
1. Someone who is presently holding an office. 2. Someone who has the legal authority to carry out the duties of an office.

incumbrance
See encumbrance.

incur
1. To become liable due to operation of law as opposed to a contract where the party becomes liable by taking an affirmative action. 2. To become liable to or subject to.

indebitatus assumpsit
(in-deb-i-TAT-uss as-SUMP-sit) Lat. Being indebted, he undertook. A common law form of action wherein the defendant has allegedly failed to satisfy a debt which he has contracted to pay.

indecent
Offensive to common tastes: obscene; vulgar. *See* indecent exposure.

indecent exposure
The intentional or negligent exposure of the body's private parts in a public place or within the public view.

indecent speech
Speech that is sexual or vulgar in nature, or that uses profane words or expressions, but that does not meet the definition of "obscenity." Indecent speech is protected by the First Amendment.

indefeasible
That which cannot be defeated, revoked, or made void.

in delicto
Lat. In fault.

indemnify
1. To insure; to secure against future loss or damage. 2. To reimburse; to compensate for past loss or damage.

indemnity
1. A contract shifting liability for a loss from one person held legally responsible to another person. 2. An insurance contract to secure a person from anticipated loss or damage. 3. Restitution; reimbursement.

indenture
1. A deed, mortgage, or other written instrument, between two or more parties in which the parties assume reciprocal obligations towards each other. The historical practice was to cut the top of the document in a wavy pattern so as to verily its authenticity. 2. A written agreement setting forth terms of issuance of debentures or bonds.

independent contractor
One who undertakes a project for another while retaining control over the means and method by which he accomplishes his goal. The employer has no control over the details of the independent contractor's work.

indeterminate sentence
1. A prison sentence for the maximum period allowed by law subject to early termination by a parole board after the minimum period has been served. 2. A prison sentence which the court allows the penal authorities to fix within the minimum and maximum time framework established by the court of law.

independent significance
Acts or documents executed without adherence to will formalities, not merely for the purpose of testamentary disposition, but also for some other reason.

index fund
A mutual fund whose portfolio of stocks is intended to match the performance of a larger index, such as the Standard & Poor's Index.

Indian Child Welfare Act
A federal law regulating proceedings regarding the custody of Native American children. The scope of the law covers foster placements, custody disputes, and adoption proceedings

Indian country
1. All land within the limits of an Indian reservation under the jurisdiction of the federal government. 2. Dependent Indian communities. 3. Indian allotments still in trust, whether located within reservations or not.

Indian tribe
An existing or historical tribe, band, nation, or group of indigenous Americans. The term in-

cludes Alaskan native villages. The federal government maintains a list of tribes that are recognized for certain programs.

indicia

(in-DISH-ee-a) Signs; indications that a particular fact or claim is probably true, though not proven certainly (*e.g.*, a document evidencing ownership of property is an "indicia of title"). The term is used synonymously with "circumstantial evidence."

indicium

(in-DISH-ee-um) Lat. An indication; a sign. Singular form of indicia.

indictable offenses

Crimes to be prosecuted under an indictment. At common law, such offenses included all felonies, capital offenses, and treason.

indictment

1. An accusation by a grand jury. 2. A written accusation drafted and submitted to the grand jury by the public prosecuting attorney charging one or more persons with a crime. The grand jury then determines whether the accusation, if proved, would lead to the conviction of the accused. If so, the indictment is adopted by the grand jury and submitted to the court. The indictment also serves to notify the accused of the charges against him with enough precision so that the defendant may prepare an adequate defense.

indigent

One who is needy and poor and has neither property nor persons able to provide support. For social welfare purposes, one is not required to be totally destitute to benefit from public assistance. One must, however, lack the means for a comfortable existence. An indigent criminal defendant who has no funds to hire a lawyer to defend him is entitled to appointed counsel.

indignity

In divorce law, a ground for divorce based on emotional and mental cruelty impacting on the subject's self-respect and personal honor as opposed to physical abuse. Examples of indignities are habitual contempt, studied neglect, intentional incivility, unmerited reproach, malignant ridicule, abusive language, and manifest disdain.

indirect evidence
Circumstantial evidence. Evidence based upon presumptions and inferences from certain facts which leans towards a particular conclusion. *See* direct evidence.

indirect tax
A tax upon some right, privilege, or corporate franchise.

indispensable evidence
Evidence which is essential to prove a fact.

indispensable party
A party whose presence in court is so essential to determining an adequate judgment that any verdict rendered in that party's absence would be incomplete or unjust. A trial cannot proceed unless all indispensable parties are joined, even if the court loses jurisdiction over the case through the joinder.

individual retirement account
A savings or brokerage account. Deposits in the account, up to a maximum amount, and interest on the account are not taxed until

withdrawn. Usually called an I.R.A.

indorsee
The person to whom an instrument or document is assigned by indorsement.

indorsement
Signature or other marking on the back of a negotiable instrument which transfers the instrument to another. An indorsement transfers the entire instrument, otherwise it is only a partial assignment. A blank indorsement does not specify the party to whom the instrument is payable. Also "endorsement."

indorser
The person who indorses an instrument or document.

inducement
1. A persuasion or influence using threats or promises. 2. In contracts: The benefit or advantage that the promisor expects to gain from the contract is the inducement for making it. 3. In pleadings: An inducement is an explanatory statement preceding the plea. 4. In criminal evidence: Motive.

ineligibility

disqualification; lacking the legal qualifications necessary to be considered for a particular position (*e.g.*, political office).

in escrow

That which is held in an escrow account, or by one who is not a party to the transaction in question, until certain conditions are satisfied. Upon the satisfaction of such conditions, the items held in escrow are transferred to the grantee, promisee or obligee.

in esse

(in ES-see) Lat. In being. That which actually exist; in essence.

in extremis

(in ex-TREE-mis) Lat. In extremity. At the end, often meaning near death. Declarations "in extremis" are dying declarations. In extremis may also characterize any situation of extreme circumstances.

infamous, infamy

1. Shameful or disgraceful. 2. Well known in a derogatory sense. 3. At common law, treason, forgery, and felony were "infamous crimes," indicating particular moral turpitude. One convicted of such a crime was denied the right to testify as a witness. 4. The legal status of one convicted of an infamous crime and involves a loss of honor and an inability to testify as a witness.

infant

A person under the age of legal majority, at common law, under 21 years of age, now usually 18 years of age. An infant is subject to various disabilities under the law (*e.g.*, an infant is precluded from suing or being sued unless he/she has a guardian ad litem, and his/her contracts are generally voidable.

infanticide

The murder of an infant soon after its birth.

in fee

Absolute ownership of an estate in land. *See* fee simple.

inference

A deduction from an admitted fact. In evidence: A fact or claim derived logically from another fact or claim which is accepted as true. Conclusions or deductions are reached through reason, common sense, and human experience rather than merely by guesswork.

inferior court

Any court whose jurisdiction is statutorily limited or special, and whose judgments are valid only if its jurisdiction is established. Any court subject to review by another court in a particular judicial system (*e.g.*, a trial court).

infeudation

Old English term for transferring full ownership in land by a ceremony called "livery of seisin." *See* enfeoffment.

infirm

Weak; sickly; feeble in mind or body. To protect the health of an infirm witness, testimony may be taken in a way that differs from regular procedures.

infirmity of mind

A disease or weakness of the mind. Something beyond a temporary disorder.

in flagrante delicto

Lat. In the act of doing the crime; "red-handed."

informal proceedings

Proceedings which do not conform to the formal rules or requirements of a normal trial (*e.g.*, some probate court proceedings, small claims court).

in forma pauperis

(in FOR-ma PAW-per-is) Lat. In the manner of a pauper. A court may allow an indigent party to proceed in forma pauperis and bear no liability for court fees or costs.

information

A written accusation submitted by a public officer, usually a prosecutor, specifying charges against an individual. An information differs from an indictment in that the former is presented by a public official on his oath while the latter is presented by the grand jury on their oath. In most states, an information may be used instead of an indictment to bring someone to trial.

information and belief

Characteristic of a statement or allegation based not on firsthand knowledge, but believed to be true from information. Such statements lack the credibility of actual knowledge, but nonetheless represent a speaker's good faith belief in their truth.

informed consent (doctrine)

1. An agreement to allow something to occur based on the knowledge necessary to make an intelligent choice. 2. In tort law: The requirement that a physician avoid possible liability for battery by disclosing to the patient what a reasonably prudent physician exercising reasonable care would disclose to the patient about the nature and risks of a proposed course of treatment, so that the patient may make an intelligent decision about whether to undergo the treatment by balancing the probable risks against the probable benefits.

informer

1. One who notifies the authorities of a violation of law. 2. In criminal law: An undisclosed person who confidentially communicates material information of a criminal activity which directs government officers in their investigation. The informer is a volunteer and the term does not refer to people who divulge

information when questioned by police or when testifying as a witness before the grand jury.

informer's privilege

The government's privilege not to disclose the identity of one who notifies authorities of a violation of the law. This privilege may be revoked, under specific circumstances, at trial.

in foro conscientiae

(in FOE-ro con-shee EN-shee-eye) Lat. In the forum of the conscience. From a moral, rather than legal, view.

infra

(IN-fra) Lat. Under; below; within. In a text, it refers to an upcoming discussion or citation, as opposed to "supra" (above or before) which refers to something already mentioned in a previous part of the text.

infraction

1. A violation or breach of a law, right, or contract. 2. A particular violation of a statute which the statute specifically identifies as an "infraction" and for which the only punishment is a fine.

infringement

1. The breach of any law. 2. An interference with the legal rights of another. 3. In copyright law: The unauthorized reproduction, performance, distribution, public display, transmission by webcast, or creation of a work derivative of a work protected by copyright. 4. In trademark law: The unlicensed use of a mark in a way that is likely to cause consumer confusion as to the source or origin of goods. 5. In patent law: Manufacturing or using a patented invention or improvement without the permission of the owner of the patent.

in futuro

(in fyoo-TOO-ro) Lat. In the future; at a later time. *Contrast* "in praesenti."

in genere

Lat. In kind. In the same genus, class or species.

ingress

The entering upon some place or something. *See* egress. (Ingress and egress are sometimes used interchangeably.)

in gross

Lat. At large. In a large quantity or sum; without deduction.

ingrossing

The act of creating a perfect copy of a document from a rough draft of it in order to use the copy for its ultimate purpose or to have it in its final form.

inhabitant

One who resides actually and permanently in a particular place and is domiciled there. Corporations are inhabitants of the state in which they are incorporated.

in haec verba

(in hike verba) Lat. In these words.

inherent defect

A defect in an object which exists regardless of the use of that object and which is not easily discoverable. Also "latent defect."

inherent powers

1. A power which has not been sanctioned by an express grant of authority. Such powers are assigned to the federal government in certain areas, even though the powers are not explicitly author-

ized by the U.S. Constitution.
2. Powers that are inherent to the idea of government, such as protecting the nation's borders from invasion.

inherent right

A right that a person possesses and which is not derived from another source.

inherently dangerous activity

An activity that involves a risk of serious harm if not done skillfully or carefully.

inherit

1. To receive property from a dead person either by descent (through intestacy laws) or by devise (a will). 2. To take as an heir solely by descent rather than by devise.

inheritance

All property, real or personal, that is received by heirs from a decedent through the laws of descent and distribution. In popular usage the term refers to property received either through intestacy or by will.

inheritance tax

A tax imposed by the government on all property, both real and personal, transferred from the dead to the living by legacy, will, or intestate succession. The tax is on the legal right to acquire property and not on the property itself. *Compare* estate tax.

in hoc

Lat. In this; respecting this.

in invitum

(in IN-vit-tum) Lat. Against the will; without consent.

initiative

1. The power of the people to propose laws, bills, and constitutional/legislative amendments and to enact or reject them by vote, independent of the legislative body. 2. The right of the people to propose laws to be enacted by the legislature. Differs from "referendum," which is the right of the people to approve or reject a law submitted to them for approval.

injunction

An equitable remedy in which the court orders a party to perform or to desist from a particular act.

Mandatory injunction commands the defendant to take a

positive action to accomplish a specific purpose (*e.g.*, the court may order a school to admit a particular student).

Restrictive injunction forbids the defendant or his agents from attempting or continuing some activity that is injurious to the plaintiff (*e.g.*, the court may prohibit a school from suspending or expelling a student).

Interlocutory injunction is any injunction issued prior to trial to prevent irreparable injury to the plaintiff while the court considers whether to grant permanent relief. Granted for a limited time only. Two types: 1. A "preliminary injunction," which is granted after the defendant has received notice and has had an opportunity to participate in a hearing on the issue, and 2. A "temporary restraining order," which is granted without notice to the defendant in situations where the plaintiff will suffer irreparably if immediate relief is not granted.

A *permanent* or *perpetual injunction* is a final disposition in the suit and is indefinite in length of time.

in jure

(in JOO-ree) Lat. In law; in right. Legally or rightfully.

injuria absque damno

(in-JOO-ree-a AB-skwee DAM-no) Lat. Wrong or injury without damage. An admitted violation of another's right which has not resulted in any damage to him. This situation will not sustain an action at law if damages must be pleaded as cause of the action. Usually refers to an injury caused through negligence since an intentional injury may entitle one to nominal or punitive damages.

injuria non excusat injuriam

(in-JOO-ree-a non ex-KOO-sat in-JOO-ree-am) Lat. One injury does not excuse another; one wrong does not justify another wrong.

injury

Damage or wrong done to another's person, property, reputation, or rights. Not synonymous with "damages," since a right may be infringed without causing any monetary loss. No action at law is maintainable without a legal injury.

in kind

The same kind; the same category, When returning a loan "in kind," one returns not the object that was loaned, but something that is the same type or the same quality as the loaned object.

in lieu of

In place of; instead of.

in limine

Lat. On the threshold; in the beginning.

in loco parentis

(in LO-ko pa-REN-tis) Lat. In place of a parent. In common law, it refers to a person who has replaced a lawful parent by assuming the responsibilities of a parent without adopting the child (*e.g.*, a minor and a residential institution or a court and a ward or orphan).

inmate

1. A person who resides with others. 2. A person who is confined to a prison or other institution.

innkeeper

One who keeps a house which provides lodging, food, and entertainment to travelers for compensation.

innocent

1. Free from guilt or wrongdoing. 2. Acting in good faith and without knowledge of defects or incriminatory circumstances.

inns of court

Four private associations of lawyers in England that give lectures, hold examinations, and hold the exclusive privilege of conferring admission to practice as a barrister.

innuendo

Lat. 1. A hint or insinuation, usually derogatory. 2. In defamation actions, the part of the complaint which explains the injurious meaning of words that are not necessarily defamatory on their face.

in odium spoliatoris omnia praesumuntur

(in O-dee-um spo-lee-a-TOR-is OM-nee-a pray-sum-un-TUR) Lat. All things are presumed to the prejudice of the despoiler or pirate. Every presumption is made against the wrongdoer.

in omnibus

Lat. In all things; in everything; in all respects.

in pais

(in PIE-ees) Fr. In the country. The phrase applies to transactions done outside the court or without a legal proceeding.

in pari delicto

(in PAR-ee de-LIK-to) Lat. In equal fault; equally culpable. In contracts: The law of equity will not help either party in an illegal transaction if they are "in pari delicto" but will leave them as it finds them.

in pari materia

(in PAR-ee ma-TEER-ee-a) Lat. In the same subject matter. In statutory construction: Statutes "in pari materia," relating to the same subject matter, should be construed together in order to derive legislative intent.

in perpetuity

Forever; perpetually.

in personam

(in per-SONE-am) Lat. Against the person. In procedure: An action taken against a person which involves his personal rights and is based on jurisdiction over him as opposed to seeking a judgment against property (in rem). Equity courts are said to give "in personam" decisions, meaning that their judgments usually command a person to do or refrain from doing something.

An action for a judgment "in personam" is initiated by giving notice to the affected party either by serving him personally or by substitute service. An example of an action in personam is a lawsuit against an individual who intentionally hit the plaintiff, because the judgment would be against the aggressor himself.

in posse

(in POS-see) Lat. In possibility; in potential but not in actuality.

in praesenti

(in pray-SEN-tee) Lat. 1. At the present time; at once. 2. Immediately effective.

in propria persona

(in PRO-pree-a per-SONE-a) Lat. In one's own person. Representing oneself in court.

inquest

1. At common law, a name for any judicial inquiry. Usually it referred to a body of people appointed by law to investigate matters before them to determine whether a crime was committed. An inquiry made by the jury was also an inquest. 2. The inquiry of a medical examiner or coroner conducted to determine whether a death that has occurred under suspicious circumstances resulted from a criminal act.

inquisition

1. A judicial inquiry or examination; an inquest. 2. An inquiry by a jury held before an officer of the Crown (inquisitor). 3. An official document recording the decision of the inquiry.

in re

(in ree *or* in ray) Lat. In the matter of. Used in the title of a judicial proceeding in which there are no opposing parties, but the matter must be decided nonetheless. This may involve the judicial disposition of a thing (*e.g.*, an estate) or of a person (*e.g.*, a neglected child).

in rem

(in rem *or* in raym) Lat. Actions against a thing (res) and not against a person. A lawsuit in rem involves settlement of a property claim without reference to the individual claimants. This judgment is binding on all claimants to the property, whether they are parties to the action or not.

insane delusion

A conception of a disordered mind that imagines the existence of facts which is not supported by any evidence.

insanity

Madness; unsoundness of mind. In criminal law, insanity is a defense to criminal charges and relieves one of all responsibility for his actions. However, everyone is presumed sane until the contrary is proved. An affirmative criminal defense.

One test for insanity is the *"M'Naghten* Rule," which defines insanity as a defect of reason, resulting from a disease of the mind, that prevents the individual from knowing the nature or quality of his act or rendering the individual incapable of determining right from wrong.

The American Law Institute has replaced the *M'Naghten* Rule with a test which requires that a person has an inability to appreciate the criminality of his actions or to conform his actions to the requirements of law due to a mental disease or detect. This test has been adopted by most federal courts and by many state courts.

in se

(in say) Lat. In itself; in and of itself.

insider

1. One who has knowledge of facts not available to the public. 2. Under the Securities and Exchange Act, any corporate officer or director, or anyone who owns more than 10 percent of a corporation's stock. The term also includes any individual who trades on inside information in violation of a duty of trust.

insider trading

Buying and/or selling of a corporate stock by a corporate insider. When an insider uses information not known to the general public to gain an unfair advantage in a transaction, he violates the Securities and Exchange Act. Insider trading is regulated by the Securities and Exchange Commission.

insolvency

1. The inability to pay one's debts as they become due. 2. The condition of a person or corporation whose liabilities exceed its assets.

insolvent

1. (n.) A person who is unable to pay his debts as they become due in the regular course of business. 2. (adj.) A corporation whose liabilities outweigh its assets is insolvent if it cannot garner sufficient resources to meet its needs either through its own assets or through credit.

in specie

(in SPEE-she) Lat. 1. In kind; in like form. 2. Specific, specifically.

inspection

1. Examination, investigation. 2. An examination of an article to determine its suitability for use or commerce (*e.g.*, food

inspections). 3. "Inspection of documents" is the right of a party in a legal action to examine and copy documents of the court or of the opposing party, to enter land, or to otherwise gather evidence through the discovery process in preparation for trial. 4. "Inspection right" is the examination of goods by the buyer, who is entitled to examine purchases to determine whether they conform to an agreement or contract.

inspection laws

1. The right of public officials to examine regulated articles or conditions in housing or industry to insure compliance with the law. 2. Regulations authorizing public officials to examine various kinds of merchandise to determine their fitness for use and compliance with prescribed standards in order to protect the public's health, safety, and welfare (*e.g.*, inspectors may investigate food for cleanliness or packages for weight and accuracy in labeling in order to admit only marketable goods and to exclude unmarketable goods from sale).

installment

1. One of the parts into which a debt is divided when payment is to be made at intervals. 2. A regular part payment of a debt.

installment contract

A contract calling for payment or performance periodically (*e.g.*, a real estate contract providing for payment of the purchase price in installments, with conveyance of title to be made upon completion of the payments).

installment sale

A sale of property in which the buyer pays for the goods over a period of time.

instant, instanter

Lat. At once; immediately: without delay. When a party is ordered to plead instanter, he must plead on that same day. Usually instanter means within 24 hours.

in statu quo

Lat. In the condition which was. To place a party in the situation that she was in before the controversy or wrongdoing. In contracts: The party in an executory contract who seeks to rescind must first place the other contracting party "in statu quo" (*i.e.*, in the position that she was in at the time of the contract's inception) before rescission can take place). Also "status quo."

instigate, instigation
To incite; to stir to some action, especially to commit a crime or to initiate a suit.

institute
1. (v.) To start or commence, as in to institute a suit. 2. (n.) An educational institution providing training for particular work. 3. A treatise on law (*e.g.*, the Institute of Justinian was a treatise on Roman law written by the emperor Justinian; the Institutes of Coke was a four-part treatise on common law written by Sir Edward Coke).

instruct, instruction
1. To advise; to direct; to order. 2. To inform a jury of the law applicable to the facts of a pending case and to point out which party has the burden of proof and any problems of proof to guide the jury in its deliberation. This statement is called a "charge" to the jury. The jury is bound to accept and apply the judge's exposition. 3. To convey information by the client to his attorney.

instrument
1. A formal document made for a legal purpose (*e.g.*, a will, a contract). An instrument may be used to create or record a legal right, to transfer money or property, or to serve as written evidence of a transaction. 2. A "negotiable instrument" is a document evidencing a right to a payment of money (*e.g.*, a check). 3. In evidence, anything, including witnesses and animate objects, presented as evidence to the court; demonstrative evidence.

insufficient evidence
A trial judge's ruling that a prosecutor's or plaintiff's evidence fails to justify going forward with the trial. Such a ruling results in a directed verdict in favor of the defendant. When an appellate court renders this decision, it results in a reversal of the decision and a dismissal of charges or the suit against the defendant.

insurable interest

1. A relationship with a person or an object upon which one can base an insurance policy. An insurance contract must involve an insurable interest; otherwise it is a form of gambling and unenforceable. 2. Any interest that will directly cause financial loss in the event of loss or damage to the person or object, or financial benefit by its continued existence, is an insurable interest. For example, if one owned a diamond ring and would suffer financially in the event of theft or loss, one has an insurable interest in the ring. However, ownership of the property is not necessary if there is a reasonable expectation of monetary advantage. In the context of life insurance, if one has a reasonable expectation of financial benefit from the life of a person (*e.g.,* a spouse or a business partner), one has an insurable interest on which to base a life insurance policy.

insurance

Act of providing against a possible loss from a specified peril by entering into a contract with a party (usually a licensed corporation) that is willing to bind itself to compensate for such loss, should it occur, in exchange for payment. The contract is a "policy." The consideration paid to the insurer or underwriter is a "premium." Types of harm protected against are called "risks" or "perils." The thing or person being protected is the "insurable interest." Fire and marine insurance is usually indemnity which means that only such sum is paid by the insurer as is actually lost and the insurer is entitled to stand in place of the insured. In life or accident insurance the insurer undertakes to pay a certain sum to the insured or his legal representative in the event of death or injury.

insured

1. Any person whose health, life, or property is covered by insurance. 2. The owner of an insurance policy.

insurer

An insurance company or underwriter who makes an insurance contract with the insured by assuming the risk or underwriting a policy.

insurrection

An uprising against political or civil authority; rebellion.

intangibles

1. Property that has no intrinsic market value but which is evidence of or representative of value or worth (*e.g* bonds, stock certificates, promissory notes). 2. Rights not related to physical articles, but based on relationships between persons that the law recognizes through sanctions.

integration

1. The act of making whole. 2. In contract law: The adoption of a writing or writings as the full and final expression of the agreement between parties. The writing or writings adopted by the contracting parties. 3. Joining disparate groups (such as races) as equals, as in the desegregation of white and black school districts.

intemperance

1. Lack of restraint in conduct or habits. 2. Excessive or habitual use of alcoholic beverages. "Habitual intemperance" is the regular consumption of liquor which results in great diminution of the attention that a person can give to his business affairs or which would inflict great mental anguish on an innocent party.

intendment of law

The true intention or meaning of a law.

intent, intention, intentional

The purpose, design, or resolve with which a person acts. Since intent is a state of mind; it can rarely be proved directly, but must be inferred from facts or circumstances. In criminal law, the "mens rea" or criminal intent requirement is that a person knows what he is doing and desires or anticipates the results of his act at the time that he commits the offense. Intent, the perpetrator's state of mind at the time of acting, differs from motive, which is what causes a person to act or refrain from acting.

In criminal law: There are two types of intent: *General intent* is the intent to commit a crime. Proof of general intent is required in all criminal prosecutions, but does not involve demonstrating that the defendant intended the precise harm which he caused (*e.g.*, shooting into a crowd is proof of general intent to commit murder, even though the accused did not intend to injure any particular person). *Specific intent* is the intent to accomplish the precise act which the law prohibits. Proof of specific intent is essential for certain crimes, such as "assault with intent to rape."

In torts: An intentional tort requires that the actor desired to cause the consequences of his act or recognizes that these consequences are substantially certain to result from his act.

In documents (*e.g.*, wills), intention is the meaning gathered from the words therein.

intentional infliction of emotional distress

A tort action for reckless or intentional conduct of an extreme or outrageous nature that causes the victim to suffer emotional distress. Also known as "outrage."

inter alia

(in-ter AL-ee-a *or* in-ter-AY-lee-a) Lat. Among other things. Used in referring to relevant parts of a statute without citing the whole text (*e.g.*, "the statute provides inter alia").

interest

1. In property: A legal concern in some property based on a right, title, claim, or legal share. The term usually denotes a right less than full title or absolute ownership in real property. 2. In commercial law: Consideration or compensation paid for the use or retention by one party of another's money. Interest is based on the amount (percentage) charged, the amount loaned, and the length of time of the loan. Interest may be simple or compounded. Simple interest is computed based on the principal only, but compounded interest uses the principal and any accrued interest as its basis for calculation. 3. A legal or monetary concern in the determination of a suit. This interest must be of a present, direct, and immediate character.

interfere, interference

1. To check; hinder; disturb; trespass; intervene; encroach. 2. To enter into the concerns of others against their wishes. 3. In

patent law: A proceeding initiated by the Patent Office to determine the priority of invention among all parties claiming the same subject matter. This takes place when a conflict in patent claims arises, such as when one person claims a patent on the whole or any part of an area already covered by an existing patent or by a pending application.

interim, interim order
Lat. In the meantime; temporary; between. An interim order is a temporary order given until a final order is entered or until some specific event happens (*e.g.*, a temporary injunction).

interim financing
A short-term debt incurred until permanent financing can be obtained.

interlineation
The act of writing between the lines (of an instrument). The writing itself that is found between the lines. An interlineation in a will raises a rebuttable presumption that the writing was made after the will was executed.

interlocking directorate
A situation wherein directors of two or more corporations sit on each other's boards. Interlocking directorates that curb competition between the corporations violate federal antitrust law.

interlocutory
Provisional; temporary; not final. A judgment is interlocutory if it does not determine all the issues relating to all the parties, but rather leaves something further to be adjudicated at a later proceeding. An interlocutory appeal is an appeal which does not resolve the controversy, but which is necessary for a later adjudication of the case on its merits.

interlocutory decree
A preliminary or provisional order. A decree made upon some point arising during a suit which is not determinative of the case on the merits, but directs further proceedings in preparation for a final decree. It is a decree made to ascertain a matter of law or fact in preparation for a final decree.

interlocutory order

An order rendered by a judge prior to a final decision. Such an order relates to an intermediate issue, and as such, does not dispose of the case on the merits.

Internal Revenue Code (I.R.C.)

Body of law which sets forth all federal tax laws, administered and enforced by the Internal Revenue Service (I.R.S.).

Internal Revenue Service (I.R.S.)

Federal agency charged with the duty of implementing and enforcing the Internal Revenue Code (I.R.C.).

international agreements

Treaties, contracts, or conventions made between nations.

International Court of Justice

The judicial body established by the United Nations. Its jurisdiction includes giving advisory opinions on matters of law and treaty construction when requested to do so by the General Assembly or the Security Council. It may also settle legal disputes between nations who voluntarily submit a controversy for adjudication. Its judgment may be enforced by the Security Council. Its judges are elected by the General Assembly and the Security Council.

International Criminal Court

A court established by international treaty to hear cases of war crimes, genocide, crimes against humanity, and aggression. The court is located in The Hague.

international law

The law or customs which regulate the conduct of nations towards each other and towards each other's citizens. The United Nations may establish tribunals to try enemies accused of offenses against international law. There are two kinds of international law: *Private international law* determines before which nation's courts a matter should be presented and by which nation's laws a matter should be tried. *Public international law* is the rules of conduct which independent, civilized states have adopted in their relations with one another.

Internet Corporation for Assigned Names and Numbers (ICANN)

A non-profit corporation that assigns and manages internet domain names and address space.

inter pares

(in-ter PAR-ays) Lat. Between peers.

inter partes

(in-ter PAR-tays) Lat. Between parties. Papers inter partes are documents in which two persons make conveyance to or engagement with the other. Judgment inter partes is a judgment against a particular person and not against a thing or right.

interpleader

A legal proceeding that enables a person holding money or property to compel the claimants to litigate the matter among themselves. When a person who possesses property in which he has no interest but to which two or more parties lay claim and he does not know which party has a right to the property, but is himself sued or expecting to be sued by one or all of the parties, he obtains relief through a court order to interplead (*i.e.*, to have the plaintiffs try their claims among themselves to determine who is entitled to the property). This is called a "stakeholder interpleader." An interpleader is an equitable remedy provided for in Federal Rule of Civil Procedure 22.

An example of interpleader is an insurance company having the court order two claimants to the proceeds of a policy to interplead their causes so that the company may turn the proceeds over to the victorious litigant without fear of a lawsuit from the other claimant.

Interpol

The International Criminal Police Organization. An international organization that gathers and shares information on transnational criminals and criminal activity among law enforcement agencies of its member nations.

interpolate

To insert words into a completed document which alter its meaning.

interpretation

The discovery of the intention of a writer or of the meaning of a document by studying the words, by conjecture, or by a combination of the two.

A "literal interpretation" ascertains the writer's intention or the document's meaning exclusively from the words used. A "rational interpretation" is a conjecture relying on probability and rationality of what the author intended when the author's language fails to express his intention precisely. A "mixed interpretation" employs both words and educated guesses to fathom the author's intention or the document's meaning when the words of the document are of doubtful meaning or do not express the author's intention when rightly understood.

interrogation

The police questioning of a suspected criminal. The subject of a police interrogation must be given a "*Miranda* warning," which includes the right to have counsel present at the time of the questioning.

interrogatories

1. A group of questions submitted to a party, witness or other person having an interest in the case. 2. In civil actions: A pretrial discovery device in which written questions are submitted by one party to the other party who must reply to the questions in writing and under oath. Unlike depositions, interrogatories can be served only on opposing parties in an action and must be answered in writing. 3. The questions on one or more specific issues of fact necessary to reach a verdict which the court may submit to a jury along with general verdict forms.

in terrorem

(in tear-ROR-em) Lat. In terror; by way of warning. This term refers to a common condition in a will, which warns a potential beneficiary not to dispute the will, or risk losing the bequest or devise. Such a condition is unenforceable in many states.

inter se

Lat. Among or between themselves. Used to distinguish rights and liabilities between two or more parties to one another from their rights or duties to others.

intersection

1. A place where two things cross. When applied to streets or highways, it refers to the area common to two streets at the point at which they cross each other as determined by a continuation of the curb. "Intersection" may also apply when one street or highway merges with another without crossing it, forming a "T" intersection. 2. The act of dividing two things by passing a line between them.

Interstate Commerce Act

The Congressional act of 1887, which regulates commerce between the states, including the transportation of people and property from within one state to another state. The Act attempts to insure that the rates of carriers are reasonable and just by prohibiting unjust discrimination, rebates, pooling of freights, or other monopolistic practices, and that the carriers publish schedules of rates. The Act created a commission (the Interstate Commerce Commission) to carry out these proposals.

Interstate Commerce Commission (I.C.C.)

Created by the Interstate Commerce Act of 1887 to regulate interstate transportation; abolished in 1995.

intervening cause

In torts, an independent cause occurring between the original negligent act or omission and the ultimate injury. If the intervening act was a foreseeable event (*e.g.,* negligent medical treatment of victim), liability attaches to the original wrongdoer. If unforeseeable, the intervening cause relieves the original tortfeasor of liability for the ultimate injury.

intervention

The procedure by which a third party not originally a litigant in an action, enters the suit as a matter of right or at the discretion of the court to protect an interest that he has in the subject matter of the dispute. The procedural grounds are delineated in Federal Rule of Civil Procedure 24.

inter vivos

(in-tair VIE-vos) Lat. Between the living. Transactions made inter vivos are made while the parties are living and are to take effect while both parties are alive. An inter vivos gift is made while the donor is living and takes effect during the donor's life, as opposed to a gift made "causa mortis" or in contemplation of death.

intestate, intestacy

Without making a will. Strictly defined, a person dies intestate if she dies without making a valid will or without otherwise indicating directions for the disposal of her property. If a person has made a will which has not completely disposed of her property, that individual is said to have died intestate as to that portion of her property not disposed of in her will. A person dies intestate if none of her heirs are available to claim her estate. An "intestate" is one who has died without leaving a valid will.

intestate succession

The disposition of property according to the laws of descent and distribution upon the death of a person who has not left a valid will or who has not ac-

counted for a portion of his estate in his will.

in toto

Lat. In the whole; wholly; completely. If an award is void in toto, then no award is allowed.

intoxication, intoxicated

1. Drunkenness. 2. The condition of impaired mental and/or physical capacity due to the excessive consumption of alcohol, drugs, or other substances. In driving while intoxicated cases, most states consider intoxication to be either the excessive use of alcohol or of drugs. In criminal law, voluntary intoxication is not a defense to general intent crimes but may refute the mens rea necessary for specific intent crimes. Involuntary intoxication which renders a person incapable of comprehending the wrongfulness of his conduct would make the actor's behavior involuntary and allow him to avoid criminal liability (*see* insanity). 3. The state of being poisoned.

intrinsic evidence

Evidence or information learned from a document without any testimony to explain the document or the purposes for which it was written or used.

intrinsic fraud

1. Fraud occurring during a trial and affecting the adjudication of the issues. Intrinsic fraud may be the result of perjury, false or forged documents, the concealment or misrepresentation of evidence, or bribery of a witness. Usually intrinsic fraud is not sufficient for setting aside a judgment resulting from it since it does not prevent the adversarial process. 2. Fraud used to obtain a transaction which makes the transaction void (*e.g.*, someone signs an instrument without having a reasonable opportunity to discover its essential terms). U.C.C. § 3-305(a)(1)(iii). 3. Fraud in the inducement.

intrusion upon seclusion

The intentional intrusion upon the seclusion or private affairs of another person in an offensive manner and without the other person's consent. The intrusion may be physical (*e.g.*, opening and reading another person's mail) or non-physical (*e.g.*, looking through a window).

inure

1. To take effect; to result. 2. To be of use or benefit to someone, especially used when the benefit is unintended. 3. Property law: To fix one's interest in a property; to vest.

in vacuo

(in VAK-yoo-o) Lat. In space.

invalid

1. Void; of no legal effect. 2. Inadequate to its purpose. 3. Lacking in authority or obligation.

invasion of privacy

Unlawful or unwarranted intrusion into one's private affairs or activities by the government or individuals. In tort law, causes of action for invasion of privacy include intrusion upon seclusion, publication of a private fact, appropriation of likeness, and false light.

invention

1. Patent law: The creation of something new by an exercise of mind exhibiting novelty and utility different in kind and in measure from anything done previously. Invention differs

from discovery in that it is not the revelation of something which existed and was not known, but rather is the creation of something which never before existed. To meet the requirement of novelty, an invention must be something not obvious to people trained in the field. 2. The article or machine so created.

inventory

1. A detailed list of goods; a list of goods designating and describing each item and indicating the quantity of each item. 2. The goods themselves, which are on the list. 3. A list of the property constituting an estate or collection drawn up by an executor or an administrator which includes the approximate value of each item. 4. Under the Uniform Commercial Code, an inventory refers to goods held for sale or lease, raw materials, and materials used in a business. The test to decide whether goods are inventory is whether the articles are offered for immediate or for ultimate sale.

in ventre sa mere

(in VEN-tra sa MARE) Fr. In the womb of the mother; an unborn child.

invest

To expend capital to acquire property or assets in the hope of securing income or profit for the investor. The word can mean purchasing goods or property for the income that it provides, or purchasing goods or property for their resale value.

investigatory powers

Authority given to governmental agencies to make inquiries into and gather information about matters that pertain to an investigation.

investiture

An old English ceremony wherein a vassal was presented with a land grant in open and notorious fashion, thus evidencing the conveyance. In times when the art of writing was not widespread, such a ceremony insured the veracity of the conveyance.

investment banker

A person or financial institution that is licensed to underwrite, buy, and sell securities. These securities transactions may involve both corporations and the general public.

investment company
A company or trust which invests in other companies. Investment companies often pool the resources of many individuals into a large fund and subsequently distribute profits made from the investment back to the individuals.

investment contract
A transaction or venture where one invests money in a common enterprise where the investor expects, or is led to expect, profits exclusively from the efforts of the promoter or a third party. The contract is based on the investor's reliance on others. A "common enterprise" is the dependent relationship of one party, the investor, on another party's performance of his part of the bargain for the investor's profits.

To be included under the federal securities acts an investment contract requires: 1) an investment of money, 2) a common enterprise, and 3) an expectation of profits solely through the efforts of others.

invitation
The act of a property owner or occupier who solicits or incites another to enter upon, remain in, or make use or his property. An invitation may be express, as when the owner or occupier uses words to invite another to enter the land or use the property thereon. It is implied when the owner's or occupier's conduct leads another to reasonably believe that the owner expects and intends others to use or traverse the land or the property thereon as they are doing (*e.g.*, the "invitation" of a shop owner to the public to enter his shop to make purchases). Today, most jurisdictions require a standard of reasonable care to all invitees.

invitee
One who is invited onto the property of another, either expressly or impliedly, to conduct business for their mutual benefit or for the benefit of the occupier, or to engage in an activity which the occupier permits to be conducted on his property (*e.g.*, a customer who enters a store is an

invitee regardless of whether he makes a purchase). In tort law, a property owner has an affirmative duty to protect the invitee not only against known dangers but also against those dangers which the owner may discover by exercising reasonable care.

invoice
1. An itemized, written record of merchandise shipped or sent to a purchaser, including the quantity and value of the merchandise as well as any additional costs. 2. A writing made for an importer specifying the goods imported and their true value.

involuntary
Acting without consent or against one's will. Involuntary acts are coerced, forced, or compelled without the consent of the actor.

involuntary manslaughter
1. The unlawful killing of a human being while committing an unlawful act not amounting to a felony or while committing a lawful act without adequate circumspection and caution. 2. Killing without malice or premeditation and without inten-

tion to kill or inflict serious bodily injury (*e.g.,* a person who hunts game without a license and shoots another hunter by mistake is guilty of involuntary manslaughter since the first hunter did not intend to kill the second hunter but did so while committing a misdemeanor by hunting without a license).

I.O.L.T.A.
Interest on Lawyers' Trust Accounts. A statute or court rule that requires that funds held in trust by an attorney be deposited in an interest-bearing account. Interest on the account is turned over to a regulatory authority.

ipse dixit
(Ip-say *or* IP-see DIK-sit) Lat. He himself said it. An assertion whose authority is based solely upon the individual who made it and not upon any precedent.

I.P.O.
Initial public offering. The first offering of securities for purchase by the public.

ipso facto

(IP-so FAK-to) Lat. By the fact itself; by the mere fact. As a consequence of an act or fact.

ipso jure

(Ip-so JOO-ree) Lat. By the law itself; merely by the operation of law.

irregular, irregularity

1. Against the rules. 2. Improper or insufficient due to a departure from or a neglect of a prescribed rule. 3. A violation or neglect of a prescribed rule or practice. An irregularity may mean a failure to do something necessary for the orderly progress of a suit or the doing of something at an improper time or in an improper manner. An irregularity is also a technical term for a defect in the mechanics of proceedings or in the way an action or defense is conducted.

irrelevant

Not material; unrelated or inapplicable to the issue. Evidence is irrelevant when it has no tendency to prove or disprove any issue involved. Irrelevant evidence is usually objected to and inadmissible at trial.

irreparable injury (damage, harm)

1. The type of injury which cannot be fully remedied by the law and, therefore, requires the equitable remedy of an injunction against the individual about to commit the injury. Demonstrating irreparable injury is usually a requirement for injunctive relief. 2. An injury which is beyond monetary compensation or damages since the damages cannot be measured by any pecuniary standard.

irresistible impulse

A term used in criminal law to mean an uncontrollable desire or urge to commit an unlawful act which cannot be controlled or resisted because a mental disease or insanity has destroyed the actor's self control or freedom of will. As a test for insanity, the irresistible impulse test allows a person to avoid criminal responsibility even though he can distinguish right from wrong and is aware of the nature and quality of his acts if he can demonstrate an inability to refrain from acting due to mental disease.

irretrievable breakdown

In jurisdictions with no-fault divorce, the grounds for the dissolution of a marital relationship. Specific legal grounds, such as infidelity or desertion, are not required.

irrevocable

That which cannot be recalled or withdrawn.

issue

1. (v.) To send forth; to put into circulation; to promulgate. 2. To send out officially, as in writs or services of process. 3. (n.) A legal point of dispute between two or more parties to the litigation which, if it is a matter of law, should be resolved by the court or, if it is a matter of fact, should be resolved by the jury. 4. All who are descended from a common ancestor. In wills, this meaning is usually narrowed to include children alone, depending on the intention of the testator. Most states allow an illegitimate child to inherit from his mother but not from his father. Many states consider an adopted child to be the "issue" of his/her adoptive parents. 5. In securities:

The offering for sale of a corporation's stock. The securities, themselves, which are being offered for sale. 6. A series or group of bonds or stock which is put into circulation at the same time.

issue preclusion

The rendering of a decision that bars the issue from being litigated again.

itemize

1. To write down in particulars. 2. To declare each item separately. Often used in the context of tax accounting.

itinerant

1. Wandering; traveling from place to place. Formerly applied to judges who made circuits. Also used in statutes to classify merchants, traders, and salesmen. 2. A person who travels from place to place.

J.

Abbreviation for justice or judge (*e.g.*, "A.J.," Associate Judge; "L.J.," Law Judge; "J.P.," Justice of the Peace).

jacitation

1. A false boast; a truthless claim; an assertion that cannot be substantiated. 2. A claim that is disputed by another.

J.A.G.

See judge advocate general.

jail

1. (n.) A prison; a place of incarceration. 2. The place of confinement where prisoners are held while awaiting trial or as punishment for misdemeanors. 3. (v.) To imprison; to detain in custody; to place in confinement.

jail credit

Credit against a criminal sentence for time spent in custody before sentence is imposed.

jailhouse lawyer

A prison inmate who studies the law informally and gives legal advice and assistance to fellow inmates.

Jencks Act

Federal statute which states that a criminal defendant in federal court may examine a witness's statements that are relevant to the testimony against him.

jeopardy

The risk or danger of conviction which a defendant faces from a criminal prosecution.

jetsam

Cargo thrown overboard to lighten a ship in distress (*e.g.*, goods deliberately thrown overboard from a ship, in a storm, to lessen the danger of the ship sinking).

jettison

To cast off or throw overboard from a ship; the act of deliberately removing cargo from a ship in distress, so as to prevent the ship from sinking.

J.J.
Abbreviation for justices or judges.

jobber
1. One who buys merchandise in bulk from manufacturers or wholesalers and then sells it to retailers in smaller lots. 2. One who trades shares on a stock exchange; a dealer in stocks or other securities. 3. A middleman.

John Doe
A placeholder name used in a legal proceeding or investigation to designate a fictitious or unidentified person.

joinder
The uniting or joining together of distinct causes of action or persons in a legal proceeding.

joinder of causes of action
The uniting or joining of distinct causes of action in a legal proceeding; under modern rules of civil procedure a party asserting a claim to relief may join as many claims as he has against an opposing party whether they are legal or equitable. *See* Federal Rule of Civil Procedure 18(a).

joint
Undivided; shared; united in interest or liability (*e.g.*, a common property interest shared by two or more persons).

joint account
Bank or brokerage account held by two or more people.

joint adventure
Business enterprise formed by a group of persons to carry out a single commercial transaction for profit whereby they pool their property, effects, money, skill, or knowledge.

joint and several
Status where rights and liabilities are shared collectively and also individually among a group of persons.

joint authors
In copyright law, two or more individuals who participate in the creation of a work with the intent to have their respective contributions merge into a single work.

joint custody
In family law, an arrangement whereby both parents share responsibility for the child. "Joint physical custody" mean

that the child spends an equal amount of time with each parent. "Joint legal custody" means that the child spends most of her time with one parent, but both parents have equal responsibility for, and control over, the child. In many jurisdictions, there is a presumption that joint custody is in the best interest of the child.

joint enterprise
Association of persons founded on an express or implied agreement to achieve a common purpose and where there is a community of interest and an equal right of control.

joint liability
Right of any party who is sued to insist that others be sued jointly with him because of their shared liability; contribution.

joint lives
A period of time which ends upon the death of any one of two or more specified persons.

joint stock company
An unincorporated business enterprise with proprietary interests represented by shares of

stock. Also called a "joint stock association."

joint tenancy
Ownership of real property, created under a single deed or instrument, whereby two or more persons have an undivided interest in the whole of the property, an equal right to share in the use and benefits of the property, and attached to which is the right of survivorship.

joint tortfeasors
Two or more persons whose negligent conduct, in concert or individually, united to injure a third person and who are therefore jointly and severally liable for the injury.

jointure
Property or estate granted to a wife upon the death of her husband, as set forth in a prenuptial agreement.

joint venture
Association of persons formed to engage in a particular commercial transaction for profit where there is a community of interest and where the right to share both in profits and losses and the right

of control is fixed by agreement. Unlike a partnership, a joint venture is of limited scope and duration. Also called a "joint adventure."

Jones Act

Federal statute enacted in 1920 providing that a sailor injured in the course of his employment can recover damages for his injuries. In such an action, all statutes modifying or extending the common law right or remedy in cases of personal injury to railway workers apply.

journalist's privilege

Law which grants members of the media a limited and qualified privilege to decline to reveal confidential sources of information. Some states have enacted such laws, which are included in so-called shield laws.

joyriding

The illegal taking of an automobile for the purpose of short-term use. In many states, joyriding constitutes a misdemeanor.

judge

Public official with the authority to preside and administer the law in a court of justice.

judge advocate corps

Staff of Judge Advocate General.

Judge Advocate General

The senior legal officer and the principal legal advisor of each branch of the United States Armed Services.

judge-made law

Common law; law that is made by judicial precedent and decision, as opposed to legislative action.

judge pro tempore

Person appointed for the term or portion thereof, during which time he performs the duties of the regular judge.

judgment

1. The decision of a court. 2. The final determination of a court on a matter submitted to it.

judgment creditor

A person who has obtained a judgment against a debtor that allows him to obtain the sum due him.

judgment debtor

A person against whom judgment has been awarded to a creditor, and who has not paid that judgment.

judgment in rem

A decision by a court which affects the status of a specific item or matter, as opposed to the person owning the item.

judgment note

A promissory note that authorizes an attorney or some other designated person to enter an appearance in court and confess a judgment against the maker for a sum therein named, upon default on payment of the note.

judgment on the merits

Decision by a court based on an analysis of the factual issues presented in a case rather than on some technical issue.

judgment proof

Status of all persons against whom judgments for money recoveries are of no consequence (*e.g.*, persons who are insolvent).

judicial

Relating or pertaining to legal proceedings or the administration of justice.

judicial activism

Behavior wherein a judge departs from judicial precedent to pursue a public policy or a judgment that the court feels is fair, given the facts of the case.

judicial bypass

A law that allows a person to obtain the court's permission for an action that normally would require the permission of someone else (*e.g.*, laws that require a minor to obtain parental permission before obtaining an abortion provide that she may instead petition the court for permission).

judicial economy

The efficiency with which a judge uses her judicial resources.

judicial immunity

The freedom of a judge from civil liability for his official acts. A judge is immune from liability for any act committed while exercising his judicial duties.

judicial notice

Decision by a court recognizing the validity of certain facts without the need for proof, thereby relieving one party of the burden of producing evidence to prove these facts (*e.g.*, a court may take judicial notice that Thanksgiving is a legal holiday).

judicial restraint

1. Behavior wherein a judge adheres to judicial precedent, rather than pursuing his or her own ideas of statutory or common law policy. 2. Deciding a case on the narrowest grounds possible without reaching other issues, such as constitutional claims.

judicial review

1. Review of a government action by a court. 2. Appellate court review of trial court decisions.

judicial sale

The sale of property made under the authority or supervision of a court, such as the sale of property ordered by a court to satisfy a tax lien.

judiciary

1. The courts of justice. 2. The branch of government entrusted with judicial power and the administration of the courts in the federal system.

judicis est jus dicere, non dare

(joo-DISH-is est joos DEE-see-ee, non DAR-ay) Lat. It is for a judge to declare the law and not to make it.

jump bail

Situation wherein an accused criminal flees after posting bail.

jura publica anteferenda privatis

(joo-ra POOB-lik-a an-tee-fer-REN-da pree-VA-tis) Lat. Public rights are to be preferred over private ones.

jural

Pertaining or relating to legal matters or jurisprudence.

jurat

Certificate of appropriate person that confirms a writing has been sworn to by the person who signed it; the certificate states when, where, and before whom the writing was sworn.

jure uxoris
(JOO-ree uks-OR-is) Lat. In the right of the wife.

juridical
1. Relating or pertaining to a legal proceeding. 2. That which is done in compliance with the laws of a country or a particular jurisdiction.

juridical day
Day on which court is in session.

juris
Lat. Of law.

jurisdiction
1. Authority by which courts and judicial officers hear and determine cases. 2. The geographic region over which a court's power to hear and determine cases extends.

jurisdictional amount
The total monetary value of the subject matter in litigation (amount in controversy) required to determine the court in which the case may be heard.

juris doctor (J.D.)
Doctor of laws. Basic professional degree in legal education.

juris ignorantia est cum jus nostrum ignoramus
(JOO-ris ig-nor-RAN-tee-a est kum joos NOS-trum ig-nor-RAM-us) Lat. It is ignorance of the law when we do not know our own legal rights.

jurisprude
A person learned in the law, especially one who makes an ostentatious display of legal knowledge.

jurisprudence
1. The science or philosophy of law. 2. A system or body of laws, such as case law.

jurist
1. Judge. 2. A legal scholar. 3. A person proficient and accomplished in law.

juror
Member of a jury; one who serves on a jury. *See* jury.

jury
A group of persons chosen from the eligible public that are convened and sworn at a trial to determine the facts in dispute.

jury box

The area in a courtroom where the jury sits during a trial.

jury list

1. Roster of jurors selected to hear a case. 2. Roster of prospective jurors summoned to attend court for purposes of jury selection.

jury nullification

A jury's deliberate refusal to follow the court's instructions in order to reach a result preferred by the jurors.

jury trial

A trial of a cause or matter before a jury. The Sixth Amendment to the U.S. Constitution guarantees this right to defendants in all criminal prosecutions.

jury wheel

Device that stores and randomly selects the names of prospective jurors.

jus

(joos) Lat. 1. Law; a legal system. 2. A right; a recognized privilege.

jus accrescendi

(joos ak-kres-SEN-dee) Lat. Right of survivorship. This right vests in the remaining joint tenants upon the death of one tenant.

jus sanguinis

(joos san-GWIN-is) Lat. Right of the blood. Rule that determines citizenship based on the citizenship of a person's parents.

jus soli

(joos SOE-lee) Lat. Right of the soil. Rule that determines citizenship according to a person's place of birth. Codified in U.S. law by the Fourteenth Amendment to the Constitution.

just

Legally proper; lawful; that which conforms to the law.

just cause

Fair and adequate cause; reasonable cause; legitimate reasons.

just compensation

Consideration that adequately indemnifies a person whose property has been taken for public use through the government's power of eminent domain.

jus tertii
(joos TAIR-tee) Lat. The right of a third person.

justice
1. Title given to judges, particularly those that sit on the United States and State Supreme Courts. 2. A standard of conduct that requires persons to fulfill their social, legal, and moral obligations to society. 3. To do that which is right or equitable. 4. Proper administration of laws.

justice of the peace
A judicial officer of lesser rank having jurisdiction as set forth by statute over minor civil matters and petty criminal offenses.

justiciable
Matter suitable for review by a court.

justifiable homicide
The killing of a person which the law sanctions or permits (*e.g.*, the killing of a person in self-defense is permitted under the law).

justification
1. Rationale. 2. Lawful excuse or reason offered for a person's conduct.

juvenile court
A court having jurisdiction over minors, especially juvenile delinquents. *See* juvenile delinquent. An adversarial system is avoided in favor of a paternal concern for the minor's well-being.

juvenile delinquent
Minor who has committed an offense punishable by criminal penalties but who is under the age, set by statute, for criminal responsibility.

kangaroo court

Spurious legal proceeding; proceeding where a person's rights and liberties are ignored and the result is a foregone conclusion.

keep

1. To maintain; to conduct; to manage (*e.g.*, to "keep" a house in good repair). 2. To record; to maintain for purposes of documentation, (*e.g.*, to "keep" financial records for a business).

key employee life insurance

Insurance that covers an employee or person essential or important to the ongoing success of the business. The insured person's employer is the beneficiary of the policy.

key numbers

Numbering system used in legal research in which each legal topic is assigned a number. The system is used by legal digest publications such as WESTLAW to categorize large bodies of legal information.

kickback

1. A payment back of a portion of the purchase price of a property by the seller to the buyer to bring about the purchase or future purchases. 2. A bribe, especially a bribe given or offered to a governmental official in exchange for a favorable contract with that unit of government.

kidnapping

To unlawfully seize and detain a person by force against his will whereby the person is taken away from the place where he was found.

kin, kindred

Relationship by blood or consanguinity.

King's (Queen's) Bench

The highest English common law court that hears both civil and criminal actions, so called because the King or Queen formerly sat there in person.

kiting
The practice of writing checks against an account where the funds are insufficient to cover them, in the hope that before they are cashed the necessary hinds will be deposited in the account.

kleptomania
An obsessive impulse to steal.

knockoff
Unauthorized, usually inferior, copy of an item.

knowingly
Consciously; with knowledge; scienter. *See* scienter.

knowledge
1. Comprehension of the truth; understanding of facts; perception of the truth. 2. Learning acquired by education.

labor
Work; to provide a service or perform a job.

labor dispute
Expression that covers any controversy concerning the terms of employment, such as wages, fringe benefits, duration of employment or conditions in the work place; more specifically, any dispute concerning an association of persons that negotiates or seeks to arrange the terms of employment with an employer.

labor organization
1. A group of workers formed for the purpose of securing favorable employment terms and conditions from employers. 2. Any organization of any kind, or any agency or employee representation committee or plan in which employees participate and which exists for the purpose, in whole or in part, of dealing with employers concerning grievances, labor disputes, wages, rates of pay, hours of employment, or conditions of work. 29 U.S.C. § 152(5).

labor union
An alliance or association of workers formed to bargain and negotiate with employers regarding the terms and conditions of employment.

laches
(LA-chess or LA-chez) An equitable defense doctrine which prevents enforcement of a claim or right which, because of neglect, lapse of time, and other circumstances, has resulted in some change in the condition or relationship of the property or parties that is prejudicial to the adverse party.

lame duck
An elected official who has lost an election but continues to serve until her successor takes office.

land
Generally, any ground, soil, or earth, including rock, waters, trees, and wetlands. More specif-

ically, land refers to real property, real estate, or any estate or interest that a person may own in land.

landlord
The person who owns real property, and leases it to a tenant. A landlord is often referred to as a lessor.

Landrum-Griffin Act
Federal statute enacted for purposes of curbing union corruption and restraining undemocratic management of internal union affairs as well as eliminating some types of secondary boycotts.

land trust
Property ownership device in which the title to real property is vested in a trustee while another agreement between the trustee and the beneficiaries allows the beneficiaries to direct the trustee and manage and receive income from the trust's property. Also "Illinois Land Trust."

lapse
1. To cease; to end. 2. The termination of a right or privilege through failure to act within a certain time period, or through failure of some contingency (*e.g.*, failure of a bequest due to devisee predeceasing testator).

lapse statutes
State statutes that prevent a legacy or devise from passing intestate or in the residue when the intended recipient dies before the testator. Generally applies only if deceased legatee or devisee is within a certain degree of relationship, usually a child, to the testator and is survived by children.

larceny
The unlawful taking and carrying away of another's personal property with intent to permanently deprive the rightful owner of possession.

larceny by trick
1. Larceny accomplished with the victim's consent which was obtained by misrepresentation. 2. Larceny by fraud or deception.

lascivious
Lewd; lecherous; salacious; indecent; obscene.

last antecedent doctrine

Principle of statutory construction that applies modifying or qualifying phrases only to the words or phrases immediately preceding, and are not to be construed as extending to or including other remote parts of a sentence, unless clearly required by context or by the reading of the entire statute.

last clear chance

Doctrine under which a defendant may be liable for injuries he caused, even though the plaintiff caused himself to be placed in a dangerous situation or was contributorily negligent, if the defendant could have avoided injury to plaintiff by exercising ordinary care.

last resort

A court from which no further appeal is allowed (*e.g.*, the United States Supreme Court).

last will and testament

Legal instrument which determines the disposition of a person's real and personal property upon his death.

latent

Hidden; concealed.

latent ambiguity

Language that appears to be clear, but upon closer examination can be interpreted to have more than one meaning. To determine the correct interpretation of such language, one must often resort to extrinsic evidence.

latent defect

A hidden or concealed flaw, such as a deficiency in a product that cannot be discovered upon casual inspection or examination.

lateral support

The right of a landowner to the natural support of his land by the adjoining land or the soil beneath.

law

A body of rules or standards of conduct promulgated or established by some authority (*e.g.*, those standards of conduct adopted by the legislative authority of a government).

lawful

That permitted or authorized by the law.

law merchant

The general body of commercial practices and customs which over time have become an established part of the law, unless displaced or modified by statute, and which relate principally to transactions involving those engaged in trade or commerce.

law of the case

Doctrine whereby courts will refuse to reconsider those matters of law in a proceeding that have been previously settled in a prior appeal, assuming that the facts in the case have not changed. *See* stare decisis, res judicata, collateral estoppel.

law of the land

Those basic principles of justice that constitute due process of law which cannot be abolished or significantly restricted; more specifically, the law as developed by the courts or statute in compliance with those principles.

Law of the Sea Treaty

United Nations Convention on the Law of the Sea. International treaty that defines the rights and responsibilities of nations in their use of the oceans. The United States has not ratified this treaty.

lawsuit

An action between two or more persons instituted in a civil court; an action or proceeding in a civil court.

lawyer

An attorney; a person licensed by an appropriate authority to practice law; a person trained and educated in the law.

layman

1. A person not a member of a religious or ecclesiastical order. 2. A person who is not a member of a particular profession (*e.g.*, one who is not a lawyer).

lay witness

A witness who lacks expert knowledge about the matters on which he or she gives testimony. Such witnesses cannot render expert opinions while testifying, but they may render opinions or inferences which are rationally based on their perceptions, and help to provide a clear understanding of the testimony or the determination of a fact at issue.

leading case
Decision which because of its legal analysis or scholarship, or the notoriety of the facts in dispute, is viewed as having settled or resolved the law on a particular subject, and as a consequence is relied on by courts.

leading question
Query which suggests to a witness the answer that is desired by the inquiring party or directs a witness towards the desired response. At trial, leading questions are permitted on cross-examination and when a hostile witness or an adverse party is being questioned.

learned intermediary doctrine
Principle of products liability law that holds that a warning to a prescribing physician of the harmful effects of a medicine is sufficient to warn the patient who ultimately uses the medicine.

lease
Agreement between two parties whereby one party, the lessor, yields his right of possession and use of some real or personal property for a specified period of time to a lessee in return for consideration. Leases of personal property in most states are governed by U.C.C. Article 2A.

leasehold
A lessee's estate or interest in real property that is created by a lease.

lease purchase agreement
An agreement for the lease of property that provides that the lessee is the owner of the property upon making the final payment.

leave and license
A defense to an action of trespass that asserts the consent of the plaintiff to the trespass alleged.

leave of court
Permission of court to take some action which, without such permission, would not be allowable.

legacy
A bequest; a disposition or distribution of personal property by will.

legal
1. That which is lawful; permitted by the law; established or

mandated by the law. 2. Relating or pertaining to the law.

legal aid
Nationwide service providing legal assistance to persons who cannot afford private legal counsel.

legal capacity to sue
The legal ability to bring a lawsuit before a court. This ability can be limited, given a plaintiff's age or soundness of mind.

legal cause
See proximate cause.

legal detriment
1. Giving up something one is privileged to retain, refraining from doing something that one is privileged to do, or doing something that one is privileged to refrain from doing. 2. Changing legal position or assuming duties or liabilities that have not been imposed. In contracts law, such detriment constitutes consideration.

legal duty
An obligation which the law or a contract requires to be done.

legal ethics
Customs and norms among members of the legal profession that relate to their professional and moral responsibilities to their profession, toward one another, to their clients and toward the courts.

legal fiction
A fact or situation assumed or created by a court so it can settle a matter before it (*e.g.*, the fiction that an unsigned agreement was properly signed so a court could enforce a contract).

legal heirs
Persons to whom law would give decedent's property if decedent had died intestate.

legalize
To make lawful.

legal representative
A person who oversees and represents the legal affairs and interests of another (*e.g.*, a court appointed guardian of a minor).

Legal Services Corporation
An entity established to provide financial support to the needy for legal assistance in noncriminal proceedings. The Legal Services

Corporation was established by the Legal Services Corporation Act of 1974, 42 U.S.C. § 2996b(a).

legal tender
1. Lawful currency that may be used for the satisfaction of any and all debts or claims. All coins and currencies of the United States, regardless of when issued, may be used to settle all debts or claims, public and private. 2. The act of making or offering to make payment on a debt or claim.

legatee
The person to whom a legacy or bequest in a will is given.

legation
A diplomatic mission that ranks below an embassy. Historically, legations were maintained in countries deemed less significant. The term has fallen into disuse.

leges posteriores priores contrarias abrogant
(LAY-gess pos-tair-ee-OR-ays pry-OR-rays kon-TRAIR-ee-as AB-ro-gant) Lat. Later laws abrogate prior laws that are in-

consistent with them. Provisions of later laws take precedence over provisions of earlier laws that conflict with their terms.

legislation
1. Laws made by a legislative body; regulations adopted by a lawmaking body. 2. The act of making or enacting laws.

legislator
A member of a lawmaking body; a person who enacts laws; a representative.

legitimate
1. That which is lawful, proper; acceptable. 2. A child born in wedlock, in contrast to a child born outside a marriage. 3. (v.) To make lawful (*e.g.*, to make an illegal alien a legal alien).

Legum Doctor (LLD)
Lat. Doctor of Laws; legal degree that is customarily awarded as an honorary degree.

lemon law
A law that requires a manufacturer or seller to repair or replace defective goods, or to refund the purchase price of the goods.

lend
To allow the use of an object for a fixed or indefinite period of time on the condition that it or something equivalent to it be returned at a time established by the parties or by law.

lesion
1. Injury; wound; diseased tissue. 2. An injury suffered by a party to an agreement where he does not receive what he is entitled to receive for what he contributes to the contract.

lessee
One who rents property; one who holds an estate in real or personal property by virtue of a lease agreement; a tenant.

lesser included offense
1. A crime that is necessarily proven by proof of a greater or more serious crime. 2. A crime that has many elements of a greater crime and which does not have any element not included in the greater crime (*e.g.*, the crime of larceny is necessarily proven by proof of the crime of robbery).

lessor
One who rents property to another; one who grants to another an estate in real or personal property for a specified duration under terms of a lease agreement; landlord.

let
1. Real property: To lease or rent property to another. 2. Contracts: To award a contract to one of several parties that have entered a bid for the contract. 3. Judicial order: It is hereby ordered (*e.g.* "Let the property be sold at public sale.").

letter
1. A communication in writing from one party to another; a written communication that is usually delivered via the postal system. 2. A written instrument that grants some authority, privilege or right.

letter of credit
A written instrument whereby one party requests that another party advance a certain sum of money or give credit to a third party, and in return guarantees repayment of the money advanced.

letter of intent

A written, preliminary understanding between parties. Such a letter constitutes not a contract or a binding agreement, but rather is a tentative expression of intentions.

letter of safe conduct

Written instrument that guarantees a person or a vessel protection and unhindered movement in a war zone, thereby preventing the person or the vessel from being seized.

letter ruling

A written statement issued to a taxpayer by the office of the Assistant Tax Commissioner (of the I.R.S.) which includes interpretations of tax laws as applied to a specific set of facts.

letters of administration

Document issued by a probate court appointing an administrator for an intestate's estate or for the estate of a testator when there is no executor.

letters testamentary

The formal document of authority and appointment issued by a court allowing a person to fulfill her duties as executor or personal representative of an estate.

leverage

Using debt to finance a large investment, to increase one's rate of return. Such a transaction usually involves a small downpayment of one's own funds.

leveraged buyout

The purchase of a business financed by loans secured by the business's assets.

levy

1. To impose; assess; tax; collect.
2. A seizure (*e.g.*, to satisfy a debt, money is raised by use of legal proceedings through seizure and sale of property).

lewd

Indecent; obscene; lascivious.

lex

Lat. A collection, system, or body of laws.

lex communis

(lex kom-MOON-nis) Lat. The common law.

lex domicilii

(lex dom-i-SILL-ee) Lat. The law of the domicile. The law of a given jurisdiction.

lex est dictamen rationis

(lex est dik_TA-men ras-see-OWN-is) Lat. Law is the dictate of reason. The common law will judge according to the laws of nature and the public welfare.

lex fori

(lex FOR-ee *or* FOR-eye) Lat. The law of the forum or court. The law of the jurisdiction where an action is brought and the law which governs the remedies that are allowed in the jurisdiction.

LEXIS

A proprietary computerized legal research service which allows a user access to a large database of legal information.

lex loci

(lex LO-key) Lat. The law of the place. The substantive rights of parties to an action are governed by the law of the place.

lex loci contractus

(lex LO-key kon-TRAK-tus) Lat. The law of the place that governs a contract. The proper law appli-cable in determining the rights and liabilities of parties to a contract.

lex loci delictus

(lex LO-key de-LIK-tus) Lat. The law of the place where the offense or wrong took place.

lex neminem cogit ad vana seu inutilia peragenda

(lex NEM-i-nem KO-jit ad VA-na soo in-oo-TIL-ee-a pair-a-JEN-da) Lat. The law will not compel one to do useless things.

lex non scripta

(lex non SKRIP-ta) Lat. The unwritten, or common law. The common law which includes customs and usages, and particu-lar local laws.

lex scripta

(lex SKRIP-ta) Lat. Written law. Law deriving its power from statute or legislative enactment.

lex semper dabit remedium

(lex SEM-per DAB-it re-MED-ee-um) Lat. Law always provides a remedy.

lex terrae

(lex TAIR-eye) Lat. Law of the land.

liability

1. Any type of obligation or debt, fixed or contingent. 2. An indebtedness owed to another party; a duty to pay another monies on funds owed. 3. An obligation or mandate to do or refrain from doing something. 4. Responsibility.

liable

1. Responsible. 2. To be obligated or accountable. 3. To be bound by law.

libel

Any false and malicious written publication printed for the purpose of defaming another's character or reputation; any written defamation of character, not privileged, which is false and malicious and which "tends to expose a person to public scorn, hatred, contempt or ridicule." *Bowie v. Evening News,* 148 Md. 569, 574 (1925). The appropriate libel standard for a public person is different than one for a private person. *See New York Times Co. v. Sullivan,* 376 U.S. 254 (1964).

libel per quod

Libel that is not actionable on its face but when considered in connection with relevant extrinsic circumstances, the meaning is defamatory.

libel per se

Words that are defamatory on their face. No special damages need be shown as the law will presume damages.

liberty

1. Freedom; lack of restraint; freedom from arbitrary control. 2. The right to exercise one's free will, except as limited by law.

license

1. (n.) A right granted to a person to do something which he otherwise could not legally do (*e.g.,* the right to operate a motor vehicle on public streets, as granted by a state). 2. (v.) To grant permission to do that which would be illegal if permission was not granted; to authorize conduct that would otherwise be improper.

licensee

1. One who enters on another's land with the possessor's permission, express or implied, for her own purpose (*e.g.,* social guest).

2. The person who receives or acquires a license.

license tax

Government charge or fee imposed for the issuance of a license to engage in a particular regulated activity.

licensor

The person who grants or bestows a license.

licentiousness

Lasciviousness, lewdness; the state of acting or functioning without moral or legal restraints.

lie detector test

See polygraph.

lien

1. A claim on another's property asserted in order to secure payment upon a debt. 2. To assert an interest in another's property until an indebtedness is discharged.

lien jurisdiction

Jurisdiction in which the title to a mortgaged property remains with the mortgagor. The mortgagee has a security interest (lien) in the property until the debt is fully paid.

lieu

Place; situation; locale. "In lieu of" means in place of.

life annuity

A fixed sum of money paid yearly during one's life or the life of another.

life estate

An ownership interest in property granted to a person for as long as he or another person lives; upon the end of the measuring life, the land will either revert to the grantor of the life estate or will go to a person holding a remainder interest in the property.

life expectancy

A person's anticipated life span, in years, given their age, gender, and various statistical factors. The figures are usually determined by actuaries.

life tenant

A person granted a life estate; a person who has an ownership interest in property for as long as she lives.

LIFO

Abbreviation for "last in, first out," an accounting method used in valuing inventories. This method assumes that the last goods bought are the first ones sold.

Lily Ledbetter Fair Pay Act
Federal law that provides that the statute of limitations for employment discrimination lawsuits based on unequal pay resets with each paycheck that is unequal. Named for the plaintiff in *Ledbetter v. Goodyear Tire & Rubber Co.,* 550 U.S. 618 (2007).

limitation
Restriction; restraint; qualification; such as to place a limitation on the amount of unemployment benefits any one person may receive.

limited jurisdiction
Jurisdiction of courts whose powers are limited to hearing certain specialized types of cases (*e.g.*, a small claims court or a probate court).

limited liability
1. The limits placed on the amount of money an investor can lose as a result of a corporation's financial losses or a lawsuit against the corporation. 2. The limits set by state and federal statute on liability for certain types of damages, or the time limit in which an action can be brought.

limited liability company (L.L.C.)
A company organized according to statutes that provide for limited liability and governance by members or directors.

limited liability partnership (L.L.P.)
A partnership in which partners are not personally liable for the actions of other partners, or of partnership employees not under his personal control.

limited partnership
A business venture in which one group of persons (called the general partners) with unlimited liability manages the venture, while another group (called the limited partners) only contributes capital and shares in profits but has no right to participate in the management of the venture.

Lindbergh Act

Federal statute which punishes kidnapping that involves the interstate movement of kidnapping victims, that is, the taking of a victim from one state to another or to a foreign country.

lineal

Direct; unbroken chain; such as being in the direct line of succession from one's ancestor (*e.g.*, lineal descent).

line of credit

The maximum amount of credit that a financial institution is willing to extend to a business or a person at any one time (*e.g.*, if a bank has lent a business the full amount of its "line of credit" it will not make any more loans to the business until some of the debt is paid off, and then only in amounts that will not exceed the business's line of credit).

lineup

A police procedure in which potential suspects with similar physical characteristics are lined up before a witness or victim, so he or she may identify the perpetrator of the crime.

liquidate

1. To resolve; to settle; to discharge; such as to discharge a debt or obligation. 2. To convert assets or property to cash. 3. To close down the affairs of a business; to settle all liabilities and obligations of an entity; to wind up the affairs of a business.

liquidated

Settled; fixed; resolved; specified.

liquidated amount

The amount readily determined by a computation that is based on the terms of the obligation.

liquidated damages

1. An amount of money specified in a contract to compensate a party for injuries suffered because of a breach of contract by the other party to the agreement. 2. The amount agreed to in advance of a breach of contract to serve as compensation for any injury or damage suffered, thereby precluding any liability in excess of the amount stipulated in the contract.

liquidation

1. The act of settling or resolving an obligation (*e.g.*, the settling of a debt). 2. The act of converting assets and property to cash. 3. The procedure whereby the financial affairs of a company are resolved. The company's liabilities and obligations are paid off and any remaining assets are divided between those persons authorized to receive them. Usually payments are made in the form of cash.

lis pendens

(lis *or* lees PEN-dens) Lat. A suit pending in court. Notice of lis pendens filed with a public records office is said to put the whole world on notice that the status of the property or matter being litigated is unsettled and therefore one should proceed with caution in entering into agreements concerning said property or matter.

listing

1. An agreement between the owner of real estate and a broker, whereby the broker agrees to secure a buyer for the owner's property. In return, the owner pays the broker a commission or predetermined fee. 2. In securities law, a contract between a firm and stock exchange regarding the trading of the firm's securities on the stock exchange.

litigant

A person involved in a lawsuit; a party to a legal proceeding.

litigation

1. Legal dispute or controversy; lawsuit. 2. Any civil action, as opposed to criminal proceeding, before a court.

litigious

1. Prone to legal dispute; inclined to file a lawsuit or initiate legal proceedings about a matter in dispute. 2. The subject of a lawsuit.

littoral rights

1. Rights and privileges that pertain to the use and enjoyment of coastal property. 2. Rights that pertain to property that abuts or borders on an ocean or a lake.

livery

1. The act of conveying legal possession of property to a party. 2. Uniform or distinctive dress of a particular profession or occupa-

tion (*e.g.*, the uniform a doorman wears). 3. The business of hiring or leasing out horses and carriages.

livery of seisin

English common law ceremony whereby real property is transferred from grantor to grantee.

living trust

A trust whose provisions are in effect during the lifetime of the person who established the trust. Also called an "inter vivos trust."

living will

Advanced health care directive. Written instructions that set out in advance a person's wishes for her medical care in anticipation of the time she is no longer able to make her wishes known.

L.J.

Abbreviation for "law judge."

loan

1. The lending of funds, under an express or implied agreement, whereby the party receiving the funds will repay the sum lent plus interest on the sum at some future date. 2. A debt that the debtor agrees is to be repaid. 3. To give or lend personal prop-

erty for temporary use by another party. Frequently, no charge is involved for the temporary use of the property.

loansharking

The practice of loaning money at usurious interest rates, often accompanied by the threat of violence as a penalty for non-payment. Such action constitutes extortion.

lobbying

1. The act of seeking to sway, influence, or manipulate the beliefs and opinions of legislators. 2. Any attempt to influence the status of proposed or existing legislation.

lobbyist

A person who attempts to influence the members of a legislative body or the status of any legislation pending before that body.

lockdown

The temporary confinement of inmates to their cells, in order to ensure the security of the entire correctional institution in anticipation of or in response to a riot, escape, or some other emergency.

lockout

The practice used by an employer in a labor dispute whereby workers are denied an opportunity to work or even enter the place of work so as to give the employer a stronger bargaining position.

locus

Place; the site where some event has taken or will take place.

locus contractus

(LO-kuss kon-TRAK-tuss) Lat. The place of a contract. The place where a contract is made or entered into.

locus delicti

(LO-kuss de-LIK-tee *or* de-LIK-tie) Lat. The place where an offense takes place. The scene or site of a crime.

locus sigilli

(LO-kuss sig-ILL-ee) Lat. The place in a written instrument where a seal is affixed.

logrolling

1. The practice of legislators combining into one large bill several smaller bills which are supported only by minority legislative factions. With the subsequent support of each of the minorities combined, the large bill passes. 2. The practice of legislators agreeing to vote on each other's bills, regardless of the bills' merits.

loiter

To be dilatory; to stand idle; to loaf; to meander; to wander about aimlessly. Most jurisdictions prohibit a person from loitering in public areas (*e.g.*, it is usually illegal to loiter on the grounds of a school).

Lone Pine order

A case management order entered by a court, usually without statutory authorization, that requires plaintiffs to provide evidence supporting a prima facie case before conducting discovery. *Lore v. Lone Pine Corp.*, 1986 WL 637507 (N.J. Super. Ct. 1986).

long-arm statutes

State legislative acts which allow local courts to obtain jurisdiction over nonresident defendants to a lawsuit where the cause of action is local in origin or has an effect in the state (*e.g.*, a nonresident corporation could be a party to a lawsuit in a jurisdiction other than its own if its goods injured residents of that jurisdiction).

long position

The ownership of a stock or security, wherein the owner holds in anticipation of a rise in the market.

Longshore and Harbor Workers' Compensation Act

Federal workers' compensation law that covers maritime employees other than sailors. Covered employees include longshoremen and stevedores.

lookout

1. The driver of a motor vehicle's ordinary watchfulness in the course of operating the vehicle, in order to avoid jeopardizing his or someone else's safety. 2. A person who participates in a criminal offense by watching at a distance to avoid detection of the crime by authorities or witnesses.

lord

In England's feudal era, the official title of a landowner who granted an estate in land to a tenant.

Lord Campbell's Act

An act existing in most states that allows wrongful death actions.

loss

Injury; forfeiture; deprivation; damage; deficiency. In its most common usage it means any reduction in value of an asset or a group of assets.

lost property

Property with which the owner has involuntarily parted through neglect, carelessness, or inadvertence. Mislaid property, by contrast, has been intentionally placed somewhere and then forgotten by the owner.

lottery

A game of chance in which individuals pay money as consideration in exchange for the opportunity to win a prize in a random drawing.

lower of cost or market

An inventory valuation method, where the choice is to use the lower of the purchase price of the item or the item's current market value.

lucid interval
Temporary period of sanity; that period of time in which a normally insane or mentally unbalanced person is in control of her faculties and can think rationally.

lump-sum settlement
A onetime payment of funds to discharge or settle a liability or an obligation. The payment covers the entire amount of any sum due.

lying in wait
Concealing or hiding for the purpose of committing a crime when the opportunity presents itself. In some jurisdictions, lying in wait contributes to a finding of premeditation.

lynch law
1. Action or conduct done without sanction or approval of law.
2. The actions of a mob that seek to punish an alleged wrongdoer without benefit of a trial, protection of the accused's civil rights, and without legal authority.
3. Vigilante justice.

machination

A crafty scheme contrived for the accomplishment of an evil purpose.

magistrate

A public officer with specific, delegated executive or judicial powers; usually a local judicial officer who conducts preliminary hearings or has limited powers to try minor criminal or civil offenses. In the federal court system, an official appointed by the judges of a district to assist with pre-trial matters, preliminary criminal appearances and motions, and other administrative duties.

Magna Charta

Lat. Great Charter. Document of English liberties granted to the barons by King John in 1215 at Runnymede, which formed the basis of many English and American constitutional liberties, including limits on taxation, the right to own property, the right to a jury trial, and the proper administration of justice. Also spelled "Magna Carta."

Magnuson-Moss Warranty Act

Federal statute requiring warranties for consumer products to disclose the terms of the warranty in fully conspicuous, simple, and easily understandable language. 15 U.S.C. § 2301 *et seq. See* lemon law.

mail box rule

Common law contracts doctrine providing that acceptance of an offer is effective when it is deposited in mail, if it is properly addressed and unless another acceptance method is otherwise agreed to.

maiming

The wrongful and intentional act which results in the loss of a limb or bodily organ of the person attacked, which is disfiguring or disabling. *See* mayhem, mutilation.

maintain
1. To continue, to uphold, to sustain. 2. To keep in its existing state or condition.

maintenance
1. Financial or other support to a spouse or children during marital separation or after a divorce, usually under court order. 2. Meddling in a legal suit by a nonparty by providing financial or other support to either party.

maintenance and cure
In maritime law, compensation paid to an injured or sick sailor. "Maintenance" refers to an allowance for onshore living expenses during the sailor's recuperation. "Cure" refers to medical expenses.

majority
1. Full age; the age when a person attains full citizenship, the right to vote, power to make a will, and the right to manage personal affairs. 2. In elections, any number greater than half the total.

majority rule
A rule or interpretation of a law followed by more than half of the courts that have considered the issue.

major life activity
An activity that an average person can perform with little or no physical effort. Examples given in the Americans with Disabilities Act include caring for oneself, performing manual tasks, seeing, hearing, eating, sleeping, walking, standing, lifting, bending, speaking, breathing, learning, reading, concentrating, thinking, communicating, and working.

maker
One who signs and becomes responsible for a promissory note (*e.g.*, the maker of a check).

mala fides
(MAL-la fieds) Lat. Bad faith, the opposite of bona fides.

mala in se
Lat. Wrongs in themselves. *See* malum in se.

malfeasance
Wrongful and unlawful conduct, especially conduct by public officials which interferes with their public duties. *Contrast* misfeasance, nonfeasance.

malfunction theory
In products liability law, a principal that allows a plaintiff to recover if she was injured by a product that malfunctioned when being used properly. Under this theory, the plaintiff does not have to show that the product was defective.

malice
Mental disposition to commit a wrongful act or injury without legal justification. "Express malice" is deliberate and actual ill will against a person. "Implied malice" is reckless disregard of the consequences of wrongful acts.

malice aforethought
1. Mental determination to commit a wrongful act or injury without legal justification, before committing the act; usually part of the charge of murder. 2. At common law, intent to kill, willful, wanton, reckless disregard, intent to cause great bodily harm, intent to commit a felony.

malicious
Having wrongful and wicked intentions without legal justification.

malicious arrest
Wrongful arrest, without grounds to believe the person has committed a crime,

malicious mischief
Destruction of personal property out of ill will against the owner.

malicious prosecution
1. Wrongful prosecution of a criminal action without grounds to believe the person has committed a crime. If the prosecution terminates in favor of the accused defendant, there is a right to recover damages. 2. Wrongfully instituting a civil action without probable cause and for motives other than adjudication of a legal claim.

malinger
To pretend sickness or insanity in order to avoid labor or military duty, or for financial gain.

malpractice
Misconduct of a doctor, attorney, accountant or other professional in the performance of professional services, through negligence or unreasonable lack of skill, prudence, or diligence.

malum in se

(MAL-um in say) Lat. A wrong in itself. An inherently evil or morally wrong act, whether prohibited by law or not (*e.g.*, murder).

malum prohibitum

(MAL-um pro-HIB-it-tum) Lat. A prohibited wrong. An act or offense which is not inherently immoral, but is prohibited by law (*e.g.*, speeding).

manager

A person who controls the business affairs of another or of a corporation.

mandamus

(man-DAY-mus) Lat. We command. A writ or order, issued by courts only in extreme necessity, to a public official or corporation, commanding the performance of some public duty required by statute. Is often used in response to judicial abuse.

mandate

1. Order of a court directing some specific action or enforcement of a judgment. 2. Bailment of property, when the bailee

agrees to do some act without pay.

mandatory

Having an obligation or command which must be obeyed.

mandatory injunction

Order of a court which compels the defendant to perform a particular act or restrain from performing an act.

mandatum

The delivery of goods, wherein the person to whom goods are delivered performs some service with regard to the goods, without recompense.

manifest

1. Document which indicates the quantity, description, origin, and destination of a ship's entire cargo, shown to United States Customs officials. 2. That which is obvious to the understanding, evident to the senses, especially to sight.

manipulation

The practice of intentionally misleading investors by buying and selling a security to affect its price, or to artificially create the impression of activity surrounding a security. Such manipulation is barred by the Securities Exchange Act of 1934. 15 U.S.C. § 78.

Mann Act

Federal statute prohibiting transportation in interstate or foreign commerce of any person for prostitution or any immoral purpose. 18 U.S.C. §§ 2421–2423.

manslaughter

Negligent or unlawful killing of a person without malice, premeditation, or deliberation. "Voluntary manslaughter" is an unlawful killing without malice, upon sudden provocation in the heat of passion. "Involuntary manslaughter" is a negligent killing with no intention to take life or to commit an unlawful act.

margin

1. Method of stock purchasing where the stockbroker purchases on the customer's account and requires only a fraction of the purchase price (or margin) to be paid by the customer, as security against losses due to price fluctuations. 2. The edge or boundary, particularly of property.

marine insurance

Insurance against losses to ships, freight, and cargo in navigation during a certain period or voyage.

marital

1. Relating to marriage. 2. The reciprocal rights and duties of spouses.

marital communications privilege

The privilege of a spouse not to disclose the content of private communications within his or her marriage. This privilege is recognized in a majority of jurisdictions, and is subject to limitations.

marital deduction

A tax deduction wherein a married person may deduct the value of the property that has been transferred to his or her spouse, or from one spouse to another. This deduction takes the form of an estate or gift tax deduction. I.R.C. §§ 2056, 2523.

maritime contract

A contract having anything to do with navigation (*e.g.*, marine insurance, seaman's wages).

maritime law

Law of the sea, concerning commerce and navigation, ships, seamen, contracts made at sea, and salvage.

marketable title

Title to property which is free from reasonable objections from a reasonably well-informed purchaser exercising ordinary business prudence. Courts may force a purchaser, who has contracted to purchase the property, to accept a marketable title, even if it is not perfect.

market price

The price of an object in an open market; a price determined by the demand for an object in relation to its supply in an open market.

market value

The price of property or goods sold in the ordinary public market of willing buyers and willing sellers.

marriage

1. Relationship established by law between two people united for life to perform the duties of spouses. 2. The ceremony creating the relationship.

marshal

1. Federal officer responsible for executing the process of the United States courts (*e.g.*, delivering summons and subpoenas). 2. In some states, a local police officer similar to a sheriff.

marshaling

Process whereby the court arranges, ranks, and disposes of competing claims to obtain the largest amount of satisfaction for all claimants. If there are two competing claims against one fund, and one of the claimants has a claim against another fund, that claimant may be ordered by the court to resort to his exclusive claim, so as to obtain the largest amount of satisfaction for both claimants (*e.g.*, marshaling of assets, marshaling of liens).

martial law

Temporary control over civilians by a military commander, usually in wartime and possible only in extreme emergency and utter necessity, during which all civil law and authority is suspended.

Mary Carter agreement

A secret settlement agreement in a multiparty civil action in which one defendant settles with the plaintiff, but continues to participate in the case as a party. The plaintiff shares a portion of any verdict or award with the settling defendant. *Booth v. Mary Carter Paint Co.*, 202 So. 2d 8 (Fla. Dist. Ct. App. 1967)

Massachusetts trust

A form of business organization wherein property is conveyed to trustees, to be held and managed for the benefit of persons who hold transferable certificates issued by the trustees. Such an organization is common among real estate investment trusts.

master

1. One who employs another to perform services with the right to control the performance of those services. 2. "Special master": Officer appointed by courts to assist the court in taking testimony, computing damages, or performing a sale.

master and servant

The relationship wherein one person employs another to do certain work, and exercises extensive control over the work, including the control to dismiss the worker; an employer-employee relationship.

master plan

A long-term plan of any organization or government agency; often utilized for municipal land use planning.

material

Important, necessary, relevant to the matter at hand.

material alteration

Any change in the terms of a written instrument which gives it a legal meaning or effect that is different from its original state.

material breach

A breach which affords the non-breaching party remedies of damages and rescission. It also discharges all of the non-breaching party's remaining duties to perform.

material fact

A fact, the consideration of which would substantially determine the ultimate decision (*e.g.*, whether to make a contract, to approve a loan, or to arrive at a verdict in a trial).

material issue
Any issue that is necessary, relevant, or of substantial legal consequence.

material witness
A trial witness whose testimony tends to prove or disprove a significant issue being considered.

maternal
That which belongs to or comes from the mother; pertaining to the mother.

matricide
1. The killing of one's mother.
2. One who has killed his or her own mother.

matrimonial action
Any action for annulment, dissolution, separation or termination of a marriage through divorce.

matter
The set of facts which constitute the basis for a claim or defense.

matter of fact
A purely factual dispute for the consideration of the jury or fact finder.

matter of law
1. A legal dispute for the judge's consideration of various statutes and legal rules. 2. The legal consequences of a particular act.

matter of record
Any fact which may be proved by reference to court records.

maturity
1. The time a legal obligation reaches full development. 2. In commercial law, the time a bill or note becomes payable.

maxim
General principle of law, traditionally and universally accepted, often used to support general legal conclusions (*e.g.*, "no one is above the law").

mayhem
The unlawful and malicious deprivation of a limb or bodily organ of another which is disfiguring or disabling. *See* maiming.

mayor

Chief executive officer of a city, town, or municipality, whose powers are defined by state law or municipal charter.

McNabb-Mallory Rule

Rule which states that if a prisoner is not promptly arraigned, any confessions or incriminating statements made by the prisoner between the time of his detention and his arraignment are inadmissible.

measure of damages

Test for determining compensation for losses occurring in a tort or breach of contract.

mechanic's lien

A claim against buildings and real property, created by statute, to secure payment to those who provide labor and materials in constructing, repairing, or making other improvements to the building or property. Also applies to automobiles and other goods as well as to structures.

mediate data

For purposes of collateral estoppel, the body of information or set of facts from which one may infer ultimate facts.

mediately

Indirectly; involving an independent or intervening agent.

mediation

1. Intervention. 2. Settlement of disputes by an objective third person who attempts to work a compromise.

Medicaid

A joint federal-state program to provide health care to those unable to afford medical services.

medical jurisprudence

1. Principles of medicine used to determine scientific or medical evidence in legal cases (*e.g.*, the cause of death, the extent of disability, the presence of poisons). 2. Forensic medicine.

Medicare

A federal program that provides medical care to the elderly.

meeting

A gathering of interested persons for the discussion and resolution of matters of mutual concern (*e.g.*, shareholders' meeting).

meeting of creditors
In bankruptcy, the first meeting of creditors at which the debtor is examined; claims may be allowed or disallowed, and a trustee is appointed. 11 U.S.C. § 341.

meeting of minds
1. In contract law, a rule of decision limiting the effect of the contract to the stated purposes and intentions of both parties. 2. Mutually agreed upon; mutual assent.

Megan's law
A law that requires persons convicted of sexual offenses to register their addresses with law enforcement when they are released from prison.

member corporation
A corporate entity engaged in the trading of securities, at least one principal of which belongs to a securities exchange (*e.g.*, the New York Stock Exchange).

member firm
A securities brokerage firm, at least one principal of which belongs to a securities exchange (*e.g.*, the New York Stock Exchange).

memorandum
1. An informal note or record of some agreement or transaction. In a law office, an informal report of the legal issues in a pending case. 2. A written argument to a court without the formal style of a brief, often requested by the judge during a trial.

memorandum opinion
A short, unanimous appellate court opinion issued when a decision follows a well-established legal principle, or when there is no point of law discussed.

mensa et thoro
(MEN-sa et THO-row) Lat. From bed and board. A partial divorce or separation, where the husband and wife will no longer live together, but the marital relation is not dissolved.

mens rea
(menz RAY-a) Lat. A guilty mind. Criminal intent; the mental state of a person committing an act which constitutes a crime.

mental anguish
The mental suffering resulting from grief, distress, fright, indignation, or shock connected with a physical injury; sometimes part of the damages in a tort action.

mental cruelty
Action by one spouse towards the other which is so cruel or harmful as to cause mental or physical damage and makes the marriage intolerable.

mental state
Condition of one's mind concerning the ability to do or refrain from doing a particular act.

mercantile
1. Concerning the business of buying and selling merchandise.
2. Trade; commerce.

merchant
1. One whose occupation involves buying goods at wholesale and selling goods at retail.
2. A person who deals in goods of the kind or otherwise by his occupation holds himself out as having knowledge or skill peculiar to the practice or goods involved in the transaction or to whom such knowledge or skill may be attributed by his employment of an agent or broker or other intermediary who by his occupation holds himself out as having such knowledge or skill. U.C.C. § 2–104(1).

merchantable, merchantability
Fit for the ordinary purposes of sale, of good and ordinary quality, and salable at the current, regular market price. "Merchantability" is the state of being merchantable.

mercy killing
An affirmative act causing painless death of a person who allegedly wishes to die because of a terminal or hopeless medical condition; euthanasia.

mere evidence rule
Now-obsolete criminal procedure principle barring authorities from seizing anything other than contraband, instrumentalities, and fruits of the crime for evidence. Evidence which did not fall under these three categories was termed "mere evidence."

merger
1. Joining of two estates or contract rights into one when the

new owner acquires both (*e.g.*, when a bank forecloses a mortgage, it achieves a merger of the mortgage right and the property). 2. In corporations, a consolidation of two or more corporations into one under the same governing organization. 3. At common law, inchoate offenses merged into the substantive offenses committed. In criminal law, lesser included offense merges into major offense upon conviction of both.

merits

Evidence and arguments relating to the substance of a legal claim, rather than the technicalities of jurisdiction, process, waiver, etc.

mesne

(meen *or* MEZ-nee) Lat. The middle. Intermediate. In common law procedure, "mesne process" refers to writs or court orders which come between the original complaint and the judgment.

metes and bounds

The boundary lines of property, including lengths and angles.

middleman

1. Person who brings together the parties to make a contract. 2. One who buys goods from a manufacturer for resale at a higher price. *See* broker.

military jurisdiction

Under the U.S. Constitution, the three types of jurisdiction granted to the military. 1. Military law, authorizing the military to govern the armed forces in both war and peace. 2. Military government, exercised in foreign wars or within the U.S. in times of rebellion or civil war. (The authority of the military government supersedes that of any local government, and is directed by the President.) 3. Martial law, called into action by Congress or temporarily by the President, in times of invasion or insurrection within the U.S., in areas where ordinary law no longer adequately secures public safety and private rights.

military law

Body of law governing members or the military services, distinguished from "martial law." In the United States, military law appeals are heard by the Court of Military Appeals.

minatur innocentibus qui parcit nocentibus

(MIN-a-toor in-no-SEN-ti-bus kwee PAR-sit no-SEN-ti-bus) Lat. He threatens the innocent who spares the guilty.

mineral estate, mineral rights

A property interest in minerals; the right to take minerals or to receive a royalty for minerals taken.

minimum contacts

The principle which refers to the degree of personal contact a defendant must have with a jurisdiction before a court may subject him to its jurisdiction in a civil matter.

minimum wage

The minimum hourly rate of compensation for work, as established by Congress (for businesses engaged in interstate commerce) or by individual states.

minister

1. One who has been ordained in the ministry of an organized religion, and undertakes to perform religious services on a regular basis. 2. One who acts as an agent for an organization or another individual in performing specified orders or duties. 3. Obsolete term for a diplomatic representative who is head of a diplomatic mission, but who ranks below an ambassador.

ministerial

Concerning official, nondiscretionary duties or functions of a government official.

ministerial act

1. Any act performed by an agent of an organization or another person, under the specific instructions of a superior, and without the actor's discretion. 2. A non-discretionary act performed by a government official according to law or regulation.

minitrial

A form of alternate dispute resolution in which the parties agree to present their cases to a neutral third-party. The third-party issues an advisory opinion on the merits, which the parties may use to guide settlement negotiations.

minor

A person who has not attained full age and citizenship.

minor breach

A partial breach; a breach which gives the non-breaching party a claim for damages stemming from the breach but which does not discharge the non-breaching party's remaining duties to perform.

minority

1. The condition of a minor. 2. A number less than half the total, especially in elections. *See* "majority."

minutes

1. In corporations, official notes or records of meetings or transactions. 2. Memorandum or record of courtroom proceedings, authorized by the judge.

***Miranda* warning**

Statement of constitutional rights which must be read by law enforcement officers when a person is arrested or taken into custody. These include the suspect's right to remain silent, that any statement made may be used against him in court, that he has a right to an attorney, and that if he cannot afford an attorney, one will be appointed for him. *See Miranda v. Arizona*, 384 U.S. 436 (1966).

misadventure

An accident (*e.g.*, a homicide by misadventure occurs when a person who is in the process of performing a lawful act unintentionally kills another person). For an action to qualify as misadventure, the action must be performed without criminal carelessness or recklessness.

misappropriation

Wrongful or unauthorized use of property or funds (*e.g.*, using trust funds other than for the beneficiary of the trust).

misbehavior

Wrongful, improper, or unlawful conduct.

miscarriage of justice

Prejudice to the rights of a party at a legal proceeding, contrary to the ends of justice, which requires reversal of the outcome or another trial.

miscegenation
Marriage, cohabitation, or sexual relations between persons of two different races. State anti-miscegenation laws were ruled unconstitutional in *Loving v. Virginia*, 388 U.S. 1 (1967).

misconduct in office
Any willful and unlawful act by a public office holder, done while acting under the color of office.

misdelivery
The delivery of goods to someone other than the person for whom the delivery was specified or authorized.

misdemeanor
A crime punishable by a fine or imprisonment for less than one year. A misdemeanor is less serious than a felony, and will usually not cause the same loss of rights (*e.g.*, voting; firearm ownership) that would be caused by a felony conviction.

misdirection
Error in the legal reasoning of a judge's instructions to the jury.

misfeasance
The improper or wrongful performance of some lawful act, *Contrast* malfeasance, nonfeasance.

misjoinder
The improper joining of parties or claims in one lawsuit.

mislaid property
Property which the owner has intentionally and voluntarily parted with, and intended to retrieve, but which the owner cannot now locate.

misnomer
Using the wrong name in legal documents or legal proceedings.

misprision
In old common law, represents several separate offenses not signified by a name, including contempt of court, sedition, disloyalty to the government, public neglect, and failure to report a crime.

misprision of felony
The offense of concealing a felony or failing to report a felony. Today this is being "an accessory after the fact."

misrepresentation

A false and misleading statement about a material fact, which may be grounds for rescinding a contract or for the recovery of damages in contract or tort.

mistake

An act or omission done out of ignorance or faulty judgment which would not have been done without an erroneous belief.

mistake of fact

An incorrect belief or ignorance of a fact, usually a reason for voiding a contract or for a criminal defense.

mistake of law

An incorrect judgment of the legal consequences of known facts, usually not a reason for a criminal defense, due to the maxim "ignorance of the law is no excuse."

mistrial

Termination of a trial due to some misconduct or extraordinary circumstance (*e.g.*, tampering with the jury, violation of ethics, or death of a juror).

mitigating circumstances

1. Circumstances surrounding the criminal act which can reduce the penalty to the defendant, in the discretion of judge and jury (*e.g.*, homicide can be reduced from murder to manslaughter if committed in a sudden heat of passion). 2. Attributes or acts of the defendant which may reduce the sentence of the crime, in the judge's discretion (*e.g.*, a first offense, good faith, good character).

mitigation

Lessening of the damages or punishment imposed by law.

mitigation of damages

1. Any lessening of the damages caused by tort or breach of contract. 2. Legal requirement that the injured person, in the exercise of ordinary care, use reasonable efforts to minimize the damages arising out of the injury.

mittimus

1. Court order to sheriff or prison warden directing him to deliver, receive, or keep a prisoner in custody. 2. Form of court order used to transfer records from one court to another.

mixed motive

An employment discrimination case in which the employment action was based in part on a discriminatory reason, and in part on a non-discriminatory reason. The defendant in such a case has the burden of showing that the same action would have been taken without the discriminatory motive.

mixed nuisance

A nuisance which disturbs both public and private people in the lawful and productive use of their property; a nuisance which simultaneously infringes upon the rights of both the public in general and specific private persons. *See* nuisance.

M'Naghten Rule

Common law test of criminal responsibility of the insane, first introduced in England in 1843 and accepted by many American courts. Under this test, insanity is grounds for acquittal if the suspect, while committing the act, was laboring under such a defect of reason from disease of the mind as not to know the nature and quality of the act he was doing, or if he did know it, that he did not know what he was doing was wrong. *M'Naghten's Case*, 8 Eng. Rep. 718 (1843).

model act

A statute proposed by the National Conference of Commissioners of Uniform State Laws. State legislatures often adopt all or part of model act or modify it for use in state (*e.g.,* Model Business Corporation Act).

Model Rules of Professional Conduct

Rules adopted by the American Bar Association in 1983, governing the conduct of lawyers. The rules replaced the Code of Professional Responsibility, and prescribe the proper behavior of attorneys in such areas as courtroom behavior and client-attorney interaction, among many others. The Model Rules have been adopted by nearly every state.

modification, modify

1. A change which alters the terms and conditions of a contract but leaves the basic purpose intact. 2. To change part of a contract.

modus operandi

(MOE-dus op-er-AN-dee *or* op-er-AN-die) Lat. Method of operating. The particular way an act is carried out (*e.g.*, murder by poisoning the victim's dinner with cyanide).

moiety

Half of something, usually half of an estate in property (*e.g.*, a joint tenant holds half an estate, or by moiety).

molestation

The offense of disturbing another and violating his or her freedom, particularly the offense of using a child for sexual gratification.

molliter manus imposuit

(MOL-it-ter MAN-us im-PO-soo-it) Lat. The gentle laying upon of hands. In a tort action, this term refers to one party using only the physical force necessary to protect himself or his property.

money

Standard means of exchange and valuation, adopted by national governments.

money demand

A claim or action arising out of an implied or express contract, tort, or statute, where the relief sought is a fixed amount of money. When money is the remedy sought, that remedy is called "damages."

money had and received

A common law action for the return of money. The money was "had" by the plaintiff, but "received" by the defendant without justification.

money judgment

A judgment, order, or decree in which the court orders the defendant to pay a sum of money.

money order

A type of instrument calling for the payment of a specified amount of money to a payee. Such orders are usually issued by and payable at a post office or bank, and are often used as a substitute for a check.

money supply

The amount of money in an economy at a given time. The U.S. Treasury Department uses three primary means of measuring the money supply (among others): (1) M-1, the money in circulation, including demand deposits and checking account balances; (2) M-2 includes M-1, plus mutual funds, savings accounts, and overnight repurchase agreements; (3) M-3 includes M-2, plus deposits at nonbank thrift institutions, longer term repurchase agreements, and time deposits exceeding $100,000.

monogamy

Marriage to one person, contrasted with polygamy or bigamy. *See* polygamy, bigamy.

monopoly

1. Exclusive privilege of manufacturing, using, or controlling the sale of a particular market commodity. 2. Business combination to fix prices of a commodity or otherwise dominate the market in restraint of free trade. In antitrust, possession of a monopoly power in the market along with acquisition or maintenance of that power is illegal under the Sherman Act. 15 U.S.C. §§ 1–7.

monopsony

Market condition wherein there is only one buyer for a particular commodity.

moot

1. A matter for argument, never decided by a court. A case is moot when it presents a pretended controversy or when a judgment by the court would have no effect upon the controversy. 2. A case where the issues have ceased to exist.

moot court

A simulated practice court where law students hear and argue fictitious ("moot") cases.

moral certainty

Certainty beyond any reasonable doubts; an assurance that excludes all reasonable doubts that a contrary conclusion may exist.

moral obligation

A duty which is not recognized by law but rests on good conscience and notions of natural justice. A moral obligation may be created by contract.

moral right

See droit moral.

moral turpitude

Intentional acts or behavior involving dishonesty, wickedness, depravity, or grave infringement of the good moral sentiment of the community.

moratorium

Delay or suspension in the obligation to perform some legal duty or in the right to have some legal duty performed, when ordered by a court or enacted by the legislature (*e.g.*, a moratorium in suits against debtors during a period of financial upheaval).

mortgage

1. Security for a loan. 2. An interest in real property given by the debtor (the mortgagor) to the creditor, loan company, or bank (the mortgagee) to secure payment of the loan. At common law, the mortgagee had the legal right to possession. Today, in most states a mortgage is a lien, therefore, the mortgagee may only have the legal right to possession after a foreclosure hearing with proof of default in payments by the debtor.

mortis causa

(MOR-tis KAW-sa) Lat. In contemplation of death. A gift may be given mortis causa by a dying person but is void if the person recovers and survives. Sometimes used as "causa mortis."

mortgage market

The state of supply and demand for mortgages. Frequently, financial institutions will buy and sell securities that are backed by large blocks of mortgages, for investment purposes.

mortgagee

The party who holds the mortgage; one who lends the money to a mortgagor and then takes a security interest in the mortgagor's real property.

mortgagor

The party who borrows money from a mortgagee. The mortgagor secures the debt with real property owned by the mortgagor.

mortmain

"Dead hand." In the old common law, represented property in perpetual ownership of the church or some corporations.

Parliament enacted the "mortmain acts" to limit the creation of perpetual ownership of property.

mortuary

A place for embalming, undertaking, or burial.

most favored nations clause

In international law, a clause in treaties which guarantees to the citizens of the participating countries the same rights and privileges given by each participating country to the most favored nations of that country. A primary result is lower import tariffs for the most favored nations.

motion

A request by a party to the court, made orally or in writing, for a favorable order, rule, or remedy, concerning a question within the judge's discretion (*e.g.*, motion to dismiss the action, motion for retrial).

motive

The reason or inducement that causes a person to act in a certain manner, contrasted to "intent," which is the purpose a person has when acting.

movable

In property, articles which can be transported away, contrasted to "fixtures" which are attached to the land.

movant

The person who makes a motion in a legal proceeding; the one who applies for an order.

move

To make a "motion" to the court for a particular order, ruling, or remedy.

mulct

1. To impose a fine or punishment on one who is guilty of an offense. 2. To assess damages against a person.

multidistrict litigation

Federal litigation in which civil actions pending in several districts are consolidated for purposes of pre-trial matters, and then tried in their original districts.

multifarious suit

A single suit wherein distinct and independent matters, having no legitimate connection, are improperly joined.

multifariousness

The improper joining of independent and distinct issues in one suit or for several unrelated defendants in one action. Also called "misjoinder." Under the Federal Rules of Civil Procedure, broad joinder of separate claims and defendants is encouraged.

multipartite

Of or relating to two or more parties or parts.

multiplicity of suits (or actions)

Grounds for the court to unite numerous separate actions or suits into one court in equity jurisdiction, where the actions are against the same defendant and concern the same right, and separate actions would be unnecessarily wasteful for the defendant.

multitudo imperitorum perdit curiam

(mul-ti-TOO-do im-pair-i-TOR-um per-DIT KOO-ree-am) Lat. A great number of unskilled practitioners ruins a court.

municipal

1. Concerning a city, town, or other local governmental or public unit. 2. In a broader sense, referring to the public and political functions of a government (*e.g.*, the "municipal purposes" of the Flood Relief Act).

municipal bond

Debt obligation issued by a state or local municipal body. Interest on such bonds is usually exempt from federal income tax, and some state and local income taxes.

municipal corporation

Local institution of government (*e.g.*, a city; a township) created by state charter for a particular geographic area, which exercises local powers delegated by the state, such as controlling transfers of property, building and maintaining roads, establishing local ordinances, and other local functions.

municipal court

Local court of limited jurisdiction to consider traffic and city ordinance violations and other minor criminal or civil offenses.

municipal ordinance

A law enacted by a municipality, the violation of which is an offense against the municipality which enacted it (*e.g.,* a zoning, traffic, or noise ordinance).

muniments

(MOO-ni-ments *or* MYOO-ni-ments) Document by which rights and privileges are proved (*e.g.,* deed, charter).

murder

An unlawful killing of another person with malice aforethought, committed either purposely or recklessly with disregard of the value of human life.

Murder is commonly divided by statute into different degrees for purposes of punishment: "First-degree murder," punishable by death or life imprisonment, is the unlawful killing of another by poison, by lying in wait, through a willful, deliberate premeditation, or during the commission or attempted. commission of a felony. "Second-degree murder" is the unlawful killing of another with malice aforethought but without premeditation (*e.g.,* result of provocation). "Felony murder" is the unlawful killing of another during the commission or attempted commission of a felony. *See* manslaughter.

mutatis mutandis

(moo-TAT-is moo-TAN-dis *or* myoo-TAT-is myoo-TAN-dis) Lat. With the necessary changes in detail to be made in compliance with one major change (*e.g.,* in renewal of a contract, details of time and delivery will be revised to comply with the new order).

mute

Unable or unwilling to speak. In criminal law, "standing mute" is the refusal to plead guilty or not guilty at the trial, which is usually construed as a plea of not guilty.

mutilation

1. In criminal law, the deprivation of another person's use of limbs or other essential parts of the body (*See* mayhem, maiming). 2. An alteration in a written document by cutting, tearing, erasing, or burning, without destroying the whole.

mutiny

1. (v.) To revolt against or to resist lawful authority, especially

on a ship at sea or in the naval forces. 2. (n.) The act constituting the revolt.

mutual

1. Common to both parties. 2. Giving and receiving in a reciprocal way; agreed to by both parties.

mutual agreement

1. A meeting of the minds on a specific matter. 2. In contracts, agreeing to the same bargain at the same time.

mutual fund

An investment fund of many public contributors, operated by a financial group which invests the contributions in securities, with the value of the fund fluctuating with the success of the investments.

mutual fund share

A security which denotes ownership in a mutual fund company. Such shares cannot be resold by the shareholder, but may be redeemed by the company.

mutual insurance company

A company which sells insurance only to its members, with the profits and losses being divided among all the members.

mutuality of contract

Principle which requires that each party to a contract have some obligation to the other party, for the contract to be enforced against that party. Neither party is bound unless the other is bound.

mutuality of estoppel

Principle by which a court will not consider a judgment conclusive against one party to a lawsuit unless it is conclusive against the other party to the lawsuit.

mutuality of obligation

Principle that both parties to a bilateral contract must perform in some specific way, otherwise the contract is invalidated for lack of consideration.

mutuality of remedy

In contract law, the principle denying a remedy to one party if the other party could not avail himself of the same remedy (*e.g.*, a court will not award specific performance to one party unless it was available to the other party as well).

mutual mistake
In contracts, a misconception or ignorance shared by both contracting parties, regarding a material fact, so that the contract does not express the parties' true intentions. Mutual mistake is grounds for the court to alter the contract.

mutual wills
See reciprocal wills.

naked

Bare; incomplete; insignificant (*e.g.*, a "naked contract" is one without consideration; a "naked trust" is one without duties for the trustee; a "naked possession" is one without proper title).

named insured

The party who is named in an insurance policy as the one protected. Often this is the same person who has contracted for the policy.

N.A.S.A.

See National Aeronautics and Space Administration.

National Aeronautics and Space Administration (N.A.S.A.)

Federal agency established in 1958 to promote space travel and technology.

nationality

1. Relationship of belonging to one nation. 2. Citizenship; involving the duty of allegiance to the nation and the reciprocal duty of the nation to protect its citizens.

NASDAQ

National Association of Securities Dealers Automated Quotations. NASDAQ offers automated price quotations for over-the-counter securities.

National Bar Association

An organization of predominantly African-American judges and attorneys that seeks to promote professionalism, education, and civil rights.

National Guard

The militia; a reserve military force composed of residents of individual states and territories.

National Labor Relations Act

Federal statute enacted in 1935 and amended in 1947 which regulates relations between employers and employees. The Act also authorized the establishment of the National Labor Relations

Board. *See* National Labor Relations Board.

National Labor Relations Board (N.L.R.B.)

Created by the National Labor Relations Act of 1935 to prevent and remedy unfair labor practices and to oversee union elections.

National Lawyers Guild

A group comprised of lawyers and members of the legal community, established for the advocacy of economic, social and political change. Much of the organization's activity pertains to the advancement of civil liberties.

National Science Foundation

Created in 1950 for the development and advancement of the sciences.

natural

1. Arising under the ordinary operation of physical laws. 2. Likely to occur in the ordinary course of things. Distinguished from "artificial" (those things requiring human action) and "legal" (those things based on legal enactments).

natural child

A child of one's body, in contrast to an adopted child. The child may or may not have been born out of wedlock.

naturalization

The act of granting citizenship and its privileges to a foreigner. In the United States, naturalization requires that the person be a lawful resident of the United States for five years, speak and write the English language, know the fundamentals of American government, adhere to the Constitution, be of good moral character, and take the oath of allegiance. *See* 8 U.S.C. § 1421.

naturalized citizen

A person born in a foreign country who has been granted full U.S. citizenship under naturalization laws.

natural law

The moral or ethical law, formulated in accordance with reason, natural justice, and the original state of nature.

natural law theory

The idea that, to understand any given legal order, one must examine the relationship between that order's positive (statutory) law and the natural law.

natural person
A human being, rather than an "artificial" being such as a corporation.

navigable
Used or capable of being used for commerce by ships and other vessels. Interstate commerce in navigable waters is subject to federal regulation and federal maritime law.

N.B.
See nota bene.

necessaries
Those articles which are actually needed for the sustenance of life (*e.g.*, food, drink, clothing, shelter, medical care). Necessaries are not limited but vary with the circumstances of age, rank, position, earning capacity, and way of living.

Necessary and Proper Clause
Clause 18 of Section 8 of Article 1 of the U.S. Constitution, which grants to Congress the power to make all laws which are "necessary and proper" to carry out the specific Congressional powers enumerated in the preceding clauses of Section 8.

necessary inference
Any inference which is inescapable or unavoidable from the standpoint of reason.

necessary parties
Those persons who must be joined in an action because without them a final order would not grant complete relief.

necessity
1. A defense to an unlawful act, where the act is compulsory and unavoidable (*e.g.*, breaking and entering to save a dying man, or shooting in self-defense). 2. In property law, a reasonable need for the use of a certain parcel of land (*e.g.*, when the only access to a public road is over another's property).

ne exeat
(nee EX-ee-at *or* EX-ay-at) Lat. No exit. A writ or order of the court to restrain a person from leaving the country, state, or jurisdiction of the court, or to restrain a person from taking property out of the jurisdiction.

negative amortization

A type of mortgage in which the payments are less than the interest for the period covered by the payment. The deficiency is added into the loan balance, so that the balance increases. Negative amortization mortgages are illegal in some states.

negative averment

An averment in some of the pleadings in which a negative is asserted.

negative easement

A right entitling its owner to compel the possessor of the servient tenement to refrain from activity on the servient tenement which, absent the easement, the possessor would be entitled to do (*e.g.*, easement for light barring construction of tall building). Similar to a restrictive covenant.

negative pregnant

A denial implying an affirmative which is beneficial to an opponent (*e.g.*, a denial that the value of goods is more than $1,000 implies that the goods are worth $1,000).

neglect

Failure to do something which one is legally, contractually, or morally required to do.

negligence

1. The inadvertent or unintentional failure to exercise that care which a reasonable, prudent, and careful person would exercise. 2. Conduct which violates certain legal standards of due care. Negligence constitutes grounds for recovery in a tort action if it is the proximate cause of injury to the plaintiff.

Contributory negligence is the negligence of the injured person which contributes to the injury and precludes his recovery in a tort action.

Comparative negligence is a proportional division of the damages between the plaintiff and the defendant in a tort action according to their respective shares of fault contributing to the injury.

Gross negligence is the failure to exercise even a minimal amount of care.

Criminal negligence is reckless, unintentional disregard for the rights of others.

Slight negligence is the failure to exercise a great amount of care.

negligence per se
An unexcused act or omission that automatically establishes the existence of a duty and breach thereof. Often results from violation of certain statutes (*e.g.,* failure to stop for red traffic signal).

negligent hiring
Lack of care in choosing and hiring an employee who is unfit for the position and whose lack of fitness creates an unreasonable risk of harm to others.

negligent homicide
Death caused by one's conduct that deviates substantially from the standard of care. Often classified as involuntary manslaughter or vehicular homicide.

negotiable instrument
A writing signed by the maker, or drawer, which contains an unconditional promise to pay on demand or at some future time a fixed amount of money to "bearer" or to "order" and containing no unauthorized undertaking or instruction by the person promising or ordering payment (*e.g.,* a check for $100, signed by the drawer and payable to the bearer). *See* U.C.C. § 3–104.

negotiation, negotiate
1. To meet and bargain over the terms and conditions of some future transaction or agreement; the meeting itself is the "negotiation." 2. To transfer an instrument in such form as to make the transferee a holder.

nemo agit in seipsum
(NEE-mo ADJ-it in say-IP-sum) Lat. No man acts against himself.

nemo dat qui (quod) non habet
(NEE-mo dat kwee [kwod] non HAB-et) Lat. He who has not cannot give (*e.g.,* a person with restrictions on his title to property cannot sell the property with a perfect title).

nemo debet bis puniri pro uno delicto
(NEE-mo-DEB-et biss PUN-eer-ee *or* PYOON-eer-ee pro oo-no de-LIK-to) Lat. No one should be punished twice for the same crime.

**nemo debet esse judex in pro-
pria causa**
(NEE-mo-DEB-et ESS-say JOO-
dex in PRO-pree-a KAW-sa)
Lat. No one should be a judge in
his own cause.

nemo est supra leges
(NEE-mo est SOO-par LEJ-is)
Lat. No one is above the law.

nemo praesumitur malus
(NEE-mo pree-SUM-i-tur
MALL-us) Lat. No one is pre-
sumed to be evil.

nemo tenetur ad impossibile
(NEE-mo-TEN-net-tur ad im-
POS-si-beel) Lat. The law requires no one to perform an
impossibility.

net
The balance remaining after all
deductions, including taxes,
expenses, discounts, etc.

net asset value
1. The net market value of a
share of stock in a mutual fund.
2. Any company's book value, or
its net worth.

net estate
The remainder of a gross estate,
after debts and expenses have

been paid and claims have been
satisfied. It is this portion of the
estate which is subject to state
and federal estate taxes.

net income
Gross income less exemptions
and deductions permitted by law.
It is this income which is subject
to state and federal income tax.

net operating loss
The excess of operating expenses
over revenues.

net profits
Profits after subtraction of all
expenses; may be considered net
before or after deductions for
taxes.

net worth
The amount by which an individual's or corporation's assets
exceed liabilities.

neutrality laws
Laws which regulate the military
or financial aid to either of two
warring nations with which the
U.S. is at peace. 22 U.S.C. § 441
et seq.

newly discovered evidence
Evidence which constitutes
grounds for a new trial if it is

discovered in all due diligence only after the first trial, is material, is not merely cumulative or minor, and would probably result in a decision contrary to that of the first trial.

new matter

Issue or substantial fact raised at the time of trial or hearing which had not been raised by either party in the pleadings. Under Federal Rule of Civil Procedure 15, parties must amend or supplement the pleadings to include the new issue or fact in the litigation.

new trial

A rehearing of a case after its dismissal during or at the close of the first hearing. Grounds for a new trial include misconduct of the jury, misconduct of counsel, error in the judge's charge to the jury, or newly discovered evidence not available previously.

New York Stock Exchange (N.Y.S.E.)

An association formed to facilitate the buying and selling of securities. It is the nation's oldest exchange.

New York Times malice

In defamation law, actual malice; publishing a falsehood about a public figure either knowing that the item published is false, or with a reckless disregard for the truth or falsity of the item.

next friend

A person who represents an infant or other legally incompetent person in litigation, not an officially appointed guardian. The next friend, often a close relative, does not become a party to the suit.

next of kin

1. In wills and trusts, the nearest blood relatives to the decedent. 2. Those entitled to inherit or acquire property under statutory distribution.

nexus

(NEK-sus) Lat. Tie; connection to.

NIFO

Abbreviation for "next in, first out," an accounting method used in valuing inventories which calculates the costs of goods sold using the replacement cost, rather than the actual cost of the goods.

nihil
(NI-hill) Lat. Nothing.

nil
Lat. Nothing. Contracted form of "nihil."

nil debet
Lat. He owes nothing. The common law defense to an action for the recovery of debt.

Nineteenth Amendment
Provision of U.S. Constitution granting women the right to vote; ratified in 1920.

Ninth Amendment
Amendment stating that the enumeration of constitutional rights shall not be construed to deny or disparage other rights retained by the people.

nisi
(NYE-sigh) Lat. Unless. A "rule nisi" or "decree nisi" will take effect unless the party against whom the rule is directed successfully appeals. A "decree nisi" is the opposite of an "absolute" rule, which absolutely takes effect.

nisi prius
(NYE-sigh PRY-us *or* PREE-us) Lat. Unless before. A "nisi prius court" is any court of original jurisdiction, where the facts of a case are first heard by a jury with judge presiding. *See* original jurisdiction.

N.L.R.B.
National Labor Relations Board. Administrative body of the United States government responsible for enforcing the National Labor Relations Act governing private employment practices.

no action letter
A letter from the staff of a regulatory agency in response to an inquiry that states that the staff will take no action against a person if the facts of her situation are as set out in the inquiry.

no bill
See grand jury.

no contest clause
A clause in a will that a legacy or devise fails if the potential beneficiary contests the provisions of the will. Such clauses are unenforceable or have limited appli-

cation in some states. Also called in terrorem clause.

no fault

1. A type of automobile insurance, required in many states, which covers all automobile damages or injuries to the insured up to a certain amount, without requiring fault on the part of the insured. 2. A type of divorce, allowed in some states, which dissolves the marriage due to "irreconcilable" differences, or an "irreparable breakdown of the marital relationship," rather than by requiring fault on the part of either spouse.

nolens volens

(no-LENZ VO-lenz) Lat. Whether willing or not willing.

nolle prosequi

(NOL-lee PROS-e-kwee *or* PROS-kwee) Lat. Unwilling to prosecute. A formal entry on the record by the prosecutor in a criminal action or by the plaintiff in a civil action, stating that he will not further prosecute the case.

nolo contendere

(NO-lo kon-TEN-der-ee *or* kon-TEN-dree) Lat. No contest. A plea in a criminal action, similar to a plea of guilty, in which the defendant does not admit the charges but will not deny the charges. If the court accepts the plea as voluntary and proper, it has the same effect as a plea of guilty (with the same punishment), but it cannot be used against the defendant in any other action (*e.g.*, a corporation's plea of nolo contendere in a criminal charge of antitrust may not be used against the corporation in a civil antitrust suit by its competitors or buyers).

nominal

1. Not real; not actual. 2. Merely named; so small or insignificant that it is barely entitled to the name given.

nominal damages

A small and insignificant sum awarded the plaintiff as recognition of a legal injury where damages are nonexistent, or where the plaintiff has not established a recoverable loss.

nominal party

A party joined to an action, not because of any claim or liability in damages, but because of technical rules of pleading.

nomination

Appointment of a person or candidate for a certain office or duty.

nominee trust

An arrangement under a written declaration of trust by which one or more persons or corporations hold title to real property for the benefit of undisclosed beneficiaries.

non-access

A defense by the alleged father in a paternity action, arguing the absence of intercourse or opportunities for intercourse with the mother. Often used to rebut the presumption of paternity of a child born during marriage.

non-age

The legal status of a minor.

nonacquiescence

An administrative agency's policy that it will not follow lower-court rulings with which it disagrees until a final ruling on the question is issued by the Supreme Court.

nonassessable stock

Any stock which has been bought at full par value or more per share. Such a stock is not liable to further assessment or taxation.

non assumpsit

Defense to the common law action of "assumpsit," in which the defendant maintains he made no promise as the plaintiff alleged.

non compos mentis

(non KOM-poes MEN-tis) Lat. Not sound of mind. Insane or mentally incompetent.

nonconforming use

In property law, use of property which was once lawful but does not conform to newly enacted zoning use restrictions. The use and the structures may be continued as actually used before the restriction but may not be enlarged or extended.

noncontestibility clause

A life insurance policy provision which bars the insurer from contesting the policy on the basis

299

of fraud or mistake after a certain date or after a specified period of time.

non culpabilis
(non kul-PA-bi-liss) Lat. Not guilty. Abbreviated as "non cul."

non damnificatus
(non-dam-ni-fi-KA-tus) Lat. Not injured. Common law defense in an action of debt on an indemnity bond, which alleges that the plaintiff has suffered no injury under the terms of the bond.

non decipitur qui scit se decipi
(non-de-SIP-i-tur kee skit say de-SIP-ee) Lat. He is not deceived who knows himself to be deceived.

nondisclosure
Failure to reveal information to a certain party, even if it has not been deliberately concealed from that party. Nondisclosure agreements are often used to prevent the disclosure of trade secrets by former employees or contractors.

nondiscretionary trust
An investment trust, wherein the trustee is permitted to buy only those securities that are set forth on a list at the time the trust is established. A trust under which trustees have no discretion as to distributions.

non est factum
Lat. It is not his deed. Common law defense which alleges that the defendant did not execute the deed or contract sued upon.

non est regula quin fallet
(non est REG-yoo-la kwinn FAL-let) Lat. There is no rule without an exception.

nonfeasance
Failure to perform a duty which one is obliged to perform. (*Contrast* malfeasance and misfeasance.) In agency law, failure of an agent to perform a duty he contracted with his principal to perform.

nonmember bank
A bank that does not belong to the Federal Reserve System.

non obstante verdicto (N.O.V.)
(non ob-STAN-tay ver-DIK-to) Lat. Notwithstanding the verdict. A judgment by the court in favor of one party notwithstanding the jury's verdict in favor of the other party.

nonperformance

Failure to perform an act stipulated in a contract or covenant.

nonobvious

In patent law, an invention that is different from prior inventions so that a person ordinarily skilled in the field relevant to the invention would not find the invention obvious.

non possessori incumbit necessitas probandi possessiones ad se pertinere

(non po-SESS-sor-ee in-KUM-bit ne-SESS-i-tas pro-BAN-dee po-sess-ee-OWN-ess as say pair-TIN-er-ee) Lat. A person in possession is not required to prove that the possessions belong to him,

nonprofit corporation

A corporation in which the members or principals do not seek or produce profits. Often, such corporations are established for or devoted to charitable, educational, or religious purposes.

non pros

Abbreviation of "non prosequitur."

non prosequitur

(non PROS-kwi-toor) Lat. He does not pursue. The defendant is entitled to judgment of "non pros" against the plaintiff if the plaintiff does not properly pursue or follow up the case. In modern practice, the plaintiff's failure to pursue the case results in a default judgment for the defendant or a dismissal.

nonpublic forum

Public property that has not traditionally been used for public speaking or expression, such as a military base.

nonrecourse

1. Lacking personal liability whatsoever (*e.g.*, a person who establishes nonrecourse in a contract wherein he is responsible for delivering goods, may return the goods without liability if the person to whom the goods were to be delivered cannot pay). 2. Status of person who holds an instrument which gives her no legal right to enforce it against prior endorsers upon dishonor.

nonresidence, nonresident

A person who resides outside of a particular jurisdiction is a "nonresident" of the jurisdiction or forum. The residence outside the jurisdiction is called "nonresidence" with respect to the jurisdiction.

non sequitur

(non SEK-wi-toor) Lat. It does not follow.

nonstock corporation

A type of corporation in which the members hold no shares (*e.g.*, fraternal organizations, mutual companies, and religious corporations).

non sui juris

(non-soo-ee JUR-is) Lat. Not his own master. Lacking legal capacity to act for oneself (*e.g.*, a minor or insane person).

nonsuit

1. Judgment against a plaintiff who does not proceed to court or prove the case. 2. A judgment without a decision on the merits or substantive issues of the case. In modern practice this is called a "dismissal."

non-support

The failure to provide support to those to whom support is legally

due (*e.g.*, the failure to provide child or spousal support).

non vult

(Abbrev. of "non vult contendere.") Lat. He will not contest. This term refers to a situation in which the criminal defendant does not admit guilt, but will not contest the charges, and subsequently agrees to be treated as one who has been found guilty.

no-par stock

Corporate stock issued without any nominal or par value.

Norris-LaGuardia Act of 1932

Federal statute restricting the federal courts' power to issue injunctions in labor disputes.

North American Free Trade Agreement (NAFTA)

An agreement between the United States, Canada, and Mexico intended to phase out trade and commercial barriers between the three nations. The Agreement was adopted in 1994.

noscitur a sociis

(NOS-si-tur a SO-shees) Lat. One is known by his companions. This term refers to the maxim of statutory construction which states that one can understand the meaning of a word when it is viewed in context.

no-strike clause

A provision in a labor contract in which employees agree not to strike during the life of the contract.

nota bene (N.B.)

Lat. Note well. When written on a document, this term indicates that the reader should pay particularly close attention to the noted section.

notary, notary public

A person who is licensed as a public officer to administer oaths, certify certain documents or signatures, take depositions, or perform other specified official acts.

note

1. To make a brief statement for the record. 2. An informal statement or memorandum. 3. A document which contains an absolute promise by the maker (or signer) to pay to the bearer a specific sum of money at a specific time. *See* negotiable instrument.

not guilty

1. Defendant's default plea in answer to a criminal charge. 2. Verdict by which the jury acquits the defendant.

notice

Communication to a person of some significant information, either by another person who has a duty to give notice, or by another proper source (*e.g.*, notice of arrest is given by the arresting officer who has the duty to give notice of arrest; notice to a defendant that an action has been filed against him is given by service or the complaint). Notice may be "actual" or "constructive" (when the person deliberately avoids inquiring or communicating about information he would have discovered otherwise).

notice of dishonor

Notice that an instrument has been dishonored. Such a notice may be given to any person who may be liable on the instrument by or on behalf of the holder or any party who has himself received notice, or any other party who can be compelled to pay the instrument. U.C.C. § 3–503.

notice of motion
Notice in writing to all parties in a cause of action, stating that one of the parties will make some motion to the court on some specified date.

notice recording statutes
Type of statute governing recording of interests in real property (*e.g.*, deeds, mortgages) which provides that a subsequent bona fide purchaser who has no actual or constructive notice of a prior unrecorded conveyance prevails over the prior grantee.

notice to quit
1. Notice in writing from the landlord to the tenant stating that the tenant must quit the premises and remove himself and his belongings, at some future time after the expiration of the lease. 2. A notice that she intends to quit the premises from the tenant to the landlord.

notorious possession
Publicly known, open, and conspicuous occupation of real property. If possession of another's property is notorious, it will constitute notice to the true owner of the property that another person is in adverse possession. *See* adverse possession.

N.O.V.
See non obstante verdicto.

novation
In contract law, the substitution of a new contract or party to a contract for an existing contract or party. A valid novation requires a valid existing contract which is extinguished and replaced by a new, valid contract with the agreement of all the parties.

NOW account
An interest-bearing checking account. NOW is the acronym for "negotiable order of withdrawal."

N.R.C.
See Nuclear Regulatory Commission.

NSF check
A check for which there are "not sufficient funds" in an account to cover. Such checks are dishonored by the drawee on presentation for payment.

Nuclear Regulatory Commission (N.R.C.)

Agency created in 1974 to regulate the uses of nuclear energy.

nudum pactum

(NOO-dum PAK-tum) Lat. Naked contract. A contract which is no more than a bare promise; made without any consideration other than goodwill or natural affection. A naked contract, one without any obligation by one party, is unenforceable.

nugatory

Void; invalid; of little or no importance or effect (*e.g.*, a judgment may be nugatory if rendered in a court that lacked proper jurisdiction).

nuisance

Anything which, in the unreasonable or unlawful use of one's property, disturbs another in the lawful and productive use of his property, endangers the health and safety of others, or violates the standards of decency. Nuisance is grounds for a tort action against the offender.

Nuisance is distinguished as "public" (that which affects the property or health of many persons or an entire community), "private" (that which affects the property of one person), and "mixed" (that which affects many, with varied consequences). Further, nuisance may be categorized as "nuisance per se" (always producing injurious effects, no matter what the circumstances) and "nuisance in fact" (producing injurious effects due *to* local conditions or factual circumstances).

nuisance per se

An act, occupation, or structure which is a nuisance at all times and under all circumstances, regardless of location or surroundings. *See* nuisance.

null

Invalid; void.

nullity

An act or proceeding that has absolutely no legal effect; one that becomes totally void.

nunc pro tunc

(nunk pro tunk) Lat. Now for then. When the court allows acts to be done after time for their performance has expired, it will issue a "nunc pro tunc order" which gives the act the same effect as if it had been performed before expiration, or as if it had been recorded at the earlier date (*e.g.*, if a party files a late appeal, a nunc pro tunc order by the court will treat the appeal as if it had been recorded on time).

nuncupative will
(nun-KYOO-pa-tiv will) A will declared or dictated orally shortly before death in the presence of sufficient witnesses. Proof of such a will thus depends on the testimony of these witnesses. Some states render a noncupative will invalid.

oath

Pledge. To fulfill a duty or obligation; profession of one's intent to carry out a responsibility entrusted to one.

oath ex officio

Old English oath in which a clergyman accused of a crime would swear his innocence to an ecclesiastical court.

obiter dicta (dictum)

Lat. Remarks made in passing. Language in a judicial opinion that does not pertain to those legal issues that are dispositive in the case; that part of a judicial opinion which does not address the central legal issues in the case.

object

1. (v.) To dispute a ruling by a court; to disagree or challenge a decision made by the court in the course of legal proceedings. 2. (n.) Goal; purpose. 3. Tangible item or thing.

objection

1. The act of objecting. 2. The reason or rationale offered by a party at trial in opposing or challenging a judge's decision or an opponent's tactics.

obligation

1. A duty owed to another. 2. A responsibility that requires a person to act in a certain manner, such as to perform a service or discharge a debt. 3. A debt; an indebtedness; a liability.

obligation of a contract

That which the parties to a contract are legally bound to perform or not to perform.

obligee

A person to whom an obligation is owed (*e.g.*, the person to whom a debt is owed); a promisee.

obligor

A person who owes an obligation to another (*e.g.*, a person who owes a debt to another); a promisor.

obliterate
1. To purposely remove a clause or a provision of a written instrument from a document. 2. Destroy; devastate; demolish.

obloquy
1. Censure, blame, reproach. 2. The state of being under censure or being disgraced.

obscene
Lewd; indecent; lascivious.

obscene material
Material which, taken as a whole, appeals to prurient interests in sex, depicts sexual conduct in a patently offensive manner, and which lacks serious artistic, literary, scientific, or political value. Such material is judged in the context of community standards. Obscene material is not protected by the First Amendment.

obscenity
See obscene material.

obsolescence
The state of disuse or uselessness. Obsolescence is caused not by physical deterioration, but by technological advances which render an object no longer useful, or of greatly diminished usefulness.

obstructing justice
To hinder, impede, or prevent the efforts of those who seek to exercise their legal rights in court or those whose duties involve the administration of justice (*e.g.*, to seek to prevent a person from testifying at a trial).

obvious
Readily understood; manifest; clear; apparent.

obvious risk
Risk that is clearly recognizable to a person of average intellect and reasonable caution.

occupancy
The act of occupying or taking possession of property.

occupant
One who takes possession, uses, or occupies a thing or premises (*e.g.*, a tenant).

occupation
1. Tenancy. 2. Possession; use and enjoyment of property (*e.g.*, to have possession of a house and its surrounding property).

3. Profession; career; how a person makes his livelihood.

occupational disease
A medical condition which is the result of employment conditions *(e.g.,* black lung disease contracted by miners).

occupational hazard
A risk that is peculiar to a particular type of occupation.

Occupational Safety and Health Administration (O.S.H.A.)
Federal agency created in 1970 to enact and enforce employment safety standards.

odd lot
A quantity of stock or bonds that is less than the established 100-share unit.

odious
Hateful; detestable; vile.

odium
1. Ill feelings toward a person; hatred or dislike. 2. The situation where a party to a judicial proceeding is so hated or loathed in a particular area that he cannot receive a fair trial in that venue.

of counsel
1. A term denoting an attorney who assists the principal attorney of record in a trial. Such attorneys are often employed for the duration of an action. 2. An attorney who is affiliated with a law firm, but who is not a regular partner or associate of the firm.

offense
A violation of the criminal laws; a felony or misdemeanor.

offer
1. (n.) A proposal to do or to abstain from doing something in the future that is binding upon the offeror upon the offeree's acceptance of the proposal. Restatement (Second) of Contracts § 24 defines offer as: "The manifestation of willingness to enter into a bargain, so made as to justify another person in understanding that his assent to that bargain is invited and will conclude it." 2. (v.) To propose; to tender; to make a proposal.

offer of proof
The presentation of evidence for admission in a hearing or trial. The term frequently refers to a situation wherein a judge sus-

tains an objection to a question. The questioning party could then proffer the purpose or answer to the question (out of the jury's presence), thus establishing the basis for an appellate court's review of the ruling.

office

1. A position of trust and authority that is conferred by election or appointment. 2. A place for the regular transaction of business.

office action

A communication by a patent examiner to an applicant stating the reasons a patent application has been denied.

officer

A person holding a position of authority, control, and influence in government, a corporation, or some other organization.

official

1. (n.) A person endowed with the authority and powers of the office that he holds. 2. (adj.) Authoritative; authorized by an officer of an organization.

officious intermeddler

One who interferes with property or business affairs without title or right. Often, an officious intermeddler will give unsolicited assistance, then seek payment from the one who benefited.

offset

1. A reduction or cancellation of a claim. 2. A counterclaim; a claim which counterbalances another claim.

oligopoly

A market condition wherein a few companies dominate the production of one class of products. Competition in an oligopolistic market is less vigorous than in a free market, but slightly more active than in a monopoly.

olograph

A legal document totally written by the person who transmits the document to another.

omission

Failure to act in the way that the law mandates (*e.g.*, the failure to report a crime to the authorities).

omnibus

Including many different things at once (*e.g.*, a legislative act that deals with two or more independent matters is said to be an omnibus bill).

omnibus clause
1. Clause in an automotive liability insurance policy which extends coverage to any drivers who are permitted by the insured to use the car. 2. A clause in a will or decree of distribution passing all property not specifically mentioned or known at the time.

on all fours
A judicial decision that is precisely on point; a decision similar in all respects to another decision.

on demand
When desired; upon request (*e.g.*, a promissory note that is payable upon request by the holder of the note).

one person, one vote
Principle that the Equal Protection Clause requires electoral districts within a state or city to have the same population.

on or about
Phrase used to denote approximation.

on the brief
Phrase which indicates all persons who participated in the writing of a brief. Such participants may not necessarily be the attorneys of record.

on the merits
Judgment rendered after consideration of the facts and evidence of the entire case. Judgments on technical or procedural issues are not judgments "on the merits."

onus probandi
(OWE-nus pro-BAN-dee) Lat. The burden of proof.

open
1. Available; visible; unobstructed. 2. (v.) To subject to inquiry or scrutiny; to begin. 3. In legal terms, an open matter is one that has not been finalized.

open account
1. An account that has not been formally settled or paid. 2. An extension of credit by a business to a customer; charge account. 3. A sale of goods in which payment is not due until a certain amount of time after the goods are delivered.

open court
A court that permits the general public to view its proceedings.

open-end contract
Agreement which allows the buyer to acquire goods over a period of time without a change in the provisions of the agreement by the seller. A "requirements contract" is a type of open-end contract.

opening statement
Presentation made by counsel at beginning of trial in which she summarizes her client's case and the evidence which she will present on the client's behalf.

open price term
Contract in which parties have not included the price term. Absent agreement on means of establishing a price, a reasonable price will be implied. *See* U.C.C. § 2–305.

open shop
Commercial enterprise in which membership in a union or a similar organization is not a condition of employment.

Open Source
A type of software license that allows users to use, copy, distribute, or modify the software without payment to the developer. *Cf.* Creative Commons.

operation of law
Process by which legal rights and obligations are transmitted to a person upon the application of established legal principles which are activated by the occurrence of a particular transaction and not by the purposeful efforts of the person.

operative part
That part of a legal instrument which creates or transfers rights from one party to another and thereby fulfills the purpose of the instrument.

opinion
1. Judicial decision which states the court's reasons for deciding a case as it did. 2. Legal advice given by an attorney to his client, in the form of a letter or other document, which states the attorney's understanding of the law with respect to a specific set of facts submitted to him for the purpose of his rendering legal advice. 3. Belief, thought, or inference, distinguished from fact.

opinion evidence
Testimony by a witness that is not based on his personal knowledge of facts but rather what he thinks or surmises with respect to the facts in dispute.

oppression
1. The wrongful punishment of a person through bodily harm, incarceration, or other injury by a public official in the exercise of his duties. 2. Any act of brutality or unfair hardship imposed on another person.

option
A privilege obtained by the payment of money or other consideration which allows a person to buy real or personal property at a stipulated price and fixed terms at any time within a specified period. Under the U.C.C., a merchant's firm offer (a type of option contract) does not need consideration.

option contract
A promise which meets the requirements for the formation of a contract and limits the promisor's power to revoke an offer (*e.g.*, contract in which a property owner promises to another the option to buy the property at a specified price within a specified amount of time). Restatement (Second) Contracts § 25.

oral
Spoken; verbal; not written.

oral contract
An agreement which has not been totally reduced to writing, but rather all or some of its terms depend on spoken words. Also called a "parol contract."

order
1. Decision of a court made in writing with regards to a matter that is not part of the case's final judgment. 2. Directive; request, *e.g.*, a request by a person made to his broker that he sell the client's stock portfolio. 3. A designation of a grouping of persons that are organized by position or class.

ordered liberty
In constitutional law, this phrase refers to the principle that only those amendments in the Bill of Rights necessary to preserve "ordered liberty" are incorporated through the due process clause of the Fourteenth

Amendment to apply to the states.

order paper
A negotiable instrument which is payable to a specified payee or any person designated by the payee through his or her indorsement.

ordinance
1. Law; statute. 2. Legislative act of a municipal government (*e.g.*, a law setting zoning standards for a community).

ordinary
Typical; common; usual; regular.

ordinary course of business
The transaction of commerce that conforms to common commercial customs, or to the norms of a community, or to the normal business activity of the individual in question.

ordinary income
For tax purposes, those earnings which emanate from a business's normal operations. For an individual, ordinary income flows from regularly recurring sources, such as interest and wages.

organic law
The fundamental law of a state, country or society, whether written or unwritten (*e.g.*, in the U.S., the Constitution espouses the nation's organic law).

organization
Any entity where a group of persons is united for some common purpose or in some common interest, such as, a corporation, a partnership, a government agency, an association.

organized crime
Criminal activity which occurs within a tightly controlled and highly planned structure.

originalism
Interpretation of the Constitution according to the intent of the drafters.

original issue
The first issue or sale of a stock or bond.

original jurisdiction
Authority of a court to recognize a suit at its beginning, act as trier of fact, and pass judgment on the case.

original package doctrine

The constitutional law doctrine which states that states may only tax imported goods after their original packages have been broken (*e.g.,* a state cannot tax goods that are in transit from one outside state to another).

orphan

A person whose parents are both deceased.

O.S.H.A.

See Occupational Safety and Health Administration.

ostensible

Apparent; supposed; seeming; outwardly evident.

ostensible authority

1. Apparent power. 2. The authority a principal induces a person to believe that the principal's agent enjoys.

ouster

The improper removal of a person or a group of persons from real property that they are legally entitled to possess.

outcome test

Test for determining whether an issue is a substantive or procedural issue in federal diversity of citizenship cases. If the issue is a substantive one, the result should be the same as if the action had proceeded in the appropriate state court. Also called "outcome determinative test."

Outer Space Treaty

United Nations Treaty on Principles Governing the Activities of States in the Exploration and Use of Outer Space. Treaty that applies norms of international law to outer space.

out-of-court settlement

Any resolution of a pending suit in which the parties agree to cease litigation without court authorization.

output contract

A contract in which one party agrees to purchase all that the other party is able to produce, in good faith.

outside director

A corporate director who is not a company officer and does not participate in the company's day-to-day management.

overbreadth

This term refers to laws which bar unlawful activity, but in so doing, also bar activity that is constitutionally protected. Such laws are struck down as being overbroad. Overbreadth doctrine originated in First Amendment law.

overdraft

A check drawn in an amount that exceeds the balance of funds present in the checking account.

overdraw

The act of seeking to obtain from a financial institution an amount of funds in excess of the balance that one has remaining in one's favor in an account with the financial institution.

overdue

Beyond an agreed time; past a fixed date; past a scheduled time (*e.g.*, a mortgage payment not paid until after the date it was originally owed).

overhead

The fixed costs of a business enterprise; the costs of a commercial enterprise that do not vary with respect to the goods produced, bought, or sold.

overreaching

1. Taking fraudulent advantage of someone through cheating, lying, or cunning. 2. Situation where one party by reason of his position or relationship with the other gains for himself any unjust or unfair advantage. 3. The practice in a commercial setting of obtaining an unfair advantage with respect to a competitor or business associate through fraud, deception, or other improper action.

overrule

Overturn; set aside; reverse; annul (*e.g.*, to reverse a judicial decision handed down by a prior court).

overt

Open; public; evident; conspicuous; not hidden.

overt act

An act done to carry out the intention to commit a crime; it must be some conduct that directly moves toward commission of the crime, more than mere preparation or planning. In conspiracy, it is something apart from the conspiracy and is an act to effect the object of the agreement.

over-the-counter market
Market in which brokers buy and sell securities that are not listed on an organized exchange. Most over-the-counter transactions are now completed through organized computer services. *See* NASDAQ.

owner
One who has legal right to possession of property; the person in whom dominion, ownership, or title is vested.

ownership
1. The state of possessing the legal right to property. 2. Possession of the complete dominion, proprietary or title right.

oyer
To hear; to ask or demand a hearing. A copy of a written instrument that is given to a party that requests it, in lieu of it being read aloud.

oyer and terminer
To hear and determine. A grant or commission of power given to judges under the English common law to hear and determine criminal cases. The name given to a senior criminal court in certain jurisdictions of the United States.

oyez
Hear ye (English term). A command given to secure a group's attention and silence (*e.g.*, the command issued by a bailiff to bring a courtroom to order before a judge begins the proceedings before the court).

P.A.
Abbreviation for professional association.

pactum; pact
Lat. A contract; an agreement. In civil law: A pact; an agreement without a title and without consideration which may, however, produce a civil obligation by its very nature. A "nudum pactum," a bare agreement, is an agreement without consideration and is therefore unenforceable.

paid-in-surplus
The amount paid for a corporate stock in excess of its par value.

pain and suffering
Type of tort damages recoverable for emotional and physical trauma that the plaintiff suffered as the result of a wrong.

painting the tape
Term which refers to a means of stock manipulation, whereby an individual or a group of people trade stock without actually changing ownership, to create the artificial impression of activity surrounding that stock.

pais
(pies) Fr. Country or district. It refers to acts done outside the court and not made as part of the record (*i.e.*, "in pais"). Trial "per pais" indicates trial "by the country" or by jury. A "matter of pais" is a matter of fact, since matters of fact are usually determined by the "country" or jury. "Estoppels in pais" are estoppels by conduct, and distinguished from estoppels by deed or record.

palimony
A court-ordered award of support similar to alimony, paid to a former partner in a nonmarital relationship.

palming off
1. Conduct which has the probable effect of deceiving the public by passing off the goods of one person as the goods of another.
2. To impose by fraud.

palpable

1. Obvious; plain; easily notice-able. 2. Easily perceptible either intellectually or through the senses.

pander

1. To pimp; to procure a person for the purposes of prostitution. 2. To exploit or cater to the lusts or prurient interests of others. "Pandering" is the crime of in-fluencing someone to become a prostitute. In obscenity, pander-ing may also refer to promoting obscene material appealing to people's prurient interests and is not protected by the First Amendment.

panel

1. A list of jurors summoned for duty. 2. A group of judges who decide a case for the entire court.

paper, papers

1. A written or printed document, instrument, or book which may be relevant to a suit, as in "pa-pers in the case" or "papers on appeal." 2. Any writing or print-ed document which the Constitu-tion protects against unreasona-ble searches and seizures in regard to one's "papers." 3. A negotiable instrument or an evidence of debt as in "commer-cial paper."

paper profit

Profit which appears on a com-pany's books, but which the company does not actually real-ize (*e.g.,* a company may show a profit from security investments, but until it sells the securities, that profit is not realized).

par

Lat. Of equal value. In negotia-ble instruments, par denotes the face value of the instrument as opposed to its market value. If a share of stock has a face value equal to its market value, then the share is "at par." If the share can be sold for more than its face value, it is "above par," and if the share can only be sold for less than its face value, it is "below par."

In mercantile law: "Par" is the established exchange value of the currency of one country in terms of the currency of another country (*e.g.,* a U.S. dollar is equal to 1.20 Canadian dollars). The exchange rate may shift depending on the demand in one country for the currency of another.

paralegal

An assistant to a lawyer or a judge who is not an attorney in his own right. A paralegal is not licensed to practice law, but is trained to perform many of the functions of an attorney.

paramount title

A superior title. In real property, a title which is superior to that with which it is compared, meaning that the latter title is derived from the former. A title which is stronger than another or which would prevail over another title which challenges it. A paramount title indicates an immediate right of possession, and is used as a basis for the eviction of a tenant by one whose rights of possession are superior to those of a tenant. The term also applies to chattels (*e.g.*, one who purchases a car has paramount title to it unless the car was stolen from its original owner).

paramour

A lover; a lover in an adulterous relationship.

parcel

1. A small package or bundle.
2. A contiguous portion of land in possession of, owned by, or recorded as the property of one person, claimant or company.

parcenary

The condition of holding title to lands jointly by parceners, joint heirs, before the common inheritance has been divided. A parcenary arises when several persons inherit as one heir from an ancestor.

parcener

1. A joint heir. 2. One who holds an estate with others in a parcenary.

pardon

1. An act of release or exemption by the executive authority (a president in federal cases and a governor in state cases) of a punishment which a person convicted of a crime has been sentenced to undergo. 2. An act by the governing power which lessens the punishment demanded by law for the crime and restores rights and privileges lost due to the commission of the crime.

parens patriae

(PAIR-ens PAT-ree-eye) Lat. Parent of the country. In the United States: the State, as sovereign, referring to its sovereign power of guardianship over persons under a disability like minors and insane and incompetent persons.

parent

The lawful father or mother of a child. The term is distinguished from ancestors, which refers to remote relatives as well as to immediate ones.

parental liability

Liability of parents for damages caused by their child, when the child's tortious act results from the parents' negligent control.

parental notification statute

Statute that requires notification of a parent before a minor may obtain an abortion. Such statutes typically contain a judicial bypass provision.

parent corporation

A corporation which owns all or a majority of the stock of another corporation so that the second corporation becomes a subsidiary of the first.

parenticide

1. The crime of murdering a parent. 2. The person who murders his/her parent.

parenting time

Term used in some states for visitation rights.

pari delicto

(PAR-ee de-LIK-to) Lat. In equal fault; in a similar offense or crime. Used when one who has participated in a wrong sues to recover in contract or tort based on that wrong, as in a suit to recover on a gambling debt. The "pari delicto" doctrine holds that courts will not enforce an invalid contract and no party can recover based on an illegal claim.

pari materia

(PAR-ee ma-TEER-ee-a) Lat. On the same matter; on the same subject. Statutes "in pari materia" deal with the same subject and must be interpreted with reference to each other.

pari passu

(PAR-ee PAS-soo) Lat. By equal steps. Equally and to the same degree; without preference. Used to refer to creditors who are equally entitled to receive payment from the same fund, without precedence over one another.

parish

1. In English ecclesiastical law, a territory administered by a parson, vicar, or other priest who tends to the religious needs of people therein. Hence, an ecclesiastical division of a town, city, or district under the administration of one minister or priest. 2. The members of the congregation of any church. 3. In Louisiana, a territorial governmental division of a state, corresponding to a county in other states.

parliament

The supreme legislative body of a nation.

parliamentary law, parliamentary rules

The generally accepted rules and usages which determine the procedure of legislative assemblies (*e.g.*, the Senate) and other deliberative bodies such as board meetings or town meetings.

parody

Using a copyrighted work to create a new work that comments on or critiques the original work. Parody may be non-infringing fair use, under some circumstances.

parol

1. A word, speech; hence, oral or verbal. 2. That which is expressed or evidenced by speech alone, and not by writing.

parole

1. In criminal law, a conditional release from prison of a prisoner who has served part of his sentence, allowing the prisoner to complete his term of punishment outside the prison if he satisfactorily complies with the terms of the parole. A parole board will grant parole where there is a reasonable probability mat the parolee will not violate laws while at liberty. 2. A release from jail or confinement after one has served part of his sentence. 3. Being in a state of supervised release from prison.

parol evidence

1. Oral or verbal evidence. 2. The kind of evidence given by

a witness in a court. 3. Evidence relating to the interpretation of an agreement that does not appear in the writing evidencing the agreement.

parol evidence rule
Rule of substantive law which states that once an agreement is reduced to writing and both parties have acknowledged this writing as the final expression of their agreement, then parol (oral) evidence of any prior or present understanding of the parties as to the terms of the agreement is inadmissible if it alters or contradicts the meaning of the written document. The basis of the rule is that a clear and unambiguous writing is the best evidence of the intent of the parties and the terms of the agreement. Agreements made subsequent to the writing, whether written or oral, are not subject to the rule. Furthermore, all evidence (whether written or oral) concerning the finality of the agreement is admissible as is evidence of fraud, duress, mistake, misrepresentation, or illegality or evidence offered to rescind or reform the contract.

parricide
1. The crime of killing one's father; patricide. 2. The person who kills his father.

particular average
In maritime law, a loss occurring to a ship, freight, or cargo which is borne exclusively by the owner who suffers the loss and is not shared proportionately by all interested parties. "Particular average" contrasts with "general average" which is a loss to one which is compensated by the other interested parties.

particularity
The method of pleading certain claims (*e.g.*, fraud), by setting forth a detailed account of the facts.

particulars
The details of a claim or the individual items of an account. A "bill of particulars" states the specific occurrences to be investigated in a criminal proceeding and details the offenses charged so that the defendant will be informed of the evidence that he faces. "Particulars of sale" is the document describing fairly and accurately all property to be sold

during an auction. Copies are distributed among the bidders. *See* bill of particulars.

partition

1. A judicial or voluntary separation of land held by joint tenants, coparceners, or tenants-in-common so that the parties may hold their estates severally and not in union with others. When partition is not an available option, the court may order a sale of the property and distribute the income proportionate to the interest held in the property. 2. Any division of real or personal property between co-owners which leads to each owner individually possessing his interests.

partner, partnership

A partner is a member of a partnership. A partnership is a voluntary agreement between two or more competent persons to place their money, effects, labor and skill, or some or all of them, in lawful commerce or business, with an understanding that any profit or loss shall be divided in certain proportions.

An association of two or more persons to carry on as co-owners a business for profit. A partnership may be implied by the parties' conduct. A general partner has unlimited liability for the debts of the partnership, but also has input in the management of the partnership. A general partner is individually liable for the debts of the partnership and his personal assets may be used to pay a debt when the partnership has insufficient assets. Partnerships are regarded as a conduit and are not taxed. The individual partners report any gains or losses on their personal income tax returns where they are subject to taxation. *See* limited partnership.

part performance doctrine

Partial performance of an oral contract in reliance on the other party's promised performance may act to remove the contract from the Statute of Frauds.

partus sequitur ventrem

(PAR-tuss SEK-wit-tur VEN-trem) Lat. The offspring follows the mother; the offspring of a slave belongs to the owner of the mother. A maxim of civil law, which the law of England has accepted for animals, but never accepted for humans.

party

1. A person officially designated as a litigant (plaintiff or defendant) in a judicial proceeding. 2. A person directly interested in the subject matter of a trial and, who, therefore, has the right to control proceedings, make a defense, assert a claim, cross-examine witnesses and appeal a judgment. With respect to litigation:

Indispensable party: One whose interest in the controversy is so essential to an equitable resolution that, in his absence, the suit cannot proceed. Federal Rule of Civil Procedure 19(b).

Necessary party: One whose interest will be affected by the suit or without whom a complete relief cannot be granted, but who need not be joined if his joinder will deprive the court of jurisdiction in the case. Federal Rule of Civil Procedure 19(a).

Party aggrieved: Any party having an interest recognized by law in a judicial proceeding and whose interest is adversely affected by a judgment is a "party aggrieved" and is entitled to appeal.

Third party: Someone other than the parties directly involved in the suit or agreement.

3. A person or entity which enters into a contract, lease, etc. 4. A political party is a group united by common political goals specifically including the nomination and election of its candidates for office.

party wall

1. A wall erected on a property boundary partly on the land of each owner as a mutual support to structures on both sides which are under different ownership. 2. A division wall between two adjacent properties belonging to two different persons and used for the mutual benefit of both parties. The wall may stand on part of the land of each owner or may stand wholly upon one lot. 3. A wall of which two neighboring owners are tenants-in-common.

par value

1. The face value of a share of stock; the value of a mortgage based on the balance owed. 2. Without discount.

pass

1. (v.) To transfer or to be transferred as in "property passing." 2. To enact or approve as in "to pass a law." 3. In negotiable instruments: To deliver or circulate. 4. (n.) Permission or license to go or come. 5. An authorized document allowing a designated individual to travel beyond certain boundaries which without such permission, she could not lawfully pass. 6. A ticket issued by a railroad or other transportation company allowing a designated individual to travel on certain routes or for a limited time.

passage

1. The act of passing; transit. 2. A way over land or water or through the air; a route. 3. An easement giving the right to pass over a privately owned body of water. 4. Enactment; the emergence of a bill as a law or a motion as a resolution, either when a bill has passed one or both houses of the legislature or when it has been signed by the President or Governor.

passion

In voluntary manslaughter cases, a state of mind incapable of premeditation. Passion includes any emotion such as rage, anger, or fear which leaves the mind incapable of cool reflection and is enough to lessen a murder charge to manslaughter.

passive

1. Inactive; permissive; consisting in endurance or submission rather than in action. 2. Subjected to a burden or charge. 3. Passive negligence is the failure to do something required by law and which failure amounts to a breach of the duty of care.

passive trust

A trust which gives the trustee no responsibilities or discretionary duties to perform; it may be terminated by a court of equity.

passport

Document issued by the government to citizens who travel to foreign countries. The passport identifies the citizen, requests foreign governments to allow the citizen to pass freely and safely, and entitles the citizen to the protection of his government's diplomatic and consular offices. In international law during wartime, the passport grants the citizen the right to remove himself from a belligerent country without being detained on account of the war.

past consideration
In contracts, a detriment to a party occurring before contract formation is generally considered insufficient consideration to support the contract (preexisting duty rule). Past consideration is sufficient to support a negotiable instrument.

past recollection recorded
This exception to the hearsay rule permits an accurate writing, previously made or adopted by the witness when the matter was fresh in her mind and of which she had personal knowledge, to be read into evidence when the witness has insufficient recollection to testify fully and accurately. *See* Federal Rule of Evidence 803(5).

patent
A grant issued by the government to an inventor, giving him the exclusive right to make, use, or sell the invention for a specified number of years, constituting a legitimate monopoly.

patent defect
A defect in personal property which is plainly visible or would be discovered in the exercise of ordinary care and prudence. *See* U.C.C. § 2–605(1).

patent infringement
The violation of another's patent rights. One is guilty of patent infringement when he makes, uses, or sells in an unauthorized manner an invention for which a patent exists.

patent troll
An owner who aggressively enforces her patents, especially one who has no intention of manufacturing or marketing the product covered by the patent.

paternity suit
A lawsuit brought to determine the father of a child born out of wedlock and to provide for paternal support of the child and the rights of the father regarding visitation and custody.

Patient Protection and Affordable Care Act
Federal medical insurance law that regulates the underwriting standards for medical insurance, requires some employers to provide medical insurance, requires some individuals to purchase medical insurance, and establishes subsidies for the purchase of insurance.

patricide
Murder of one's father; parricide.

Patriot Act
Federal law giving law enforcement broad powers to gather and share information for the purpose of investigating terrorism. The full acronym is USA PATRIOT Act (Uniting and Strengthening America by Providing Appropriate Tools Required to Intercept and Obstruct Terrorism).

patronage
1. Support. 2. A political officeholder's support of political cronies, friends, and family members.

pauper
A person in poverty, who is allowed to sue and defend cases without paying court costs, or who is represented by the public defender in a criminal case.

pawn
1. To give goods or property to another (usually a pawnbroker) as security for a loan or existing debt. 2. The action of pawning goods as security. 3. The goods or property pawned.

pawnbroker
A person in the business of lending money to those who pawn goods or personal property to him as security for the loan.

payable
The amount of money which a person is under a legal obligation to pay.

payee
The person to whom money, checks, orders, promissory notes, or bills of exchange are paid.

payment
1. The performance of an obligation or promise. 2, The satisfaction of a monetary debt.

payment in due course
Payment made in good faith to the holder of an instrument at or

after its maturity and without notice that the title is defective.

payment into court

A deposit of money or the subject matter of a suit, made to the court. The judge redistributes the deposit to the parties pursuant to the resolution of the matter.

payor

One who pays a debt, or is obligated to pay a debt (*e.g.*, one who makes payment of an instrument such as a check).

peace

1. State of international relations opposite of war. 2. Public safety, comfort, and happiness represented by good order, obedience to the law, and public tranquility.

peaceable possession

Possession of real estate which is not disturbed by adverse suits or hostile action intended to oust the possessor.

peculation

Fraudulent misappropriation of money or property for one's own use by one who was legally entrusted to care for it.

pecuniary

Monetary; related to money and finances. A "pecuniary loss" is one which can be valued entirely in monetary amounts.

peer

1. In old English law, the ranks of the nobility (*e.g.*, duke, marquis, earl, baron). 2. Those in each rank sat in court as judges of those of equal rank being tried. A "jury of his peers" in America means a jury of citizens, all citizens in America being equal.

penal

Having to do with punishment or penalties.

penal action

1. A criminal prosecution. 2. Civil actions brought to enforce a penalty arbitrarily created by statute for some act or omission of the defendant (*e.g.*, a fine or penalty payable to the aggrieved party).

penal institution

Any place of confinement for one convicted of a crime (*e.g.*, jail, prison, house of correction, etc.).

penal law, penal code, penal statute

1. Generally, state and federal laws which define criminal offenses and create punishment of fines or imprisonment. A "penal code" is a collection of all the state's criminal laws. 2. Laws which proscribe certain public conduct and create penalties for violation of that conduct. Laws which provide the injured party with a "right of action" for damages are called "remedial;" laws which impose penalties are "penal."

penalty

1. Payment of a sum of money or other punishment imposed by the law for the commission of an offense or the neglect of a duty. 2. Provision in a contract or bond setting forth a sum of money as punishment for default or as security for actual damages occurring in case of default.

penalty clause

A clause in a contract requiring one who defaults to pay a specific sum to the other party or parties to the contract. Such clauses are common in loan agreements and savings instruments, among others.

pendente lite

(pen-DEN-tay leet) Lat. Pending the suit. Contingent upon the determination of the lawsuit; (*e.g.*, in an action to determine the ownership of property, the property itself is "pendente lite").

pendent jurisdiction

A principle of federal court jurisdiction, in which a party may join a state cause of action to a federal cause of action if the action arose from the same transaction, even if the cause would not independently meet the diversity requirements for federal jurisdiction. Now part of supplemental jurisdiction.

pending, pendency

During the occurrence of something; before the completion. A suit is said to be "pending" or in its "pendency" from its beginning until judgment is given.

pen register

A device that records the numbers dialed on a telephone. It does not detect conversations.

pension

Systematic payments made to retired persons, based on length of service and the level of past salary.

Pension Benefit Guaranty Corporation

Created in 1974 by the Employee Retirement Income Security Act of 1974 (ERISA) to guaranty pension benefits in covered private plans if the plans terminate with insufficient assets.

pensioner

The person who receives pension payments.

penumbra

1. Area or vicinity. 2. Civil liberties not explicitly guaranteed by the Bill of Rights, but implied by the Amendments.

per

Lat. By or through.

per annum

Lat. By the year (*e.g.*, salaries, interest rates, and business growth statistics are measured "per annum").

per autre vie

(per OWE-ter vee) Fr. For the lifetime of another person. *See* pur autre vie.

per capita

(per KAP-it-ta) Lat. By the head. Equally divided among all the people. 1. Used in the old law of inheritance, "per capita" means an equal division of the estate among those who stand in equal rank to the deceased; the opposite of "per stirpes." 2. Used in statistics, "per capita income" is the average income per person in a society, calculated by dividing the total income by the number of people.

per curiam

(per KOO-ree-am *or* KYOO-ree-am) Lat. By the court. Term used to distinguish an opinion of the whole court from that written by any one judge; often used in brief or unimportant decisions.

per diem

Lat. By the day. Term used to signify an allowance or expense account with a specific "per diem" amount allocated for each day of service.

peremptory

Absolute; final; conclusive of the matter. *E.g.*, the "peremptory challenge" in jury selection is the means by which each side may conclusively reject a certain number of potential jury members in a trial without giving a reason for the challenge.

peremptory writ

1. In old English law, a writ which ordered the sheriff to compel the defendant to appear in court, after the plaintiff had given the sheriff a deposit to secure the prosecution of his or her claim. Its modern day counterpart is the summons. 2. A type of mandamus requiring the subject of an order to perform the act completely and without debate.

perfect

1. (adj.) Complete and executed (*e.g.*, a security interest is "perfected" when collateral is taken, notice is filed, or a purchase money interest in the goods (in consumer credit sales) is retained). 2. (v.) To create a perfected security interest; to "perfect." A creditor holding a per-

fected security interest has priority against other creditors.

performance

1. The complete fulfillment of one's obligations according to the contract. 2. "Part performance" is the fulfilling of only some of the contract obligations. 3. "Substantial performance" is performance of the essential purpose of the contract, although insignificant deviations from the strict obligations of the contract may remain.

performance bond

A contractor's bond, whereby the contractor guarantees the completion of the work. Should the contractor fail to complete the work, the client may use the proceeds of the bond to pay for its completion.

peril

The risk or cause of loss which is covered by an insurance policy.

per infortunium

(per in-for-TOO-nee-um) Lat. By misfortune; by accident.

perjury

The criminal offense of making a false statement under oath in a legal proceeding with no sincere belief in its truth, when it is relevant to a material issue in the proceeding. Some states have broadened the reach of perjury by statute, to include any false statement made under oath in a legal instrument or legal setting (*e.g.*, in the pleadings, affidavits, interrogations, or license applications).

permanent disability
A physical disability which causes loss of earning power and which will last or is expected to last for the rest of the disabled person's life.

permission
Formal consent, authorization, or license without which an act would be unlawful.

permissive
Allowed; endured.

permissive counterclaim
See counterclaim.

permissive waste
Waste or damage to a building caused by a tenant's failure to make necessary repairs. *See* waste.

permit
1. (n.) A license which allows some act, such as the building of a house. 2. (v.) To give permission.

per my et per tout
(per mee ay per too) Lat./Fr. By half and by all. This phrase refers to the unity in possession of a joint tenancy.

perpetuity
1. Something lasting forever. 2. Real property: The limitation of the disposition of property for longer than the life of a person then living, plus 21 years. *See* Rule Against Perpetuities.

per quod
Lat. Whereby. A libel or slander action is either "actionable per se" or "actionable per quod." "Per se" means the words themselves constitute the injury; "per quod" means that special circumstances caused the injury or that special damages resulted, whereby the defendant should be liable.

per se

(per say) Lat. By itself. Considered alone; unconnected with other matters.

per se violation

A trade practice that is considered inherently anticompetitive and harmful to the public without a determination that market competition has been harmed.

person

1. An existence capable of having rights and duties, be it a human being (natural person) or a corporation (artificial person). Partnerships, associations, foreign governments, and municipalities are persons. 2. Related to the body.

personal

1. Pertaining to a human being. 2. Limited to an individual person.

personal effects

Movable property which is intimately associated with a person, often the decedent (*e.g.*, clothing, jewelry, furniture).

personal holding company

A corporation owned by a limited number of shareholders, which earns mostly passive income such as interest, royalties, and annuities. Such companies are subject to federal personal holding company tax, which prevents high income taxpayers from using this corporate structure for tax avoidance.

personal injury

1. Injury to the body. 2. A violation of a personal right (*e.g.*, injury to a person's reputation).

personal judgment

A judgment imposed against a defendant, whereby the defendant must part with a specified portion of his or her assets.

personal property

All property not real estate. The two categories of personal property are "corporeal," consisting of movable objects such as furniture or jewelry, and "incorporeal," consisting of the interest one has in something, such as in a corporation by the ownership of stock. *See* chose in action, personalty.

personal recognizance

Pretrial release from custody on the arrestee's promise to appear for trial. No surety bond is required.

personal representative
An executor or administrator who handles the estate of a deceased person, though, according to the intent of the user, it may also include heirs, assignees, grantees, receivers, and trustees.

personalty
Personal property; movable property; property that is not real estate. If personalty is affixed to real estate, it becomes part of the real estate if removing it would damage the realty.

per stirpes
(per SITR-peez) Lat. By the roots. In the law of inheritance, "per stirpes" means division of the property by representation according to the relative number of heirs in each class; the opposite of "per capita." Under per stirpes, grandchildren would inherit only their parents' share; under per capita, all grandchildren would inherit equally.

pertinent
Relevant; significant; applicable. Evidence is pertinent if it tends

to prove or disprove an allegation.

per tout et non per my
(per toot ay non per mee) Lat./Fr. By all and not by the half. This phrase refers to the notion that when a man and a wife own an estate, they are neither joint tenants nor tenants in common, because they are considered to be one person by the law. Rather, they both own the estate in its entirety.

petition
A formal written request for something to be done (*e.g.*, a petition to a court is a request to find relief for some wrong committed against one, or for authority to do something; a petition in bankruptcy is a request by a creditor or debtor to the bankruptcy court to find that a debtor is unable to pay his debts and is entitled to the provisions of the Bankruptcy Act).

petitioner
One who presents a petition to a court or any official body or office, seeking relief.

petition in bankruptcy
A petition filed in bankruptcy court, wherein an insolvent debtor seeks protections set forth by the Bankruptcy Code.

petit jury
A common trial jury of usually 12 persons which renders a verdict in civil and criminal cases, as opposed to a grand jury which has a greater number of persons and whose role is not to render a verdict but to determine whether an indictment is justified. Also called "petty jury."

petit larceny
Unlawful taking and carrying away of personal property valued below an amount set by statute, with the intent to deprive its owner of its use. Also called "petty larceny." *Compare* grand larceny.

petty jury
See petit jury.

petty larceny
See petit larceny.

physical fact
A fact perceived by the senses.

physician-patient privilege
The patient's right not to disclose communications between himself and his physician, or have the physician disclose the contents of their communications. The privilege is inapplicable when the patient has put her physical condition in issue (*e.g.*, in a personal injury action).

picket
The practice of attempting to influence someone by patrolling a location, usually with signs or placards. This is often done by labor in disputes with management to publicize grievances, to promote a strike, or to promote union membership by employees. The right to picket is constitutionally protected when done peaceably, but may be unlawful when it is not a truthful representation of the facts, or if it is dangerous to the public safety.

pickpocket
One who secretly steals money or other valuable property from the person of another.

piercing the corporate veil
Phrase referring to a court's refusal to grant immunity to

corporate officers or entities for their wrongful acts. Such refusal is an exception to the general rule that individuals are shielded by their corporate employers from personal liability for wrongful acts done while in the corporate purview. Courts will do so when, among other instances, the corporation is engaged in fraud.

Pierringer release

A release of one co-defendant in which the plaintiff agrees to reduce her recovery from the remaining defendants by the amount of consideration received from the released defendant. *Pierringer v. Hoger,* 21 Wis. 2d 182, 124 N.W. 2d 106 (1963).

pilferage

1. Stealing something of small value 2. Petty larceny. 3. Stealing a small part of something rather than the whole.

pimp

Person who procures customers for prostitutes; a panderer.

piracy

1. Act of robbery and violence committed on the high seas or in the air. 2. Infringement of copyright by making and selling unauthorized copies of a work.

P.J.

Abbreviation for "presiding judge."

plagiarism

Copying and publishing as one's own work all or part of the work of another. Plagiarism does not exist if work alleged to be copied is arrived at independently. Certain uses of copyrighted material are allowed under the "fair use doctrine" of the Copyright Act without the consent of the copyright owner.

plain error

Rule which requires a retrial if, during the trial, an error occurred which plainly affected the defendant's rights and which, if uncorrected, would result in a miscarriage of justice. The retrial is compulsory even if the defendant failed to object at the time of the error.

plaintiff

1. Person who brings a lawsuit; the complainant. 2. The prosecution in a criminal case.

plain view

Unconcealed; immediately apparent. This term refers to a maxim of police search and seizure, wherein officers may seize objects which are in plain view, and are clearly evidential in nature, if the officers are justified in being in the viewing area.

plat

A map showing the boundaries and location of real estate in a town, village or subdivision, and the streets and parcels which are adjacent to the property.

plea

1. In common law pleading, a defendant's formal response to a criminal charge or a civil suit. Pleas in equity are either "dilatory" or "peremptory." Dilatory pleas seek to defeat the plaintiff's case based on a matter not connected with the merits of the case. Peremptory pleas are based on the merits of the action. These equity pleas are now obsolete with the adoption of the Rules of Civil Procedure. 2. Criminal pleas are guilty, not guilty, and "nolo contendere."

plea bargaining

Process by which a defendant's attorney and a prosecutor bargain for a mutually satisfactory disposition of a criminal case. Often this involves the defendant's pleading guilty to a lesser offense or to only some counts in a multi-count indictment in exchange for a lighter sentence. The plea bargain arrangement is subject to court approval.

plead

To formally answer a criminal charge or a plaintiff's complaint in a civil action; to make a pleading.

pleading

A written statement by a plaintiff or defendant setting forth the material facts on which he bases his case. Under the Federal Rules of Civil Procedure the pleadings consist of a complaint, an answer, a reply to a counterclaim, an answer to a cross-claim, a third-party complaint, and a third-party answer. *See* Federal Rule of Civil Procedure 7(a). Pleadings consist of simple, concise and direct averments of claims for relief, defenses, and denials. *See* Federal Rule of Civil Procedure 8.

pledge

1. Act of delivering personal property to a creditor to be held as security for payment of a debt or performance of an obligation.
2. The property so delivered.

plenary

Absolute; complete, full (*e.g.*, a "plenary action" is a complete, formal action heard on the merits; a "summary proceeding" is a shortened, simplified process used to expedite the disposition of a case).

plurality

A greater number. A plurality of votes received by a winning candidate in an election with more than two candidates is greater than the number received by any other candidate. A plurality opinion of an appellate court is that opinion held by the greatest number of judges while not being a majority.

pocket veto

A situation in which an executive chooses not to approve or veto legislation that has been passed by the legislature. When the legislature adjourns, the legislation dies as a result of the executive's inaction.

P.O.D. account

Pay on death; an account payable to person during her lifetime and upon her death, payable to another person or persons.

point

1. A proposition or question of law raised in a suit. 2. In real estate: A charge for lending money, collected at the time the loan is made, equal to 1% of the principal amount of the loan. 3. In the stock market, a point means $1; in the bond market, it means $10.

point and click agreement

A type of license to download or use software. A person gives her assent to the terms of the license by pointing and clicking on an area of a web page (usually, the words "I agree").

point reserved

An issue which a court decides provisionally, thereby reserving it for possible future argument (*e.g.*, at a hearing on a motion for a new trial), so that the matter at hand may proceed.

poison pill
A defensive tactic used to protect a corporation from a takeover. A typical poison pill defense allows shareholders to buy additional shares at a discount if one shareholder acquires a certain percentage of the corporation's stock.

police court
1. A local or municipal court. An inferior court with jurisdiction over minor offenses.

police power
A broad, flexible term for the authority possessed by the state to regulate private actions in order to promote and maintain the public health, safety, welfare, and order.

policy
1. The general principles which guide a government's actions; the course of action taken (*e.g.*, foreign policy, domestic policy). 2. The intention or objective of a statute or law as distinguished from the letter of the law. "Public policy" means the public

good. 3. A contract for insurance. 4. A lottery, a numbers game.

political
Related to government. Political rights or liberties are those which a citizen has to participate in government. A political crime is a crime against the government.

political party
An association of individuals united to pursue political goals, such as the nomination and election of a candidate, whose members usually possess certain common beliefs about governmental policy.

political question
A legal issue which is so political in nature that courts will decline to adjudicate, leaving it instead to the legislative or executive branches to resolve.

poll
1. (v.) To question each juror individually as to his verdict. 2. To question the electorate for the purpose of forecasting the result of an election. 3. To vote or to receive a vote. 4. (n.) A head; an individual. 5. a list of individuals, as of jurors or of

persons who may vote in an election.

poll tax

A tax levied on certain classes of people as a prerequisite to voting. Illegal in all federal and state elections.

polyandry

The condition of a woman who has more than one living husband.

polygamy

The condition of a man or woman who has several living spouses. It is illegal in all states.

polygraph

A lie detector test. An electro-mechanical instrument that records changes in physiological processes during questioning. Polygraph results are inadmissible as evidence in some jurisdictions.

Ponzi scheme

(PON-zee *or* PON-zeye scheme) A type of investment fraud in which investors' returns are paid by funds contributed by subsequent investors, rather than by a return on investments.

pool

A group or combination of persons or corporations engaged in the same business, who combine resources so as to eliminate competition among themselves or control the market. Any pooling arrangement which thwarts competition within an industry violates the Sherman Antitrust Act.

pornography

Any obscene material which appeals to the prurient interest, depicts sexual conduct in a patently offensive way, and lacks serious literary, artistic, political, or scientific value.

positive evidence

Direct evidence that can prove a fact without any presumption (*e.g.*, eyewitness testimony). It is distinguished from "circumstantial evidence."

positive law

Law specifically created and enforced by a proper authority for the government of society. Also, those laws established by tacit approval of society.

positivism
The theory that one best judges a legal system by viewing its positive law.

posse
(pos-see) 1. Lat. A possibility. A thing "in posse" may possibly exist. "In esse" means it actually exists. 2. A group of persons that assists a sheriff with his duties, such as the arrest of a suspect. Same as "posse comitatus."

posse comitatus
Lat. The power of the country. This includes all able-bodied men who may be called to assist a sheriff with his duties. Such persons have the same protection of the law that the sheriff has when they act under the sheriff's orders. Same as "posse."

possession
Exclusive dominion and control over property. Possession is more than actual physical custody, which is mere keeping and caring, but it involves an assertion of a *right* to exercise dominion and control. The two kinds of possession are "actual" and "constructive." Someone who has direct physical control over

something has actual possession of it. Constructive possession is where someone has the power and intention of exercising control over something while it is not in his actual possession. A tenant who occupies an apartment is in actual possession of it while the owner of it is in constructive possession of it.

possessory action
A lawsuit to obtain actual possession of property, as distinguished from a "petitory action" in which a plaintiff seeks to establish title. An eviction is a possessory action. *See* eviction.

possessory interest
The right to exert control over specific land to the exclusion of others, coupled with the intent to exercise that right.

possibility of reverter
Reverter or reversion is a future interest kept by someone who transfers property. "Possibility of reverter" is such an interest remaining only as a possibility because it is dependent on the occurrence of a future contingency. Thus, when a grantor or testator conveys an estate by

conditional or determinable fee, there remains only the possibility of reverter because the estate does not "revert" back to her until a specified condition is breached or an event occurs.

POOSSLQ

Census Bureau acronym for "persons of opposite sex sharing living quarters." While intended to refer only to unmarried couples, the literal definition includes married couples as well.

Postal Regulatory Commission

An independent agency established to regulate and determine postage rates.

post-conviction relief proceedings

Procedure in which a convicted prisoner may challenge alleged constitutional violations, after the defendant has exhausted the normal review process. Also "PCR actions."

post date

To date an instrument, such as a check, later than the actual date on which it is signed. This does not affect the negotiability of the instrument. U.C.C. § 3–114.

post hoc ergo propter hoc

(post hock air-go PROP-ter hock) Lat. After this, therefore because of this. This term refers to the fiction that because one event happened after another, the preceding event caused the subsequent event.

posthumous child

Child born after the death of its father.

posting

1. The act of mailing an object or document. 2. The act of displaying for public view. 3. The procedure by which a bank pays a negotiable instrument (*e.g.,* a check) and records its payment.

post mortem

Lat. After death. Term usually refers to an autopsy; an examination of a dead body.

postnuptial agreement

Agreement between spouses made after marriage regarding division of property upon occurrence of event, such as divorce or separation.

post-trial motions

Motions permitted after trial ends (*e.g.,* motion for new trial).

pot

Slang for marijuana.

potentia non est nisi ad bonum
(poe-TEN-shee-a non est NEE-see ad BOW-num) Lat. Power does not exist, except for the public good.

pourover

A provision in a will which directs the distribution of money or other valuables into a previously established trust. This term less often refers to a provision in a trust placing the assets of the trust into a will.

power

The right, ability, or authority to do something, such as to change a legal relation or to dispose of property. Powers are classified as "naked" and "coupled with an interest" (*e.g.*, when authority is granted to a stranger to dispose of property in which the stranger had and continues to have no interest, the authority is "naked power;" authority granted to a person who has a present or future interest in property is called power "coupled with an interest"). *See also* constitutional power, corporate power.

power of appointment

Authority given to a person (donee) by deed or will to dispose of property, or interest therein, vested in someone other than himself. A donee with "general power of appointment" is unrestricted as to whom he may appoint to receive the property. "Special power of appointment" limits the donee's choice of beneficiaries. *See* power.

power of attorney

Document by which a person (principal) grants authority to another (agent) to perform specified acts on the principal's behalf. Also called "letter of attorney" and "warrant of attorney."

power coupled with an interest

A power or right to perform an act, accompanied by an interest in the property which is subject to the power.

power of acceptance

An offeree's capacity to create a binding contract upon accepting the terms of an offer.

practice

1. Custom; habit; usual procedure. 2. Court procedure (*i.e.*, the

formal steps of a judicial proceeding). 3. (v.) To engage in a
profession, such as medicine or
law.

praecipe
(PREE-sip-ee) 1. A command;
an order; a written note ordering
a person to do something or
show cause why he should not.
2. A note stating the particulars
of a writ one wishes to be issued
by a court officer (*e.g.*, for summons). 3. An order to the clerk of
the trial court ordering preparation of the trial record for review
by an appellate court.

prayer (for relief)
1. The request made by a person
seeking relief, or redress of an
alleged wrong. 2. The part of a
pleading in which a request for
relief is made.

preamble
A clause at the beginning of a
constitution, statute, document,
or ordinance which states the
purpose for its enactment. A
preamble is explanatory and is
not an essential part of a document.

precatory words
Words expressing advice, recommendation, wish, or request,
rather than those that command.
Term is used to describe certain
language in a trust or will. A
"precatory trust" is one that uses
such language. It can be interpreted as being unenforceable
due to its mild, nonobligatory
language; or it can be held as a
valid, enforceable trust if the
language on the whole might be
construed as imperative and the
subject of the request and the
person(s) intended to benefit
from it are clear.

precedent
1. A previously decided case
which is used as an example or
authority for similar cases which
subsequently arise. (*See* stare
decisis.) 2. A rule of law established for a certain type of case.
3. A "precedent condition" or
"condition precedent" is a condition that must exist before something, such as a contract or an
estate, can take effect.

preceding estate
An estate after which a future
interest arises.

precept

An order, command, or writ given by one in authority to another to perform a duty within his power; a warrant; a process (*e.g.*, a precept is given by a judge to the police to bring a person to court).

precinct

A police or election district.

predecessor

One who goes or has gone before another; correlative of "successor."

preemption

1. A doctrine based on the Supremacy Clause of the U.S. Constitution (Article VI, clause 2) which holds that federal legislation overrides state legislation when both deal with the same subject matter. 2. Act of buying something, such as stock, before all others.

preemptive rights

A stockholder's privilege to buy issues of the corporation's new stock, and thereby maintain a constant percentage of ownership.

preference

Act of preferring one over another, especially as in an insolvent's payment of some of his creditors over others.

preferential transfer

Transfer to a creditor by an insolvent debtor shortly before the debtor files bankruptcy. A creditor who receives a preferential transfer receives a greater share of the debtor's assets than he would otherwise be entitled to receive.

preferred stock

Type of capital stock of a corporation that gives its holder priority over common stockholders in the distribution of dividends, or of company assets upon dissolution. Shares of this stock are called "preferred shares."

prejudice

1. Bias; preconceived opinion; a leaning in the mind toward one side of an issue without justification. 2. Prejudice in a judge refers to a mental disposition he has toward a party to the litigation and not toward its subject matter. It renders him unable to make an impartial decision.

3. Detriment, deprivation of a right or interest, as in a change of position for the worse after relying on another's promise.

prejudicial error
Error by a court which detrimentally affects the legal rights of a party and which, if uncorrected, would result in a miscarriage of justice. This may be grounds for a new trial or for a reversal of a decision of a lower court. Same as "reversible error."

preliminary hearing
An initial hearing conducted to determine whether probable cause exists to justify holding a person for trial. In felony cases, it is a hearing conducted before an indictment. Same as "preliminary examination."

premeditation
Thinking about and deciding to do something before doing it; plotting. The thought may be for any length of time. It is one of the elements of first-degree murder. *See* malice aforethought.

premise
The underlying proposition upon which an argument or conclusion is based.

premises
1. Land, building, and the surrounding environs (*e.g.*, in criminal law, a search warrant covers the premises owned by the suspect; in insurance law, insurance covers the premises. 2. In workers' compensation: Wherever business activity occurs. 3. The statements or clauses put before (*e.g.*, in pleading, the "premises" are the earlier clauses in the pleading).

premises liability
The legal responsibility of the owner or occupier of land for injuries occurring to people on the land.

premium
1. The amount paid by the insured for an insurance policy. 2. The excess of the market price of stock over its par value. 3. A reward; bonus.

prenuptial agreement
An agreement entered into by prospective spouses which sets

forth the financial and property rights of both in anticipation of death or divorce; antenuptial agreement.

preparation

In criminal law, consists of planning or arranging means or acts necessary for commission of crime. *Contrast* attempt offense, which requires conduct actually directed toward commission after preparation.

preponderance

In civil litigation, when all the evidence more clearly and more probably favors one side than the other, that side has established a "preponderance of the evidence" which satisfies its burden of proof.

preponderance of the evidence

Standard of proof necessary to prevail at judgment in a civil action. When one proves something to the preponderance of the evidence, it is more likely to be true than not.

prerogative

An exclusive power or privilege, exhibited by an official or branch of government (*e.g.*, the power to veto legislation is the president's prerogative).

prerogative writ

In the old common law, discretionary writs of the court issued not as a matter of right but for good cause (*e.g.*, writs of mandamus, certiorari, procedendo, quo warranto, and habeas corpus). Today, many of these writs are specifically established and regulated by statute, and the old discretionary prerogative writs are abolished.

prescription

1. Remedy for disease; drugs and medicine. 2. The process of acquiring an easement (the right to use part of another's property, water, or light) by continuous use, rather than by asking the owner of the property. "Prescription" applies to easements as "adverse possession" applies to real property.

present

Now existing; now occurring (*e.g.*, a "present estate" is one in which the owner now possesses the estate; a "present sale" is one in which the property exchanges hands when the contract is made).

pre-sentence report
The report prepared by a probation department to assist the court in passing sentence on a convicted defendant.

presentment
1. A written accusation made by the grand jury, instructing the prosecutor to issue an indictment against the accused. 2. The production of a negotiable instrument (*e.g.*, a check) to the party liable for payment or to the drawee for acceptance.

present recollection revived
The use of a writing to refresh a witness's present recollection of a past event. The writing is not admissible evidence.

presents
Term used in a legal document to designate that document (*e.g.*, "By these presents the parties agree . . . .").

president
1. Chief officer or executive of an organization or corporation who presides at meetings, administers the business of the organi-

zation, and supervises employees. 2. Chief executive of a nation or state, usually elected by the citizens (*e.g.*, President of the United States).

presumed intent
One is presumed to intend the natural and probable consequences of her voluntary acts (*e.g.*, criminal intent can be presumed from the act, except in specific intent crimes).

presumption
In litigation, an assumption of fact arising from a basic fact and based on a rule of law, created by statute or by the courts. The presumption is a rule of evidence that shifts the burden of proof or the burden of producing evidence to the party against whom the presumption is made, to prove that the fact assumed is not true (*e.g.*, in a criminal trial, the defendant is entitled to the presumption of innocence (based on a rule of law) and the prosecutor must prove him guilty).

Presumptions are either "conclusive" or "rebuttable." Conclusive presumptions are, as a matter of law, final against the parties and the opposing party may introduce no evidence on the matter. Rebuttable presumptions may be attacked by the opposing party, who may introduce evidence on the matter.

presumption of innocence
The maxim that a person is innocent of a crime until proven guilty.

presumptive evidence
Prima facie evidence, or evidence that is not conclusive, which is treated as true until and unless it is rebutted by other evidence (*e.g.*, evidence which a statute regards as presumptive of another fact unless rebutted). Also "prima facie evidence."

pretermitted heir
Offspring of the testator omitted in the testator's will or born after the will was made. Some states provide by statute that the pretermitted heir be included in the distribution of the testator's property.

pretrial conference
1. In a civil suit, a conference held after pleadings and before the trial, wherein parties outline the issues to be tried, the evidence to be introduced, and discovery procedures. 2. In a criminal case, this conference takes place after indictment and before the trial, and is much more narrow in scope because of the defendant's right against self-incrimination.

pretrial intervention
Rehabilitation procedure in which selected criminal defendants are excused from prosecution and placed instead in remedial, probationary programs. Upon completion of the "PTL" program, a charge is erased from the defendant's record.

prevailing party
The party in whose favor a legal judgment is rendered.

prevarication
Evasion of the truth; deceitful conduct.

preventive detention
Pretrial confinement imposed on a party while awaiting trial. Preventive detention is generally imposed against criminal defendants who have threatened to escape, or against mentally ill defendants who pose a risk to

themselves or others and are thus held without bail.

price
The amount a seller charges for his goods or a buyer pays for goods purchased; consideration given for goods received.

price discrimination
The practice of selling the same product to different buyers at different prices. Price discrimination is prohibited under the Clayton Act where it interferes with fair competition, unless costs of production are different between the buyers, the products are obsolete, or the price was lowered in good faith to meet the competition.

price fixing
The cooperative and unlawful setting of prices by manufacturers or dealers in a market. Such activity violates the Sherman Antitrust Act.

priest-penitent privilege
One's right not to disclose communications between oneself and a member of the clergy, or have the clergy member disclose the contents of their communications.

primae impressionis
(PREE-mai im-pres-see-OWN-is) Lat. First impression.

prima facie
(PRIME-a FAY-shee) Lat. On its face. Describing a fact convincing on its face, without any further proof of validity.

prima facie case
A case in which the plaintiff has presented sufficient evidence to entitle him to a decision by the judge or jury; a case which compels a favorable decision when no contrary or rebutting evidence is presented.

prima facie tort
An unjustified intentional infliction of harm that results in damage to another person, by doing something that would otherwise be lawful.

primary
1. First in time or importance.
2. Elections.

primary caregiver
The parent who has had the greatest responsibility for the

day-to-day care and rearing of a minor child. The laws in many states give preference to the parent who is the primary caregiver when determining the physical custody of a child.

primary evidence
Original or "best evidence" which is the most satisfactory way of proving a point in issue (*e.g.*, the real gun in a murder case, the eyewitness's testimony, or the original contract).

primogeniture
(pry-mo-JEN-i-chur) Ancient common law rule of inheritance in which the eldest son of the deceased would inherit all the property. By contrast, "gavelkind" inheritance gave all sons an equal share.

principal
1. Most important or highest in rank. 2. In agency law: one who directs or allows another to act for his benefit, subject to his direction and control. The principal may be "disclosed" (known to third parties); "partially disclosed" (when third parties know only that the agent is acting for some principal); or "undis-

closed" (when third parties do not know that the agent is acting for any principal). 3. In criminal law: one who commits a crime, as opposed to an "accessory," who may aid the crime but is not present at the commission of the crime. 4. In commercial law: the amount of the loan or investment, not including any interest. 5. In trust law: the money and property in the trust, not including any profit. 6. In the law of guaranty and surety: the one who is obligated to perform a contract which the surety guarantees.

principle
A fundamental rule or doctrine of law which guides judicial decisions.

prior appropriation
Rule that allows the earliest riparian landowner who uses water to take all she can use before other landowners have a right to it.

prior inconsistent statement
In evidence, statements made by a witness which contradict his or her testimony in court. Such statements may be used to impeach the witness.

priority
A legal preference; a right to go first (*e.g.*, in a bankruptcy action, creditors with "priority" are entitled to the first proceeds of the assets).

prior lien
A first or superior lien, which is not necessarily antecedent in time.

prior restraint
The governmental prohibition of a publication or speech prior to its expression. The First Amendment bars such restraint in all but the most extreme circumstances.

prisoner
One who is forcibly held in captivity.

privacy
The right to be let alone, protected by law. The various rights of privacy include the confidentiality of private communications and letters, the freedom to make personal decisions (*e.g.*, marriage and abortion), the right to enjoy private property, and the interest against false publicity. Some states provide for penalties and civil remedies for breach of privacy.

private attorney general
A person who brings a lawsuit that benefits a large number of people or that vindicates an important public policy and is important to the public as a whole. A private attorney general is often entitled to recover her attorney's fees in the litigation.

private judge
An individual hired by private parties to act as a judge and resolve a dispute.

private nuisance
Interference with one's use and enjoyment of his own property, through unreasonable or unlawful means.

private offering
The sale of a security directly to a private person or favored clients such as large institutional investors, outside of a public offering.

privatization
Turning a governmental activity or function over to private individuals or businesses.

privies

Those joined together in interest or in relation to a thing (*e.g.*, privies to contract (those who signed the contract), privies to estate (lessor and lessee), or privies of blood (blood relatives)).

privilege

1. Some advantage or benefit enjoyed by one person or a particular group of persons; a benefit which all citizens do not share. 2. A specific immunity (*e.g.*, physician-patient privilege).

privileged communication

Statements made by one person or another which may be withheld as confidential by that other person when he is a witness in court regarding the conversation (*e.g.*, patient-physician, client-attorney, penitent-priest, or husband-wife communications are protected).

privilege from arrest

The privilege, granted by government, of specific persons to be immune from arrest for certain acts.

privileges and immunities

The basic rights common to all U.S. citizens, as established by the Privileges and Immunities Clause in Article 4 of the Constitution, and reinforced in the Privileges and Immunities Clause of the 14th Amendment. These provisions guarantee that when citizens move from one state to another, they may enjoy the same rights as the native citizens of that state.

privity

A relationship of common interests or common legal rights (*e.g.*, a privity of contract is required in a breach of contract action; the defendant must be a party in interest to the plaintiffs contract).

privy

One person who has privity with another.

pro

Lat. For.

probable cause

The existence of certain facts which would lead a person of reasonable intelligence and prudence to believe that a crime has been committed. Probable cause is required before an arrest or search warrant is issued by the judge.

probate
The legal procedure necessary to prove that a will was legally made; more generally, the whole legal process having to do with legal administration of wills and estates.

probation
In criminal law, the sentence imposed by the judge when the defendant is not imprisoned but instead is required to report periodically to the probation officer who supervises the probation, ensuring that the person on probation is productively employed and out of trouble with the law. "Parole," in contrast, is release of the defendant after he has served part of his prison sentence.

probative
Serving to establish or prove the truth.

pro bono publico
(pro bone-o PUB-lik-o) Lat. For the public good (*e.g.*, a lawyer engaged in "pro bono publico" activities represents, without charge, those who cannot afford legal services).

procedendo
(pro-she-DEN-do) Lat. Duty to have proceeded. Refers to a superior court writ commanding an inferior court to proceed to judgment. Also "remand."

procedural due process
Constitutional guarantee that a person whose right to life, liberty or property is to be affected is entitled to reasonable notice and an opportunity to he heard and present a defense to the proposed action before a fair and impartial decision-maker. *See* due process of law.

procedure
The process by which lawsuits are resolved; the rules regulating the pleadings, service of process, trial practice, evidence, and appeal. In contrast, "substantive" rules create and define legal rights and duties.

proceedings
The events which take place in court connected with a lawsuit. More generally, all the actions of

legal officials (judges, clerks, magistrates, officers) from the commencement of a lawsuit until the enforcement of the final judgment.

process

1. The formal papers used to notify a defendant in a civil suit that he must appear at trial. 2. The method by which a court exercises its jurisdiction over persons or property connected with the action.

proclamation

1. An official announcement, usually made by a high government official (*e.g.,* president, governor). 2. The document containing such a public declaration. 3. A bailiff's declaration that something is about to be done.

proctor

1. Person appointed to manage another's affairs or to represent him in court; a procurator, attorney, or proxy. 2. Originally, an officer who performed the duties of an attorney in ecclesiastical or admiralty courts.

procuration

1. Act by which one person gives another authority to act in his behalf; agency; proxy. 2. Act of procuring a person for sexual purposes.

procurator

An agent; attorney; proctor; anyone who, under power of attorney, acts in another's behalf. *See* proctor, procuration.

produce

1. (v.) To show; to bring forth; to furnish, such as to produce evidence. 2. To yield, as in to produce dividends. 3. (n.) Something that grows or is found in the earth (*e.g.,* fruits, vegetables, gas, oil).

product liability

Responsibility which manufacturers and sellers of merchandise have to persons injured or damaged due to defects in their products. The manufacturer or seller is liable even though he has not been negligent (*i.e.,* he is "strictly liable"). *See* strict liability.

professional corporation (P.C.)

A corporation established for the purpose of practicing a profession (*e.g.*, lawyers, accountants, doctors).

proffer

To offer or present, as in to produce and offer a document to support a cause of action.

profiling

A law enforcement officer's use of impermissible factors such as race or ethnicity as grounds to stop or detain a person.

profit

Gain, benefit, or advantage realized in money or money's worth. In business transactions, it is the difference between income and expenditures. "Gross profit" is the money made from the sale of goods minus the cost of the goods to the seller, excluding expenses and taxes. "Net profit" is money made from the sale of goods minus all costs to the seller.

profit à prendre

(PROF-fit a PRAWN-dre) Fr. A right to enter another's land and to profit from the removal of designated products it yields, such as minerals, trees, or game.

profiteering

Practice of acquiring excessive profits. This is usually done by taking advantage of unusual circumstances, and thus the term carries a derogatory connotation.

profit sharing plan

An employee benefit plan that allows eligible employees to share directly in the employer's profits.

pro forma

Lat. As a matter of form, or for the sake of form. Term is used to mean a decree or judgment was rendered to facilitate further proceedings, not because it was necessarily right. It is also used to describe financial statements that are based on assumed or anticipated facts.

pro hac vice

(pro hak VEE-chay) Lat. For this one particular occasion. Courts may permit certain acts on a "pro hac vice" basis (*e.g.*, allowing an out-of-state attorney to argue a single case), although such an act generally violates a jurisdiction's norms.

prohibition

Short for a "writ of prohibition." An order issued by a court of superior jurisdiction to an inferior court or quasi-judicial tribunal preventing the latter from dealing with matters outside its jurisdiction.

prolixity

The use of unnecessary words; the state of being verbose. Applied especially to wordiness in pleadings and affidavits. Adj. is "prolix."

promise

An expression of an intention to do or not do something. A promise binds a person in honor, conscience, or law, and it may be written or oral. A promise made by deed is called a "covenant." A reciprocal exchange of promises, or a promise made in exchange for consideration, is called an "agreement."

promissory estoppel

Doctrine in equity that states that a promise is binding if the person who made it (promisor) could reasonably expect another (promisee) to rely upon it in a substantial way, and that the promisee did indeed rely upon it. The promisor is "estopped," or barred, from denying his promise created a contract, even though one has not been made in the normal way. *See* estoppel.

promissory note

A negotiable instrument by which the maker unconditionally promises to pay a sum of money. It may be made out "to the order of" a person named on it or simply to "bearer," and it may be payable on demand or by a specified date.

promoter

Person who takes the initial steps in the formation of a corporation. These steps include issuing a prospectus, writing a charter, and selling stock.

promulgation

1. Publication. 2. Act of officially announcing.

proof

1. The result of evidence; that evidence which establishes the existence of a fact, that which is required to convince a judge or jury as to the truth of something. (For distinction between proof

and evidence, *see* evidence.)
2. Summary of the oral testimony a witness is expected to give at trial. This testimony is given to the witness's counsel before trial to guide counsel during the trial.

property

1. The exclusive right one has to possess, use, enjoy, and dispose of anything he owns. 2. Anything that is owned, be it land, personalty, or an incorporeal right. 3. In criminal law, property means anything that has value. 4. When used in reference to trusts, an interest in something and not the thing itself. *See* personal property, real property, community property, chattel.

property settlement

The division of marital property upon divorce, either by a court-sanctioned agreement between the parties or by a court ruling.

proportional representation

A voting system that guarantees that minority interests will be represented in the government.

proposal

An offer; an expression of intention to do something. A proposal

is not always an offer, but may only be an initial statement made for consideration by another. When this is the case, a proposal does not ripen into a contract as an offer does.

propound

To propose; to offer; to put something forth for consideration (*e.g.,* to propound a will is to offer it to the probate court with the request it be declared valid).

proprietary

1. Owned exclusively. 2. Belonging to a corporation or individual.

proprietary functions

Acts performed by a municipality or state for the particular benefit of its citizens (*e.g.,* owning and operating a parking garage). *Contrast* with governmental functions.

proprietor

The one who exclusively owns a proprietorship; owner.

pro rata

Lat. According to the rate; in proportion to some rate or standard; proportionately (*e.g.,* an insolvent may have his assets divided among his creditors on a "pro rata" basis, meaning each would receive payment in equal proportion to what he is owed).

pro rate
To divide, distribute, or assess proportionately. *See* pro rata.

prorogation
1. Act of putting off something to another day, especially a legislative or court session. (*See* continuance.) 2. Civil law: An agreement to extend time beyond which was previously allowed.

pro se
(pro say) Lat. For himself; in her own behalf. A person who appears in court "pro se" does not have a lawyer and represents herself.

prosecution
1. The process of initiating and proceeding with a criminal or civil lawsuit; process of trying formal charges against an alleged offender. Verb is "prosecute." 2. The government's side of a criminal suit. *See* prosecutor.

prosecutor
Public official who prosecutes a person accused of a crime. A prosecutor acts as the trial lawyer on behalf of the government and may be elected or appointed. A prosecutor for the state is called a District Attorney, County Attorney, or State's Attorney depending on the jurisdiction. A federal prosecutor is called a U.S. Attorney.

prospective
Concerned with or related to the future. A prospective law applies to situations in the future, as opposed to a retrospective or retroactive law which encompasses the past.

prospectus
1. A document published by a company that describes the company and the securities it offers for sale to the public. By law, a prospectus must be furnished to a potential buyer before he purchases any securities. 2. More broadly, prospectus means any communication, either printed or broadcast, that offers securities for sale or confirms the sale of securities.

prostitute
One who engages in sexual activity for pay.

prostitution

Act of offering, agreeing to, or actually engaging in sexual intercourse, or any unlawful sex act, for pay.

pro tanto

(pro TAN-to) Lat. For so much; to such an extent. 1. Partial payment on a claim. 2. Commonly used to describe the government's partial payment for property taken under right of eminent domain.

protect

To prevent from being injured, attacked, or harmed.

protected activity

Conduct that a person may engage in without lawful retaliation (*e.g.*, cooperating with a discrimination investigation against an employer).

protected class

In employment discrimination law, a group of people protected from discrimination based on their membership in the class. Protected classes under federal law include race, color, sex, national origin, religion, age, pregnancy, genetic makeup, or disability.

protective custody

The holding of a person by authorities, to protect him or her from either self-inflicted harm or harm by another.

protective order

1. Any court order intended to protect a party from abuse or harassment by another person. 2. An order limiting the scope or methods of pre-trial discovery.

pro tem

Lat. Short for "pro tempore," for the time being; temporarily (*e.g.*, a mayor who serves "pro tem" serves on a provisional basis until he, or someone else, is officially elected).

protest

1. Written expression of disagreement with the legality or justice of a payment, or the amount of a payment, made to protect oneself against the effects one's payment would imply (*e.g.*, taxes are sometimes paid in full but under protest, protecting the taxpayer's right to have his taxes readjusted). 2. Statement

written by a notary public at the request of a holder of a negotiable instrument, that states the instrument was presented for payment or acceptance, and that same was refused. In the statement, the notary "protests" against all parties to the instrument, and declares them liable for losses or damage due to their "refusal of payment or acceptance." 3. A statement written by an importer contesting the amount of the duty charged on his goods. 4. Maritime law: A written statement by the master of a vessel stating the weather-related or natural causes of damage to his ship or cargo.

prothonotary

Title sometimes given to a chief clerk or registrar of a court.

protocols

1. First or original drafts of an agreement between countries or records of preliminary negotiations. 2. Accepted methods of procedure among diplomats or heads of state. 3. Ceremonial rules and procedures. 4. Formalities.

province

1. A colony or geographical division of a country (*e.g.*, the Canadian province of Quebec). 2. Duty, function, power, responsibility, or sphere of activity of a profession.

provisional

Temporary; preliminary; made or existing for a time or until something further is done; tentative (*e.g.*, provisional remedy is a court order which helps to enforce the law on a temporary basis).

proviso

"It being provided;" condition or stipulation; qualification; limitation. Usually a clause in a contract, statute, deed, or lease which imposes a condition that must be met in order for the instrument to be valid.

provocation

1. An act by one person that incites or influences a second person to perform a particular act, usually an illegal one. 2. An act by one person that so enrages a second person that he loses self-control and commits an act he would not ordinarily commit.

Provocation may reduce the severity of a crime, such as reducing murder to manslaughter.

proximate cause
1. Something that produces a result in the natural sequence of events and without which the result could not have occurred. One's liability is generally limited to results "proximately caused" by his actions. 2. Real cause; direct cause; legal cause.

proxy
Person who is authorized by another person to act for him, usually to vote for him at a meeting (*e.g.*, one permitted to vote for a shareholder of a corporation). Written authorization given by one person to another so that the second can act for the first.

proxy statement
Information required by the S.E.C. that must be given to stockholders prior to solicitation of their shares.

prudent person rule
Investment principle that states that a fiduciary may buy securities that any prudent person of discretion and intelligence would buy, in order to earn a reasonable income and preserve capital. In some states where this rule is eschewed, fiduciaries must buy securities from an established seller or broker.

prurient interest
A shameful or morbid interest in sex, nudity, or excretion. *See* obscenity.

public
1. All of the citizens of a state, nation, city, or community. 2. That which belongs to the people at large. 3. That which affects, or is open to or related to all persons, as distinguished from private. 4. The body politic.

publication
1. Making public; the offering of anything to the public at large. 2. In defamation law, the communication of defamatory material to someone other than the person defamed. 3. A printed book, circular, magazine, or newspaper. 4. The acknowledgment by a testator in the presence of witnesses that an instrument is his last will.

public defender
An attorney paid by the government to defend indigent criminal defendants.

public domain
1. Land owned by the government, as opposed to private property. 2. Free for anyone to use; not protected by patent or copyright.

public figure
Figures who have achieved public fame or notoriety (*e.g.*, athletes, entertainment celebrities, artists). Public figures must prove actual malice on the part of the press, in order to win damages in a defamation action.

public forum
A place open to the public that has been designated or has traditionally been used for free speech and expression.

public policy
Flexible, vague term often meaning "what is good for (or will not harm) the general public;" principle of law holding that no person can do that which has a tendency to harm the general public.

public property
That which is owned or controlled by the government and/or dedicated to public use.

public safety exception
Exception to the *Miranda* rule that allows law enforcement officers to ask questions of a detained person if there is an immediate need to protect the public (*e.g.,* "Where's the gun?") without first advising the person of his right to remain silent.

public use
The use of government-condemned property in such a way that it confers a benefit to the whole community. The government must prove that a proposed taking is for a public use before it may invoke eminent domain.

public utility
A privately owned business which is granted the exclusive right to provide an important service to a particular area, and therefore must adhere to government regulation of some of its business practices (*e.g.*, pricing).

publish

1. To make or effect a publication. 2. To give publicity to. 3. To print for general circulation. 4. To print a manuscript.

puffing

Statement made by a seller which is not a representation of fact, but rather an exaggeration concerning the quality of goods; generally bragging about the product rather than a legally binding representation.

punishment

Penalty imposed for wrongdoing by authority of the law (*e.g.,* a fine or incarceration).

punitive damages

Award of damages not related to actual harm caused to plaintiff, but instead intended to punish the defendant and deter future wrongdoing. Usually awarded when a tort is aggravated by evil motives, actual malice, deliberate violence, or oppression. Also called "exemplary damages" or "vindictive damages."

pur autre vie

(purr OWE-ter vee) Fr. For or during the life of another. Also

"per autre vie." An "estate pur autre vie" is an estate held for the life of a third person.

purchase

1. To acquire title to property by voluntary act and agreement and for valuable consideration; to buy. 2. Acquisition of property by any means other than by descent.

"Purchase" includes taking by sale, discount, negotiation, mortgage, pledge, lien, issue or reissue, gift or any other voluntary transaction creating an interest in property. U.C.C. § 1–201(32).

purchase money security interest (PMSI)

A security interest in goods sold retained by the seller or a lender to secure a loan of the purchase price. *See* U.C.C. § 9–107.

purchaser

One who obtains real or personal property in exchange for valuable consideration.

purge

1. To cleanse; clear. 2. To exonerate from some criminal charge or imputation of guilt or from a contempt.

purloin

To pilfer, steal, filch, commit larceny.

purport

1. (v.) To imply; claim; mean; convey; give the impression. 2. (n.) The meaning, intent, purpose, or objective of something.

purposely

Intentionally or deliberately; not accidentally.

pursuit of happiness

The right to apply one's energies so as to maximize his or her prosperity and enjoyment of life, within the bounds of the law. This right is mentioned in the Declaration of Independence as an "inalienable" right.

purview

1. The purpose, scope, and design of a statute or other enacted law. 2. The enacting part of an act, as distinguished from other parts such as the preamble.

putative

Reputed; supposed; commonly esteemed; believed; assumed (*e.g.*, a putative father is the man believed to be the father of a child born out of wedlock).

pyramiding

The use of investment profits from securities to finance new holdings.

pyramid scheme

A business model that charges participants a fee for participation, and then promises additional payment as they recruit new participants, and as those participants in turn recruit other participants. A pyramid scheme is unsustainable, due to the large number of participants who must be recruited in order for the scheme to remain profitable.

Q

qua

Lat. In the character or capacity of.

quaere

(KWEE-ree) Lat. A question, query, doubt. Indicates that the proposition is open to question.

qualification

1. Possessing the qualities, property, or other circumstances which make a person eligible to fill a public office or profession. 2. Limitation or restriction.

qualified domestic relations order

Abbreviated QDRO ("quid-row"). A court order or judgment in a domestic relations case that provides for an alternate payee's right to receive payments from a pension or profit-sharing plan. Such an order must meet the

requirements of the Internal Revenue Code.

qualified endorsement (indorsement)

An endorsement on the back of a negotiable instrument by which the endorser excludes her liability, usually by adding the words "without recourse" after the signature. U.C.C. § 3-415(b).

qualified privilege

Conditional privilege. Protects a libel defendant from liability only if statements were made without actual malice.

qualify

1. To prepare or make oneself fit to exercise a right, franchise, or office. 2. To restrict, limit, modify.

quantum damnificatus

(KWAN-tum dam-ni-fi-KAT-tus) Lat. How much was he damaged? The issue for determining the amount of compensation to be awarded to the plaintiff.

quantum meruit

(KWAN-tum MARE-oo-it) Lat. As much as he deserves. An equitable doctrine that allows a party to recover for the value of his labor and materials furnished to another even though there was no actual contract so that the other party will not be unjustly enriched. The suit is based on an implied promise to pay.

quantum valebant
(KWAN-tum VAL-e-bant) Lat. As much as they are worth. Form of pleading for payment for goods sold and delivered, based on implied promise by the buyer to pay the seller as much as the goods are reasonably worth.

quarantine
1. Enforced isolation for the purpose of preventing the spread of contagious or infectious diseases. 2. Isolation of a vessel arriving in a foreign port pending formal permission to disembark. 3. Forty-day period during which persons, goods, or animals on a ship where there is a contagious disease must wait before being allowed to land. 4. Privilege of a widow to use a portion of her husband's estate before the estate is settled.

quare
Lat. Wherefore; why; on what account; because.

quare clausum fregit
(KWAR-ray KLAW-sum FREG-git) Lat. Wherefore he broke the close. Action for trespass to recover damages for the unlawful entry upon land of another.

quash
Vacate; set aside; annul; suppress; make void (*e.g.*, to quash an indictment).

quasi
(KWA-zee) Lat. As it were; as if; having the qualities of; related to. Frequently used to show similarities between two subjects, but indicating that there are differences (*e.g.*, quasi-contract).

quasi-contract
1. Contract created by law based on relationship of parties or their actions. 2. An implied contract. Quasi-contract is used to prevent unjust enrichment. Based on theory of quantum meruit.

quasi-judicial
Functioning like a judge. Term is applied to the case-deciding functions of an administrative

agency or an authority which are not really courts of law. The action may include investigating facts, holding hearings and drawing conclusions from them by exercising discretion and judgment of a judicial nature.

query
Question; an inquiry.

Queen's Bench
Superior English common law court, so called because the king or queen formerly sat there in person. It was called Queen's Bench during the reign of a queen.

question
1. Problem; the issue to be decided in a court of law; matter about which opposing parties in a suit disagree; point in controversy. 2. An interrogatory or query put to a witness.

question of fact
Disputed factual contention; question of the truth to be decided usually by a jury after hearing evidence on both sides of a case.

question of law
Disputed legal contention; matter for the court to decide based on interpretation or application of existing laws.

quia timet
(KWEE-a TIM-met) Lat. Because he fears or apprehends. Technical name of a bill in equity practice filed by a party seeking an injunction "because he fears" injury to his rights or property in a pending case.

quick
1. Rapid. 2. The living status of a being.

quickening
That point in a pregnancy at which the fetus first moves.

quid pro quo
(kwid pro kwo) Lat. What for what; something for something. Synonymous with consideration, as in the mutual consideration in a contract which makes the contract binding and valid.

quid pro quo harassment
A type of sexual harassment in which the victim is offered some benefit of employment (*e.g.*, a raise or promotion) in exchange for sexual favors.

quia emptores, statute of
(KWEE-a *or* KEE-a emp-TORE-ays) Lat. An old English act abolishing the feudal era's restraints upon transfer of land.

quiet enjoyment
Covenant in a lease or conveyance by which the lessor or grantor warrants that the lessee or grantee shall enjoy the possession of the premises in peace and without disturbance.

quiet title
An action in court, in which a plaintiff seeks to resolve a real-property ownership dispute with the defendant, who is the adverse claimant to the title.

qui tam
(kee tam) Lat. Who also share. This term refers to an action in which the plaintiff may recover on his own behalf and on behalf of the state.

quitclaim deed
Deed by which the grantor releases all his interest in property by passing any interest, claim, or title in the property which he has. The grantor makes no warranties or covenants for title in a quit-claim deed. The deed only purports to convey such title as the grantor has.

quittance
Lat. Abbreviation of "acquittance;" release.

quo animo
Lat. With what mind, intent, motive.

quorum
1. Majority of the entire body.
2. Minimum number of persons required to be present in order for a deliberative body, such as a committee, board of directors, or shareholders, to legally transact business.

quotation
1. In commercial usage, the stated price of an item. 2. Word-for-word repetition of a statement from some authority, case, law, or statute.

quotient verdict
An improper verdict resulting from the jurors individually determining a damages amount, adding those amounts together and dividing by the number of jurors to obtain a final amount.

quo warranto

(kwo war-RAN-to) Lat. By what authority. 1. A writ by which the court inquires into the right of a person or corporation to hold an office or to exercise a franchise. 2. A legal proceeding to determine whether a person (*e.g.*, a public official), is exercising unlawful authority.

race

A group of people united or classified on the basis of ancestry.

race notice recording statutes

Type of statute for recording interests in real property under which a prior unrecorded conveyance is invalid against a subsequent bona fide purchaser for value who records first without knowledge of the prior instrument.

race recording statutes

Statutes governing recording of interests in real property which provide that the party who records first has priority. Actual notice of prior conveyances is irrelevant. Very few states have this type of statute.

racketeering

An organized conspiracy to commit or attempt crimes of extortion or coercion and other illegal enterprises. Racketeering-related activities are prohibited by the federal Racketeer Influenced and Corrupt Organizations Act (RICO).

radar

A device used to determine the speed, position, or range of objects. Frequently used by police departments to prove the speed of a motor vehicle.

raised check

A check which has been unlawfully altered without the drawer's authorization, to show an amount higher than the original figure.

ranked choice voting

A system of voting in which voters do not select one candidate, but rank the candidates on the ballot according to their preferences. Also called "instant runoff voting" or "preferential voting."

ransom

1. The money or other consideration paid for the release of a

kidnapped person. 2. The return of illegally held property or persons in exchange for payment.

rape

Under common law, unlawful sexual intercourse by a man with a woman committed without her consent and through the use of fear or force by the man against the woman. "Statutory rape," in modern usage, is unlawful sexual intercourse with a female under a certain statutory age, with or without her consent. Under some modern statutes, rape is classified as criminal sexual assault and is gender neutral. Some statutes further enlarge the classification by making rape of a spouse a crime.

rape crisis counselor privilege

A rape counselor's right not to disclose communications, notes, or records regarding an incident of sexual assault. This privilege is limited, is relatively new, and is accordingly recognized by a minority of jurisdictions.

rape shield law

A law that prohibits a defendant from introducing evidence of a sexual assault victim's prior sexual conduct to impeach the character of the victim.

ratable

Subject to taxation; proportional; capable of being estimated.

rate

Proportional or relative amount (*e.g.*, the "rate of interest" is the percentage of the whole which will be paid in interest; the "price rate" is the price amount relating to each specific unit or quantity).

rate of return

A return on an investment, expressed as a percentage of the original investment.

ratification

1. The acceptance or confirmation of a prior act done by oneself or another for one's benefit, which authorizes the prior act as if it had been originally authorized. 2. The approval by state legislatures or popular conventions of proposed constitutional amendments. 3. Subsequent approval by a principal of an agent's unauthorized act.

ratio decidendi
(RAT-ee-o des-i-DEN-dee) Lat. The reason for decision. The grounds or rationale in a case which determine and support the court's decision.

ratio legis est anima legis
(RAT-ee-o LEJ-is est an-NEE-ma LEJ-is) Lat. The reason of law is the soul of law.

rational basis test
Method by which courts determine the constitutionality of a law. Under this test, the legislature must have had a rational basis for enacting a law, and the law must reasonably relate to a legitimate governmental objective, for it to be constitutional. This is the most permissive of tests used by courts for constitutional questions.

ravish
Archaic: To rape. To have carnal knowledge of a woman against her will and with force.

real
1. In civil law, referring to a "thing," as distinguished from a "person." 2. In evidence, referring to the actual, physical objects used by the parties or witnesses. 3. In property law, referring to land, buildings, and estates, as distinguished from "personal" property such as jewelry, objects, etc.

real estate
Land and permanent attachments to the land, including buildings, fences, and all the permanent attachments to the buildings, including heating, plumbing, lighting, masonry, etc.

real estate investment trust (REIT)
A corporation formed by a group of at least 100 shareholders, for the purpose of investing in real estate. REITs are exempt from corporate taxes, as income is taxed directly to shareholders.

Real Estate Settlement Procedures Act (RESPA)
Federal law that requires lenders in residential real estate transactions to disclose the costs of settlement to the borrowers.

real evidence
Evidence submitted during a trial which represents the actual, physical thing sought to be

proved (*e.g.*, the murder weapon, the stolen goods, the heroin, the scar on the victim's body). Real evidence is distinguished from "demonstrative evidence" which can only demonstrate conclusions made from the real thing (*e.g.*, maps, charts, diagrams, scale models).

realization

To obtain the advantage or benefit of a thing or an action (*e.g.*, to receive returns on an investment). The realization of income is a taxable event.

real party in interest

1. The party with the legal right under the applicable substantive law to prosecute or defend the contemplated legal action. 2. The party who is actually interested in the outcome of the action.

real property

Land (including buildings and other permanent attachments to the land) and the rights arising out of land. Real property is distinguished from "personal property," which is temporary and movable in nature. A "leasehold interest," the right to rent land for a particular time, is

characterized as personal property because it is thought to be temporary.

realty

Another term for real estate or real property.

reapportionment

The redistribution of representation in a legislative district, as a result of population changes. Reapportionment must satisfy the Constitution's one person, one vote standard.

reargument

Additional argument of a decision or principle of law about which there has been a misapprehension of facts, or which would have a controlling effect and which has been overlooked.

reasonable accommodation

Under the Americans with Disabilities Act, a modification or adjustment to a job or the work environment that enables a person with a disability to perform essential job functions.

reasonable belief

1. Criminal law standard similar to probable cause. Under this standard, an officer may make an

arrest without a warrant if the officer relied on personal knowledge of facts and circumstances which are reasonably trustworthy, and that would justify a person of average caution in the belief that a felony has been or is being committed. 2. In tort law, this phrase denotes that the actor believes a fact exists and the circumstances which he knows would cause any reasonable person to so believe.

reasonable care

The degree of care which a person of ordinary prudence would ordinarily or usually exercise.

reasonable doubt

In a criminal trial, that doubt which is direct and reasonable in light of all the evidence presented at the trial, which would justify the jury in reaching a verdict of "not guilty." Where the evidence presents a case of guilt beyond all reasonable doubt, the evidence justifies the jury in reaching a verdict of "guilty." A reasonable doubt is more than a mere skepticism but does not need to be represented by clear evidence; it need only be that

doubt which reasonable people would consider.

reasonable person

Any person who exercises qualities of attention, knowledge, intelligence and judgment which society requires of its members for the protection of their own and others' interests. One must meet this standard to avoid liability for negligence. Also "reasonable man."

reasonable time

In contract law, when contracting parties do not set a time for "acceptance" or for "performance," it must be done within a reasonable amount of time, that time which is not unreasonable depending on the nature and circumstances of each case.

rebate

A discount or refund of money given for purchases, prompt payment, overpaid taxes, or rate charges, given back to the payer after he has already paid the full, original sum.

rebut

To defeat, refute, or prove the contrary of an assumption or inference made at trial (*e.g.*, if a plaintiff introduces evidence which raises the presumption that the defendant had notice of a particular fact, the defendant may rebut that presumption with evidence that she had no such notice).

rebuttal, rebutting evidence
Evidence that defeats, refutes, or proves the contrary of facts or presumptions offered in evidence by the opposing party. Rebuttal evidence may be offered at the close of the opponent's case.

rebutter
An early English pleading by the defendant in response to a plaintiff's surrejoinder.

recall
1. Procedure in which a public official, including a judge, may be removed from office through popular vote or through a circulating petition. 2. Procedure in which purchasers of a particular product are notified to take the product back to the seller for adjustments or examinations, usually when the seller or manufacturer believes the product is defective or dangerous.

recall a judgment
To vacate or reverse a judgment for matters of fact.

recapitalization
The restructuring of a corporation's capital structure, (*e.g.*, through major changes in its securities portfolio.)

recaption
At common law, the peaceful recovery of one's property when one is legally entitled to it and when one finds it in another's wrongful possession.

recapture
Situation in which the government requires a taxpayer to pay an amount which he or she had avoided through tax deduction or credit in a previous tax return. The government is said to have "recaptured" that amount.

receipt
Written and signed document, showing the taking or receiving of money or goods. A receipt is not conclusive evidence at court of the taking or receiving, and it may be supplemented in court with oral evidence.

receiver

A court-appointed custodian of assets that are subject to litigation or to a bankruptcy action. The receiver will hold and preserve property of the parties or of the bankrupt while awaiting the court's ruling. In the case of corporations, a receiver may not only manage the assets but will sometimes, upon the court's order, manage the operation of the business.

receivership

A remedy where the court appoints a receiver to hold, preserve, or manage property subject to litigation or to a bankruptcy action. The property or corporation controlled by a receiver is said to be in "receivership."

receiving stolen goods (or stolen property)

The criminal offense of receiving property that has been unlawfully stolen by another, when the person who receives the property knows it to be stolen and acts with fraudulent intent.

recess

1. The time when a trial or hearing is suspended for a short period, for meals, overnight, over the weekend, or for a short investigation. Any period longer than three days is generally called a "continuance." 2. The time between court sessions or between legislative sessions, without a final adjournment of the body.

recidivist

A habitual criminal; a repeat offender. Many states have "recidivist statutes" which subject the repeat offender to longer sentences.

reciprocal wills

Wills made by two or more persons (*e.g.*, husband and wife), with identical provisions and each will favoring the other person. If done in one will, it is a joint and reciprocal will.

reciprocity

A relationship between corporations, persons, or nations, where privileges and benefits are granted by each entity to the other (*e.g.*, "trade reciprocity" is where one country will sell a commodity to another country and that country will sell another commodity of equal worth to the first country).

recitals

Specific statements in a document, deed, or statute, listing the reasons or basis for enacting the document, usually beginning with the word "whereas."

reckless

Careless; inattentive; indifferent. The meaning of "reckless" varies, depending on the circumstances, from merely negligent or careless action to willful disregard of the consequences of an act. "Reckless" conduct indicates a conscious disregard of the substantial risks of certain conduct which a reasonable person would recognize.

reckless disregard

1. Generally, action by one who is aware of the danger of the action, but nonetheless lacks concern for consequences. 2. In a libel action, the publication of work despite serious doubts regarding the truth of the work, or the veracity of the sources on which the writer relied.

reckless driving

Recklessness in operating a motor vehicle, with the knowledge that one's acts will result in probable injury to others, or with wanton disregard of the safety of others.

reclaim

To demand the return of one's property.

recognition

Acceptance or acknowledgment of another's act by one who has authority to approve that act.

recognizance

Formal obligation entered into at court by which a person agrees to perform some act in the future. Courts may or may not require the person to post a bond. In a criminal case, the defendant may be released if he promises to appear for a future hearing. *See* release on recognizance. "Personal recognizance" occurs when the court does not require a bond.

reconciliation

1. Defense to a divorce action that alleges the reuniting of husband and wife with the resumption of marital duties and the cessation of enmity and discord. The defense does not apply in states that have adopted no-fault divorce laws. 2. In accounting,

the process of adjusting the records to conform with each other, to correct possible errors.

reconveyance
The transfer or sale of real property back to its previous owner.

record
1. The precise history of a lawsuit from its commencement to its termination, including all pleadings, evidence, testimony, and judicial decisions. This history is also known as the "record of appeal" and the appellants are usually restricted to those facts in the record. 2. The writing, the memorandum, the item which holds the information preserved (*e.g.*, the sales slip, the transcript, the letter). A "public record" is one prepared and used by a public agency as required by law (*e.g.*, birth and death records). A corporation's records include its charter, bylaws, meeting minutes, contracts, and other accounts of the official business of the corporation which are kept in the regular course of business. 3. (v.) To record; to preserve information in a writing (*e.g.*, to record a deed).

record date
The date on which a person must be registered as a shareholder on the books of a company in order to receive dividends or other benefits, such as the right to vote on company affairs.

recording acts
State statutes providing for the official recording of land or estate interests, as a means of giving constructive notice of ownership. *See* notice recording statute, race notice recording statute, race recording statute.

record owner
1. The owner of real property as stated on public records. 2. The owner of a security as stated on corporate records.

recoupment
Defendant's right to recover part of the plaintiff's award of damages by reducing the plaintiff's claim due to previous payment by the defendant or plaintiff's own wrongful or defective performance of the contract.

recourse
The right of the person who holds a negotiable instrument to

recover against someone who is secondarily liable (*e.g.*, the endorser or cosigner of the instrument).

recover
1. To gain back that which is lost (*e.g.*, to recover one's property). 2. To collect the amount of the court's judgment against the other party.

recrimination
In a divorce case, a charge made by the defendant against the plaintiff that alleges the same or similar marital misconduct (*e.g.*, adultery or cruelty). Recrimination traditionally blocked the divorce (*e.g.*, if the husband sued the wife for a divorce on grounds of adultery and the wife alleged that the husband also committed adultery, he would not be entitled to a divorce). Many states have abolished this doctrine in "no-fault divorce" statutes.

recusation; recusal
The process by which a judge excuses herself or is disqualified from an action, due to prejudice, self-interest, or bias.

reddendum
1. In old English law, rendering; yielding. 2. The clause in the conveyance used by a grantor to denote that he is reserving something for himself, such as rents from the land.

redeem
To buy back; to repurchase; to pay the debts. To redeem a mortgage means to pay the outstanding value of the mortgage and hence achieve full control over the property. A corporation may redeem stock held by shareholders by purchasing it with cash.

redeemable bond
A bond which the issuer may recall for payment. Also "callable bond."

redemption
The repurchase of property or the cancellation of debt (*e.g.*, the purchase of a loan or of a corporation's own shares of stock, or the payment of the outstanding balance of a mortgage). The "right of redemption" is the right of the mortgagor to buy back the property after a "foreclosure" or forced sale, which is a limited

right created and regulated by state statute.

red herring
1. Something that calls attention away from the central issue. 2. A preliminary stock prospectus that has not yet been approved by government securities authorities.

redlining
The illegal and discriminatory practice of rejecting a qualified mortgage or insurance applicant because the property to be mortgaged or insured lies in a specified, often impoverished, area.

redress
Payment or compensation for damages or injuries.

reductio ad absurdum
Lat. Reduced to the absurd. An argument showing that the logical consequences of another argument would be absurd.

reentry (right of)
The right of the grantor to resume possession of land granted to another, due to some condition reserved in the lease (*e.g.*, death of the tenant, nonpayment of rent, expiration of the lease). In the old common law, reentry was always allowed for nonpayment of rent, but today it must be reserved in the lease. Also, the old common law allowed the grantor to enforce his right of reentry, but today he must initiate legal proceedings to do so.

reexamination
The examination of a witness which immediately follows cross-examination, and relates to matters of that examination; also known as redirect examination.

referee
Quasi-judicial officer appointed by the court for a specific purpose, who may hear testimony, decide factual disputes, and report his findings.

referee in bankruptcy
Before the 1978 Bankruptcy Act, the officer appointed by the courts who administered bankruptcy proceedings. Today these functions are performed by judges of the Bankruptcy Court or by trustees appointed by the court.

reference
1. The act of referring a legal case to a "referee" or "master"

for resolution. 2. The agreement between parties to a contract to submit their disputes to arbitration. 3. A person who will provide information regarding another's character, credit, or abilities.

referendum
1. A popular election held for consideration of a law proposed or passed by the state legislature or of a proposed constitutional amendment. 2. An election for public approval of the issuance of bonds by a taxing district for public improvements (*e.g.*, construction of school). 3. A report by an ambassador to his country concerning matters that she cannot decide without further orders.

refinancing
The act of financing again (*e.g.*, for the purpose of satisfying existing debts with funds raised from new debt).

reform
To amend, correct, modify, or rectify.

reformation of contract
An equitable remedy used to change a written contract so that it conforms to the actual agreement of the parties, when either by mistake of both parties or by mistake of one party with fraud by the other party, the writing does not conform to the contract as actually made.

refreshing memory
Allowing a witness who once had knowledge about some act or transaction, but has insufficient recollection to be able to testify fully, to consult his own records or memoranda made near the time of the act or transaction, to refresh his memory. *See* Federal Rule of Evidence 803 (5) (present recollection revived).

refunding
The replacement and retirement of outstanding securities (*e.g.*, bonds, through the sale of a new issue).

refusal
The act of rejecting something that one has a right or obligation to accept.

regional stock exchange

A securities exchange located outside of New York City (*e.g.*, the Philadelphia Stock Exchange).

register

1. To formally record a matter, as on a list. 2. The public record of facts (*e.g.*, births and deaths, patent filings, wills, deeds). 3. The public officials who keep public records.

registered agent

A person designated by a corporation or limited liability company to receive service of process on behalf of the corporation or company. A registered agent is not necessarily an employee of the company or corporation.

registered representative

A person authorized by law or a securities exchange to sell securities to the general public.

registrar

Private officer who keeps a register or registry (*e.g.*, at a school, a list of students; at a hospital, a list of patients; at a corporation, a list of shareholders).

registration

1. The creation of a register. 2. The making of a list catalog, schedule, or register for the purpose of official record keeping.

registration statement

Document describing the securities offered by a company and giving detailed financial data regarding the business. Such statements are subject to approval by the Securities and Exchange Commission prior to a public offering of new securities.

registry

The book containing the recording of facts and documents, authorized and maintained in accordance with the law (*e.g.*, registry of deeds, registry of ships at a customs house).

regulation

A rule or order of the executive branch of government which has the same force of law as if issued by the legislative branch (*e.g.*, a tax regulation issued by the Internal Revenue Service that dictates the proper payment of specific tax receipts).

Regulation A

The Securities and Exchange Commission regulation for small securities offerings, which allows for simplified registration filing requirements.

Regulation Fair Disclosure

The Securities and Exchange Commission regulation that requires disclosure of material information to all investors at the same time. Also called Regulation FD.

Regulation T

The Federal Reserve Board regulation limiting the amount of credit that securities brokers may extend to customers.

Regulation U

The Federal Reserve Board regulation limiting the amount of credit that banks may extend to customers for the purpose of buying regulated securities.

Regulation Z

The regulations included in the Truth-In-Lending Act and implemented by the Federal Reserve Board.

regulatory agency

Government body responsible for overseeing the implementation of specific legislation.

regulatory offense

Any crime that is not inherently evil, but is nonetheless proscribed by statute (*e.g.*, public consumption of alcohol).

rehabilitation, rehabilitate

1. The restoring or reinstatement of something or someone to its former capacity or position; to restore or reinstate (*e.g.*, in corporation law, to administer the assets of an insolvent corporation and to continue the business in hopes of its eventual return to solvency). 2. In litigation, a witness may be "rehabilitated" after a cross-examination, through redirect examination, to improve his standing, credibility, or integrity.

rehearing

A retrial or reconsideration of the issues of a case by the same court in which the suit was originally heard (*e.g.*, when a party alleges oversight in the first hearing, or when new evidence is discovered).

reimburse

To pay another person for costs and expenses incurred on one's behalf.

reinstate, reinstatement

To restore someone or something to its former position; the restoration (*e.g.*, in insurance, a restoration of the insured person's rights and benefits under a policy which had expired or been canceled).

reinsurance

1. An insurance contract between two insurers (or insurance companies) to insure one of them against risk of loss in insurance policies with its insured persons. 2. The substitution of another insurer for the original insurer on an insurance policy, with the consent of the insured person.

rejoinder

In common law pleadings, the defendant's second formal pleading, in answer to the plaintiff's replication to the defendant's first pleading.

related proceeding

In bankruptcy law, an action that involves a claim that will affect the administration of the estate, but that does not arise under the Bankruptcy Code (*e.g.*, a tort claim against the debtor).

relation

1. A relative or kinsman, by blood or marriage. In a restrictive sense, it means only blood relatives. When used in a will, it means only those who would inherit the estate under the state statute of distributions. 2. Generally, the connection between two persons (*e.g.*, the "marital relation" between husband and wife; the "agency relation" between master and servant). 3. A narrative, given by the "relator." 4. Doctrine of legal fiction whereby some act is considered to have taken place at some time earlier than it actually did occur, sometimes called "relation back."

relation back

The rule that one may amend a pleading to allege a new or different claim or defense if it is based on, related to, or arose from the original claim, transaction or occurrence set forth. If these conditions are met, the amended pleading "relates back" to the original filing date, for statute of limitations purposes.

relator

1. An informer. 2. An interested person who complains and instigates litigation against a defendant in the name of the state (*e.g.*, in *State ex rel. Jones v. Smith,* Jones is the relator and Smith is the defendant).

release

1. The giving up of some claim, right, or interest before the court or in writing between the parties (*e.g.*, a person injured by another may sign a release which is his promise not to sue in court for damages). 2. In property law, the owner of property or an interest in property may release his interest to another, usually a person who has a different interest in the same property.

release on recognizance (ROR)

Release of a criminal suspect from custody on her promise to appear at a later hearing. The court will decide whether to release the suspect upon an examination of the nature of the charge, the suspect's family ties, employment, character, past

criminal record, etc. Also called RPR (release on personal recognizance).

relevant, relevant evidence

Evidence that tends to prove or disprove an issue in controversy. "Relevant evidence" is any evidence having any tendency to make the existence of any fact that is of consequence to a final determination more or less probable than it would be without the evidence. *See* Federal Rule of Evidence 40.

relevant market

A geographically specified market made up of commodities that are reasonably interchangeable, given price, quality, and use. Such a market is identified for the purpose of determining antitrust violations.

reliance

Confidence or belief which causes a person to act to his detriment on the promises, acts, or representations of another. Reliance is often an element in legal actions (*e.g.*, in an action for fraud, the plaintiff must prove he relied on the defendant's fraudulent misrepresentation that caused injury).

relict

A widower or widow; technically, the relict of the marriage is the one who survives the union after the other is deceased.

reliction

The withdrawal or recession of waters, causing the exposure of land previously covered by water.

relief

1. The assistance or redress that a person seeks of the court (*e.g.*, an "injunction" against wrongs, or "specific performance" on the contract). 2. Public assistance given to the poor or indigent. 3. In feudal property law, the sum paid to the lord by a deceased tenant's heirs for the right to inherit the tenant's lands.

religious freedom, religious liberty

Guarantee in the First Amendment to the United States Constitution of the right to worship God according to the dictates of one's conscience, including the right to do or not do any act of religious observance not inconsistent with the peace and order of society.

relinquish, relinquishment

To abandon or surrender; the act of abandoning or surrendering. Relinquishment will occur when a federal court refuses to hear certain cases which it will "relinquish" to the state courts. *See* abstention.

remainder

In property, an interest or estate in land that will take effect when the immediately preceding estate terminates. Thus, if *A* grants Greenacre to *B* for 10 years with the "remainder" to *C*, *C's* estate will begin 10 years after the original grant, on the condition that *C* is existing and ascertained at the time her estate is due to commence. A remainder can only be valid when the previous estate is less than a "fee simple," when the previous estate terminates regularly, when the remainder is created in the same grant as the previous estate, and when the remainder "vests" (or becomes ascertained) during the previous estate.

A *contingent remainder* is one that is subject to a condition precedent, (*e.g.*, a remainder "to the children of *D*" when *D* has no children at the time of the grant, or a remainder "to *E* if *E* marries" when *E is* unmarried). The remainder is said to "vest" when the condition occurs (*e.g.*, when *D* has children, or when *E* marries).

A *vested remainder* is one to a person in existence who is certain to take immediate possession of the estate when the immediately preceding estate terminates.

remainderman
One who is entitled, by grant of the original owner, to a future estate in a remainder of land at the termination of the previous estate.

remand
1. To send a case from a higher court back to a lower court for a new hearing consistent with the higher court's decision. 2. Act of judge sending a prisoner back to prison after denial of habeas corpus relief.

remedial statute
A law passed by the legislature that creates or expands the methods and legal measures that private parties can use to obtain relief or compensation for damages,

remedy
The methods used by a court to redress an injury or protect a right. (*e.g.*, the court may order the defendant to pay money to the injured party, or the court may issue an "injunction," which orders a party to cease some activity which violates the plaintiff's rights).

Remedies may be "legal" or "equitable." Equitable remedies (*e.g.*, an injunction or specific performance on a contract) are available only in "courts of equity." "Provisional remedies" are those employed by the court during the cause of action and before a final decision in the case (*e.g.*, a preliminary injunction or a restraining order).

remission
1. The release of a debt. 2. The forgiving of an offense or injury.

remit

To send or send back; to relinquish (*e.g.*, to remit money borrowed).

remittance

Money one person sends to another.

remitter

The relating back from a defective title to an earlier valid title (*e.g.*, to restore good title to one who entered upon the land with less than the original good title which he or she held).

remittit damna

(ree-MIT-it DAM-na) Lat. Entry in the record that the plaintiff has remitted or given up part of the damages awarded by the jury.

remittitur

The power of the judge to order the plaintiff to remit, or accept a reduction in the amount of the damages awarded in the jury's verdict, when the judge believes the verdict is excessively high as a matter of law. The judge may order a retrial if the plaintiff does not accept the reduction.

removal

1. Generally, the transfer of a person or thing to another state. 2. In federal civil procedure, a case may be "removed" on the defendant's request from a state court to the federal district court if the case could have been originally brought in the federal court. *See* 28 U.S.C. § 1441.

render

1. To announce or declare (*e.g.*, to render the verdict of the jury). 2. To return, surrender, or yield.

renewal

1. The revival of a right that has expired. 2. The substitution of a new right or obligation for an old one, which extends the time for performance of the right or obligation (*e.g.*, the renewal of a debt means the rewriting of the original debt to extend the deadline to repay).

rent

Payment to the owner for the possession by the tenant of land, buildings, or tenements.

rent strike

An organized movement by tenants to refuse to pay their rent until their disputes with the owner are settled.

renounce

To reject by formal announcement; an affirmative declaration of abandonment (*e.g.*, of a title).

renunciation, renounce

1. The abandonment of a contract right of one party, often without payment or other consideration. 2. In criminal law, voluntary abandonment of the intention to commit a crime, prior to the actual commission of the crime. Renunciation is usually an affirmative defense to the charges of attempt, conspiracy, solicitation, and accessory. Renunciation is not valid as a defense if it is motivated by a possible failure of the crime, an increased risk of detection, or a mere desire to postpone the crime. *See* affirmative defense.

renvoi

(RON-voy) Fr. 1. A dismissal; a sending back. 2. Method used by the courts in cases involving potential conflict of laws between two or more jurisdictions. The courts must determine whether to utilize the law of the forum (where the court is located), the law of the domicile (where the party resides), or the law of the place where the act or injury occurred. 3. "Doctrine of renvoi" refers to doctrine under which a court is referred in a particular matter to the rules of foreign law as to conflict of laws which in turn refers court back to the law of the forum.

reorganization

1. In corporation law, reorganization is achieved by transferring all the assets of an insolvent corporation to a newly formed corporation with substantially the same stockholders as the old corporation. 2. Chapter 11 bankruptcy.

repair and deduct

A statutory remedy in some states that allows a residential tenant to make repairs to serious conditions in the rented premises when the landlord does not do so, and then deduct the cost of those repairs from rental payments.

reparable injury

An injury that may be cured sufficiently through payment of damages or similar relief.

reparation

Aid in relief of injuries, given by the one who caused the injuries.

repatriation

Returning to one's home nation after an extended period in a foreign country. *See* expatriation.

repeal

The complete rescinding of a statute by a subsequent act of the legislature. An "express repeal" is one that specifically revokes a statute. An "implied repeal" is caused by creating a statute that conflicts with and overrides a previous statute.

replevin

An action to recover the possession of personal property that has been unlawfully taken from the plaintiff. *Compare* trover.

replevy

To deliver goods or personal property back to the rightful owner, usually in connection with a "replevin action."

replication

In common law pleading, the plaintiff's pleading following the defendant's first pleading. In modern practice this is called the "reply."

reply

In modern civil procedure, the plaintiff's pleading following the defendant's answer. The reply may respond only to the defendant's counterclaims unless the court orders the plaintiff to respond to the defendant's answer or a third-party answer. *See* Federal Rule of Civil Procedure 7(a).

reporter

1. The person who officially reports or publishes a court's decisions. 2. The unofficial or commercially printed volumes of the cases decided by a court, sometimes also called "reports."

reports

1. Printed volumes of cases decided by a court (*e.g.*, Supreme Court Reports, Pennsylvania Superior Court Reports). Also includes volumes of administrative agency decisions. 2. Formal statement of activities or facts

(*e.g.*, annual report, credit report).

repossession

The process of taking back items by the seller or by a lender because the purchaser or borrower failed to pay as promised. Before actually taking the items back, the repossessor must follow, in most states, requirements to give notice, identify the goods, and meet timing deadlines.

represent

1. To exhibit; to appear in the character of; impersonate (*e.g.*, "the diagram represents the scene of the crime") 2. To speak or act with authority on behalf of another. *See* agent.

representation

1. Any statement of fact or conduct that implies a particular fact. 2. In an action for fraud, a statement or conduct designed to mislead others. 3. In contract law, an express or implied statement made before the signing of the contract regarding some fact influential in the decision to sign the contract. A representation is "material" when the parties would not have made the contract without the representation. *See* misrepresentation. 4. The act of representing another.

representative

1. One who represents another. *See* agent. A representative may be an agent, an executor, an administrator, a receiver, a trustee, a director, an officer, etc. 2. A person elected by the voters to serve in a legislative body.

representative action

Method for a large group of interested persons to be represented in an action by one or more of its members who will represent the entire group or class. Also called "class action." The class must be ascertainable, must have similar interests, must be too numerous to be heard in one court, and must be adequately represented by one named member. *See* Federal Rule of Civil Procedure 23.

reprieve

In criminal law, a delay in the execution of a sentence. A "reprieve" merely postpones the sentence, while a "pardon" totally abrogates it.

reprisal

1. The taking or doing of one thing, in satisfaction for another. 2. One nation's deprivation of another nation's rights or property in retaliation for an injury committed by the other nation. Reprisals may be "positive" (actual seizing of property) or "negative" (refusing to honor a valid contract right).

republic

A nation with the sovereign power in the people, or citizens, who elect representatives to a national legislature to govern the nation.

republication

The second publication or reestablishment of a will by a testator who earlier had revoked it.

repudiate, repudiation

1. To reject or deny a claim, right, or privilege; the rejection or denial. 2. In contract law, "repudiation of a contract" is the unequivocal declaration before performance is due that performance will not be made.

repugnancy, repugnant

1. An inconsistency or opposition between a clause in a contract, deed, statute, or other writing, and a previous clause in the same writing. 2. In pleadings, the affirmation of a cause of action in one count and the denial of same in another. Inconsistent claims or defenses are permitted under Federal Rule of Civil Procedure 8.

requirements contract

A contract where the buyer agrees to purchase all her requirements of a particular item for use in her business over a period of time. The uncertainty of a requirements contract does not destroy its validity. *See* U.C.C. § 2–306.

requisition

1. Seizure of property by government. 2. Demand of one government for a fugitive criminal located within the bounds of another government. 3. Generally, any formal request.

res

(race) Lat. 1. A thing. 2. The subject matter of a trust or will. 3. The object of an action "in rem" brought to determine the legal status of the object or thing. In an action of title, the res is the land; in an action to determine ownership of tangible personal property, the res is the property. The purpose of the res is to establish the jurisdiction of the action; the action must be brought in a court in the jurisdiction where the res is located.

rescind

To abrogate, annul, avoid, or cancel a contract, and in so doing, to restore the parties to the position they occupied before the contract was made.

rescission

The abrogation or voiding of a contract, removing all obligations of the parties, and restoring them to their original positions.

rescript

The written statement from an appellate court, giving its decision and orders to the trial court.

rescue

1. In common law, to free a prisoner, using force, from lawful custody without his aid or to unlawfully or forcibly retrieve

goods lawfully taken in securing rent payment or cure for damages. 2. Act of saving from peril or hazard.

rescue doctrine

In tort law, doctrine that one who imperils the life of another through negligence is also liable for injuries to a third party who attempts to rescue the victim if such a rescue is not rash or extremely reckless.

reservation

1. A clause in a deed retaining some right or interest for the grantor (*e.g.*, the right of reentry). 2. Land area set aside for a specific purpose (*e.g.*, wildlife conservation, Native American tribal lands).

reservation of rights

A statement to an insured that his insurer is not waiving its right to deny or contest coverage of a claim, even though it is providing the insured with a defense to the claim.

reserve

1. (v.) To keep back for a future use or for a special purpose. 2. (n.) Funds kept to meet future

expenses, losses, claims, liabilities, or contingencies.

reserve clause

A clause in sports contracts in which the team that first signs a player has a right to that player's future service.

res gestae

(res JES-tai *or* GES-tai) Lat. Things done. The events which form the litigated act. Statements made as part of the "res gestae" are admissible in evidence under an exception to the hearsay rule, when the statement accompanies an event that is otherwise admissible and explains the event (*e.g.*, a driver states, during an automobile accident, "My gas pedal was stuck."). *See* Federal Rules of Evidence 803(1), 803(2). "

residence

A person's dwelling place. "Residence" differs from "domicile" in that the domicile is a person's legal home for tax and voting purposes, and the residence is where the person lives.

residuary

Making up the surplus of an estate after all debts, devises, and costs are taken out. The surplus, or "residue," includes devises that are invalid or impossible to take effect.

residuary bequest/devise

A bequest/devise that disposes of the entire contents of the estate after all debts, devises, and costs are distributed.

residuary estate

That part of an estate which remains after the payment of charges, debts, legacies, and devises.

residuum

1. In general, what is left after a separation. 2. In wills, the content of the estate after all grants, debts, and devises are taken out.

res ipsa loquitur

(race IP-sa LO-kwi-tur) Lat. The thing speaks for itself. Doctrine in tort cases which creates a permissible inference of negligence unless the defendant can prove otherwise when (a) the defendant had exclusive control of the thing producing injury and (b) the injury would not normally occur without negligence (*e.g.*, a baby exhibits clear dog bite marks and the defendant owns the only dog in the neighborhood).

resisting arrest

The crime of opposing or obstructing a police officer who is making a lawful arrest.

res judicata

(race joo-di-KAT-ta) Lat. A thing already judged. Doctrine that a final judgment of a court is conclusive against the same parties in any further, identical cause of action between the parties.

resolution

Formal statement expressing the opinion of a legislative body. A resolution differs from a law or ordinance because it expresses only an opinion and does not permanently control or direct citizens.

resort

1. To seek help; a person or thing from which help is sought (*e.g.*, a "court of last resort" is a court whose decision is final and without further appeal). 2. To frequent; a place frequented by

persons, usually for legal or illicit activities.

Resource Conservation and Recovery Act (RCRA)

A federal law governing the disposal and management of solid and hazardous waste.

respite

1. A delay in the execution of a sentence. *See* reprieve. 2. A delay in the payment of debts, granted by the court or by the creditor to a debtor. It is "voluntary" if granted by the creditor and "forced" if granted by the court.

respondeat superior

(ray-spon-day-AT soo-PEER-ee-or) Lat. Let the superior answer. Doctrine that a principal (master or employer) is liable for injuries proximately resulting from the negligent acts of his agent (servant or employee) when the acts are committed within the scope of the agent's authority or apparent authority of employment. The principal, who is deemed to act through his agents, maintains a duty to conduct his affairs so as not to injure others, and is thus liable for the negligent acts of his agents.

respondent

1. One who argues against an appeal by the petitioner. 2. Defendant in a civil action. 3. One who answers a bill or pleading in equity.

responsive

Answering the allegations directly and completely without introducing new allegations (*e.g.*, in an answer to a complaint, pleading new matters is nonresponsive to the complaint).

responsibility

The state of being personally accountable for an action, or the discharge of a duty.

rest

1. When the party has no more witnesses to present at a trial, she will "rest" her case, and may offer only rebutting evidence afterward. 2. Lapse of activity; repose. 3. The "residue" of an estate.

restatement

A series of legal writings that clarify the current status of the law in various subjects (*e.g.*, Restatement of the Law of Contracts). The series is overseen by the American Law Institute, which assigns each Restatement to highly respected legal experts in a given field.

restitution

1. A common law remedy by which the court can, in its discretion, restore the injured party to a previous position, return something to the rightful owner, or restore the status quo. 2. The measure of actual damages.

In contracts, restitution occurs when a party recovers monetary payments already made or when a party is ordered to pay the value of performance already rendered. In torts, restitution is used to prevent unjust enrichment at the expense of others. In criminal law, restitution may be part of the sentence, when the offender is required to pay the victim in some way.

restorative justice

A penalty for a crime that avoids incarceration in favor of making the offender responsible for repairing the harm done. Examples of restorative justice sentences include restitution, community service, or a requirement that an offender write the victim a letter of apology.

restrain
To impede, hinder, or repress.

restraining order
An order of the court, after an application for injunction is filed, forbidding the defendant from doing some particular act until the court holds a hearing on the propriety of issuing the injunction sought.

restraint of trade
In antitrust law, contracts or combinations designed to thwart business or commercial competition, achieve a monopoly, affect prices, or in any other way obstruct free trade as it would occur in a natural economy, are illegal under the Sherman Antitrust Act. *See* 15 U.S.C. §§ 1–7.

restraint on alienation
A restriction written into a conveyance agreement, in which the grantee is barred from conveying his or her interest in the real property. Such restrictions are frequently unenforceable.

restricted securities
Securities that cannot be distributed openly to the general public. The prohibition against such a public offering can emanate from statute or contract.

restrictive covenant
1. In a deed, a promise to restrict the use of real property, which is a covenant said to "run with the land." Restrictive covenants that prohibit selling property to a person of a certain race are unenforceable by the courts under the due process clause of the Fourteenth Amendment. 2. In a contract, a promise by the employee or partner to refrain from performing similar work after the contract terminates, which is valid if limited to a reasonable geographical area and period of time.

restrictive indorsement
An indorsement which restricts the negotiability of an instrument, by creating a condition, restricting transferability, including restrictive words (*e.g.*, "for deposit only"), or limiting the use of the instrument (*e.g.*, "for accounts payable only").

resulting trust

Implied in law, this occurs when a trust must be created to fulfill the apparent intentions of the parties, who dispose of property for another's benefit without expressly creating a trust. A "resulting trust" differs from a "constructive trust" which is created contrary to the parties' intentions, often in the presence of fraud.

retail installment contract

Any contract between a buyer and seller in which the buyer makes periodic payments for the property. At the completion of the payments, the seller conveys title or his interest in the subject of the transaction to the buyer.

retainer

Advance deposit paid to an attorney for representing a client, including full or partial fees, expenses, and the agreement not to represent the client's adversary.

retire, retirement

1. To redeem, to pay off, or to cash in (*e.g.*, to retire a bond is to turn it in for cash). 2. To withdraw voluntarily from employ-

ment. 3. In a trial, after the parties present their cases and the judge instructs the jury, the jury will then retire to deliberate its verdict.

retirement plans

Any benefit plan provided by an employer or a self-employed person for retirement. Participation in a qualified retirement plan often results in tax advantages for the employer and the beneficiary.

retraction

To withdraw a statement made earlier (*e.g.*, to withdraw an offer before acceptance, or to correct a defamatory statement).

retraxit

(ree-TRAKS-it) Lat. He has withdrawn. A plaintiff's open and voluntary renunciation of his or her suit in court, which results in the forfeiture of future action.

retreat, duty to

The duty to retreat from dangerous situations, rather than resort to deadly force in self-defense. This duty is recognized in a minority or jurisdictions, and does not apply to all dangerous situations.

retrial

A new trial of an action that has previously been tried.

retroactive

Refers to a law which affects rights or acts that were fully legal in the past. Retroactive includes both "retrospective" and "ex post facto" laws. Retrospective technically applies only to civil laws which impair vested rights or create new duties. Ex post facto applies to criminal laws that make illegal something which was legal when the act occurred. Ex post facto laws are unconstitutional under the U.S. Constitution, Article 1, § 10.

retrospective

Refers to a civil law that affects rights which were fully legal in the past. A retrospective law impairs vested rights, creates new obligations, imposes new duties, or applies a new disability to a valid transaction.

return

1. Report of a sheriff or other official stating whether or not he was able to carry out a court order. A "false return" is one in which the official falsely reports that he has carried out the order when in fact he has not. 2. A report of information filed with the government (*e.g.*, tax return).

return day

The day, noted in a writ or process, when the officer must make a "return" of the writ or process.

revenue

Income from property, commerce, or investment (*e.g.*, rents from land, proceeds from the sale of merchandise, interest on savings accounts). "Public revenue" is the government's income from taxes, duties, customs, or fines.

revenue bills

Legislative acts that levy taxes for government operations.

revenue ruling

A ruling published by the I.R.S., setting forth a specific set of facts and the tax laws that would apply to those facts. I.R.C. § 7805.

reversal

The appellate court's changing or annulling of a lower court's decision. Distinguished from "remand," where the appellate court returns the case to the lower court for further proceedings.

reverse

To change or annul a lower court's decision, by ruling against the winning party in the lower court.

reverse discrimination

Any situation in which members of the nation's racial majority (*i.e.*, whites) claim to be disqualified from obtaining employment or another benefit because of their race.

reverse engineering

Learning how an invention or device works by disassembling it and studying the mechanism. Reverse engineering is a lawful way to learn a trade secret.

reverse mortgage

A transaction in which a property owner sells her equity in the property but continues to occupy it. Payment is not due until the owner vacates the property or dies.

reversible error

A legal error which, if not redressed, would injure the appellant and create a miscarriage of justice. Such an error justifies reversing the judgment of the court in which the error occurred.

reversion

In property law, the residue of an estate returns to the grantor by operation of law upon the termination of the estate granted. The reversion takes effect when the owner grants an estate less than his own; the grantor or his heirs take possession upon the natural termination of the estate granted (*e.g.*, if *A* grants to *B* a life estate, when *B* dies, *A* or his heirs will take possession by operation of law). *See* remainder.

revert

To return to the original owner. In property law, the residue of an estate will "revert" to the grantor, under operation of law, upon the termination of the estate granted if it is less than the grantor's whole estate. *See* reversion.

reverter

"Possibility of reverter" exists in a grantor when he conveys a defeasible estate subject to a special limitation. Reversions exist in a grantor when he conveys a lesser estate and does not dispose of the remaining interest. Similar to "reversion."

revest

1. To vest again in the same person. 2. The return of an estate to the grantor, upon the termination of the estate which he or she has granted.

review

1. A reexamination by the court or administrative body of its previous decision in a case. 2. The examination of an appellate court of the decision of a lower court or administrative body.

revised statutes

Statutes which have been altered, reorganized, changed, rearranged or reenacted.

revival

1. The renewal of an unexecuted judgment of a court when that judgment may not be executed without a new process or court order. 2. The renewal of an expired contract obligation by giving a new promise or acknowledgment of the contract.

revocable

That which may be voided, withdrawn, or canceled.

revocation

The cancellation or rescinding of power or authority granted to another (*e.g.*, revocation of an offer to contract; revocation of a will; revocation of a deed or instrument).

revocation of a will

The annulment or voiding of an existing will through an affirmative act of the testator.

revoke

To cancel or rescind a power or authority granted to another; to rescind privileges formerly granted (*e.g.*, the state board of examination may revoke a medical practitioner's license for good cause).

revolving credit

Consumer credit plan whereby the creditor extends continually renewable credit to the borrower, as long as the amount owed remains below a certain level.

rex

Lat. The king. Used in the names of English criminal prosecutions (*e.g.*, *Rex v. Smith*).

rex non potest peccare

(rex non POE-test PEK-ar-ray) Lat. The king can do no wrong. Old English legal maxim that parties could not sue the king or his government in a tort or breach of contract action.

R.I.C.O.

Racketeer Influenced and Corrupt Organizations Act. A federal or state law that allows criminal prosecutions and civil suits against individuals and enterprises involved in racketeering activities.

rider

An addition to a statute or contract which is annexed to the document and considered a part of the document, without having to rewrite the entire document (*e.g.*, a clause added to an insurance policy which specifically modifies the policy but does not necessitate revising the entire policy).

right

1. Inherent power or privilege to freely act; an inherent privilege or interest which is recognized and protected by the power of law (*e.g.*, in the United States, the Bill of Rights guarantees the right to worship freely and the right against self-incrimination, etc.; "civil rights," which belong to all American citizens, include the right to vote, the right to own property, the right to sue in court). 2. A legally enforceable claim of one person against another (*e.g.*, the right to exclude others from one's property, the right to have a contract performance, the right to receive damages for injuries received by another). 3. An interest in real or personal property, including the rights to freely use or convey the properly.

right of action

The legal right to sue another which arises out of certain facts or conditions (*e.g.*, a breach of contract gives rise to a right of action to sue for performance on the contract).

right of election
The right of a surviving spouse to choose either what the spouse gave under a will or what the law allows the survivor to take. *See* election.

right of entry
The right to possess or to regain possession of real property by peacefully entering the property upon breach of a condition created in the conveyance of certain defeasible estates.

right of first publication
Under former copyright law, the rule which protected against unauthorized publication of a work before it was published by the author. This was also called the "common law copyright" because the statutory copyright only protected works after publication. The right of first publication does not apply to works created after January 1, 1978.

right of publicity
An individual's right to control the use of her name, image, or likeness.

right of way
1. The right of one to pass over or use the land of another. *See* easement. 2. The strip of land upon which one exercises his right of way. 3. In highway safety law, the right of one driver to proceed without stopping at an intersection when another driver approaches from a different direction.

right to die
The right of an ill or injured person to refuse life-sustaining medical treatment.

right to know law
A law that requires disclosure of certain information, especially a law that requires the producer of toxic or hazardous substances to give information about the substance to its employees and to the community in which the substances are produced or stored.

right to work laws
Statutes which eliminate as a condition of employment the requirement that the employees join or pay dues to a labor union. Such statutes are permissible under section 14(b) of the Na-

tional Labor Relations Act, and exist in over 20 states.

rigor mortis
The stiffening of the muscles after death.

riot
A public disturbance involving the disorderly behavior of three or more people, threatening violence or acting in violence, which produces an injury to life or property or has the clear and present danger of producing injury to life or property.

riparian rights
The legal rights of owner of land adjacent to a stream or river to use the natural flow of the stream for reasonable purposes which do not obstruct another's use of the stream. The right includes land beneath the stream; it is limited to waterways, not including oceans or seas.

ripe for judgment
The stage in an action where the matter is ready for final determination, everything having been done that ought to be done before final adjudication.

ripeness doctrine
Constitutional law principle in which federal courts may not hear an action unless it is an actual, present controversy which is neither speculative nor hypothetical in nature. Generally, the case will not be heard unless the plaintiff has been harmed or is threatened with immediate harm.

risk
1. Uncertainty about the future.
2. The degree of danger or hazard associated with loss of life or property.

risk capital
That portion of an investor's money or property which is invested either in stocks, or any business over which the investor has no control.

risk of loss
The financial responsibility for destruction or damage of property as it is being transferred between the seller and the buyer. U.C.C. § 2–509.

robbery
The taking of property from the person or in presence of another by the use of force or by threat-

ening the imminent use of force. Aggravated robbery is generally defined by statute as robbery committed with a deadly weapon.

Robinson-Patman Act
Section 2(a) of the Clayton Act, which prohibits a seller to engage in price discrimination against any customer, where the effect of such discrimination may be to injure, destroy or prevent competition.

rogatory letters
A formal request from one judge to a second judge within another jurisdiction to take the testimony of a witness located within that jurisdiction.

roll
1. List of persons or property for a particular purpose (*e.g.*, "tax roll" of those subject to a particular tax). 2. Record of the actions of a court (*e.g.*, "judgment roll," which includes the pleadings, admissions, orders, and judgment of every case decided by a court).

round lot shareholders
Individuals who own stocks in standard 100-share units, or bonds with par value of $1,000 or $5,000.

royalty
Payments to the owner of property for the business use of that property, expressed as a percentage of the profits or gross product (*e.g.*, payments to an author for the right to publish and distribute his copyrighted work; payments to the owner of mineral lands for the right to extract minerals).

rubric
1. A heading or title of a statute, or a chapter in a legal codebook. 2. An authoritative rule or established tradition.

rule
1. To decide the law; to require a certain action. 2. A principle or standard established by authority (*e.g.*, the Supreme Court established the rights of a criminal defendant in *Miranda v. Arizona).*

Rule Against Perpetuities

In property law, the ancient rule that a future (or contingent) interest which, by any possibility, may not vest within 21 years after a life or lives in being at the time of its creation is void from the time it is created. The rule was introduced to promote the free transfer of land and to restrict tying up the land indefinitely for some unknown claimant.

Rule in Shelley's Case

See Shelley's Case, Rule in.

Rule in Wild's Case

See Wild's Case, Rule in.

rule nisi

(rule NYE-sigh) A proposed rule, introduced by one party, which will be made absolute and final unless the other party, against whom the rule is directed, shows cause why it should not be made final.

rule of necessity

When a judge is the only judge with the power to decide a matter in which she has a direct interest, the rule requires her to hear the matter. Also applies when all judges in a court system have an interest, (*e.g.,* legality of statute affecting state pension benefits for all judges).

rulemaking power

Broad discretionary power of Congress and legislatures to delegate power to promulgate rules to administrative agencies and courts. The delegation must include clear and intelligible standards and must not violate the separation of powers doctrine.

rule of reason

In antitrust law, a rule that states that a trade practice is unlawful only if economic factors show that it is an unreasonable restraint of trade.

running with the land

An obligation or right "runs with the land" when it passes to all future owners and assignees of the land. A covenant or easement running with the land is valid if it affects the use or value of the land and is intended by the parties who form the covenant or easement.

sabotage
To purposely destroy or ruin property (*e.g.*, the destruction of a manufacturer's equipment by employees during a labor dispute).

safe harbor
1. A protected area. 2. A provision of a law or regulation that allows a person who complies with that provision to have protection from liability.

safe haven law
A law that provides protection from prosecution for a parent who abandons an infant at a designated location, such as a hospital.

Safety Appliance Act
Federal law regulating the equipment used by railroads.

said
Already referred to; aforementioned.

salable
1. Able to be sold in an open and free market. 2. Ordinarily marketable.

salary
Compensation for employment, usually calculated on a monthly or yearly basis, as opposed to an hourly basis.

sale
Transaction between buyer and seller in which real or personal property is transferred from the seller to the buyer in exchange for some form of consideration. Sales of goods are governed by Article 2 of U.C.C.

sale and leaseback
Transaction in which a property owner sells his or her property to another, who immediately leases the property back to the former owner.

sale on approval
A form of conditional sale which becomes final only when the buyer, after a trial period, is satisfied with the goods. Ap-

proval may be implied by the buyer keeping the goods past a reasonable time. U.C.C. §§ 2–326(1), (2).

sale or exchange
The conveyance of property in a value-for-value exchange, as distinguished from a conveyance by contribution, gift, etc. A gain or loss from such a transfer is recognized for tax purposes.

sale or return
A type of sale under which the goods, although conforming to the contract, can be returned by the buyer if he does not resell them. U.C.C. § 2–326(1), (3).

sales tax
A consumption tax calculated as a percentage of the price of an article, and added to the price paid by the purchaser.

salvage
1. To save property from loss or destruction. 2. Personal property or goods that survive some destructive event, such as a flood. 3. Compensation for a person who voluntarily helps to save a vessel or its cargo.

sample
A small portion that is representative of a whole class.

sampling
In copyright law, incorporating a small portion of a sound recording into another recording. The portion taken may be manipulated or edited. Sampling may constitute copyright infringement.

sanction
1. To approve; to confirm; to ratify. 2. To punish; to rebuke; to censure. 3. A criminal penalty. 4. A measure, such as a trade embargo, adopted by one nation against another in order to punish the latter for a violation of international law.

sane
Rational; reasonable; of sound mind.

sanity hearing
1. A preliminary hearing to determine the mental competency of a person to stand trial, which may be commenced anytime during trial. 2. A statutory proceeding to determine whether a

person should be committed to an institution.

satisfaction

The fulfillment of an obligation; the elimination of a debt owed. *See also* accord and satisfaction.

satisfaction contract

A contract that makes acceptance of one party's performance conditional on the other's approval of that performance.

save harmless

To indemnify; to protect from liability.

saving

An act of fiscal economy that seeks to prevent waste or financial loss; preservation from forfeiture.

saving clause

1. A provision in a legislative act which maintains the validity of the act even though certain clauses of the act may be held invalid by a court. 2. A provision in a legislative act which excepts a specific item or concern from the general body of things mentioned in an act (*e.g.*, a clause that preserves legal remedies at common law from an act that

repeals a prior statute and its statutory remedies).

saving to suitors clause

Federal law that allows maritime suits to be brought in state courts.

S.B.A.

See Small Business Administration.

scab

Strikebreaker; a person who crosses a picket line during a strike.

scandalous subject matter

In trademark law, a proposed mark that is shockingly offensive to social mores. The Patent and Trademark Office will refuse to register such a mark.

schedule

1. A listing; a roster; a timetable. 2. A writing attached to a legal document which lists in detail the items referred to in the document, (*e.g.*, a listing of the prior owners of a parcel of property referred to in a deed).

scholarships and fellowships

Gifts of money or other aid to help a student meet the financial requirements of attending institutions of higher learning, or pay for activities which advance the pursuit of a degree. With some exceptions, recipients of such gifts are not required to treat such assistance as income, for tax purposes.

scienter
(sigh-EN-ter) Lat. Knowingly; intentionally; purposely; with knowledge.

scintilla
Lat. A spark; a trifle. The "scintilla doctrine" holds that if there is any evidence at all in a case that tends to support a material issue the case should not be taken from the jury, but left to their decision.

scire facias
(SEE-ree FASH-ee-as) Lat. You have cause to know. A judicial writ that requires a person bound by a judgment to show cause why the person bringing the writ should not have advantage of the judgment.

scope of authority
In the law of agency, the range of acts which the agency has not only explicitly authorized the agent to perform, but also those acts which are apparently or impliedly delegated to the agent.

scope of employment
The duties or conduct of an employee that fall within the parameters of his job or position.

scorched-earth
In corporate law ,the sale of a corporation's most valuable assets, in order to defeat a takeover bid.

scrip
1. Paper currency issued for temporary use. 2. A writing which entitles the bearer to receive something of value (*e.g.*, the right to exchange the scrip for shares of stock).

scrivener
A writer; one who prepares and writes out legal instruments, such as contracts of sale.

scroll
1. A rolled-up parchment which contains writing, frequently a formal legal document. 2. Mark made with a pen, intended to take the place of a seal.

scutage

In feudal law, money paid by landholders to their lord in lieu of knight service.

seal

Any symbol or mark that indicates a legal document has been formally executed.

sealed instrument

An instrument of writing which the party has signed and to which the party has attached his or her seal.

sealing of records

The act of closing public access to records of court proceedings. Such action is performed in many states to prevent the opening of a former youthful offender's records without a court order. Also occurs with regard to adoption records.

seaman

An individual engaged or employed in any capacity onboard a vessel, except for scientific personnel, sailing school instructors, or sailing school students.

search

An investigation of property or person with the purpose of seeking to find prohibited articles.

search and seizure

In a criminal investigation by law enforcement officials, the practice of searching persons or property and confiscating any items found during the search that are relevant to the investigation. Unreasonable searches and seizures are proscribed by the Fourth Amendment.

search incident to arrest

A police officer, having the right to arrest a person, may search that person and the immediate area ("wingspan") for weapons. *Chimel v. California,* 395 U.S. 752 (1969).

search warrant

Written court order issued by a judge to a law enforcement official granting permission for the official to search and confiscate any property that is material evidence with respect to a criminal investigation. Warrant must be supported by probable cause.

seasonable

In a reasonable amount of time; timely; in due season or time.

seasonal

Relating to a particular time of the year; dependent on a particular season.

seaworthiness

Word that describes a ship's ability to sail and to engage in those activities that it was designed to engage in.

S.E.C.

See Securities Exchange Commission.

Second Amendment

Amendment to the U.S. Constitution which states: "A well-regulated militia, being necessary to the security of a free state, the right of the people to keep and bear arms shall not be infringed." This right may be subject to state and federal regulations.

secondary boycott

Any association of two or more persons formed to exert pressure on the customers of a business with the purpose of causing the customers or the suppliers of the business not to deal with it.

secondary distribution

The organized sale of a stock after it has been initially sold by the issuer and held by another.

secondary evidence

Evidence that is not original or first-hand evidence, (*e.g.*, a photocopy of an agreement).

secondary meaning

In trademark law, the association that a merely descriptive trademark or tradename has acquired with a particular product.

secondary party

One who is liable to pay a debt if the person who incurred the debt defaults.

second mortgage

A mortgage over which the first mortgage takes priority.

secretary

The corporate employee or officer in charge of corporate records, such as the minutes of board meetings.

Secretary of State

1. The principal appointed official in the federal government charged with carrying out American foreign policy. 2. In most

state governments, the elected official charged with registering corporations and other formal duties with respect to licensing and recording.

secundum
(sek-KUN-dum) Lat. According to.

secured creditor
A creditor who holds security that ensures the payment of his or her debt, should the debtor default.

securities
Written certificates indicating obligations owed or ownership of property and assets.

Securities Acts
Phrase referring to the federal Securities Act of 1933 and the Securities Exchange Act of 1934, which together regulate the issuance and trading of corporate securities.

Securities Exchange Commission (S.E.C.)
Established in 1934 to regulate the trading and sale of stocks, bonds, and other securities.

Securities Investor Protection Corporation (S.I.P.C.)
Nonprofit organization created by Congress to protect investors and give financial assistance to dealers and brokers in certain circumstances.

securitization
The practice of pooling contractual debt ,such as mortgages, and reselling them to investors.

security
1. A written certificate that indicates an indebtedness is owed or ownership in property (*e.g.*, a share of stock or a debenture). 2. Collateral; assurance of payment; deposit.

security agreement
An agreement granting a security interest in personal property to a creditor.

security deposit
Funds given by a lessee to a lessor to guarantee his compliance with the terms of the lease.

security interest
Any interest in property which is obtained by a creditor to guarantee payment of a debt.

sedition

Any communication which advocates treasonous conduct or the illegal overthrow of any lawfully constituted government.

seditious libel

A writing intended to incite illegal action against the government (*e.g.*, the violent overthrow of government). The First Amendment generally protects such "political speech," if it does not incite imminent lawless action.

seduction

The act of one person inducing another to engage in sexual intercourse without the use of force. Common-law rights of action for seduction have largely been abolished by statute.

segregation

The act of separating or isolating. Often the term refers to the illegal separation of groups based on their race (*e.g.*, the separation of blacks from whites in housing or educational contexts).

seigneur

(SAY-nyur) Fr. Master, lord (*e.g.*, lord of a fee).

seised

(seezed) The state of legal ownership and possession of real property.

seisin

(SEE-zin *or* SAY-zin) Ownership and possession of real property under lawful title.

seizure

Confiscation of property; the taking of property by a law enforcement official (*e.g.*, the taking by legal process of a person's property to satisfy a judgment against him).

selective incorporation

The policy of extending to the states only selected protections guaranteed by the Bill of Rights. These protections are said to be "incorporated" to apply to the states through the Fourteenth Amendment.

selective prosecution

In criminal law, a prosecutor's use of personal discretion, instead of regular criteria, to decide whether to prosecute a particular offense. The term refers especially to exercising the discretion to prosecute based on race or exercise of a protected constitutional right.

Selective Service System
Federal agency created in 1940 to organize a system for military conscription.

self-dealing
1. Situation where a fiduciary or trustee uses confidential information obtained from her position of trust for her own personal enrichment. 2. Insider trading.

self-defense
Right of a person to take any reasonable action necessary to protect himself or his family from harm by another.

self-help
A situation wherein a person redresses or prevents a wrong personally, without resorting to the legal process for assistance. State and federal laws impose strict limits on such action.

self-incrimination
Any action or admission made by a person that implicates that person in the commission of a crime, either before trial or at trial.

self-incrimination, privilege against
Under the Fifth Amendment, one may choose not to implicate himself in a crime, by refusing to answer questions or testify before or during trial. This right also has been extended to apply to the states.

self-insurance
Setting aside a calculated sum of money as protection against future loss. Self-insurance is usually allowed for compulsory insurance (*e.g.*, motor vehicle insurance; workers' compensation insurance), but the self-insurer must demonstrate to the appropriate regulatory authority that he has set aside sufficient funds to meet likely obligations.

self-proving
In probate law, a will or affidavit that will be accepted by the court without the need for additional proof of its validity.

seller
1. Person who exchanges goods or property in return for money or its equivalent. 2. Vendor.

selling short
Sale of a security or commodity that one has a contract to own, and that one expects to buy back at a later date and at a lower price.

Senate
1. The upper chamber in a bicameral state legislature. 2. The upper chamber in the United States Congress, composed of two elected Senators from each state.

senile dementia
Lat. The progressive deterioration of an elderly person's mental faculties, often associated with Alzheimer's disease.

senior status
The status of a semi-retired judge who continues to perform judicial functions that she is willing and able to perform.

sentence
A court judgment that imposes a penalty upon a person convicted of a crime (*e.g.*, a prison term imposed on a person found guilty of bribery).

sentencing guidelines
Standards for determining criminal punishment. Guidelines typically consider the severity of the offense for which the defendant was convicted and the defendant's criminal history. The purpose of guidelines is to make criminal sentences uniform among similarly situated offenders.

separability clause
A common clause providing that if one or more provisions in a document should fail, the rest of the instrument remains in force. Used in contracts and legislation.

separable controversy
Within a complex legal action, a claim or cause of action which is capable of being removed and independently adjudicated.

separate but equal
Doctrine adopted in response to early civil rights legislation, providing that equality is achieved when races are given substantially equal facilities, even though the facilities are separate. This doctrine has been held unconstitutional when applied to numerous contexts in-

cluding public education. *E.g.,*
Brown v. Board of Education,
347 U.S. 483 (1954).

separate estate

The real or personal property
solely owned by a person who
also owns other property jointly
with another person in a marital
or business relationship.

separate maintenance

Funds paid by one married person to another for support and
financial assistance if they are no
longer living together as a married couple.

separate property

Those assets solely owned by a
married person and which are not
jointly owned by both partners in
the marriage. *Compare* community property.

separation

1. A division; a split. 2. Situation
where a married couple lives
apart from each other though
they do not divorce.

separation agreement

Compact between a married
couple that is about to divorce or
separate that divides up property,

allocates income, and determines
who has custody of any children.

separation of powers

Division of authority between the
three branches of government
(judicial, legislative, executive).
One branch of government is not
permitted to impinge on the
duties of another (*e.g.,* the judici-
ary is not permitted to legislate
and enact laws, which is the
domain of the legislature).

sequester

To isolate; to quarantine; to keep
from the public (*e.g.,* to keep
members of a jury from the
public while a trial is in progress).

sequestration

1. The attachment of property or
money by the court, pending the
outcome of an action. 2. The
occasional isolation of a jury
during a trial, to guard against
improper contact. 3. The separation of witnesses while outside
the courtroom, to ensure untaint-
ed testimony.

sergeant at arms

Person appointed by a legislative
body or other organization to

keep order while the legislative body is in session or while the organization is meeting.

seriatim

(sair-ee-A-tim) Lat. Severally. Individually; one by one; in order.

serious health condition

For purposes of the Family and Medical Leave Act, an illness, injury, impairment, or physical or mental condition that involves a defined period of incapacity, or that requires periodic medical treatments.

servant

1. Employee; a person who works for another person; a person in the employ of another. 2. An agent.

service

1. To perform a job. 2. To render labor for the benefit of another. 3. A department or agency of government (*e.g.*, the armed services). 4. The delivery of any communication.

service mark (SM)

A word, phrase, symbol, or design, or some combination thereof, that identifies and distinguishes the source of services. *Compare* trademark.

service of process

The delivery of a summons, a complaint, or any notice of a legal proceeding to a person.

services

In the old English system of feudal tenure, the acts performed by a tenant for his lord, in exchange for property granted to him by his lord.

servient

Subject to a servitude; encumbered by an obligation (*e.g.*, a servient estate is an estate that is obligated to provide a benefit for another estate).

servitude

1. A burden or an obligation imposed upon one estate for the benefit of another estate (*e.g.*, an estate that must provide water to another estate free of charge). 2. State or condition in which a person willingly or unwillingly is a servant for another.

session

A meeting of a legislative or judicial body for a specific period of time (*e.g.*, a court's daily sitting).

session laws

Laws enacted by a state legislature, published during the legislative session and bound in order of enactment.

set aside

1. To reverse a judgment; to vacate a prior court's decision. 2. To reserve funds for a specific purpose.

set-off

A counterclaim demand brought by a defendant, extrinsic to the cause of action, to reduce the amount of the plaintiff's recovery (*e.g.*, a counterclaim demand based on breach of contract brought by a defendant in a tort action for the purpose of reducing plaintiff's possible recovery).

settle

To resolve a dispute; to agree to terms; to reach agreement.

settlement

An agreement which resolves conclusively a dispute or conflict between two or more persons, with judicial approval usually not required.

settlor

1. A person who creates a trust. 2. The person who furnishes the corpus for a trust.

Seventh Amendment

U.S. Constitutional amendment which guarantees the right to a jury trial "where the value in controversy shall exceed twenty dollars . . . and no fact tried by a jury shall be otherwise re-examined in any Court of the United States, than according to the rules of the common law."

sever

1. To separate, divide. 2. Bifurcate (*e.g.*, to separate a cause of action into a trial to determine liability and a trial to fix damages). 2. To order separate trials for criminal codefendants.

severable

Capable of being divided or separated (*e.g.*, an estate that can be divided into smaller estates).

severable contract

One in which a party may breach some part of the contract without breaching the entire agreement.

severable statute

A statute which has been deemed to contain invalid components by a court, the remainder of which is nonetheless valid and enforceable.

several

More than two; distinct; various; separate.

severalty

To have individual or sole control over something (*e.g.*, severalty in estate means that a person owns an estate exclusively and not with any other person).

severance

The state of being divided or separated.

severe

Harsh; to an extreme degree; causing extreme distress.

sex offender registry

A list of the names and addresses of sex offenders who have been released from custody, made available to the public. *See* Megan's Law.

sexual harassment

A type of employment discrimination that involves harassment based on sex or sexual orientation.

shall

Denoting obligation or mandatory action. In some instances, the word denotes permissive action, at the discretion of the actor. Such a reading is given when required by public policy or the context of the writing.

sham

Without merit; spurious; bogus; false (*e.g.*, a sham pleading is a pleading that is spurious and has no legal basis).

share

1. A person's interest in the ownership of some asset or entity; the portion of some benefit or liability that is allotted to a person. 2. A single unit of stock that represents ownership in a business entity.

share and share alike

To distribute in equal portions. This phrase often denotes division on a per capita basis.

shareholder agreement

An agreement between shareholders of a corporation to vote the same way in elections for members of the board of directors.

sharia
(sha-RYE-a) Arabic. The moral code and religious law of Islam.

Shelley's Case, Rule in
Early English common law rule that holds that conveyance of an estate for life to a person, and with the remainder to the grantee's heirs, in fact gives the grantee title in fee simple absolute and the heirs get nothing (*e.g.*, Red, owner in fee simple of Blackacre, conveys Blackacre to Blue for life and the remainder to the heirs of Blue, Blue takes Blackacre in fee simple absolute, getting both the life estate and the remainder). Rule is now abolished in most states.

sheriff
Chief law enforcement official of a county.

sheriff's sale
The sale by a sheriff or court official of a party's property, pursuant to a court-ordered decree of execution or foreclosure (*e.g.*, sale of attached property in

order to satisfy an unpaid judgment).

Sherman Antitrust Act
Federal statute that prohibits any contract, combination, or conspiracy in restraint of interstate or foreign trade or commerce and which also prohibits any monopoly or attempt to monopolize interstate or foreign trade or commerce.

shield laws
1. State statutes which grant to media members a limited and qualified privilege to decline to reveal confidential sources of information. (*See* journalist's privilege.) 2. Statutes which grant to potential witnesses the privilege not to testify about certain matters (*e.g.*, a rape victim's qualified privilege not to answer questions about past sexual behavior). 3. Statutes protecting child victims of sexual assault from having to testify in the courtroom, subject to stringent standards.

shifting the burden of proof
Transferring from one party to another the responsibility of producing evidence to support a

claim. That is, when the party who first had the burden of proof has made out a prima facie case or defense by evidence, the other party must rebut by producing evidence.

shoplifting

Larceny of merchandise from store.

short rate

To rescind an insurance policy and renegotiate for a new policy with the same coverage, but with a shorter term and lower earned premium.

short sale

A sale of shares of stock which the seller does not own or control at the time the sale is negotiated but which she acquires at a lower price prior to the time the delivery of the shares to the buyer is required.

short swing profits

Profits made by insider through the buying and selling or selling and buying of shares within a six-month period. Practice is prohibited by S.E.C. rules.

show cause

Give proof; provide a reason.

show up

A one-to-one confrontation between a suspect and a witness to a crime, for the purpose of identifying the suspect.

shrink-wrap license

A contract deemed accepted by a buyer of software when she opens the package containing the software.

shyster

A deceitful person; an unethical individual; most commonly used to refer to an unethical and unscrupulous lawyer.

sic

Lat. Thus; in such manner; as it appears. The word is used in written texts to indicate that a misspelling of a word or a grammatical error found in a quotation can also be found in the original text and is to be read as it appears.

sick pay

Pay given to an employee who is away from the job due to injury or illness.

side-bar

The area at the side of the judge's bench, which is out of

the hearing range of the jury and witnesses. Side-bar conferences are held to discuss issues that are inappropriate for the jury and/or witnesses to hear. Such discussions are recorded for purposes of appeal.

sight draft

A bill of exchange for the immediate payment of money (*i.e.*, a bill which is payable on demand).

signature

A person's name as written by himself. Under the U.C.C., any mark is sufficient if the signer intends it as his signature.

silent partner

One who owns a share of a business, but is not actively involved in the operation of the business, or not known to other owners.

silver platter doctrine

Now-obsolete doctrine allowing evidence seized illegally by state actors to be used against federal criminal defendants. This doctrine was ruled unconstitutional.

simple contract

1. A contract that is agreed to informally, without a seal. 2. An oral contract.

simple negligence

The failure to exercise the needed degree of care in a particular situation as would be exercised by the typical careful person in the same situation.

simplex commendatio non obligat

(SIM-plex com-men-DAT-ee-o non ob-li-GAT) Lat. Mere recommendation does not bind. Used with respect to sellers' representations. A recommendation of a good by a vendor does not create an obligation like a warranty. The rule has been superseded by the implied warranty of fitness for a particular prupose.

simpliciter

(sim-PLIS-i-ter) Simply; directly.

Simultaneous Death Act

A uniform law adopted by most states which provides for the distribution of property, when distribution depends on the time of death of more than one person and there is not enough evidence to deduce that they died other than simultaneously. The Act provides that, if two or more people die within 120 hours of one another, each is considered to have predeceased the others., unless a will or other document provides otherwise.

sine
(SEE-nay) Lat. Without.

sine die
(SIGH-nee dye) Lat. Without day. Without assigning a day for holding the next meeting (*e.g.*, when the United States Senate adjourns without fixing the date on which it will next meet).

sine qua non
Lat. Without which not. An essential qualification or requirement (*e.g.*, a person must be 35 years of age to be elected President of the United States).

single publication rule
In cases involving a libelous statement in print form, the plaintiff has but a single cause of action, although the number of copies distributed may affect damages.

sinking fund
Government or corporate funds intended for the repayment of debt or replacement or improvement of equipment.

situs
(SIGH-tus) Lat. Situation. The place of the occurrence or the location of a thing.

Sixth Amendment
U.S. constitutional amendment which ensures the right to speedy and public trial by an impartial jury, the right to confront witnesses, the right to be informed of the nature of the accusation, the right to assistance of counsel and the right to have compulsory process for obtaining witnesses in one's favor.

skiptracing
Locating missing persons or assets.

S.L.
Abbreviation for "session laws," or "statute laws."

slander

Oral defamation; spoken words that defame a person in front of others and that cause harm or some damage.

slander of title

An erroneous and malicious statement that asperses a person's legal title to and ownership of real or personal property.

SLAPP suit

Strategic lawsuit against public participation. A lawsuit brought by a private party to stifle public criticism or protest. Although a SLAPP suit may be frivolous or meritless, the defendant will often have insufficient resources to fight the suit.

slip decision

A separate and early printing of a court's opinion before it is printed in the court reporters.

Small Business Administration

A federal agency whose mission is to encourage, promote, and protect the interests of American small business.

small claims court

Court established to deal solely with civil suits involving small amounts of money. Also called "conciliation court."

smart money

Punitive damages awarded a plaintiff in a civil action because of the defendant's extremely improper behavior.

Smith Act

Federal statute which prohibits any seditious activity, including the advocating of the overthrow of the government by violence or other unlawful means.

smuggling

The crime of bringing goods in or out of a country that are either prohibited or where there has been a failure to pay custom charges owed on the goods.

socage

Under medieval English law, land occupied by a person who rendered certain services other than military services to the owner in fee simple of the property for the right to occupy and enjoy the property.

Social Security Act

Federal statute which provides supplemental income to the retired, the disabled, or the survivors of a person who was covered by the Act. The social insurance programs that fall within the Act's guidelines are funded by mandatory contributions from employees and employers at a rate established by Congress.

sodomy

Copulation by a person with a person of the same sex or an animal, or unnatural copulation with a member of the opposite sex. Laws that made consensual sodomy between adults a crime were declared unconstitutional in *Lawrence v. Texas,* 539 U.S. 558 (2003).

solar easement

An easement granted to ensure the dominant estate has access to sunlight for generating solar energy.

solatium

Compensation; damages awarded; payment made to a person who has suffered an injury (*e.g.*, compensations paid to a person whose feelings have been hurt).

Soldiers' and Sailors' Civil Relief Act

Federal statute that alters, or even defers, the civil liabilities of a person who is in the military and that sets forth specific procedures for persons who want to enforce their claims against persons in the military.

sole

Only; exclusive; one; single; individual.

solemnity of contract

The notion that two people may enter into any agreement they wish, and that contract will be enforceable if it is free of defects or defenses.

sole proprietorship

A non-incorporated business owned entirely by one person.

solicitation

To entreat a person to engage in a specific type of behavior; to importune; to implore; to ask a person to do something; to request something of a person (*e.g.*, to implore a person to make a statement in court with respect to his opinion of a person's reputation). Solicitation to commit a crime is a punishable offense.

Solicitor General

A federal official whose duty it is to represent the United States Government before the Supreme Court.

solvency

1. Capacity to pay debts as they are due. 2. Ability to meet financial obligations.

solvent

Capable of meeting the financial obligations one owes. A person who can pay his debts as they come due is solvent.

Sonny Bono Copyright Term Extension Act

Federal law enacted in 1998 that retroactively extends the time of copyright protection.

Son of Sam law

State law that prohibits convicted criminals from profiting from their crimes by selling the rights to their stories.

sound

1. Valid; reliable; whole; true. 2. Solvent; in good condition. 3. Noise; utterance.

sounds in

1. Associated with; concerning; in connection with. 2. Brought under a theory of law (*e.g.*, a lawsuit that sounds in tort).

sovereign

1. One that exercises supreme authority. 2. A monarch, ruler, or chief of state.

sovereign immunity

Doctrine that holds that a government or sovereign is immune or exempt from tort liability because of its status in society. Most jurisdictions have waived tort immunity to a certain extent

special agent

1. A person engaged by another to execute or conclude a particular deal or transaction (*e.g.*, a person hired by a corporation to sell a particular factory). 2. A law enforcement officer assigned to a specific area or project.

special appearance

The presence of a party to a legal proceeding by judicial summons before a court for the sole purpose of denying the jurisdiction of the court over his person with respect to the legal proceeding in question.

special damages

Damages which are the direct result of defendant's actions but are not the necessary or typical result of such conduct and therefore must be specifically pleaded by plaintiff in the cause of action and proven at trial.

special demurrer

A demurrer filed by a defendant in opposition to a plaintiff's cause of action which attacks with specifics the flaws in the composition or form of the plaintiff's pleading.

special hazard rule

Rule that states an employee is covered by workers' compensation for injuries sustained traveling to and from her workplace if the route is not ordinarily used by the general public except in dealing with the employer, and the route contains unique hazards and risks.

special indorsement

An indorsement that states to whose benefit a financial instrument is payable and therefore

requires his signature for it to be exchanged for cash or other assets.

special legislation

Laws enacted to benefit particular persons, districts or things, as distinguished from general legislation, which benefits the general public.

specialty

1. A legal instrument or agreement that is under seal; such as, a contract that is under seal. 2. An area of expertise or proficiency (*e.g.*, a lawyer who has an area of expertise in the practice of admiralty law).

special use permit

An allowed exception to a zoning ordinance.

special verdict

Special finding by the jury on each material issue of the case, leaving the application of the law to the court (*e.g.*, in a negligence case, the jury finds that defendant was driving too fast under the circumstances).

special warranty deed

A deed in which the grantor of real property only agrees to

defend and protect the grantee's interest in and title to the property against all claims that arise out or the grantor's interest in the property.

specie

(SPEE-she) Coins which have value independent of their stamped value (*e.g.*, gold or silver coins). *See also* in specie.

specification

A detailed description or statement of some matter or item, (*e.g.*, provisions of a contract detailed in a separate schedule).

specific bequest

The giving of a gift of a specific item of personal property to a person as set forth in the provisions of a will.

specific performance

1. Equitable remedy granted by a court where there has been a breach of contract and where damages would be inadequate to compensate the injured party so that the court requires the breaching party to fulfill his obligations under the contract.
2. The fulfillment or achieve-

ment of one's obligations under a contract.

Speech or Debate Clause

Clause in Article I, section 6, clause 1 of the U.S. Constitution which grants immunity to members of Congress "for any speech or debate in either House."

speedy trial

The Sixth Amendment constitutional right of a person accused of a crime to a swift and expeditious trial.

spending power

Congressional power to spend money to provide for the states' general welfare. This power is enumerated in Article I, section 8, clause 1 of the U.S. Constitution.

spendthrift trust

A trust established for the benefit of a person that has restrictions attached to it so as to guard against that person's misuse or wasting of the trust's proceeds.

spin-off corporation

A subsidiary of a parent corporation created by transferring part of the parent's assets to the new corporation and the new corporation's stock is distributed to the shareholders of the parent corporation without surrender of the parent's stock.

spite fence
A fence constructed for the sole purpose of annoying the owners of adjoining property.

splitting a cause of action
The separation of a cause of action into several different parts, claims, or actions.

spoliation
The destruction or severe modification of evidence.

spoliatus debet ante omnia restitui
(spo-lee-AT-tus DEB-bet AN-tay *or* AN-tee OM-nee-a RES-ti-twee) Lat. A party despoiled ought first of all to be restored. A person unjustly dispossessed of his property should be restored to possession.

spousal disqualification
Now obsolete maxim that disqualified one spouse from testifying in any action to which the other spouse was a party. *See* marital communications privilege.

squatter
A person who occupies and takes possession of real property without title or legal authority to do so.

squeeze-out
The elimination or diminution of a corporation's minority shareholders by the corporation's controlling interests. Often, such action is accomplished through stock transactions.

stakeholder
1. A third party selected by two or more parties to hold money or some property until one of the parties can establish their legal right to it. *See also* interpleader. 2. A person who has an interest in a business other than an ownership interest (*e.g.*, an employee; a regular supplier).

stale check
A check whose date of issue is so much earlier than the date on which it is presented for satisfaction that it will not be accepted.

stamp tax
The charge for getting legal documents certified or approved by a government official (*e.g.*,

the cost of getting a contract certified by a county clerk).

stand
1. To remain valid; to be viable; to be in force. 2. To present oneself; to submit oneself (*e.g.*, to present oneself as a candidate for public office). 3. To remain upright; to be still; to remain motionless.

standard of care
A standard of behavior used in negligence law, which takes into consideration the degree of care that a reasonable person of ordinary prudence would exercise in similar circumstances.

standard of review
The amount or level of deference given to a lower court's order or decision by an appellate court.

standby counsel
Counsel appointed to remain available to assist a pro se defendant in a criminal case as needed or requested by the defendant.

standing
1. To have the right to bring a suit or other legal action before a court of justice (*i.e.*, having a

stake in the outcome); to be eligible to bring a cause of action against another party in a court of justice. 2. A person's status, rank, or position within society, an organization, or government.

standing mute
A defendant's refusal to plead in a criminal trial. Such action is regarded as a plea of not guilty.

Star Chamber
A medieval English court that principally heard criminal cases without the use of a jury that could fix any penalty but death. It was eventually abolished because of abuses perpetrated on defendants.

stare decisis
(star-RAY de-SIGH-sis) Lat. To abide by decided cases. Judicial doctrine that holds that legal precedent will not be set aside unless there is good cause to do so.

state
1. A geographic region with its own government; a nation; a country; a commonwealth (*e.g.*, the United States of America or

the State of Illinois). 2. To assert; allege; express; aver.

state action

1. Action taken by a state or state agency. The term refers to claims brought under the Civil Rights Act and the Due Process Clause of the Fourteenth Amendment, in which a private citizen must show "state action" in order to seek a remedy for an improper governmental intrusion. To determine whether the government agent's action constitutes "state action," courts look for a close nexus between the state and the challenged action. 2. In antitrust law, a state law or regulation that has the effect of limiting competition. State action does not violate antitrust laws.

statement

1. A declaration of fact; an allegation. 2. One of various legal declarations. *See* opening statement.

state of the art

In products liability law, the level of relevant scientific and technical knowledge existing at the time of a product's manufacture.

state or municipal bonds

Debt instruments issued by the state or local government entities. Such bonds are generally regarded as tax-exempt by the federal government and some states.

state secret

Concealed, nonpublic information that is vital to the welfare and well-being of a country.

state's evidence

Testimony presented to a court by a party to a crime that incriminates others in the commission of a crime for the purpose of his receiving immunity from prosecution or a lesser sentence for his criminal conduct.

status

Condition; position; situation; rank.

status crime

An offense which punishes not a wrongful action or inaction, but rather proscribes a certain personal status (*e.g.*, a law against being a drug addict). The punishment of such "offenses" is unconstitutional.

status quo
Lat. The existing state of affairs; the condition of things at a certain time.

statute
A law; legislative enactment; codified rule of law.

Statute of Frauds
Law that holds that certain contracts may not be enforced unless there is some writing signed by the defendant to the dispute indicating that there was an agreement.

statute of limitations
Law that prohibits the bringing of any civil action or criminal prosecution after a specified period of time has elapsed from when the right to bring the action or prosecute the crime started.

statute of repose
Law that prohibits bringing a lawsuit after a specified time since the defendant acted, even if the cause of action has not accrued.

Statute of Uses
An old English law preventing the separation of legal and equitable estates in land, upon the creation of a common law use.

Statute of Wills
Medieval English law that set forth the manner in which property could be bequeathed by a person to others upon his death.

Statutes at Large
The official listing of legislative enactments passed by Congress in a particular session.

statutory
Based on statute; derived from or referring to a legislative enactment.

statutory construction
The process by which courts interpret statutes which have been enacted by a legislature. *See* strict construction.

statutory offense
Crimes which are created by statutes, as opposed to those established by common law.

statutory rape
Formerly, the crime of engaging in sexual intercourse with a female who is under the age of consent. Most states now redefine the offense to include engag-

ing in certain types of sexual activity with a either male or female under a certain age.

stay

The stopping of legal proceedings for a temporary period by court order.

stay of execution

The stopping or suspending of the performance of a court judgment for a temporary period (*e.g.*, the stopping of the performance of the death penalty upon a convicted murderer).

stealing

Theft; the felonious appropriation of another's personal property; the crime of taking another's property.

sterility

Inability to reproduce and have offspring.

stipendiary estate

Estate or real property given to a person for services rendered, generally of a military kind.

stipulation

1. Admission, or agreement between opposing parties in a judicial proceeding. 2. Agree-

ment as to facts. 3. A condition, term or proviso of an agreement.

stirpes

(STIR-pees) Lat. Descents, root; the base or stock of a tree. Used in reference to the descendants of a particular person or family. *See* per stirpes.

stock

1. Capital invested in a corporation; the equity interest in a business enterprise. 2. A person's equity and ownership interest in a corporation. 3. Merchandise; goods; inventory.

stockbroker

A person who acts as an agent for another in the selling and buying of stock and other securities.

stock certificate

A written instrument which indicates ownership of a designated number of shares of stock.

stock clearing

The process by which securities are physically delivered to the buyer and payment is physically delivered to the seller.

stock dividend

Dividend distributed by a company to its stockholders in the form of the company's stock and which involves a transfer from the surplus capital to the stock account on the corporation's balance sheet in an amount equal to the dividend distributed.

stock exchange

A market at which securities are bought and sold.

stock option

The option holder's right to buy or sell stock at a future date for a certain price. A "put" option is a contract to sell, while a "call" option is a contract to buy.

stock split

The division of a corporation's outstanding shares, such that the total number of shares increases, but the proportion of each shareholder's ownership interest is unchanged. Stock splits are frequently performed to lower the security's per share market price.

stockholder/shareholder

A person who owns shares of stock of a corporation and there-

fore has an ownership interest in the corporation.

stockholder's derivative action

A suit brought by a stockholder on behalf of her corporation against a third party to recover for injuries suffered by the corporation. The stockholder initiates the suit because the corporation refuses to file suit against the third party.

stop and frisk

A police officer's search for concealed weapons on a suspected criminal, in which the officer runs his or her hands over the suspect's outer clothing. A stop and frisk search does not require probable cause.

stop order

A directive given by a stockholder to his stockbroker to buy shares of stock or other securities at a specified price above or to sell such securities at a specified price below their current market price.

stoppage in transit

The right of a person who sells goods on credit to stop the transfer and transport of the goods to the buyer and to regain possession and control of the goods until he receives payment or suitable guarantee from the buyer.

straddle

Investment strategy in which one owns an equal number of put options and call options on the same stock or commodity, with the same price. *See* hedging.

stranding

The running aground and stopping of a ship on a shore, sandbar, or other barrier.

stranger

An outsider; a person who has no privity to a relationship, transaction, or agreement.

straw man

A person who secretly acts on behalf of others while at the same time he represents himself to third parties as acting in his own behalf (*e.g.*, a person who buys a building in his own name from a third party but who is in fact purchasing the building on behalf of someone else).

street name

Where a security is held in the broker's name rather than the owner's name.

strict construction

The process by which courts interpret statutes so that the interpretation of the law adheres closely to the literal meaning of the text.

strict liability

Legal doctrine that holds a manufacturer or a seller liable for all the defects and injuries caused by his products regardless of the degree of care that it exercised.

strict scrutiny

Method by which courts determine the constitutionality of a law, when a law affects a fundamental right (*e.g.*, the right to equal protection). Under the strict scrutiny test, the legislature must have a compelling interest to enact the law, and the measures prescribed by the law must be the least restrictive means possible to accomplish the legislature's goal.

strictissimi juris
(strik-TIS-sim-ee JUR-is) Lat. Of the most strict law. To strictly and literally apply the law to a situation or person.

strike
1. Work stoppage engaged in by employees as a means to get better terms of employment from their employer. 2. To remove; delete; expunge. 3. To hit, beat.

strike suit
A suit brought against a corporation by a shareholder who owns a small amount of that corporation's shares. Such suits are most often brought with the sole intention of forcing the corporation to privately settle the suit, rather than spend a large sum of money to defend.

struck jury
A special jury convened to hear an important, profound or complex legal question.

sua sponte
(SOO-a SPON-tee) Lat. Of his own will. To take a course of action without the suggestion of another (*e.g.,* a court may raise an issue sua sponte, that is, on its own.

sub
Lat. Under; upon.

Subchapter S corporation
An elective provision allowing certain small business corporations to be taxed as if they were individual proprietorships.

subcontractor
A person who enters into an agreement with a contractor to perform part, or all, of the work the contractor has undertaken (*e.g.,* a person who handles the electrical wiring in a building that is being constructed).

subdivision
The division of a lot, parcel, or tract of land into two or more parcels.

subinfeudation
In feudal England, the process whereby feudal tenants granted smaller estates out of their holdings to others.

subjacent support
The support of surface land by the land which lies underneath.

439

subject matter

The topic or issue that is being considered; the issue in dispute before a court, legislature, or an administrative body.

subject matter jurisdiction

The power of a court to hear and determine cases involving particular subjects.

subject to open

In property law, the future interests of a class of people, when the number of people in the class is subject to change.

sub judice

(sub joo-DISH-ee *or* joo DISS-ee) Lat. Before a court for its consideration.

sublease

Agreement whereby a lessee grants his rights and interest in a lease to a third person for a period of time less than the lease.

sublet

A situation wherein a tenant leases property to a third party, called the subtenant.

submission

1. Agreement between two or more persons to submit a dispute to a court for judicial resolution. 2. The acquiescing and giving in to the power or authority of another person or a government (*e.g.*, an escaped convict who turns himself into law enforcement officials).

submit

To yield to the will of another; to present.

sub modo

Lat. Subject to a condition or under a restriction.

sub nom/sub nomine

Under the name of.

subordinate

1. To make subservient; to place at an inferior rank. 2. To put in an inferior class (*e.g.*, to place a mortgage in a junior position to another mortgage loan).

subornation of perjury

The crime of inducing another person to make a false oath before a court.

subpoena

A judicial order requiring a person to appear in court and to give testimony with respect to a dispute before the court.

subpoena duces tecum
(subpoena DOOK-ess TAY-kum) A judicial order requiring a person to bring all documents in her possession that pertain to the matter in dispute to the court.

subrogation
The placement of one person in the place of another so that he succeeds to that person's rights and obligations with respect to a third person.

subrogee
A person who acquires the legal rights of another person by subrogation.

subrogor
A person whose legal rights are acquired by another through subrogation.

sub rosa
Privately; secretly.

subscribe
1. To sign a legal document or other agreement. 2. To agree to buy a portion of the initial stock offering of a corporation. 3. To pledge or contribute money to a cause.

subscriber
One who agrees in writing to buy a corporation's initial stock offering.

subscription rights
A shareholder's right to buy any additional stock offered by the corporation.

subsidiary
1. Secondary in importance; subordinate in position or influence. 2. A company having more than 50% of its stock owned by another company.

subsidy
Financial aid and assistance given to a business enterprise or other organization by government.

sub silentio
(sub sigh-LEN-shee-o) Lat. Silently.

substance
The material aspect or part of something (*e.g.*, the essence of a legal argument).

substantial performance
The fulfillment of the material obligations that a person has under a contract so as to excuse

441

complete performance of the condition. The contract remains enforceable as long as the omission is minor although damages may be available to the other party. Rule is often applied to construction contracts.

substantive due process

The essence of due process requires that no person be deprived of life, liberty, or property by unreasonable and arbitrary laws.

substantive law

Statute or common law that creates, defines, and regulates a person's rights in a particular area.

substituted judgment

Allowing a surrogate to make decisions on behalf of an incapacitated person, based on the surrogate's best determination of what the person would decide if she were not incapacitated.

substituted service

Service of process upon a person by any authorized means other than personal delivery of the legal order to the person.

substitution

The putting of a person or thing in the place of another person or thing.

subtenant

1. A person who rents all or part of leased premises from the original lessee of the property for a period less than the term of the original lease. 2. Sublessee.

succession

1. Procedure by which property of a deceased person is transferred to another person, either by operation of statute or will. 2. The act of following in sequence (*e.g.*, the replacement of a retired judge by his successor to the bench).

successive terms

Terms that follow one another in uninterrupted order.

successor

One who immediately follows another (*e.g.*, one who takes an incumbent's place or position after the incumbent departs).

sudden passion

Anger or fury that is the immediate and direct result of an incident. Most commonly referred to with respect to the definition of manslaughter (*i.e.,* "heat of passion").

sue

To institute legal proceedings; to bring a civil action against another person; to file a cause of action against another.

sue out

To apply for and obtain a writ, process, or court order.

suffrage

The right or privilege to vote.

suicide

The intentional taking or destruction of one's own life.

sui generis

(swee JEN-er-is) Lat. Of its own kind. To be unique and different from all others.

sui juris

(swee JOOR-is) Lat. Of his own right. The capacity or ability to control one's life and make decisions with respect to how one's life will be ordered.

suit

1. Any legal proceeding initiated by a person. 2. A civil action

brought in a court of law to redress a wrong.

suitor

The person who brings a legal action; a claimant.

sum certain

The fixed, exact, settled, or stated amount in a contract, damages judgment, or negotiable instrument.

summary

1. (n.) A concise description of a legal argument. 2. Digest of a judicial decision. 3. (adj.) Concise; condensed; brief.

summary judgment

Judgment rendered in favor of a party to a legal proceeding on an issue in dispute upon a motion by that party for judgment, because there is no genuine issue of material fact and he is therefore entitled to prevail on the issue as a matter of law. Judgment may be directed to all or part of the cause of action.

summary proceeding

Proceeding by which a legal dispute is settled promptly through the use of abbreviated judicial procedures, such as limited discovery and the use of a bench trial rather than a trial by jury (*e.g.*, a small claims court proceeding).

summing up

The restatement and summarization of evidence and arguments presented by counsel at the end of a trial by jury.

summons

Judicial writ issued by a court that orders a person to appear before the court so a civil action brought against the person by another party may be adjudicated.

Sunday closing laws

Laws restricting the Sunday operations of certain types of businesses (*e.g.*, retail liquor establishments). Also "blue laws."

sunset law

Law that provides that a government agency or program will cease to exist on a certain date unless the legislature acts to continue it.

sunshine laws

Laws that require government meetings to be open and accessible to the public.

suo nomine

(SOO-oh NOM-in-nee) Lat. In his own name.

supersede

To replace; to set aside; to displace (*e.g.*, to set aside a prior court ruling).

supersedeas

(soo-per-SEE-dee-as) Judicial writ issued by an appellate court that stays or suspends lower court proceedings or decisions.

superseding cause

Conduct of a person that is so substantially responsible for an injury suffered by another person that the prior negligent conduct of other persons that also caused the injury is waived in determining liability. *See* intervening cause, supervening cause.

supervening cause

The source or origin of an injury that is independent of all other causes and is the direct and proximate cause of the injury.

supplemental
That which is added to complete a thing.

supplemental pleading
A pleading that sets forth facts arising after the original pleading was filed. *Contrast* with an amended pleading, which corrects errors in form or substance in original pleading.

supplementary proceedings
Judicial hearing that follows a judgment issued by a court on behalf of a creditor against a debtor which has as its purpose the ascertainment of the assets and property of the debtor that are available to satisfy the judgment.

support
1. (v.) To sustain; to bolster; to validate by the offering of additional proof (*e.g.*, to bolster a legal argument advanced by another person). 2. (n.) Sustenance; maintenance provided for the upkeep of a person or a family; to furnish the necessary means so a person may go on living.

suppress
To forcibly put a stop to; to prevent; to subdue.

suppression of evidence
1. The exclusion of evidence by a trial judge because it was illegally obtained. 2. The refusal to produce evidence, or to interfere with the production of evidence.

suppressio veri, expresso falsi
(soo-PRESS-ee-o VAIR-ee ex-PRES-so FAL-see) Lat. Suppression of the truth is the same as the expression of what is false.

supra
(SOO-pra) Lat. Above. The word is used to refer to a prior passage in a legal text.

Supremacy Clause
Clause in Article VI, section 2 of the U.S. Constitution which establishes that the laws, treaties and actions of the federal government pursuant to the Constitution are superior to those of the states. Thus, if a federal and state law conflict, federal law governs.

Supreme Court
The highest judicial body in the United States and in most states.

surcharge
1. To impose an additional tax; to inflict a supplementary cost on an individual or a corporation.
2. To hold a fiduciary liable for her improper and negligent conduct in the carrying out of her fiduciary duties.

surety
A person who agrees to fulfill a financial obligation of another person upon that person's default of his obligation.

surname
A person's last name; a person's family name (*e.g.*, John Smith's surname is Smith).

surplus
That which exceeds the necessary or required amount. In finance, this term refers to the excess of assets over liabilities.

surplusage
Extraneous material; nonessential matter.

surprise
1. (n.) An unexpected event or happening (*e.g.*, an unexpected occurrence during a trial). 2. (v.) To stun or catch unaware.

surrebutter
Under common law pleading, the plaintiff's answer of fact to the defendant's rebutter.

surrejoinder
Under common law pleading, the plaintiff's answer of fact to the defendant's rejoinder.

surrender
To give up; yield; relinquish (*e.g.*, to relinquish a claim against property).

surrogate
1. Person who takes the place of another; a substitute. 2. Title given to a judicial officer entrusted with the responsibility of supervising probate matters.

surrogate parent
1. A person other than a parent who stands in place of a natural parent, and thereby assumes parental rights and responsibilities. *See* in loco parentis. 2. A woman who agrees to provide her uterus to carry an embryo to term and bear the child for another person or couple. The surrogate agrees to surrender any and all parental rights to the child.

surtax

An additional tax imposed on top of another tax.

surveillance

The close observation of another person or place (*e.g.,* police observation of a criminal suspect in order to gather evidence).

survival statute

A statute that insures the continuance of a cause of action after the death of the injured person who instituted the action. In case of the injured person's death, the estate would continue the action and collect damages related to the injury.

survivorship

Right to property or some other interest that a person possesses because he has outlived another.

suspect

1. (v.) To have a vague idea concerning. 2. (n.) One who is suspected of committing a crime.

suspect classification

A classification in a statute based on race, national origin, or alienage. Suspect classifications are subject to strict-scrutiny for equal protection purposes.

suspended sentence

Criminal penalty of imprisonment that is imposed on the convicted person but which he is not immediately required to serve.

suspension

An interruption; a postponement (*e.g.,* the interruption of a lawyer's right to practice law because of her improper conduct).

sustain

To uphold; maintain; to approve (*e.g.,* to uphold a lower court judgment).

sweetheart deal

A collusive contract, especially a collective bargaining agreement that is unusually favorable to the employer.

Swiss Verein

(swiss fair-AIN) A type of organization recognized by Swiss law similar to a voluntary association. The members of the Verein have limited liability for the actions of other members. Several multinational law and accounting firms have adopted this form of organization.

syllabus
A summary outline of a decision or an argument.

symbolic delivery
The transferring of possession of real or personal property from one person to another by the transfer of some token object.

symbolic speech
Communication of ideas through conduct (*e.g.*, wearing black arm bands as war protest), which may be constitutionally protected.

syndicate
A group of persons who join together for the express purpose of conducting a commercial transaction (*e.g.*, a group of brokers).

imposed certain duties on unions, established unfair labor practices for unions, abolished the closed shop, established the rights of employees to revoke the union as their bargaining agent, and provided for the equal treatment of independent and affiliated unions.

table
In legislative or parliamentary practice, to defer consideration of a matter until and unless brought up for consideration at a later time.

tacit
1. Implied understanding. 2. Silent agreement without any opposition.

tacking
1. In property law, the joining of periods of possession of consecutive adverse possessors, for purposes of establishing title by adverse possession. 2. Generally, any joining or adding together of elements.

Taft-Hartley Act
Federal labor legislation enacted in 1947, amending the Wagner Act of 1935, by limiting the power of labor unions. The Act

tail
In property law, an "estate in tail" or "fee tail" is an estate which, at the death of the owner, goes to the lineal descendants or the "heirs of the body" of the owner, as long as there are lineal descendants. Today, the fee tail is rarely used in the United States.

taking
The act of laying hold upon an object; transfer of possession or control. In criminal law, one need not remove the object for a taking to occur.

taking the Fifth
The exercising of one's right not to answer a question that is self-incriminating. This phrase refers to the Fifth Amendment to the U.S. Constitution, which protects such action.

talesman

(TAL-es-man *or* TAY-lees-man) A person added to the jury from among the bystanders at the courthouse, rather than being summoned in the normal manner.

Talmud

The authoritative body of Jewish law and tradition.

tampering

1. Illegally altering a document or product. 2. Attempting to influence another through improper means, such as bribery.

tangible

Having a definite, physical existence. In property law, "tangible property" includes things like objects, buildings, and money. In evidence, "tangible evidence" refers to physical evidence which can be seen at trial (*e.g.*, the gun, the contract, the photographs).

tangible property

In property law, referring to things with a definite physical existence (*e.g.*, an object, a building, a bank account). "Intangible property" is not physical (*e.g.*, a copyright, an easement, goodwill, or rights under a contract).

tariff

The payment of customs or duties on goods imported into the United States. The "tariff schedule" lists rates for the various imports which are subject to the tariff. Tariffs may be "protective" (to help United States businesses against foreign competition) "retaliatory" (to force another nation to reduce its tariffs on United States goods) or "fiscal" (to raise revenue).

tarnishment

Unauthorized use of a trademark in such a way as to diminish the mark's distinctive qualities.

tax

The money or rate of money paid to government by its citizens for governmental services. A tax may be assessed on income, property, business, sales, inheritances, roads, mining, gifts, excess profits, capital gains, etc.

taxable estate

The gross estate of a decedent, reduced by allowable deductions. I.R.C. § 2051.

taxable gift

The value of a gift, after adjusting for any allowable deductions (*e.g.*, charitable deductions).

taxable income

The amount of income taxed, at varying rates depending on the amount. For individuals, taxable income is adjusted gross income minus deductions and exemptions. For businesses, taxable income is gross income.

taxable year

The time period during which tax liability is calculated; generally, tax liability is calculated on either a calendar or fiscal year basis.

tax avoidance

Paying only the minimum amount of taxes required.

tax benefit doctrine

Rule which states that amounts deducted from gross income in an earlier tax year and recovered in later years may be recognized as income, but only to the extent that the earlier deductions generated a tax savings.

tax court

An independent federal court that hears disputes involving deficiencies or over-payments in taxes, as determined by the I.R.S.

tax credit

A reduction in the amount of tax owed by a taxpayer. As opposed to deductions, a tax credit reduces tax liability dollar for dollar, while a deduction simply reduces the amount that is subject to tax.

tax deduction

An allowable subtraction from gross income, made to determine the net amount subject to tax.

tax deferred

Income that will not be taxed until some future date.

tax evasion

Illegally paying less tax than the law requires, a crime under Internal Revenue Code § 7201.

tax exempt

That which is not subject to tax (*e.g.*, funds used for charitable purposes).

tax expenditure

Situation wherein the federal government chooses not to tax

certain activity or persons, allowing those persons to keep the forsaken tax. The practical effect is the same as if the government had taxed the activity and made an expenditure to support that activity.

taxing power

The power of Congress to "lay and collect taxes, imports and excises." The power is enumerated in Article I, section 8, clause 1.

taxpayer

One who is liable for tax.

tax-preference items

Items which are deducted in the course of determining taxable income, then added back in the course of determining taxable income for alternative minimum tax purposes.

tax rate

The amount of tax imposed on the taxpayer.

tax shelter

A financial device by which a taxpayer reduces or defers his or her tax liability (*e.g.*, certain real estate investments, certain limited partnership agreements).

teller

An official counter. In banks, tellers take deposits and disburse withdrawals of money. In legislatures, tellers count the votes.

temporary

Of a limited amount of time; not permanent.

Temporary Emergency Court of Appeals

A court created in 1971 with jurisdiction to hear appeals of cases arising under the wage and price control provisions of the Economic Stabilization Act of 1970 and the Emergency Petroleum Allocation Act of 1973. The court was abolished in 1992.

temporary injunction

A remedy granted temporarily by the court at the start of the litigation to prevent future injury to the person seeking the injunction, until the court has had an opportunity to make a final decision in the case. Also called "interlocutory injunction."

temporary restraining order (T.R.O.)

A remedy granted temporarily by the court only in exceptional circumstances when the court cannot hold an immediate hearing. A T.R.O. is granted to prevent further immediate and irreparable injury to the person seeking the order. The order may be granted without advance notice to the adverse party and lasts only until the court holds a hearing. *See* Federal Rule of Civil Procedure 65(b).

tempore

(tem-PORE-ay) Lat. At the time. *See* pro tem.

tenancy

The right to possess real property under a lease, subject to another's valid title. The landlord, who holds title, leases the exclusive right of possession to the tenant, withholding the landlord's right to enter to demand rent or to make repairs.

tenancy by the entirety

Ownership of property by a husband and wife together so that upon the death of either spouse the other will take full and complete ownership of the entire property. Neither spouse can sell the property without the consent of the other. A divorce terminates the tenancy by the entirety and creates a "tenancy in common."

tenancy in common

Undivided ownership in property by two or more persons, each having the same right to the use and possession of the property. Thus, each owner may separately partition, convey, sell, or dispose by will his share of the property.

tenant

1. One who possesses real property. 2. One who possesses real property under a lease given by the owner or "landlord," subject to the landlord's title.

tenant at sufferance

One who continues to possess real estate after his right to possession has terminated; also called a "holdover tenant." A tenant at sufferance has no estate and no privity with the landlord; he is not entitled to stay unless the landlord agrees to extend the lease. However, he may not be sued for trespass unless the landlord enters and demands possession.

tenantable

Fit for habitation.

tenant at will

One who possesses real estate under a lease which does not set a fixed term of tenancy. The tenancy may be terminated, upon proper notice, by either the landlord or the tenant at any time.

tenant for life

One who possesses real property for the term of his life, or the life of another person.

tenant in fee simple

One who holds an estate in land without any Limitations on it, giving the owner absolute power of disposition. *See* fee simple.

tender

1. Unconditional offer to pay or perform one's duties under a contract, along with the present ability to carry out the offer. If the other party refuses the offer, that party is in default, and the tendering party then has a right to sue for breach of contract. 2. To make payment of money. 3. To deliver a deed. 4. To deliver stock certificates.

tender offer

In securities law, a corporation's direct offer to the shareholders of another corporation to purchase a certain number of shares at a given price or at a maximum price, in order to achieve control of the corporation. Tender offers are public and are regulated by federal and state securities laws.

tender years doctrine

In family law, the former presumption that the custody of very young children should be awarded to the mother, unless she is shown to be unfit. The doctrine has largely been replaced by the "best interests of the child" test.

tenement

1. Any structure permanently attached to land (*e.g.*, buildings, houses, apartments). 2. At common law, any real property which might be possessed permanently. 3. Slum housing for the poor.

Tennessee Valley Authority (T.V.A.)

Established in 1933 to conduct a unified resource development program to promote economic growth in the Tennessee Valley area.

tenor

In pleadings, used to mean that the exact language of the deed or contract is included, rather than a paraphrasing of the language (*e.g.*, "the tenor of the contract that . . .").

Tenth Amendment

U.S. constitutional Amendment reserving to the states or people any powers not delegated to the federal government.

tenure

1. The right to possess property. 2. The duration of the right to hold public office (*e.g.*, federal judges hold tenure for life subject to good behavior). 3. The right of some employees (*e.g.*, teachers) to hold their positions permanently, subject only to removal for cause or for economic necessity (*e.g.*, declining enrollment).

term

1. A fixed period of time in contracts or deeds (*e.g.*, time to make payments, time of employment, time of lease). 2. Any segment of a contract concerning a particular item (*e.g.*, price term, delivery term, payment term). 3. The period of time a court is mandated by law to hear cases. A "session" is the period of time a court actually hears cases.

terminable interest

Any interest in property that is subject to termination at a specified time or upon the occurrence of a specified event (*e.g.*, upon the death of the holder). The transfer of such an interest generally does not qualify for the marital deduction.

termination of parental rights

A court order severing all legal bonds between a parent and a child, and taking from the parent all rights and responsibilities regarding the child. Such orders may be entered voluntarily, as when a parent consents to the adoption of a child by another, or involuntary, in cases of abuse or neglect.

term of art

A word or phrase having a special meaning when used in a particular occupation or business.

term of court

The time period as defined by law or statute during which the court performs its functions.

territorial court

Court established by Congress which adjudicates matters pertaining to "the rules and regulations respecting the territory or other property belonging to the government," as set forth in the U.S. Constitution, Article IV, section 3, clause 2. Generally, this term refers to a court in the U.S. judicial system in U.S. territory.

territorial jurisdiction

The territory over which a court or government subdivision has jurisdiction.

territorial waters

Designated waters which are within the legal and political control of a nation, including inland rivers, waters within the tides, and seawaters extending three miles beyond the shore.

territory

Geographical area under control of an outside power. In the United States, territories are lands which are not part of any state, have not been admitted as a state, but are organized with legislatures and executive officers appointed by the president. *See U.S. Constitution, Article IV, section 3.*

terroristic threat

A threat to use violence with the purpose of terrorizing another, causing the evacuation of a building or facility, causing serious public inconvenience, or with a reckless disregard of the risk of causing such terror or inconvenience.

Terry stop

A stop-and-frisk search. *Terry v. Ohio,* 392 U.S. 1 (1968).

testacy

The condition of having left a will at one's death, opposed to "intestacy," having died without leaving a will.

testament

Formerly, one's statement regarding disposition of his personal property at his death, distinguished from a "will" which controlled disposition of real property (*e.g.,* "last will and testament"). Today, the word "testament" is unnecessary, since a will may dispose of both real and personal property.

testamentary
1. Concerning a will or testament. 2. Describing a deed, contract, instrument, gift, etc., which takes effect only upon the death of the maker.

testamentary capacity
The measure of mental capacity one must possess while making a will in order for that will to be legal. To satisfy this standard, a testator must generally understand the nature of his or her business and comprehend the nature and extent of the property and the persons who are the objects of his or her bounty.

testamentary disposition
Disposition of property by gift, will, deed, or contract, which takes effect only upon the death of the grantor.

testamentum omne morte consummatur
(tes-ta-MEN-tum OM-nee mort con-soo-MAT-tur) Lat. Every will is perfected at death. Princi-

ple that a will must take effect only upon the death of the testator.

testate
Having left a will at one's death, opposed to "intestate," having died without leaving a will.

testator
A man who dies having left a will or testament.

testatrix
A woman who dies having left a will or testament.

test case
A court action, the outcome of which establishes an important legal principle or the validity of a law. Often a test case is an action chosen out of a large pool of similar pending actions, whereby all the litigants agree to be bound by the decision of this one action. Also "test action."

testes ponderantur, non numerantur
(TES-tes pon-DARE-en-tur non NOO-mer-ran-toor) Lat. Witnesses are weighed, not numbered. Principle that the credibility and strength of testimony should determine conflicts in the

evidence, not the number of witnesses each side presents.

testify
1. To make a statement under oath. 2. To submit testimony or bear witness for the purpose of establishing a fact.

testimony
Statements by a witness under oath or affirmation, usually in court, connected with a legal proceeding. Testimony is one form of evidence.

theft
The illegal taking of another's property without the owner's consent, with the intent to permanently deprive the owner of its use. *See* larceny and robbery.

theory of the case
The line of reasoning and theory used by a litigant in a suit.

third degree
Illegal conduct using extended periods of interrogation, threatening violence, or employing actual violence when trying to extract a statement or confession from a criminal suspect. *See Miranda* warning.

third party
A person not involved in the specific litigation, contract, or transaction under consideration, but who may have incidental rights or interests to assert.

third party beneficiary
One who may receive a benefit under a contract without being a party to the contract (*e.g.*, the beneficiary under a life insurance policy stands to receive the proceeds of the policy, but never signs or agrees to the policy). Two parties may validly contract to confer benefits on a third party, even though the third party provides no consideration.

third party plaintiff
A defendant who files a pleading against a non-party, making the non-party a third-party defendant.

Thirteenth Amendment
U.S. constitutional amendment which prohibits slavery and involuntary servitude, and which grants to Congress the power to enforce the Amendment.

threat
Statement of intention to injure person or property through an unlawful act, along with the ability to injure, in order to coerce another.

three-mile limit
The distance offshore of three nautical miles (one marine league equals 5.6 KM), representing the waters which are within the legal and political control of the nation inhabiting the shoreline.

three-strikes law
A law that imposes an enhanced penalty for an offender's third felony conviction. The enhanced penalty often is life imprisonment.

thrift institutions
Any savings bank or savings and loan association.

ticket
1. In contracts, a receipt indicating that the holder has a specific and described right (*e.g.*, pawn tickets, baseball tickets, discount tickets). 2. Form for recording violations of the motor vehicle laws.

tide land
Land over which water ebbs and flows.

tie-in arrangement
See tying arrangement; tying into.

time is of the essence
Phrase in a contract which denotes the absolute necessity of one party performing an act within a specified period of time, or else that party breaches the entire contract.

time immemorial
A time beyond the reach of memory, record, or tradition.

time, place and manner restriction
A governmental restriction on when, where, and how public communication or assembly may be made that does not depend on the content of the speech or the purpose of the assembly.

timesharing
Arrangement whereby joint owners or tenants alternate their periods of occupancy. Occupancy commonly lasts less than a month.

tippee

Persons given advance information by corporate insiders concerning nonpublic matters that may affect the price of securities. Tippee may be liable under S.E.C. rule 10b-5.

tithe

One-tenth of one's income, given to support a charitable or religious organization. A tax or levy of 10 percent.

title

1. In property law, the right to own and possess real and personal property. Usually applied to real property, "title" identifies the legal owner of the land. 2. Designation at the beginning of a pleading, identifying the court and the name of the parties. 3. Any mark or designation (*e.g.*, a book title, a patent title, or the title of an official).

title jurisdiction

Any jurisdiction in which title to a mortgaged premises passes to the mortgagee, reverting to the mortgagor only upon the completion of payments.

Title IX

Popular name for Title IX of the Educational Amendments of 1972, 20 U.S.C.A. § 1681 *et seq.*, the federal law prohibiting sex discrimination by schools that receive federal funds.

title search

The examination of all public records pertaining to the title of a property, for the purpose of determining the validity of the title. Title is said to be valid, or good, when it is clear of defects such as liens.

Title VII

Popular name for Title VII of the Civil Rights Act of 1964, 42 U.S.C.A. § 2000e *et seq.*, the federal law prohibiting employment discrimination based on race, sex, pregnancy, religion, and national origin.

to have and to hold

The traditional phrase used in a conveyance which signifies the estate granted (*e.g.*, "To *A* and his heirs, to have and to hold Blackacre, unto and for the use of *A* and his heirs forever.") Often referred to as a "habendum clause."

toll
1. A charge for the use of public highways. 2. To end; to defeat (*e.g.*, the statute of limitations "tolls" the right to sue after a specified period of time). 3. To temporarily stop or suspend (*e.g.*, the statute of limitations is tolled during plaintiff's incapacity).

tombstone ad
Advertisement taken out by corporations, announcing an offering of public securities. The ad is not an official offer to buy or sell, but is merely an announcement of a forthcoming prospectus. The layout of text in such ads is similar to that seen on tombstones.

tonnage
The carrying capacity of a ship, in tons or cubic feet.

tontine
A special kind of financial agreement, sometimes used in insurance policies, by which a group of investors share all the benefits exclusively. When any of them dies or defaults, the benefits are equally divided among those remaining.

Torrens title
A system of land title where a register of property ownership maintained by the state guarantees indefeasible title to those included in the register. Land ownership is transferred through registration of title. Nine states have adopted Torrens systems for some land.

tort
A wrongful injury; a private or civil wrong which is not a breach of contract. A tort is some action or conduct by the defendant which results from a breach of a legal duty owed by the defendant to the plaintiff, which proximately causes injury or damage to the plaintiff. Torts may be "intentional" (when the defendant intends to violate a legal duty) or "negligent" (when the defendant fails to exercise the proper degree of care established by law).

Tort Claims Act
Statute adopted in 1946 which declares that the U.S. government waives its right to be immune from tort liability, and establishes the conditions for bringing tort claims against the

federal government. The Act provides for a number of exceptions to the general waiver of sovereign immunity. Most states have similar enactments.

tortfeasor
The person who commits a tort.

tortious
Describing action or conduct that results from a breach of a legal duty which may subject the actor to liability.

total disability
The disability which prevents the employee from performing the substantial, gainful work required in his usual occupation, resulting in a loss of earning power, whether or not the disability is permanent, crippling, or physical.

totality of the circumstances test
Test which incorporates all circumstances of a particular case, to determine whether a police search was constitutional.

total loss
In fire insurance policies, the complete destruction of the building or property, so that there

are no substantial remains to reconstruct or restore to the original condition.

Totten trust
A trust arrangement by which the creator of the trust becomes the trustee for the beneficiary of the trust. The Totten trust may be revoked by the creator until the death of the creator or until the creator transfers control to the beneficiary.

touch and concern
A property law standard used to determine the validity of a covenant which runs with the land. Any covenant that enhances the enjoyment of one piece of property by burdening the enjoyment of another "touches and concerns" the land.

to wit
Namely; that is to say. Phrase used to introduce an explanation, (*e.g.*, "Defendant breached the contract, to wit, she did not deliver the goods.").

town
A civil and political division of a state. In many states, the town is the unit of local government; in

others, the county is the unit of local government and a town is part of the county.

township

1. In the United States government public lands survey, a six-mile square tract of land. 2. In many states, a political unit for local government.

trade disparagement

Intentionally belittling or demeaning another person's business by statements that are false and misleading, but not necessarily defamatory.

trade fixture

Any personal property used by a tenant in the conduct of a business. The tenant retains ownership of such property after the termination of the tenancy.

trademark

Any mark, picture, symbol, or stamp used to designate a certain product of a certain manufacturer and to distinguish it from other manufacturers' similar products. The trademark must be adopted by the manufacturer or merchant and affixed to the product. Generic names are not valid trade-marks. Personal names, place names, and common adjectives are valid trademarks only if they have acquired a secondary meaning identifying them with a product. The federal government gives trademark holders exclusive rights to use the trademark for a period of years that may be renewed indefinitely; actions for infringement of trademark may be brought in federal court.

trade name

1. The name under which a business operates. 2. A description, including words or symbols, of the dealer or manufacturer of particular goods, distinguished from a trademark which is a description of the goods.

trade practice

A customary way of doing business in a particular industry.

trade secret

1. A secret formula or other kind of information used in one's business for commercial advantage (*e.g.*, the recipe for Coca-Cola). 2. Information that derives independent economic value from not being generally known to or ascertainable by other per-

sons, and that is the subject of reasonable efforts to maintain its secrecy. Uniform Trade Secrets Act § 1.4.

trade union
An organization of workers in the same trade or related trades with the purpose of achieving better wages, hours, or conditions of employment (*e.g.*, United Steelworkers, Ladies Garment Workers).

trade usage
The practice and customs of the participants in a particular trade relating to the forming and performing of contracts.

traditionary evidence
Evidence which is based on longstanding facts or statements by deceased persons, to prove pedigree and ancient boundaries. Such evidence is used in the absence of testimony from living persons.

transaction
The activities around which a contract, crime, or some other legal matter develops, including negotiations, business management, other conversations, or events.

transactions or occurrence test
Test used in a civil action, to determine whether a compulsory counterclaim must be brought. If a potential counterclaim arises from same transaction or occurrence as the opposing party's claim, it must be brought.

transcript
Anything transcribed or copied from an original (especially original legal documents). A "trial transcript" is a copy of the questions, answers, and statements made at a trial and recorded by the court reporter.

transfer
1. To convey, sell, or in any other way give possession or control of land to another. 2. The act of conveying, selling, or giving away property.

transfer agent
One who facilitates the transfer of publicly traded stock, by registering the name, address, and number of shares owned by a buyer or seller. The transfer agent also issues new stock cer-

tificates and facilitates the cancellation of old certificates.

transferred intent

Legal principal used in tort law which states that if a person intends to harm *A* and instead harms *B*, he is liable to *B* in tort even though the intent was not directed to *B*. The principle is also used in criminal law: when a person intends to murder *A* but instead murders *B*, the requisite intent for murder of *B* may be established.

transferee liability

Tax liability of one who is the transferee of property. In some situations, a transferee is liable for the property tax when the I.R.S. cannot collect the tax from the transferor.

transfer tax

Tax on the transfer of property, whether by sale or gift. The tax may be placed on the deed, on the gift, on the inheritance, or on securities.

transformative use

In copyright law, the use of a work to create a new work that provides a new expression, meaning, or message.

transitory action

A cause of action which may be pursued in several places, as opposed to a "local" action which may be brought only in one place. Property and criminal actions are "local"; contract and tort actions are generally transitory.

transnational law

Law applicable to all persons, businesses, or nations that perform or have influence across national borders.

trauma

A physical injury to the body, including any wound, shock, or psychological damage resulting from a particular emotional disturbance.

traverse

In common law pleading, a denial of the preceding pleading. The traverse may be "common" (a denial of all allegations with no argument) or "special" (including an affirmative argument or explanation).

treason

Rebellion against one's own civil government. Treason against the United States is defined as "levying war against them, or, in adhering to their Enemies, giving them Aid and Comfort." U.S. Constitution, Article III, section 3.

treasure trove

Any money, coin, gold, silver, plate, bullion, or valuable item found hidden in the earth or a private place, whose owner is unknown.

treasury

1. A place in which funds are kept, managed, and disbursed. 2. That part of the government responsible for keeping and managing public funds.

treasury bill

A short-term obligation of the U.S. Treasury. Such bills mature within a year and are generally sold at a discount from face value.

treasury bond

1. A bond issued by a corporation, then bought back by the same corporation. 2. A long-term

obligation of the U.S. Treasury, which matures after 10 years and pays interest semi-annually.

treasury notes

Promissory note with interest-bearing coupons issued by the United States for one to five years.

treasury shares

Stock issued to shareholders by a corporation, then bought back by the same corporation for various purposes (*e.g.,* a stock bonus plan for managers). Also "treasury stock."

treaty

In international law, an agreement between two or more nations relating to international or external affairs. In the United States, the President may make a treaty which must be approved by the Senate before it takes effect.

treble damages

Damages awarded to the plaintiff three times the amount of his actual injury as found by the jury. Treble damages may be given only by statute (*e.g.,* they are awarded in antitrust cases

466

under section 4 of the Clayton Act, 15 U.S.C. § 15).

trespass

1. Wrongful interference with or damage to another's real or personal property, including entering onto land, physical assault, or destruction of legal rights. 2. In common law pleading, any type of broad civil wrong or tort.

trespasser

One who wrongfully enters, interferes with, or damages another's property.

trial

Courtroom proceedings before a judge or judge and jury to examine evidence, hear arguments, and decide the factual and legal questions presented in making a final decision.

trial court

Any court of original jurisdiction where all evidence is first heard.

trial de novo

A new trial in which the entire cause is retried as if no prior trial had occurred.

tribal court

A formalized system established by American Indian and Alaska Native tribes for resolving criminal and other legal matters.

tribunal

A court, composed of several judges, each with legal authority to decide cases.

tripartite

Having three parts.

TRIPs

Agreement on Trade-Related Aspects of Intellectual Property Rights, an international agreement strengthening and harmonizing national laws on patents, trademarks, copyrights, and trade secrets. The agreement is administered by the World Trade Organization.

T.R.O.

See temporary restraining order.

trover

An old common law pleading to recover damages for a wrongful taking of property or to recover actual possession of the property. Trover originally developed for the recovery of lost property and later expanded to include taken property.

true bill

An indictment approved by the grand jury which indicates it is satisfied that the evidence presents a prima facie case against the accused.

trust

Property held by one person as trustee for the benefit of another. The trustee holds the legal title of the trust property and the beneficiary or "cestui que trust" holds the "equitable title" of the property. *See* constructive trust, precatory trust, and resulting trust.

trust deed

1. Document by which one person gives legal title to real property to another person as trustee where the property is given as security for the payment of a debt or performance of an obligation. 2. A mortgage deal.

trustee

The person appointed to hold and manage property in trust for the benefit of another.

trustee in bankruptcy

Person who is assigned to take control of the property of the debtor, by running his business, liquidating his assets, defending his suits, contesting the claims, and eventually distributing his assets.

trust fund

The property or money held by the trustee in a trust for the benefit of another. Also called the "corpus" or the "res" of the trust.

trust indenture

The document which states the terms and conditions of the trust and the conduct of the trustee.

trustor

One who creates a trust. Also "settlor."

trust receipt

A receipt stating the security arrangements surrounding bank-funded commercial sales of goods. The bank holds title, under the trust receipts, to the goods until the debt is paid by the buyer.

Truth-In-Lending Act

Federal law requiring commercial lenders to provide to customers accurate and understandable information regarding credit terms. Among other things, the Act requires lenders to express the cost of credit in terms of an annual percentage rate computed on the unpaid balance of the amount financed.

try

To examine or present evidence in courtroom proceedings in order to decide the issues raised.

try title

To enter into a legal action to determine the legitimacy of title to property.

turpis causa

(TUR-pis KAOW-sa) Lat. Base cause. Immoral or base consideration is invalid to support a contract (*e.g.*, prostitution, embezzlement, or kidnapping).

turpitude

Conduct which is inherently immoral or dishonest. Some statutes provide that a witness may be impeached with evidence of a crime involving moral turpitude because it tends to contradict his credibility.

tutor

In civil law, the guardian appointed for a minor child.

T.V.A.

See Tennessee Valley Authority.

Twelve Tables

The earliest surviving record of Roman legislation, dating from the 5th century B.C.E.

tying arrangement

The sale or lease of a product on the condition that the buyer or lessor also take another product. Such arrangements often violate antitrust laws.

tying in

Unfair contracting by a seller with substantial market power who refuses to sell a certain product unless the buyer also buys another product from the seller. Tie-in sales are illegal under the Clayton Act.

ubi
(OO-bee) Lat. Where.

ubi supra
Lat. Where stated above.

ukase
(YOO-kase) Russian. An arbitrary or final decree by a governmental authority.

ultimate facts
Final and resulting facts inferred from evidentiary facts presented to a court and which are essential for a court to reach a decision.

ultimatum
Lat. The last. 1. The last and conclusive offer asserted by a person (*e.g.*, the last offer made by a person who is negotiating an employment contract). 2. The final proposal advanced by a party involved in negotiations or a dispute.

ultra
Lat. Beyond. Extreme (*e.g.*, a person who is an ultraconservative is extremely conservative in his beliefs).

ultrahazardous activity
Any action taken out of the course of common usage, involving a risk of serious harm to the person, land or chattels of others, which cannot be eliminated by the exercise of utmost care. Such activity is subject to strict liability.

ultra vires
(ul-TRA VEE-res *or* VIE-res) Lat. Beyond granted powers. Conduct that exceeds the powers granted to an entity, most commonly used in reference to corporate actions that exceed the powers granted to the corporation through its articles of incorporation or by state law.

unbundling
Regulations that require incumbents in a market to make facilities available to new market entrants (*e.g.*,. Federal Communications Commission rules that required telecommunications

carriers to allow access to their networks by new carriers).

unclean hands

Doctrine that asserts that a person who has defrauded her opponent in a transaction may not seek to avail herself of the equitable powers of a court with respect to that transaction.

unconscionability

Contract doctrine holding that where a commercial transaction or contract is so one-sided and beneficial to one party in the transaction that the contract will be voided because its terms when applied are onerous, burdensome, and oppressive to the other party. The court may void the entire contract or that portion which it finds offensive.

unconscious

A state of mind that renders a person unaware of her acts.

unconstitutional

That which violates or contravenes the provisions of a constitution (*e.g.*, a state statute which violates the First Amendment of the United States Constitution).

under-lease

1. A sublease; the leasing of property by a lessee to another person for a period of time less than the full term of the lease.
2. The subleasing of a portion of the property leased by the lessee to another person for the duration of the lease.

under protest

A payment made or an act done under an obligation while reserving the right to object to the payment or act at a later date.

understand

To perceive; discern; realize; know.

understanding

A contract; an agreement; an informal agreement, either written or oral, based upon the express provisions of a contract.

undertake

To engage in; to enter into (*e.g.*, to enter into a compact with another person).

undertaking

1. Compact; promise; agreement.
2. Enterprise; venture. 3. Business endeavor.

underwrite

1. To insure against losses; to guarantee against loss or destruction (*e.g.*, to insure property). 2. To assume financial responsibility; to insure the sale of stock or other securities.

underwriter

1. A financial institution or business, and any person associated with such entity, that insures the sale of stock or other securities issued by a business, government, or a public agency. 2. In insurance, the one who assumes the risk in exchange for the payment of a premium.

undisclosed principal

A person who engages an agent to act on his behalf in regard to a transaction while the other party to the transaction is not aware that the agent is acting on behalf of someone else.

undivided interest

An interest or right in property, in which the tenant has an equal right to use and enjoy the entire property (*i.e.*, joint tenancy, tenancy in common, and tenancy by the entirety).

undue influence

Inappropriate persuasion of another person which destroys that person's opportunity to make a rational choice (*e.g.*, the improper inducement of a person so that his last will and testament does not reflect his own wishes).

unearned surplus

Corporate surplus that is not included in earned surplus calculations. Unearned surplus includes paid-in surplus, revaluation surplus, and donated surplus.

unethical conduct

Behavior that does not comport with the rules of conduct or standard of morality in a given situation (*e.g.*, conduct engaged in by a lawyer that does not meet the accepted and recognized standards of the profession).

unfair competition

1. Improper business conduct; dishonest commercial practices. 2. Fraudulent or deceptive business activities.

unfair labor practice

Action taken by an employer that violates an employee's rights as set forth in the National Labor

Relations Act (*e.g.*, the interference by an employer in the internal affairs of a labor union).

unfit
Unqualified; inappropriate; unsuitable for a particular purpose.

uniform
1. Unchanging; invariable; consistent. 2. The distinctive wardrobe of a group or organization (*e.g.*, the wardrobe worn by members of a police department).

uniform acts or laws
Statutes in particular subject areas that are drafted, formulated, and approved by the Commissioners on Uniform State Laws and which are enacted, in whole or in part, by state governments.

Uniform Child Custody Jurisdiction and Enforcement Act
Uniform act revising standards for jurisdiction in child custody cases, and providing an enforcement mechanism for interstate custody and visitation disputes. The law has been adopted by nearly all U.S. jurisdictions.

Uniform Commercial Code (U.C.C.)
Statute drafted, formulated, and approved by the Commissioners on Uniform State Laws that sets forth the rules that control commercial transactions and contracts. The statute has been enacted in its entirety by all states except Louisiana.

Uniform Consumer Credit Code (U.C.C.C.)
A Uniform Law adopted by some states which simplifies consumer credit laws and norms. Among other reasons, the Code was adopted to increase consumer understanding of credit transactions, protect consumers, and foster competition among creditors. Also "U.3C."

Uniform Crime Reports
Annual statistical and criminological report on offenses and crime and arrest rates prepared by the FBI.

Uniform Probate Code
A Uniform Law adopted to standardize and modernize probate procedures. Every state has adopted some provisions of the

Code, but only sixteen states have adopted it in its entirety.

Uniform Transfer to Minors Act

A Uniform Law adopted by most states which provides for the means of making a gift in trust to minors. The Act includes statutory methods for managing such trusts. The Act replaced the Uniform Gifts to Minors Act.

unilateral

Pertaining to or involving one person, object or thing; one-sided.

unilateral contract

Agreement whereby one person makes an express promise to perform upon actual performance by the other party. The agreement is the exchange of a promise for an act.

unilateral mistake

Misunderstanding or erroneous judgment made by only one party to a contract with respect to the contract's terms or provisions.

uninsured automobile insurance

Insurance provided by car owner's primary insurer to cover the risk of injury/damages caused by an uninsured driver. Coverage is mandatory in many states.

union shop

Place of employment where all employees belong to a union.

unissued stock

Corporate stock that is authorized but not issued.

unitary business

A business that has subsidiaries in several jurisdictions and that pays tax in each jurisdiction based on the percentage of its business done there. A unitary business has functional integration and centralized management, and employs economies of scale.

United Nations

International political organization whose major purposes are the promotion of peace and justice and the protection of human rights.

United States Code Annotated (U.S.C.A.)
Legal publication, in multi-volume form, that is comprised of the complete text of all federal statutes, brief summaries of federal and state court decisions that refer to the statutes, and historical and research references that relate to the statutes.

United States Code of Military Justice
Body of law that provides both the substantive and procedural law that governs the United States military and its members.

United States Commissioners
Officers of a federal district court, appointed by a judge of that court, who handle preliminary trial matters. This position has been replaced by that of United States Magistrate.

United States Courts of Appeals
Federal appellate courts. There is a court of appeals for each of the 11 federal circuits. The judges who sit on these courts of appeals are appointed by the President subject to approval by the United States Senate.

United States International Trade Commission (U.S.I.T.C.)
Established in 1916; among other things, it has been called upon to carry out provisions of the Tariff Act of 1930, the Agricultural Adjustment Act of 1934, the Trade Expansion Act of 1962, the Trade Act of 1974, the Trade Agreements Act of 1979, the Trade and Tariff Act of 1984, the Omnibus Trade and Competitiveness Act of 1988, and the Uruguay Round Agreements Act.

United States of America
Sovereign nation located in the Western Hemisphere which is composed of 50 states and other territories.

unit investment trust
An investment company organized under a trust indenture, contract of agency, contract of custodianship, or a similar instrument. 15 U.S.C.A.§ 80a-4(2).

unity
1. Oneness. 2. Concurrent interests. 3. The condition of being one in interest or possession of real or personal property.

unity of interest
The condition that cotenants' shares in a joint tenancy be equal and that they be acquired in the same transaction.

unity of possession
One of the essential properties of a joint estate, which requires that each joint tenant hold the same undivided possession of the whole.

unity of title
Phrase that recognizes that cotenants in a joint tenancy own their property under the same legal title.

universal agent
Person who has the power to act on behalf of another in all areas and who also has the authority to entrust this power of agency to another person as well.

universal partnership
Partnership where the partners agree to pool all of their assets for the benefit of the partnership for the length of their association.

unjust enrichment
Improper acquisition of property or money by a person at the expense of another which neither equity nor justice would condone, and is, therefore, a legally sufficient cause for failure to enforce a contract or infer a remedy (*e.g.*, constructive trust).

unlawful
Illegal; criminal conduct; extra-legal activity.

unlawful assembly
The illegal meeting of a group of persons for the purpose of causing a civil disturbance or similar strife.

unlawful detainer
The illegal possession of real property by a person whose once valid right to possess the property is now extinguished.

unlawful entry
Unconsented entry upon someone else's property by a willful wrong such as fraud.

unlisted security
A stock or bond that is not listed on an organized stock exchange, and is thus traded on over-the-counter markets.

unnecessary hardship

A standard used in granting zoning variances. "Unnecessary hardship" exists when the property's physical characteristics preclude its use for a permitted purpose, or when such use would be prohibitively expensive.

unreasonable

Not governed by reason; arbitrary; capricious; exorbitant; confiscatory; immoderate.

unreasonable search and seizure

The examination of one's person, premises, papers, or effects in violation of search and seizure protections guaranteed by the U.S. Constitution.

unsound mind

Unhealthy intellect; infirm or sick mind.

untenantable

Not fit for occupancy or habitation.

unwritten law

1. Case law. 2. Any rule of law not set forth by statute or regulation enacted by a legislative body.

upset price

The minimum price for which real or personal property that is to be sold at an auction may be purchased.

urban survival syndrome

An enhanced fear of being a victim of violent crime caused by living in a high-crime urban environment. The syndrome is often used to bolster a claim of self-defense, on the theory that the defendant's fear led her to believe that her violent acts were necessary for survival.

usage

Customary practice; habitual act (*e.g.*, a well-known local custom in trade or business).

USA PATRIOT ACT

See Patriot Act.

use

1. (n.) Practice; employ; usage.
2. (v.) To utilize; employ, operate.

usufruct

(OO-soo-frukt) The privilege possessed by a person to the benefits of property owned by another.

477

usurious contract
One in which the charged interest rate exceeds the legal limit.

usury
The lending of funds at an exorbitant interest rate or at a rate above that permitted by law.

utility
1. Serving a beneficial function.
2. In patent law, the capacity to perform a function or achieve a result.

utmost care
The highest degree of care.

utmost resistance
The degree of resistance offered by the victim, in order for a rape charge to be upheld against the attacker. Most states have abandoned this requirement.

utter
1. To speak; to make a sound.
2. To issue; publish; emit (*e.g.,* to issue a forged security under the pretense that it is legitimate).

uxor
Lat. A wife.

uxoricide
The killing of a wife by her husband.

v.

Abbreviation for "versus" in the name of a case; also used as an abbreviation for "vide" (see); "voce" (voice); "verb"; or "volume."

V.A.

See Department of Veterans' Affairs.

vacant

Empty, unoccupied.

vacate

1. To cancel; annul; set aside; rescind. 2. To make an act void as "to vacate a judgment." 3. To move out as in "vacating premises."

vagrancy

The state or condition of being idle and/or roaming aimlessly, without employment or other means of support, although physically and mentally capable of sustaining employment. State statutes prohibiting vagrancy vary widely, and many have been voided for vagueness.

vagrant

1. An idle wanderer. 2. A person who is capable of maintaining himself by lawful labor, but who refuses to work and lives without labor or on the charity of others.

vague

1. Indefinite; uncertain; imprecise. 2. Not capable of being understood.

vagueness doctrine

A law that does not give reasonable notice as to what acts are required or prohibited is unconstitutional as violative of due process.

valid

1. Legally binding; executed with proper formalities. 2. Authentic. 3. Authorized by law. 4. Incapable of being rightfully overthrown or set aside.

valuable consideration

1. A type of consideration upon which a promise may be founded. Some right, interest, profit, or benefit accruing to one party, or

some forbearance, detriment, loss, or responsibility given, suffered, or undertaken by the other. 2. Consideration in money or something which has monetary value.

value

1. The utility or worth of an object. 2. An abbreviation for "valuable consideration," such as in the phrases "purchaser for value" and "holder for value."

value added tax

A consumption tax that is added to the price of an article at every stage at which value is added to the article. Value added taxes are common in the European Union.

value received

Phrase denoting that consideration has been given; usually used in a bill of exchange or promissory note to denote that lawful consideration has been given for it.

variance

1. In pleading, a discrepancy between two instruments or two allegations in the same cause, which should by law be consonant, such as a disagreement between the statements in the pleadings and the evidence adduced in proof thereof. 2. In zoning, permission to use property in such a way as is otherwise prohibited by the zoning-law.

vassal

1. A feudal landholder who received land from his lord in return for services. 2. Subordinate; usually meant in a derogatory way.

vel non

Lat. Or not.

venal

Susceptible to bribery or corruption.

vend

To sell; to transfer to another for a pecuniary equivalent.

vendee

A purchaser or buyer; one to whom anything is sold. Term generally refers to one who buys land. One who buys goods is usually called a "buyer."

vendor

A seller; one who sells anything. Generally refers to one selling real estate. One who sells goods is usually called a "seller."

vendor's lien
In equity, a lien belonging to a vendor for the unpaid purchase price of property where the vendor has not taken any other lien or security.

venire facias
(VEN-eer-ay FASH-ee-as) Lat. Make to come. A writ to a sheriff to summon a jury.

venire facias de novo
Lat. 1. A writ to summon a jury for a new trial. 2. A writ to compel a new trial of an action.

venue
1. The neighborhood. 2. The particular county or geographical area in which a court with jurisdiction may hear and determine a case. 3. In common law pleading and practice, the place, neighborhood, or county in which an injury took place. Spelled "visne" in older common law documents.

veracity
Truthfulness; adherence to truth; accuracy.

verdict
The formal decision of a jury concerning the matters submitted to it in the trial of a cause. A verdict may be general or special. In a "general verdict" the jury decides which side wins, and how much, if applicable. A "special verdict" is when the jury is given specific questions of fact to answer and based on those answers the court determines which party is to have judgment.

verification
Confirmation of the correctness, truth, or authenticity of something (such as a pleading) by means of an affidavit, oath, or deposition.

versus
Lat. Against. In the title of a case the plaintiff's name is put first followed by "versus" and the defendant's name. Commonly abbreviated as "v." or "vs." (*e.g.*, *Smith v. Jones*).

vessel
In maritime law, a watercraft or other artificial contrivance used, or capable of being used, as a means of transportation on water.

vest

To give an immediate, fixed right of present or future enjoyment.

vested

Fixed, accrued, absolute, fixed in interest, indefeasible, not contingent. Generally used to describe any right or title to something which is not dependent upon the occurrence or nonoccurrence of some condition precedent. The right must be more than a mere expectation; it must become a title, legal or equitable, to the present or future enforcement of some demand (*e.g.,* pension plan benefits are vested if they are not contingent on the employee continuing to work for the employer).

Veteran's Administration (V.A.)

Former official name for the U.S. Department of Veterans' Affairs (q.v.), still used colloquially.

veto

Lat. I forbid. To refuse to sign a law enacted by the legislative branch of the government.

vexatious litigation

Proceeding instituted which is not bona fide, but which is instituted without probable cause, maliciously, or with the intent to harass the opponent.

viable

Capable of living. Generally term is applied to a newborn or unborn child to denote the power it possesses to continue or maintain an independent existence.

vicarious liability

1. The liability of one person for the acts of another. 2. Indirect legal responsibility (*e.g.,* the liability of the employer for the acts of an employee).

vice

1. (n.) A fault, defect, or imperfection. 2. Immoral conduct, practice, or habit. 3. (adj.) Lat. Instead of; in the place of (*e.g.,* vice president).

vice crimes

Crimes involving conduct that offends community morality standards (*e.g.,* gambling, prostitution, and pornography).

vicinage

Vicinity; neighborhood. In modern usage, this term refers to the area where a trial is held, the jurors are chosen, or a crime is committed.

victim impact statement

An oral or written statement made a part of the record during a criminal sentence proceeding that informs the court and jury of the physical, financial, and emotional effect the defendant's crime had on the victim.

victualer

One who supplies food that is ready to eat.

victuals

Food that is ready to eat.

viduitate

(vid-YOO-i-tate) Lat. Widowhood.

vi et armis

(VEE et ar-MISS) Lat. With force and arms.

villenage

A form of feudal tenancy involving tenants of the lowest order who were obliged to perform any services demanded by their lord.

violation

1. Breach of right, duty, or law. 2. Injury. 3. Rape.

violence

The exercise of physical force for the purpose of violating, injuring, or abusing another person or object.

vir

(veer) Lat. Man.

vis

Lat. Force or violence.

visa

The endorsement on a passport or other official document by foreign authorities allowing a person to enter another country.

visitation rights

The right of a parent to visit his or her child. Such rights are frequently granted to a noncustodial parent in a divorce or custody action. Often called "parenting time." In some states, other family members such as grandparents may be granted visitation rights.

vis major

Lat. A higher force, an irresistible force (*e.g.*, a storm or earthquake).

Visual Artists' Rights Act (VARA)

Federal law that gives the authors or creators of certain works of visual art moral rights in their work that go beyond copyright. The additional rights include the right to be identified as the author of a work, and the right to prevent distortion or mutilation of a work. 17 U.S.C. § 106A.

vitiate

1. To destroy the legal or binding effect of something, such as an act or instrument (*e.g.*, fraud vitiates a contract). 2. To invalidate; to impair.

viva voce

(VEE-va VO-chay) Lat. The living voice; by word of mouth. 1. In evidence, term means oral testimony as opposed to written evidence such as affidavits or depositions. 2. In relation to voting, term means voting by outcry rather than by written ballots.

viz

Lat. Abbreviation of "videlicet." Namely; that is to say; to wit.

voice exemplar

Voice identification test, in which a recording of one's voice is compared to another. Once inadmissible, voice exemplars have been held by the Supreme Court to be valid identification procedures.

void

Of no legal force or binding effect, null, nugatory, incapable of being ratified. *Contrast* voidable.

void ab initio

Void from the beginning. A contract is void at its inception if it seriously offends law or public policy.

voidable

Defective, but capable of confirmation or ratification, such as a minor;s contract. A minor does not have the capacity to enter into a contract; therefore, any contract he makes is voidable. However, the contract is not void, and, therefore, it is binding on the competent party unless the minor repudiates it. A voidable transaction is one that can be affirmed by a party entitled to void it.

void for vagueness

A doctrine used to invalidate laws which are so obscure that persons of average intelligence must guess at the law's meaning and application. Such laws violate due process. *See* vagueness doctrine.

voir dire

(vwar *or* vore deer) Lat. To speak the truth. 1. An examination of a person as a prospective juror to test her competency and prejudice. 2. Preliminary examination of a witness in order to determine her competency to speak the truth.

volenti non fit injuria

(vo-LEN-tee non fit in-JOO-ree-a) Lat. To a willing person no injury is done. Torts maxim meaning that one cannot usually claim damages when he, knowing and comprehending the danger, consented to the action that caused the damage.

Volstead Act

Federal law passed under the Eighteenth Amendment to the U.S. Constitution which prohibited the manufacture, sale, or transportation of liquor. Repealed by the Twenty-first Amendment.

voluntary

1. Acting without compulsion, intended. 2. Acting on one's own initiative without being paid to do so. 3. Not impelled by another's influence. 4. As used in statutes, often implies knowledge of essential facts.

volunteer

1. A person who acts without an express or implied promise or remuneration. 2. A person who enlists in the armed services without being compelled by a military draft. 3. An intruder who intermeddles.

voting right

A qualified citizen's right to vote in open elections, without discrimination based on race, color or previous condition of servitude.

485

Voting Rights Act
Federal law guaranteeing the right of qualified citizens to vote, without discrimination based on race, color or previous condition of servitude. 42 U.S.C. § 1971.

voting trust
An arrangement by which shares of stock in a corporation are pooled and held in trust for the purpose of voting them at stockholder's meetings. Voting trusts are generally created for the purpose of electing officers or controlling the activities of the corporation.

voucher
1. A receipt or other evidence of payment. 2. Written proof of a transaction. 3. A book of accounts containing the company's receipts. 4. A document giving evidence of an expenditure.

wager

A gamble or bet; an agreement between two persons that one will pay the other a sum of money or other stake if a certain thing happens or does not happen. The parties have no interest in the event except that arising from the possibility of such gain or loss.

wager of law

Obsolete common law procedure by which a defendant would give security in an action on a debt that he would "wage" his law, meaning that he would appear at the set time and would give an oath as to his innocence, and bring with him 11 neighbors (called compurgators) to swear that they believed his truthfulness.

Wagner Act

The National Labor Relations Act, the federal law giving employees the right to organize, to form unions, and to bargain collectively with employers. The Act also set up the National Labor Relations Board to help enforce the new labor laws. *See* 29 U.S.C. § 151 *et seq.*

wait and see statutes

Type of statutes enacted by some states to lessen the harsh effect of the Rule Against Perpetuities by determining the validity of an interest when the contingency (future estate) occurs rather than at the time of its creation. Also called second look statutes.

waiting period

The time period that must expire before one may pursue some legal right or remedy.

waive

To voluntarily give up, relinquish, renounce, or disclaim a privilege, right, or benefit. It is often assumed that one who waives a right does so intentionally and with full knowledge of the facts.

waiver

The voluntary and intentional giving up or renouncing of a known right, benefit, or privilege. A waiver may be either "express," such as an oral or written statement, or "implied" from circumstances.

waiver of counsel

In criminal law, a defendant's relinquishment of the right to be represented by counsel at some stage of the proceedings against him. In order to be valid, such a waiver must be made voluntarily, knowingly, and intelligently.

wanton

1. Reckless, heedless, malicious. 2. Extreme recklessness or foolhardiness. 3. Disregardful of the rights or safety of others or of consequences.

war crime

Conduct that violates international norms governing armed conflict, especially conduct that violates the Geneva Convention.

ward

1. A person, usually a minor or incompetent, who is under guardianship. 2. Subdivision of a city, borough, county, or parish for election and other purposes.

warden

Guardian; keeper; guard; the superintendent of a prison.

ward of the court

Person whose rights and safety are guarded by the court (*e.g.*, minors and mentally incompetent individuals).

wardship

The state of guardianship (*e.g.*, wardship over a minor).

warehouseman

A person who is engaged in the business of accepting and storing goods for compensation or profit. *See* U.C.C. § 7–102.

warehouse receipt

A receipt issued by a person engaged in the business of storing goods for hire. *See* U.C.C. § 1–201 (45).

War Powers Resolution

Federal law limiting the power of the President to commit U.S. troops to an armed conflict without congressional approval. 50 U.S.C.A. § 1541 *et seq.* The consequences for a violation of the resolution are not clear.

warrant

1. Written authority. 2. An order from a court or other authorized body to an officer, directing the officer to arrest a person, search a house, etc. 3. In commercial and property law, to state that something is true; act of guaranteeing, assuring. 4. An order authorizing a payment of money by one person to a third person.

warrantless arrest

An arrest of a person made without a warrant. Such an arrest is legal when the officer has probable cause (*e.g.*, reasonable grounds to believe that the suspect committed a felony).

warranty

1. Promise that certain facts are true. 2. Guarantee concerning goods or land, that is expressly or impliedly made to a purchaser by the vendor. 3. Statement or promise made as part of a transaction upon which the transaction depends (*e.g.,* in an insurance contract, the insurance company could refuse to pay a claim if a statement made in the

application is false). 4. An agreement to be responsible for all damages that arise from the falsity of a statement or assurance of a fact.

warranty deed

Deed in which the grantor warrants that the title is free of encumbrances (unless noted in the instrument). The usual warranties included are seisin, right to convey, quiet enjoyment, freedom from encumbrances and defense of title against all claims.

warranty of fitness

Where the seller has reason to know any particular purpose for which the goods are required, and that the buyer is relying on the seller's skill or judgment to select or furnish suitable goods, there is, unless excluded or modified, an implied warranty that the goods shall be fit for such purpose. *See* U.C.C. § 2–315.

warranty of merchantability

Warranty made by a merchant seller that the goods sold are, among other things, reasonably fit for general purposes for which they are sold. *See* U.C.C. § 2–314.

Warsaw Convention

International agreement regarding claims for injuries arising out of international air travel.

wash sale

1. The sale and repurchase of securities or assets with equal or nearly equal value within a short time period. Often, such transactions are conducted to create the artificial appearance of tax losses; consequently, they are strictly regulated by the I.R.S. 2. The simultaneous sale and purchase of securities by traders, to create the impression of activity surrounding a stock. Such action is prohibited by law.

waste

Abuse, destruction, misuse, alteration, or neglect of property in one's rightful possession, but belonging to somebody else. Waste may be "permissive" (mere neglect or omission to do what is necessary to prevent injury), "voluntary" (doing some act which causes the damage), or "ameliorative" (making unauthorized, unnecessary improvements).

wasting asset

An asset which will be consumed through its use (*e.g.*, oil wells and coal mines). Such assets are amortized for tax purposes by depletion.

watercourse

A stream of water flowing in a definite direction or channel with banks.

watered stock

Stock that is issued by a company as though it were paid in full when it has not been (*e.g.*, shares issued for no consideration or at a discount).

weapon

An instrument used for offensive or defensive combat (*e.g.*, gun, knife, club, or any device for inflicting harm or for protecting oneself against an attacker). Often defined by state statute.

wear and tear

Deterioration of property from ordinary, reasonable use of the property.

week

1. Seven consecutive days. 2. For purposes of wage and hour laws,

a period of 168 consecutive hours.

weight of the evidence
The balance or preponderance of evidence; the weight of the evidence is that which is more believable and is superior to the evidence submitted by the other side in a case. "Weight" does not refer to quantity, but rather to how convincing is each side's evidence.

Welfare Clause
Article I, section 8 of the U.S. Constitution empowering the federal government to promulgate laws for the general welfare of the people. Basis for implied powers necessary to perform express provisions of the Constitution. *See also* Necessary and Proper Clause.

wergild, wergeld
In Saxon law, the fine or price imposed for homicide or other atrocious personal offense. Part of the fine went to the king for the loss of a subject and part went to the relatives of the deceased.

wharfage
Compensation for the use of a wharf; money paid for landing goods upon or loading them from a wharf.

wharfinger
A person who owns or keeps a wharf for the purpose of receiving and shipping goods thereon for hire.

Wharton rule
An agreement by two or more persons to commit a crime cannot be the basis for a conspiracy prosecution if the crime by definition requires the participation of two or more persons (*e.g.*, dueling).

when issued
In securities law, short for "when, as and if issued," a phrase used as a condition of sale for a stock that has not yet been authorized for issuance.

whereas
When in fact; that being the case; considering that; because; in view of the following facts; a word introducing the recital of a fact.

whiplash injury

A personal injury involving the neck where the head is thrown violently forward and back or from side to side. Commonly caused by an automobile accident.

whistleblower law

Federal or state law that prohibits employers from retaliating against employees who report or disclose wrongdoing by the employer.

white-collar crime

Nonviolent crimes committed by corporations, business persons, or individuals, often involving fraudulent financial activity (*e.g.*, bribery, embezzlement, stock manipulation).

white slaver

1. The interstate transportation of females for immoral purposes. 2. Holding females for prostitution. *See* Mann Act.

wholesaler

One who sells goods in large quantities, frequently for distribution to other distributors or retailers.

wildcat strike

A strike by union workers that is not authorized by union officials.

Wild's Case, Rule in

In property law, a rule of construction that a devise to *B* and his children or issue, *B* having no issue at the time of the devise, gives him an estate tail; but if he has issue at the time, *B* and his children take as joint tenants, or as tenants in common according to the other words of the will. *See* 77 E.R. 277 (1599).

will

A person's declaration of how she wishes her property to be disposed of after her death. A will is revocable during the testator's or testatrix's lifetime. Most states require that it be in writing and be witnessed. Minors and persons of unsound mind have no legal capacity to make a will.

willful, wilful

1. An act which is intentional, deliberate, knowing, or voluntary, as distinguished from accidental. 2. With evil motive or unlawful intent; malicious.

winding up

The liquidation of a partnership or corporation by finishing current business, settling accounts, turning property into cash, and splitting up the assets. Winding up may be either voluntary or involuntary, such as when it is court ordered. Liquidation procedures are usually prescribed by state statutes.

wiretap

A concealed recording and listening device, used by law enforcement officials to eavesdrop on the communications of others. Wiretapping is strictly regulated by federal and state law.

withdrawal

1. Removal of money or security from the place where it is deposited, such as a bank. 2. The abandonment of a crime by a coconspirator. Withdrawal requires that the coconspirator must evidence disapproval of or opposition to the criminal activities and communicate it to the coconspirators or give complete disclosure to authorities.

withholding

The portion of an employee's wages that is deducted by the employer and remitted to the government, usually for tax or social security purposes.

without prejudice

Phrase declaring that no rights or privileges of the contesting parties have been affected by the disposition of the matter before the court. A dismissal "without prejudice" allows a new suit to be brought on the same cause of action without being affected by res judicata.

without recourse

Phrase used in a qualified endorsement of a negotiable instrument, stating that the indorser will not be responsible for payment if the party primarily liable does not pay. *See U.*C.C. § 3-415(b).

with prejudice

Disposition of a matter before the court "with prejudice." Dismissal with prejudice is as conclusive of the parties' rights as if the cause had proceeded to final judgment; bars refiling of the cause.

witness

1. One who sees or perceives an act or event being done. 2. One who testifies under oath at a trial or hearing as to what he has seen, heard, or otherwise observed. 3. To be present at the signing of, and often to sign, a legal document such as a deed or a will. 4. One who is a witness to a signature on a will or deed and attests to its authenticity.

witness protection

Relocating and giving a new identity to a witness to protect her from retaliation for her testimony.

words of art

Terms that are used in a special way by members of a profession, line of work or study (*e.g.*, legal words of art have either no meanings or different meanings outside of a legal context).

words of limitation

A clause in a conveyance which declares how long the estate transferred thereby shall continue. Words of limitation actually indicate the type of estate transferred. Phrases such as "heirs" or "heirs of the body" are words of limitation.

words of purchase

Words in a property transfer which denote the person who takes the estate.

worker's compensation laws

Statutes that provide funds to pay workers for injuries or illnesses arising out of or in the course of employment, regardless of whether the injury was due to the fault or negligence of the employee. The statutes generally establish the liability of the employer and, if the injury is covered by the statute, the employee's only remedy against the employer is that which the statute provides.

workfare

A system that requires recipients of public assistance benefits to earn their benefits by working at a job assigned to them.

work-product

In civil practice, a class of materials which are given protection from discovery, such as work done by an attorney in the process of representing his client.

The adverse party may obtain discovery only upon a showing of substantial need of the materials in preparation of his case and that he is unable without undue hardship to obtain the substantial equivalent by other means. *See Richards-Wilcox Mfg. Co. v. Young Spring & Wire Corp., 34 F.R.D. 212,* 213 (N.D. Ill. 1964).

work release program

Correction program wherein the prisoner works for compensation or voluntarily engages in a training or educational program in the community for limited time periods during his or her incarceration.

worthier title, doctrine of

Common law rule whereby, if a gift by devise to one's heir constituted the exact same interest in land that the heir would have taken by descent, the heir would take by descent, since that was considered the "worthier title." This rule has been abandoned by many states.

wound

1. (n.) An injury to the body usually involving the breaking of the skin or mucous membranes as the result of violence. 2. (v.) To inflict a cut, laceration, or bruise.

wraparound mortgage

A second mortgage which is added onto a previous mortgage. Often, such mortgages are offered to borrowers with low first mortgage interest rates. The face amount of the wraparound mortgage is the amount due on the wraparound mortgage, plus the amount due on the first mortgage.

writ

A formal written command or authorization of the court issued to an officer, directing him to act in some way.

writing, written

1. Printing, typewriting, or any other intentional reduction to tangible form. 2. A document as opposed to mere spoken words. *See* U.C.C. § 1–201(46).

writ of assistance

An equitable remedy issued to enforce a court decree transferring real property where the title has been previously adjudicated.

writ of certiorari
Order issued by an appellate court when the court has discretion as to whether to take an appeal. *See* certiorari.

writ of coram nobis
In our presence; before us (*i.e.*, before our court). Writ used to obtain review, in the rendering court, of a judgment for the purpose of correcting errors of fact in a criminal or civil proceeding. Also referred to simply as "coram nobis."

writ of error
A writ issued from an appellate court to the judges of a court of record, requiring the judge or judges to remit the records of the case for appellate review of alleged errors of law. This is a writ of right, and applies only to cases in which jurisdiction is exercised according to the course of common law (unless otherwise stated by statute).

writ of execution
Court's order to the sheriff to enforce a judgment of the court issuing the writ.

writ of mandamus
See mandamus.

writ of prohibition
Writ issued by a superior court, preventing an inferior court or judicial (or quasi-judicial) body from exceeding its jurisdiction.

writ of quo warranto
See quo warranto.

writ of right
A writ granted as a matter of right.

written instrument
Anything that has been reduced to writing (*e.g.*, to give formal expression to an agreement or contract).

wrong
A violation or invasion of the legal rights of another or of a legal duty. A wrong may be private, which would allow for compensation to an individual, or public, such as a crime.

wrongful act
Any act which in the ordinary course will infringe upon the rights of another to her damage, unless it is done in the exercise of an equal or superior right.

wrongful death statute

Statute which allows a survivor or executor of a decedent's estate the right to sue for any wrongful act or negligence that caused the decedent's death. Wrongful death statutes exist in every state. At common law the death of an individual could not be a cause of action in a civil suit.

wrongful life

A tort action pertaining to child-birth, brought on the child's behalf. In a wrongful life action, the plaintiffs allege that the child would not have been born (or would not have been born with defects) if not for the negligent treatment or advice given by the defendant to one or both parents.

X

A mark used as a signature by
one who is unable to write his or
her name. Such a mark constitutes a valid signature.

year and a day

1. Common law rule whereby a criminal defendant was liable for another's death only if the death occurred within a year and a day of the wrongful conduct. This rule has been abandoned by a number of jurisdictions. 2. In some states, the minimum sentence that distinguishes a felony from a misdemeanor.

year books

Annual reports of old English cases from the time of King Edward II to Henry VIII (1268-1535).

yellow dog contract

Employment contract which states that an employee will not join a labor union under penalty of dismissal. Such contracts are now illegal under NLRA.

yield

1. To give up, relinquish, surrender, succumb, submit, cease opposition. 2. Return from an investment or expenditure of money or labor. 3. Real property law: To perform a service due by a tenant to his lord.

yield to maturity

A calculation of a bond's yield, indicating the overall rate of return an investor would receive if he or she held the bond until maturity, and interest rates remained unchanged.

youthful offender

Criminal who is older than a juvenile but younger than an adult. Youthful offenders often receive alternative sentences that involve training, education, and the like, to foster rehabilitation.

zoning
Legislative action dividing a city or county into areas for the purpose of limiting the use to which land may be put, minimum size of lots, building types, etc.

zero tolerance
A policy that states that all acts of a certain type will be punished.

zone of danger
A dangerous area created by a tortfeasor's actions. A person who was severely frightened by the actions may recover damages if she was within the zone of danger.

zone of employment
The physical area within the workplace and the area surrounding the workplace which is under the employer's control. If an injury occurs outside one's "zone of employment," one cannot seek worker's compensation.

zone of privacy
Privacy rights implied by the specific guarantees of the Bill of Rights.

APPENDIX A

Constitution of the United States of America

WE THE PEOPLE of the United States, in Order to form a more perfect Union, establish Justice, insure domestic Tranquility, provide for the common defence, promote the general Welfare, and secure the Blessings of Liberty to ourselves and our posterity, do ordain and establish this Constitution for the United States of America.

ARTICLE I.

Section 1. All legislative Powers herein granted shall be vested in a Congress of the United States, which shall consist of a Senate and House of Representatives.

Section 2. The House of Representatives shall be composed of Members chosen every second Year by the People of the several States, and the Electors in each State shall have the Qualifications requisite for Electors of the most numerous Branch of the State Legislature.

No person shall be a Representative who shall not have attained to the Age of twenty five Years, and been seven Years a Citizen of the United States, and who shall not, when elected, be an Inhabitant of that State in which he shall be chosen.

Representatives and direct Taxes shall be apportioned among the several States which may be included within this Union, according to their respective Numbers, which shall be determined by adding to the whole Number of free Persons, including those bound to Service for a Term of Years, and excluding Indians not taxed, three fifths of all other Persons. The actual Enumeration shall be made within three Years after the first Meeting of the Congress of the United States, and within every subsequent Term of ten Years, in such Manner as they shall by Law direct. The Number of Representatives shall not exceed one for every thirty Thousand, but each State shall have at Least one Representative; and until such enumeration shall be made, the State of New Hampshire shall be entitled to chuse three, Massachusetts eight, Rhode Island and Providence Plantations one, Connecticut five, New York six, New Jersey four, Pennsylvania eight, Delaware one, Maryland six, Virginia ten, North Carolina five, South Carolina five, and Georgia three.

When vacancies happen in the Representation from any State, the Executive Authority thereof shall issue Writs of Election to fill such vacancies.

The House of Representatives shall chuse their Speaker and other Officers; and shall have the sole Power of Impeachment.

Section 3. The Senate of the United States shall be composed of two Senators from each State, chosen by the Legislature thereof, for six Years; and each Senator shall have one Vote.

Immediately after they shall be assembled in Consequence of the first Election, they shall be divided as equally as may be into three Classes. The Seats of the Senators of the first Class shall be vacated at the Expiration of the second Year, of the second Class at the Expiration of the fourth Year, and of the third Class at the Expiration of the sixth Year, so that one third may be chosen every second Year; and if Vacancies happen by Resignation, or otherwise, during the Recess of the Legislature of any State, the Executive thereof may make temporary Appointments until the next Meeting of the Legislature, which shall then fill such Vacancies.

No person shall be a Senator who shall not have attained to the Age of thirty Years, and been nine Years a Citizen of the United States, and who shall not, when elected, be an Inhabitant of that State for which he shall be chosen.

The Vice President of the United States shall be President of the Senate, but shall have no Vote, unless they be equally divided.

The Senate shall chuse their other. Officers, and also a President pro tempore, in the Absence of the Vice President, or when he shall exercise the Office of President of the United States.

The Senate shall have the sole Power to try all Impeachments. When sitting for that Purpose, they shall be on Oath or Affirmation. When the President of the United States is tried the Chief Justice shall preside:

And no Person shall be convicted without the Concurrence of two thirds of the Members present.

Judgment in Cases of Impeachment shall not extend further than to removal from Office, and disqualification to hold and enjoy any Office of honor, Trust or Profit under the United States: but the Party convicted shall nevertheless be liable and subject to Indictment, Trial, Judgment and Punishment, according to Law.

Section 4. The Times, Places and Manner of holding Elections for Senators and Representatives, shall be prescribed in each State by the Legislature thereof; but the Congress may at any time by Law make or alter such Regulations, except as to the Places of choosing Senators.

The Congress shall assemble at least once in every Year, and such Meeting shall be on the first Monday in December, unless they shall by Law appoint a different Day.

Section 5. Each House shall be the Judge of the Elections, Returns and Qualifications of its own Members, and a Majority of each shall constitute a Quorum to do Business; but a smaller Number may adjourn from day to day, and may be authorized to compel the Attendance of absent Members, in such manner, and under such Penalties as each House may provide.

Each House may determine the Rules of its Proceedings, punish its Members for disorderly Behavior, and, with the Concurrence of two thirds, expel a Member.

Each House shall keep a Journal of its Proceedings, and from time to time publish the same, excepting such Parts as may in their Judgment require Secrecy; and the Yeas and Nays of the Members of either House on any question shall, at the Desire of one fifth of those present, be entered on the Journal.

Neither House, during the Session of Congress, shall, without the Consent of the other, adjourn for more than three days, nor to any other Place than that in which the two Houses shall be sitting.

Section 6. The Senators and Representatives shall receive a Compensation for their Services, to be ascertained by Law, and paid out of the Treasury of the United States. They shall in all Cases, except Treason,

Felony and Breach of the Peace, be privileged from Arrest during their Attendance at the Session of their respective Houses, and in going to and returning from the same; and for any Speech or Debate in either House, they shall not be questioned in any other Place.

No Senator or Representative shall, during the Time for which he was elected, be appointed to any civil Office under the Authority of the United States, which shall have been created, or the Emoluments whereof shall have been encreased during such time; and no Person holding any Office under the United States, shall be a Member of either House during his Continuance in Office.

Section 7. All Bills for raising Revenue shall originate in the House of Representatives; but the Senate may propose or concur with Amendments as on other Bills.

Every Bill which shall have passed the House of Representatives and the Senate, shall, before it become a Law, be presented to the President of the United States; If he approves he shall sign it, but if not he shall return it, with his Objections to that House in which it shall have originated, who shall enter the Objections at large on their Journal, and proceed to reconsider it. If after such Reconsideration two thirds of that House shall agree to pass the Bill, it shall be sent together with the Objections, to the other House, by which it shall likewise be reconsidered, and if approved by two thirds of that House, it shall become a Law. But in all such Cases the Votes of both Houses shall be determined by Yeas and Nays, and the Names of the Persons voting for and against the Bill shall be entered on the Journal of each House respectively. If any Bill shall not be returned by the President within ten Days (Sundays excepted) after it shall have been presented to him, the Same shall be a Law, in like Manner as if he had signed it, unless the Congress by their Adjournment prevent its Return, in which Case it shall not be a Law.

Every Order, Resolution, or Vote to which the Concurrence of the Senate and House of Representatives may be necessary (except on a question of Adjournment) shall be presented to the President of the United States; and before the Same shall take Effect, shall be approved by him, or being disapproved by him, shall be repassed by two thirds of the Senate and House of Representatives, according to the Rules and Limitations prescribed in the Case of a Bill.

Section 8. The Congress shall have Power To lay and collect Taxes, Duties, Imposts and Excises, to pay the Debts and provide for the common Defence and general Welfare of the United States; but all Duties, Imposts and Excises shall be uniform throughout the United States;

To borrow Money on the credit of the United States;

To regulate Commerce with foreign Nations; and among the several States, and with the Indian Tribes;

To establish a uniform Rule of Naturalization, and uniform Laws on the subject of Bankruptcies throughout the United States;

To coin Money, regulate the Value thereof, and of foreign Coin, and fix the Standard of Weights and Measures;

To provide for the Punishment of counterfeiting the Securities and current Coin of the United States;

To establish Post Offices and post Roads;

To promote the Progress of Science and Useful Arts, by securing for limited Times to Authors and Inventors the exclusive Right to their respective Writings and Discoveries;

To constitute Tribunals inferior to the supreme Court;

To define and punish Piracies and Felonies committed on the high Seas, and Offences against the Law of Nations;

To declare War, grant Letters of Marque and Reprisal, and make Rules concerning Captures on Land and Water;

To raise and support Armies, but no Appropriation of Money to that Use shall be for a longer Term than two Years;

To provide and maintain a Navy;

To make Rules for the Government and Regulation of the land and naval Forces;

To provide for calling forth the Militia to execute the Laws of the Union, suppress Insurrections and repel Invasions;

To provide for organizing, arming, and disciplining, the Militia, and for governing such Part of them as may be employed in the Service of the United States, reserving to the States respectively, the Appointment of the Officers, and the Authority of training the Militia according to the discipline prescribed by Congress;

To exercise exclusive Legislation in all Cases whatsoever, over such District (not exceeding ten Miles square) as may, by Cession of particular States, and the Acceptance of Congress, become the Seat of the Government of the United States, and to exercise like Authority over all Places purchased by the Consent of the Legislature of the State in which the Same shall be, for the Erection of Forts, Magazines, Arsenals, dockyards, and other needful Buildings; And

To make all Laws which shall be necessary and proper for carrying into Execution the foregoing Powers, and all other Powers vested by this Constitution in the Government of the United States, or in any Department or Officer thereof.

Section 9. The Migration or Importation of such Persons as any of the States now existing shall think proper to admit, shall not be prohibited by the Congress prior to the Year one thousand eight hundred and eight, but a Tax or duty may be imposed on such Importation, not exceeding ten dollars for each Person.

The Privilege of the Writ of Habeas Corpus shall not be suspended, unless when in Cases of Rebellion or Invasion the public Safety may require it.

No Bill of Attainder or ex post facto Law shall be passed.

No Capitation, or other direct, Tax shall be laid, unless in Proportion to the Census or Enumeration herein before directed to be taken.

No Tax or Duty shall be laid on Articles exported from any State.

No Preference shall be given by any Regulation of Commerce or Revenue to the Ports of one State over those of another; nor shall Vessels bound to, or from, one State, be obliged to enter, clear, or pay Duties in another.

No Money shall be drawn from the Treasury, but in Consequence of Appropriations made by Law; and a regular Statement and Account of the Receipts and Expenditures of all public Money shall be published from time to time.

No Title of Nobility shall be granted by the United States; And no Person holding any Office of Profit or Trust under them, shall, without the Consent of the Congress, accept of any present, Emolument, Office, or Title, of any kind whatever, from any King, Prince, or foreign State.

Section 10. No State shall enter into any Treaty, Alliance, or Confederation; grant Letters of Marque and Reprisal; coin Money; emit Bills of Credit; make any Thing but gold and silver Coin a Tender in Payment of Debts; pass any Bill of Attainder, ex post facto Law, or Law impairing the Obligation of Contracts, or grant any Title of Nobility.

No State, shall, without the Consent of the Congress, lay any Imposts or Duties on Imports or Exports, except what may be absolutely necessary for executing its inspection Laws: and the net Produce of all Duties and Imposts, laid by any State on Imports or Exports, shall be for the Use of the Treasury of the United States; and all such Laws shall be subject to the Revision and Controul of the Congress.

No State shall, without the Consent of Congress, Lay any Duty of Tonnage, keep Troops, or Ships of War in time of Peace, enter into any Agreement or Compact with another State, or with a foreign Power, or engage in War, unless actually invaded, or in such imminent Danger as will not admit of delay.

ARTICLE II.

Section 1. The executive Power shall be vested in a President of the United States of America. He shall hold his Office during the Term of four Years, and, together with the Vice President, chosen for the Same Term, be elected, as follows.

Each State shall appoint, in such Manner as the Legislature thereof may direct, a Number of Electors, equal to the whole Number of Senators and Representatives to which the State may be entitled in the Congress: but no Senator or Representative, or Person holding an Office of Trust or Profit under the United States, shall be appointed an Elector.

The Electors shall meet in their respective States, and vote by Ballot for two Persons of whom one at least shall not be an Inhabitant of the same State with themselves. And they shall make a List of all the Persons voted for, and of the Number of Votes for each; which List they shall sign and certify, and transmit sealed to the Seat of the Government of the United States, directed to the President of the Senate. The President of the Senate shall, in the Presence of the Senate and House of Representatives, open all the Certificates, and the Votes shall then be counted. The Person having the greater Number of Votes shall be the President, if such Number be a Majority of the whole Number of Electors appointed; and if there be more than one who have such Majority, and have an equal Number of Votes, then the House of Representatives shall immediately chuse by Ballot one of them for President; and if no Person have a Majority, then from the five highest on the List the said House shall in like Manner chuse the President But in chusing the President, the Votes shall be taken by States, the Representation from each State having one Vote; A quorum for this Purpose shall consist of a Member or Members from two thirds of the States, and a Majority of all the States shall be necessary to a Choice. In every Case, after the Choice of the President, the Person having the greatest Number of Votes of the Electors shall be the Vice President. But if there should remain two or more who have equal Votes, the Senate shall chuse from them by Ballot the Vice President.

The Congress may determine the Time of chusing the Electors, and the Day on which they shall give their Votes; which Day shall be the same throughout the United States.

No Person except a natural born Citizen, or a Citizen of the United States, at the time of the Adoption of this Constitution, shall be eligible to the Office of President; neither shall any Person be eligible to that Office who shall not have attained to the Age of thirty five Years, and been fourteen Years a Resident within the United States.

In Case of the Removal of the President from Office, or of his Death, Resignation, or Inability to discharge the Powers and Duties of the said Office, the same shall devolve on the Vice President, and the Congress may by Law provide for the Case of Removal, Death, Resignation or Inability, both of the President and Vice President, declaring what Officer shall then act as President, and such Officer shall act accordingly, until the Disability be removed, or a President shall be elected.

The President shall, at stated Times, receive for his Services, a Compensation, which shall neither be increased nor diminished during the Period for which he shall have been elected, and he shall not receive within that Period any other Emolument from the United States, or any of them.

Before he enter on the Execution of his Office, he shall take the following Oath or Affirmation: 1 do solemnly swear (or affirm) that I will faithfully execute the Office of President of the United States, and will to the best of my Ability, preserve, protect and defend the Constitution of the United States.

Section 2. The President shall be Commander in Chief of the Army and Navy of the United States, and of the Militia of the several States, when called into the actual Service of the United States; he may require the Opinion, in writing, of the principal Officer in each of the executive Departments, upon any Subject relating to the Duties of their respective Offices, and he shall have Power to grant Reprieves and Pardons for Offences against the United States, except in Cases of Impeachment.

He shall have Power, by and with the Advice and Consent of the Senate, to make Treaties, provided two thirds of the Senators present concur; and he shall nominate, and by and with the Advice and Consent of the Senate, shall appoint Ambassadors, other public Ministers and Consuls, judges of the supreme Court, and all other Officers of the United States, whose Appointments are not herein otherwise provided for, and which shall be established by Law: but the Congress may by Law vest the Appointment of such inferior Officers, as they think proper, in the President alone, in the Courts of Law, or in the Heads of Departments.

The President shall have Power to fill up all Vacancies that may happen during the Recess of the Senate, by granting Commissions which shall expire at the End of their next Session.

Section 3. He shall from time to time give to the Congress Information of the State of the Union, and recommend to their Consideration such Measures as he shall judge necessary and expedient; he may, on extraordinary Occasions, convene both Houses, or either of them, and in Case of Disagreement between them, with Respect to the Time of Adjournment, he may adjourn them to such Time as he shall think proper; he shall receive Ambassadors and other public Ministers; he shall take Care that the Laws be faithfully executed, and shall Commission all the Officers of the United States.

Section 4. The President, Vice President and all civil Officers of the United States, shall be removed from Office on Impeachment for, and Conviction of, Treason, Bribery, or other high Crimes and Misdemeanors.

ARTICLE III.

Section 1. The judicial Power of the United States, shall be vested in one supreme Court, and in such inferior Courts as the Congress may from time to time ordain and establish. The Judges, both of the supreme and inferior Courts, shall hold their Offices during good Behaviour, and shall, at stated Times, receive for their Services, a Compensation, which shall not be diminished during their Continuance in Office.

Section 2. The judicial Power shall extend to all Cases, in Law and Equity, arising under this Constitution, the Laws of the United States, and Treaties made, or which shall be made, under their Authority; to all Cases affecting Ambassador, other public Ministers and Consuls; to all Cases of admiralty and maritime Jurisdiction; to Controversies to which the United States shall be a Party; to Controversies between two or more States; between a State and Citizens of another State; between Citizens of different States, between Citizens of the same State claiming Lands under Grants of different States, and between a State, or the Citizens thereof, and foreign States, Citizens or Subjects.

In all Cases affecting Ambassadors, other public Ministers and Consuls, and those in which a State shall be Party, the supreme Court shall have original Jurisdiction. In all the other Cases before mentioned, the supreme Court shall have appellate jurisdiction, both as to Law and Fact, with such Exceptions, and under such Regulations as the Congress shall make.

The Trial of all Crimes, except in Cases of Impeachment, shall be by Jury, and such Trial shall be held in the State where the said Crimes shall have been committed; but when not committed within any State, the Trial shall be at such Place or Places as the Congress may by Law have directed.

Section 3. Treason against the United States, shall consist only in levying War against them, or in adhering to their Enemies, giving them Aid and Comfort. No Person shall be convicted of Treason unless on the Testimony of two Witnesses to the same overt Act, or on Confession in open Court.

The Congress shall have Power to declare the Punishment of Treason, but no Attainder of Treason shall work Corruption of Blood, or Forfeiture except during the Life of the Person attainted.

ARTICLE IV.

Section 1. Full Faith and Credit shall be given in each State to the public Acts, Records, and judicial Proceedings of every other State. And the Congress may by general Laws prescribe the Manner in which such Acts, Records and Proceedings shall be proved, and the Effect thereof.

Section 2. The Citizens of each State shall be entitled to all Privileges and Immunities of Citizens in the several states.

A Person charged in any State with Treason, Felony, or other Crime, who shall flee from Justice, and be found in another State, shall on Demand of the executive Authority of the State from which he fled, be delivered up, to be removed to the state having Jurisdiction of the Crime.

No Person held to Service or Labour in one State, under the Laws thereof, escaping into another, shall, in Consequence of any Law or Regulation therein, be discharged from such Service or Labour, but shall be delivered up on Claim of the Party to whom such Service or Labour may be due.

Section 3. New States may be admitted by the Congress into this Union; but no new State shall be formed or erected within the Jurisdiction of any other State; nor any State be formed by the Junction of two or more States, or Parts of States, without the Consent of the Legislature of the States concerned as well as of the Congress.

The Congress shall have Power to dispose of and make all needful Rules and Regulations respecting the Territory or other Property belonging to the United States; and nothing in this Constitution shall be so construed as to Prejudice any Claims of the United States, or of any particular State.

Section 4. The United States shall guarantee to every State in this Union a Republican Form of Government, and shall protect each of them against Invasion; and on Application of the Legislature, or of the Executive (when the Legislature cannot be convened) against domestic Violence.

ARTICLE V.

The Congress, whenever two thirds of both Houses shall deem it necessary, shall propose Amendments to this Constitution, or, on the Application of the Legislatures of two thirds of the several States, shall call a Convention for proposing Amendments, which, in either Case, shall be valid to all Intents and Purposes, as Part of this Constitution, when ratified by the Legislatures of three fourths of the several States, or by Conventions in three fourths thereof, as the one or the other Mode of Ratification may be proposed by the Congress; Provided that no Amendment which may be made prior to the Year One thousand eight hundred and eight shall in any Manner affect the first and fourth Clauses in the Ninth Section of the first Article; and that no State, without its Consent, shall be deprived of its equal Suffrage in the Senate.

ARTICLE VI.

All Debts contracted and Engagements entered into, before the Adoption of this Constitution, shall be as valid against the United States under this Constitution, as under the Confederation.

This Constitution, and the laws of the United States which shall be made in Pursuance thereof; and all Treaties made, or which shall be made, under the Authority of the United States, shall be the supreme Law of the Land; and the Judges in every State shall be bound thereby, any Thing in the Constitution or Laws of any State to the Contrary notwithstanding.

The Senators and Representatives before mentioned, and the Members of the several State Legislatures, and all executive and judicial Officers, both of the United States and of the several States, shall be bound by Oath or Affirmation, to support this Constitution; but no religious Test shall ever be required as a Qualification to any Office or public Trust under the United States.

ARTICLE VII.

The Ratification of the Conventions of nine States, shall be sufficient for the Establishment of this Constitution between the States so ratifying the Same.

ARTICLES IN ADDITION TO, AND AMENDMENT OF THE CONSTITUTION OF THE UNITED STATES OF AMERICA, PROPOSED BY CONGRESS, AND RATIFIED BY THE LEGISLATURES OF THE SEVERAL STATES, PURSUANT TO THE FIFTH ARTICLE OF THE ORIGINAL CONSTITUTION.

Amendment I.

Congress shall make no law respecting an establishment of religion, or prohibiting the free exercise thereof; or abridging the freedom of speech, or of the press; or the right of the people peaceably to assemble, and to petition the Government for a redress of grievances.

Amendment II.

A well regulated militia, being necessary to the security of a free State, the right of the people to keep and bear arms, shall not be infringed.

Amendment III.

No Soldier shall, in time of peace be quartered in any house, without the consent of the owner, nor in time of war, but in a manner to be prescribed by law.

Amendment IV.

The right of the people to be secure in their persons, houses, papers, and effects, against unreasonable searches and seizures, shall not be violated, and no warrants shall issue, but upon probable cause, supported by oath or affirmation, and particularly describing the place to be searched, and the persons or things to be seized.

Amendment V.

No person shall be held to answer for a capital, or otherwise infamous crime, unless on a presentment or indictment of a Grand Jury, except in cases arising in the land or naval forces, or in the militia, when in actual service in time of war or public danger, nor shall any person be subject for the same offence to be twice put in jeopardy of life or limb; nor shall be compelled in any criminal case to be a witness against himself, nor be deprived of life, liberty, or property, without due process of law; nor shall private property be taken for public use, without just compensation.

Amendment VI.

In all criminal prosecutions, the accused shall enjoy the right to a speedy and public trial, by an impartial jury of the State and district wherein the crime shall have been committed, which district shall have been previously ascertained by law, and to be informed of the nature and cause of the accusation; to be confronted with the witnesses against him; to have compulsory process for obtaining witnesses in his favor, and to have the assistance of counsel for his defence.

Amendment VII.

In Suits at common law, where the value in controversy shall exceed twenty dollars, the right of trial by jury shall be preserved, and no fact tried by a jury, shall be otherwise reexamined in any Court of the United States, than according to the rules of the common law.

Amendment VIII.

Excessive bail shall not be required, nor excessive fines imposed, nor cruel and unusual punishments inflicted.

Amendment IX.

The enumeration in the Constitution, of certain rights, shall not be construed to deny or disparage others retained by the people.

Amendment X.

The powers not delegated to the United States by the Constitution, nor prohibited by it to the States, are reserved to the States respectively, or to the people.

Amendment XI.

The Judicial power of the United States shall not be construed to extend to any suit in law or equity, commenced or prosecuted against one of the United States by Citizens of another State, or by Citizens or Subjects of any Foreign State.

Amendment XII.

The Electors shall meet in their respective states and vote by ballot for President and Vice President, one of whom, at least, shall not be an inhabitant of the same state with themselves; they shall name in their ballots the person voted for as President, and in distinct ballots the person voted for as Vice President, and they shall make distinct lists of all persons voted for as President, and of all persons voted for as Vice President, and of the number of votes for each, which lists they shall sign and certify, and transmit sealed to the seat of the government of the United States, directed to the President of the Senate; the President of the Senate shall, in the presence of the Senate and House of Representatives, open all the certificates and the votes shall then be counted; The person having the greatest number of votes for President, shall be the President, if such number be a majority of the whole number of Electors appointed; and if no person have such majority, then from the persons having the highest numbers not exceeding three on the list of those voted for as President, the House of Representatives shall choose immediately, by ballot, the President. But in choosing the President, the votes shall be taken by states, the representation from each state having one vote; a quorum for this purpose shall consist of a member or members from two-thirds of the states, and a majority of all the states shall be necessary to a choice. And if the House of Representatives shall not choose a President whenever the right of choice shall devolve upon them, before the fourth day of March next following, then the Vice President shall act as President, as in the case of the death or other constitutional disability of the President. The person having the greatest number of votes as Vice President, shall be the Vice President, if such number be a majority of the whole number of Electors appointed, and if no person have a majority, then from the two highest numbers on the list, the Senate shall choose the Vice President; a quorum for the purpose shall consist of two-thirds of the whole number of Senators, and a majority of the whole number shall be necessary to a choice. But no person constitutionally ineligible to the office of President shall be eligible to that of Vice President of the United States.

Amendment XIII.

Section 1. Neither slavery nor involuntary servitude, except as a punishment for crime whereof the party shall have been duly convicted, shall exist within the United States, or any place subject to their jurisdiction.

Section 2. Congress shall have power to enforce this article by appropriate legislation.

Amendment XIV.

Section 1. All persons born or naturalized in the United States, and subject to the jurisdiction thereof, are citizens of the United States and of the State wherein they reside. No State shall make or enforce any law which shall abridge the privileges or immunities of citizens of the United States; nor shall any State deprive any person of life, liberty, or property, without due process of law, nor deny to any person within its jurisdiction the equal protection of the laws.

Section 2. Representatives shall be apportioned among the several states according to their respective numbers, counting the whole number of persons in each State, excluding Indians not taxed. But when the right to vote at any election for the choice of electors for President and Vice President of the United States, Representatives in Congress, the Executive and Judicial officers of a State, or the members of the Legislature thereof, is denied to any of the male inhabitants of such State, being twenty-one years of age, and citizens of the United States, or in any way abridged, except for participation in rebellion, or other crime, the basis of representation therein shall be reduced in the proportion which the number of such male citizens shall bear to the whole number of male citizens twenty-one years of age in such State.

Section 3. No person shall be a Senator or Representative in Congress, or elector of President and Vice President, or hold any office, civil or military, under the United States, or under any State, who, having previously taken an oath, as a member of Congress, or as an officer of the United States, or as a member of any State legislature, or as an executive or judicial officer of any State, to support the Constitution of the United States, shall have engaged in insurrection or rebellion against the same, or given aid or comfort to the enemies thereof. But

Congress may by a vote of two-thirds of each House remove such disability.

Section 4. The validity of the public debt of the United States, authorized by law, including debts incurred for payment of pensions and bounties for services in suppressing insurrection or rebellion, shall not be questioned. But neither the United States nor any State shall assume or pay any debt or obligation incurred in aid of insurrection or rebellion against the United States, or any claim for the loss or emancipation of any slave; but all such debts, obligations and claims shall be held illegal and void.

Section 5. The Congress shall have power to enforce, by appropriate legislation, the provisions of this article.

Amendment XV.

Section 1. The right of citizens of the United States to vote shall not be denied or abridged by the United States or by any State on account of race, color, or previous condition of servitude.

Section 2. The Congress shall have power to enforce this article by appropriate legislation.

Amendment XVI.

The Congress shall have power to lay and collect taxes on incomes, from whatever source derived, without apportionment among the several States, and without regard to any census or enumeration.

Amendment XVII.

The Senate of the United States shall be composed of two Senators from each State, elected by the people thereof, for six years; and each Senator shall have one vote. The electors in each State shall have the qualifications requisite for electors of the most numerous branch of the State legislatures.

When vacancies happen in the representation of any State in the Senate, the executive authority of such State shall issue writs of election to fill such vacancies: *Provided,* That the legislature of any State may empower the executive thereof to make temporary appointments until the people fill the vacancies by election as the legislature may direct.

This amendment shall not be so construed as to affect the election or term of any Senator chosen before it becomes valid as part of the Constitution.

Amendment XVIII.

Section 1. After one year from the ratification of this article the manufacture, sale, or transportation of intoxicating liquors within, the importation thereof into, or the exportation thereof from the United States and all territory subject to the jurisdiction thereof for beverage purposes is hereby prohibited.

Section 2. The Congress and the several States shall have concurrent power to enforce this article by appropriate legislation.

Section 3. This article shall be inoperative unless it shall have been ratified as an amendment to the Constitution by the legislatures of the several States, as provided in the Constitution, within seven years from the date of the submission hereof to the States by the Congress.

Amendment XIX.

The right of citizens of the United States to vote shall not be denied or abridged by the United States or by any State on account of sex.

Congress shall have power to enforce this article by appropriate legislation.

Amendment XX.

Section 1. The terms of the President and Vice President shall end at noon on the 20th day of January, and the terms of Senators and Representatives at noon on the 3rd day of January, of the years in which such terms would have ended if this article had not been ratified; and the terms of their successors shall then begin.

Section 2. The Congress shall assemble at least once in every year, and such meeting shall begin at noon on the 3rd day of January, unless they shall by law appoint a different day.

Section 3. If, at the time fixed for the beginning of the term of the President, the President elect shall have died, the Vice President elect shall become President. If a President shall not have been chosen before the time fixed for the beginning of his term, or if the President elect shall have failed to qualify, then the Vice President elect shall act as President until a President shall have qualified; and the Congress may by law provide for the case wherein neither a President elect nor a Vice President elect shall have qualified, declaring who shall then act as President, or the manner in which one who is to act shall be selected, and such person shall act accordingly until a President or Vice President shall have qualified.

Section 4. The Congress may by law provide for the case of the death of any of the persons from whom the House of Representatives may choose a President whenever the rights of choice shall have devolved upon them, and for the case of the death of any of the persons from whom the Senate may choose a Vice President whenever the right of choice shall have devolved upon them.

Section 5. Sections 1 and 2 shall take effect on the 15th day of October following the ratification of this article.

Section 6. This article shall be inoperative unless it shall have been ratified as an amendment to the Constitution by the legislatures of three-fourths of the several States within seven years from the date of its submission.

Amendment XXI.

Section 1. The eighteenth article of amendment to the Constitution of the United States is hereby repealed.

Section 2. The transportation or importation into any State, Territory, or possession of the United States for delivery or use therein of intoxicating liquors, in violation of the laws thereof, is hereby prohibited.

Section 3. This article shall be inoperative unless it shall have been ratified as an amendment to the Constitution by conventions in the several States, as provided in the Constitution, within seven years from the date of the submission hereof to the States by the Congress.

Amendment XXII.

Section 1. No person shall be elected to the office of the President more than twice, and no person who has held the office of President, or acted as President, for more than two years of a term to which some other person was elected President shall be elected to the office of the President more than once. But this Article shall not apply to any person holding the office of President when this Article was proposed by the Congress, and shall not prevent any person who may be holding the office of President, or acting as President, during the term within which this Article becomes operative from holding the office of President or acting as President during the remainder of such term.

Section 2. This article shall be inoperative unless it shall have been ratified as an amendment to the Constitution by the legislatures of three-fourths of the several States within seven years from the date of its submission to the States by the Congress.

Amendment XXIII.

Section 1. The District constituting the seat of Government of the United States shall appoint in such manner as the Congress may direct:
A number of electors of President and Vice President equal to the whole number of Senators and Representatives in Congress to which the District would be entitled if it were a State, but in no event more than the least populous State; they shall be in addition to those appointed by the States but they shall be considered, for the purposes of the election of President and Vice President, to be electors appointed by a State; and they shall meet in the District and perform such duties as provided by the twelfth article of amendment.

Section 2. The Congress shall have power to enforce this article by appropriate legislation.

Amendment XXIV.

Section 1. The right of citizens of the United States to vote in any primary or other election for President or Vice President, for electors for President or Vice President, or for Senator or Representative in Congress, shall not be denied or abridged by the United States or any State by reason of failure to pay any poll tax or other tax.

Section 2. The Congress shall have power to enforce this article by appropriate legislation.

Amendment XXV.

Section 1. In case of the removal of the President from office or of his death or resignation, the Vice President shall become President.

Section 2. Whenever there is a vacancy in the office of the Vice President, the President shall nominate a Vice President who shall take office upon confirmation by a majority vote of both Houses of Congress.

Section 3. Whenever the President transmits to the President pro tempore of the Senate and the Speaker of the House of Representatives his written declaration that he is unable to discharge the powers and duties of his office, and until he transmits to them a written declaration to the contrary, such powers and duties shall be discharged by the Vice President as Acting President

Section 4. Whenever the Vice President and a majority of either the principal officers of the executive departments or of such other body as Congress may by law provide, transmit to the President pro tempore of the Senate and the Speaker of the House of Representatives their written declaration that the President is unable to discharge the powers and duties of his office, the Vice President shall immediately assume the powers and duties of the office as Acting President.

Thereafter, when the President transmits to the President pro tempore of the Senate and the Speaker of the House of Representatives his written declaration that no inability exists, he shall resume the powers and duties of his office unless the Vice President and a majority of either the principal officers of the executive department or of such other body as Congress may by law provide, transmit within four days to the President pro tempore of the Senate and the Speaker of the House of Representatives their written declaration that the President is unable to discharge the powers and duties of his office. Thereupon Congress shall decide the issue, assembling within forty-eight hours for that purpose if not in session. If the Congress, within twenty-one days after receipt of the latter written declaration, or, if Congress is not in session, within twenty-one days after Congress is required to assemble, determines by two-thirds vote of both Houses that the President is unable to discharge the powers and duties of his office, the Vice President shall continue to discharge the same as Acting President; otherwise, the President shall resume the powers and duties of his office.

Amendment XXVI.

Section 1. The right of citizens of the United States, who are eighteen years of age or older, to vote shall not be denied or abridged by the United States or by any State on account of age.
Section 2. The Congress shall have power to enforce this article by appropriate legislation.

Amendment XXVII.

No Law, varying the compensation for the services of the Senators and Representatives, shall take effect, until an election of Representatives shall have intervened.

Appendix B

Abbreviations of Governmental Agencies and Departments

ACDA	Arms Control and Disarmament Agency
ACE	Army Corps of Engineers
ADAMHA	Alcohol, Drug Abuse, and Mental Health Administration
AFDC	Aid to Families with Dependent Children
AFIS	American Forces Information System
AID	Agency for International Development
Amtrak	National Railroad Passenger Corporation
ANA	Administration for Native Americans
AOUSA	Administrative Office of the U.S. Courts
APS	Administration for Public Services
ATF	Bureau of Alcohol, Tobacco, Firearms, and Explosives
BEA	Bureau of Economic Analysis
BIA	Bureau of Indian Affairs
BJS	Bureau of Justice Statistics
BLM	Bureau of Land Management
BLS	Bureau of Labor Statistics
CAB	Civil Aeronautics Board
CBP	Customs and Border Protection
CBO	Congressional Budget Office
CDC	Centers for Disease Control
CEA	Council of Economic Advisers

CENTO	Central Treaty Organization
CEQ	Council on Environmental Quality
CETA	Comprehensive Employment and Training Act
CIA	Central Intelligence Agency
CIS	Citizenship and Immigration Service
Comcen's	Federal Communications Centers Agency
Conrail	Consolidated Rail Corporation
COPS	Community Oriented Policing Services
CRS	Community Relations Service
CSC	Civil Service Commission
DEA	Drug Enforcement Administration
DHS	Department of Homeland Security
DIA	Defense Intelligence Agency
DNA	Defense Nuclear Agency
DOD	Department of Defense
DOE	Department of Energy
DOI	Department of the Interior
DOL	Department of Labor
DOS	Department of State
DOT	Department of Transportation
DVA	Department of Veterans' Affairs
ED	Department of Education
EDA	Economic Development Administration
EEC	European Economic Community
EEOC	Equal Employment Opportunity Commission
EIA	Energy Information Administration

EPA	Environmental Protection Agency
ERISA	Employee Retirement Income Security Act
ESA	Employment Standards Administration
EU	European Union
FAA	Federal Aviation Administration
FAO	Food and Agriculture Organization of the United Nations
FBI	Federal Bureau of Investigation
FCA	Farm Credit Administration
FCC	Federal Communications Commission
FCIC	Federal Crop Insurance Corporation
FDA	Food and Drug Administration
FDIC	Federal Deposit Insurance Corporation
FEC	Federal Election Commission
FEMA	Federal Emergency Management Agency
FHA	Federal Housing Administration
FHWA	Federal Highway Administration
FIC	Federal Information Centers
FMC	Federal Maritime Commission
FOIA	Freedom of Information Act
FRA	Federal Railroad Administration
FRS	Federal Reserve System
FSLIC	Federal Savings and Loan Insurance Corporation
FTA	Federal Transit Administration
FTC	Federal Trade Commission
GAO	General Accounting Office

GPO	Government Printing Office
GSA	General Services Administration
HHS	Department of Health and Human Services
HSA	Health Services Administration
HUD	Department of Housing and Urban Development
IAEA	International Atomic Energy Agency
ICC	Interstate Commerce Commission
ICJ	International Court of Justice
ICS	Immigration and Customs Enforcement
IFC	International Finance Corporation
IG	Inspector General
ILO	International Labour Organization
IMF	International Monetary Fund
INS	Immigration and Naturalization Service
INTERPOL	International Criminal Police Organization
IRS	Internal Revenue Service
ITA	International Trade Administration
JAG	Judge Advocate General
JCS	Joint Chiefs of Staff
JOBS	Job Opportunities in the Business Sector
LEAA	Law Enforcement Assistance Administration
LOC	Library of Congress
LSC	Legal Services Corporation
MBDA	Minority Business Development Agency
MDL	Judicial Panel on Multidistrict Litigation
MSHA	Mine Safety and Health Administration

MSPB	Merit Systems Protection Board
NARS	National Archives and Records Service
NASA	National Aeronautics and Space Administration
NATO	North Atlantic Treaty Organization
NBS	National Bureau of Standards
NCI	National Cancer Institute
NFIP	National Flood Insurance Program
NHTSA	National Highway Transportation Safety Administration
NIH	National Institute of Health
NIMH	National Institute for Mental Health
NLRB	National Labor Relations Board
NOAA	National Oceanic and Atmospheric Administration
NRC	Nuclear Regulatory Commission
NSA	National Security Agency
NSC	National Security Council
NSF	National Science Foundation
NTSB	National Transportation Safety Board
NWS	National Weather Service
OAS	Organization of American States
OCC	Office of the Comptroller of Currency
OCSE	Office of Child Support Enforcement
OFR	Office of the Federal Register
OJARS	Office of Justice Assistance, Research and Statistics

OLC	Office of Legal Counsel
OMB	Office of Management and Budget
OOG	Office of Oil and Gas
OPM	Office of Personnel Management
OSHA	Occupational Safety and Health Administration
PAHO	Pan American Health Organization
PHS	Public Health Service
PRC	Postal Rate Commission
PTO	Patent and Trademark Office
RFE/RL	Radio Free Europe/Radio Liberty
RRB	Railroad Retirement Board
RSVP	Retired Senior Volunteer Program
SALT	Strategic Arms Limitation Talks
SBA	Small Business Administration
SCORE	Service Corps of Retired Executives
SCOTUS	Supreme Court of the United States
SCS	Soil Conservation Service
SEA	Science and Education Administration
SEATO	Southeast Asia Treaty Organization
SEC	Securities and Exchange Commission
SIPC	Securities Investors Protection Corporation
SLS	Saint Lawrence Seaway Development Corporation
SSA	Social Security Administration
SSS	Selective Service System
TSA	Transportation Safety Administration

TVA	Tennessee Valley Authority
UCPP	Urban Crime Prevention Program
UIS	Unemployment Insurance Service
UMTA	Urban Mass Transportation Administration
UN	United Nations
UNESCO	United Nations Educational, Scientific and Cultural Organization
UNICEF	United Nations Children's Fund
US CERT	United States Computer Emergency Readiness Team
USCG	United States Coast Guard
USDA	United States Department of Agriculture
USGS	United States Geological Survey
USPS	United States Postal Service
VA	Veterans Administration
VETS	Veterans Employment and Training Service
VISTA	Volunteers in Service to America
VOA	Voice of America
WHO	World Health Organization